Ethnic and Multicultural Drug Abuse: Perspectives on Current Research

Ethnic and Multicultural Drug Abuse: Perspectives on Current Research

Joseph E. Trimble
Catherine S. Bolek
Steve J. Niemcryk
Editors

Ethnic and Multicultural Drug Abuse: Perspectives on Current Research, edited by Joseph E. Trimble, Catherine S. Bolek and Steve J. Niemcryk, was simultaneously issued by The Haworth Press, Inc., under the same title, as special issues of *Drugs & Society*, Volume 6, Numbers 1/2 and 3/4 1992, Bernard Segal, Journal Editor.

Routledge
Taylor & Francis Group
New York   London

ISBN 1-56023-023-1

First published by
The Haworth Press, Inc., 10 Alice Street, Binghamton, NY 13904-1580

This edition published 2013 by Routledge
711 Third Avenue, New York, NY 10017
2 Park Square, Milton Park, Abingdon, Oxon OX14 4RN

Routledge is an imprint of the Taylor & Francis Group, an informa business

Ethnic and Multicultural Drug Abuse: Perspectives on Current Research has also been published
as *Drugs & Society*, Volume 6, Numbers 1/2 and 3/4, 1992.

Library of Congress Cataloging-in-Publication Data

Ethnic and multicultural drug abuse : perspectives on current research / Joseph E. Trimble,
Catherine S. Bolek, Steve J. Niemcryk, editors.
    p. cm.
    Includes bibliographical references and index.
    ISBN 1-56024-321-X (alk. paper)–ISBN: 1-56023-023-1 (alk. paper)
    1. Minorities–United States–Substance use. 2. Minorities–United States–Substance use–Re-
      search. 3. Minorities–United States–Drug use. 4. Minorities–United States–Drug
      use–Research. I. Trimble, Joseph E. II. Bolek, Catherine S. III. Niemcryk, Steve J.
HV5824.E85E87 1992
362.29'08693–dc20   92-23858
                                                        CIP

Ethnic and Multicultural Drug Abuse: Perspectives on Current Research

CONTENTS

Ethnic and Multicultural Drug Abuse: Perspectives on Current Research

ABOUT THE EDITORS

Joseph E. Trimble, PhD, is Professor of Psychology at Western Washington University and Research Associate in the Center for Cross-Cultural Research. He is also Research Associate at the National Center for American Indian and Alaska Native Mental Health Research at the University of Colorado Health Science Center. Throughout his research career he has concentrated his work toward understanding the psychosocial characteristics of native people experiencing problematic life events and identifying strategies that assist them in coping with these experiences. For the past decade, Dr. Trimble has been working collaboratively on drug and alcohol prevention research models intended for use with American Indian youth.

Catherine S. Bolek, MS, was Associate Director of Special Populations Research at the National Institute on Drug Abuse for several years before taking her current position as Director of the Office of Sponsored Research at the University of Maryland Eastern Shore. Ms. Bolek has a long standing commitment to the advancement of drug use research among ethnic-minority groups. While at the National Institute of Drug Abuse, she was instrumental in developing and promoting research training programs to increase the participation of ethnic-minority researchers in the drug abuse fields. She has edited and co-edited several books and monographs on drug abuse research.

Steve J. Niemcryk, PhD, is an epidemiologist in the Office of Science and Epidemiology in the Health Resources Services Administration. His graduate studies focused on preventive medicine and community health. He continues to conduct research in the areas of medicine, epidemiology, and the behavioral sciences.

Foreword

Over the course of the past few decades use of psychoactive drugs has increased to the point that it reached crisis level proportions in the late 1980's. Recent research findings suggest though that drug use among America's youth is slowly declining. Nonetheless use of psychoactive drugs continues to be a problem especially among America's ethnic-minority populations. The research literature shows that ethnic-minorities were and continue to be overrepresented in drug abuse reporting files and data tracking systems, although no one is quite certain why. Moreover no one is quite certain why ethnic-minorities are more affected by drug use than the dominant society in the United States. Even more puzzling is the paucity of findings related to etiological causes among certain ethnic groups (Trimble, in press; Tucker, 1985).

The data that are available suggest that ethnic-minorities are highly represented in alcohol and drug treatment programs and in drug related emergency hospital admissions. For example, the National Institute on Drug Abuse's (NIDA) Drug Abuse Warning Network (DAWN) and the Client Oriented Data Acquisition Process (CODAP) systems alone show that ethnic-minorities are disproportionately represented in the case files when compared with the prevalence rates for the dominant population. And while the results from a 1990 survey show that the dominant culture's youths are declining in their rates of drug use, other researchers indicate that the rates of certain ethnic groups have at best stabilized but are not declining.

Our knowledge concerning ethnic-minority drug-use is thin, uneven in its explanations, almost devoid of theory, and, in some cases, lacks sufficient data from which one can generalize. Combine the knowledge base with the existing drug-use rates and one can get a glimpse of one of the reasons why the use rates continue to be a problem. Yet there is an additional reason to be concerned. Ethnic-

xiii

minorities will constitute ''one third of the nation's'' population by the mid-1990s. The American Council of Education (1988) reports that within the next decade one-third of all school age children, 42 percent of all public school students, and 21.8 million of the 140.4 million projected to be in the labor force will be of ethnic-minority background. The long history of oppression, racism and discrimination experienced by these groups will no doubt be exacerbated by the rapid population increase. There is little reason to doubt that drug use will continue to be a problem in the communities, too.

The prevalence and incidence of drug abuse among America's ethnic minority groups have not gone unnoticed. Research in the areas of prevention, intervention, etiology, and epidemiology is occurring largely through the efforts of the National Institute on Drug Abuse (NIDA) and the Office of Substance Abuse Prevention (OSAP). Unfortunately and despite the efforts on the part of NIDA and OSAP the amount of useful data is very limited and restricted to distinct ethnic populations residing in certain sections of the country. In addition there is a noticeable paucity of well trained ethnic minorities working in the field, particularly evident by the relatively few ethnic minority researchers who have received research grants from NIDA.

In 1985, in response to the paucity of ethnic minority researchers NIDA through the Office of Special Populations Research, embarked on a mission to increase the numbers by sponsoring a series of ongoing training seminars. The primary objective of the seminars was to provide training opportunities for promising ethnic minority researchers. Areas of training included grant writing, drug abuse research methodologies and procedures, and knowledge of the research and development opportunities available through NIDA. From 1985 to 1991 numerous ethnic minority researchers were provided training in one form or another through the efforts of NIDA consultants and staff. During that time and as a result of the training close to a dozen participants received research grant awards through NIDA's normal grant submission and review process.

During the training venture it became clear to certain NIDA staff, their consultants, and the participants that there was a distinct and noticeable absence of resource materials dedicated specifically to the subject of ethnic minority and cross-cultural drug abuse research. The number of data based journal articles published on the topic since 1954 is rather slim (see Iiyama, Nishi, & Johnson, 1976; Tucker, 1985; Austin, Johnson, Carroll, & Lettieri, 1987; Trimble, Padilla, & Bell, 1987; and Trimble, in press). To close the gap, the editors of this book invited several drug abuse researchers to submit articles focusing on their respective interest in the field. Several contributors to this volume were participants in the training seminars, and the content of much of their work was inspired by their training experiences. The motives for compiling this edited volume go beyond serving as a showcase of exemplary ethnic minority research: the editors also wanted to (1) include articles that defined the status of drug abuse research with specific ethnic minority groups such as Asian Pacific Americans and Hispanics; (2) provide a summary of the research in the field; (3) provide some guidelines for developing competitive research proposals; and (4) offer some suggestions for plausible and effective ways to conduct research with ethnic minority populations.

· The volume contains 13 articles representing the collective efforts and contributions of 29 researchers, the majority of whom are of ethnic minority background (i.e., African American, American Indian, Asian Pacific American, or Hispanic). The first three articles focus on the research development process. The opening article by Bolek, Bielawski, Niemcryk, Needle, and Baker identifies and describes the various components involved in preparing a research application intended for review by one of the institutes associated with the United States Public Health Service (PHS). Along with the descriptions the authors point out a number of critical elements involved in preparing and writing a grant application. The authors conclude their article with a description of a prototype software program, HUGO, which has been designed to assist a researcher in developing a PHS (RO1 type) research grant application. The authors include an all important research check list to guide the grant writer-researcher in preparing and organizing an application. The next article prepared by Rebach is an annotated review of selected ethnic minority drug abuse literature. Most of the articles listed in the review emphasize empirical findings. The author provides a critique of many of the research articles and draws attention to their strengths and weaknesses. Closing out the first triage of the volume's contents is Collins' article that emphasizes the methodological issues involved in conducting drug abuse research with ethnic minorities. Collins effectively identifies a variety of methodological problems that crop up in conducting research with culturally different populations including sampling, the "myth" of homogeneity, socioeconomic status, acculturation, identifying and developing culturally sensitive measures, research design considerations, and appropriate considerations in analyzing results.

The remaining ten articles emphasize a variety of ethnic minority research themes. The first three articles of the series present research findings and research recommendations for Blacks or African Americans. To lead off the section, Maton and Zimmerman present the results of their prospective study of 150 urban Black adolescents. Using hierarchical regression analysis the researchers found that lifestyle indicators were strong predictors of marijuana and alcohol use at both points in their measurement process. They also found that leaving school prematurely led to increased use of alcohol when contrasted with a subsample of those who remained in school. Overall their research is one of a few studies that examine substance abuse predictors among high risk urban Black youths. The article closes with a set of recommendations intended to guide possible intervention approaches. In the second article of the ethnic specific series Milburn and Booth describe in detail their work among Black adult homeless populations in the Washington, D.C. area. Attention is devoted to the drug use and abuse characteristics of this population. The findings suggest that drug abuse is more of a problem among homeless Black adults in shelters than among non-homeless Blacks in the general population. Details summarizing their seminal work are illustrated in a series of nine tables. The third article by Pena and Koss-Chioino describes a treatment model intended for use with Black cocaine abusers from various New Orleans communities. The authors begin their article with a general plea for researchers and practitioners to consider carefully the generalizability of work done with ethnic minority groups, particularly the importance of ethnic and cultural factors that influence the lifestyle preferences of participants and clients. The article then focuses on the use of treatment modalities presumed to be sensitive to the cultural lifeways of drug abusing clients. The authors then expand their perspective to suggest that clinical research can be considered invalid if researchers do not examine the influence of stylized ethno-specific adaptations often exhibited by ethnic specific populations in treatment.

The next three articles discuss drug abuse research issues mainly existing among Asian Pacific Americans and Hispanics. Zane and Sasao address the myth that Asian Pacific populations do not experience drug abuse problems. Although there is scant published literature on the topic, the authors point out that clinical case files and anecdotal evidence strongly suggest that indeed a serious drug use problem exists in many Asian Pacific communities. Evidence for their contention is provided through a review of a number of research findings however limited they may be. The authors explore the various issues that are involved in conducting drug abuse research with Asian Pacific Americans. They close their article with a discussion of the treatment issues involved in delivering intervention services to the Asian Pacific client. Chavez and Swaim in the next article provide a brief review of the epidemiological issues involved in drug research with Hispanics. The authors then discuss various research problems often encountered in conducting drug abuse research with America's fastest growing ethnic minority population. Castro, Barrington, Sharp, Dial, Wang and Rawson provide research findings in the last article of the series that emphasize the effects of cocaine abuse on the lifestyles of a comparative sample of Blacks, Hispanics, and non-Hispanic Whites. Castro et al. hypothesized that illnesses increase as one continues to abuse cocaine. In testing out their lifestyle shift hypothesis the researchers found that Hispanics exhibited the greatest unhealthy deviations from a normal healthy lifestyle; moreover the authors found that the less acculturated Hispanic experienced a worse health status. Castro et al. remind the reader that their findings are based on a rather small sample.

Using structural modeling techniques King, Beals, Manson, and Trimble explored the causal effects of life stressors, social support, and depression on drug use patterns among a sample of American Indian boarding school youth. The results from their comprehensive study show that a degree of life stress is significantly related to depression and drug use. Indian students who experience a high level of stress are likely to feel more depressed and use drugs than those who do not. To the contrary students who experience minimal stress appear to receive greater support from their families and are less likely to use alcohol. In the next article of the volume Segal provides results from an extensive study of drug use among Alaskan youth. The author found that drug involvement was highest for Alaska Native and American Indian youth in Alaska while Blacks and Asian Pacifics reported the lowest use rates. What is significant about Segal's findings is his claim that drug use among Alaskan youth collectively is higher than comparable age groups in the lower 48 states. The author offers a few plausible explanations for his results.

The last two articles in the volume deal with theory and development. E. R. Oetting proposes an intriguing and compelling model for guiding our understanding of deviant behavior and drug using adolescents. Oetting takes the position that deviant attitudes and behaviors are psychosocial in origin. They are the product of psychological, social, and cultural characteristics. The model is grounded in peer cluster theory and has strong potential for use in guiding prevention research and development. The last article in the volume is actually three short summaries of research and development activities that occured as a result of initiatives sponsored by the National Institute on Drug Abuse. Bolek, Debro and Trimble provide summaries of training activities and conference proceedings. The last part of their article contains a series of recommendations for increasing the number of ethnic-minority drug abuse researchers and research devoted to this segment of America's population.

The contents of this volume by no means reflect the wealth of drug abuse prevention and intervention efforts that are occurring in ethnic minority communities across the country. Many of the tireless efforts of local community leaders and their supporters go unnoticed as the summation of their work usually does not find its way into the usual publication outlets. Hopefully the information provided in this volume will be useful for those who are deeply concerned about drug abuse problems. In addition it is our hope that the contents of this volume will serve as a guide and inspiration to those contemplating a career in the drug abuse research field.

Finally the senior editor wishes to acknowledge the assistance of the Tri-Ethnic Center for Prevention Research at Colorado State University (funded by NIDA grant P50 DA07074) for their assistance in providing support for the preparation of this volume.

Joseph E. Trimble
Catherine S. Bolek
Steve J. Niemcryk

REFERENCES

American Council on Education. (1988). *One-third of a nation.* Washington, DC: Author.

Austin, G.A., Johnson, B.D., Carroll, E.E., & Lettieri, D.J. (Eds.). (1987). *Drugs and minorities (Research Issues 21).* Washington, DC: U.S. Government Printing Office.

Iiyama, P., Nishi, S.M., & Johnson, B.D. (1976). *Drug use and abuse among U.S. minorities: An annotated bibliography.* New York, NY: Praeger.

Trimble, J.E., Padilla, A.M., & Bell, C.S. (Eds.). (1987). *Drug abuse among ethnic minorities (DHHS Publication No. ADM 87-1474).* Washington, DC: U.S. Government Printing Office.

Trimble, J.E. (in press). Ethnic minority substance abuse research perspectives: A literature review with commentary. In J.E. Trimble, C.S. Bolek, & S. J. Niemcryk (Eds.), *Conducting cross-cultural substance abuse research: Emerging strategies and methods.* Binghamton, NY: The Haworth Press, Inc.

Tucker, M.B. (1985). U.S. ethnic minorities and drug abuse: An assessment of the science and practice. *International Journal of the Addictions,* 20(6&7), 1021-1047.

Developing a Competitive Research Proposal

Catherine S. Bolek
Larry Bielawski
Steve Niemcryk
Richard Needle
Steve Baker

Gaining access to Federal research funds can represent a major challenge to even the most sophisticated scholar. Competition for research funds is on the increase; the peer review of grant applications is becoming more complex; academic careers are more dependent on grant awards; and to make matters worse costs associated with preparation and review of grant applications are escalating. To be competitive in this environment, potential grantees and applicant institutions will have to develop new strategies to improve the probability that research proposals receive meritorious priority scores.

In an attempt to address some of these challenges, this chapter will present a series of discussions on research development and the grants process, including: (a) an overview of the grants process from preproposal through submission to review and award; (b) a summa-

---

Catherine S. Bolek is Director, Office of Sponsored Research, at the University of Maryland Eastern Shore, Princess Anne, MD. Larry Bielawski holds the Decker Chair in Information Technology at Goucher College, Towson, MD. Steve Niemcryk is an Epidemiologist at the Health Services Research Administration, Rockville, MD. Richard Needle is Staff Fellow at the National Institute on Drug Abuse, Rockville, MD. Steve Baker is Project Manager at Capital Consulting Corporation, Rockville, MD.

The contents of this chapter represent the opinions of the authors and as such are not intended to represent the policies, regulations, practices or opinions of the authors' employers.

1

ry of critical elements in behavioral/clinical research design; (c) budget preparation strategies; (d) a discussion of how to present a powerful research argument; and, (e) a brief discussion of the value of using micro-computers for research development.

OVERVIEW OF THE GRANTS PROCESS

Developing the Grant Application

Research applications funded by the National Institutes of Health (NIH) and the Alcohol, Mental Health, and Drug Abuse Administration (ADAMHA) are highly competitive; based on robust research designs; targeted to the mission of the funding institute; and evaluated in accordance with a well established peer review system. In general, these institutes are committed to increasing the participation of underrepresented scholars interested in examining issues of importance to the understanding of various public health problems and to the development of improved methods for assessment, prevention and treatment of these problems. To meet these goals, the institutes provide a number of research support mechanisms including grants and contracts.

Since application, review, and funding practices differ from one institute to another and from one funding mechanism to another, investigators should develop a basic understanding of the rules and expectations governing these entities. Early in the proposal development process, investigators should visit with university officers who are responsible for–and knowledgeable about–opportunities for sponsored research activities. Where possible, a visit to a funding institute is recommended as a valuable means of receiving targeted technical assistance. When these options are not available, an investment of a few hours with funding documents (see Federal Register, NIH Guide to Grants and Contracts, The Catalogue of Federal Domestic Assistance, Guide to Research Support, Annual Register of Grant Support) or on-line data searching systems (see Fedix), available in many university and community libraries may prove highly profitable.

Having identified the appropriate funding institute (for example,

National Heart, Lung and Blood Institute (NHLBI) and research mechanism (for example, RO1 Investigator Initiated) investigators should develop a preproposal based on the institute's instructions, generally included in a Program Announcement (PA) or Request for Application (RFA). The preproposal should include a brief statement of the problem(s), proposed design including information on sampling methods, data collection and analysis techniques, and anticipated budget and research team. This document should be submitted to the funding institute's project officer whose responsibilities include providing technical assistance to prospective grant applicants. Feedback from the project officer should include: (a) the level of interest the institute may have regarding support for research as outlined in the preproposal; (b) updates on relevant program announcements and submission dates; (c) in some cases, suggestions for improving the quality of the design; and, (d) other information aimed at strengthening the subsequent grant application. In most cases, the project officer can provide copies of the Public Health Service Grant Application Kit (a.k.a. PHS 398) and instructions on completing the form.

Reviewing the Grant Application

The Division of Research Grants (DRG), NIH serves as the receipt and processing center for grant applications submitted to the NIH and ADAMHA Institutes. DRG staff apply institute grant referral guidelines to determine assignment of applications to a specific NIH or ADAMHA institute. In turn, institute staff determine assignment to specific peer review committees, also known as Initial Review Groups (IRGs). The IRG Executive Secretary assigns peer reviewers from among the members of the scientific community. Membership on the IRG is " . . . based on respect among peers, the quality of research accomplished, independent publications in referred scientific journals, and other significant scientific activities, achievements, and honors. Usually a doctoral degree or its equivalent is required" (ADAMHA, 1987).

IRG members are charged with the task of assessing the scientific strengths and weaknesses of the grant applications. Although additional criteria may be imposed on the process, general review criteria include: (a) significance of the proposed work; (b) feasibility of the approach; (c) the training and experience of the project team; (d) adequacy of the facilities and other resources; and, (e) where appropriate, adequacy of steps taken to protect human subjects and animals.

After the primary and secondary reviewers have presented their reviews, the full committee (generally consisting of 12 or more members) will discuss the application under consideration and vote for a given recommendation. The process results in one of three recommendations: (a) approval, (b) disapproval, or (c) deferral. If approved, the grant application will receive a priority score ranging from 100 (most meritorious) to 500 (least meritorious). These scores serve as important indicators of the quality of the application and ultimately as guides to the funding institute regarding the awarding of grants. If disapproved, the application request will not result in an award; however, resubmission is possible. Deferrals generally result in a written communication by the Executive Secretary on behalf of the IRG requesting additional information or clarification of specific aspects of the proposal. Infrequently, a deferral will result in a site visit to the applicant institution.

Following the IRG meeting, the Executive Secretary prepares Summary Statements (Pink Sheets) that reflect the Committee's discussions and deliberations leading to the final recommendations. Summaries contain the following information: (a) applicant's abstract of the proposed work; (b) a resume of the committee's recommendations; (c) a statement on the adequacy of human/animal protection; (d) a critique of the strengths and weaknesses of the proposed work; and (e) statements on the adequacy of personnel, resources, environment, and budget.

With a small number of exceptions, the results of the IRG reviews are presented at national advisory council meetings. The councils provide oversight of the IRG process, make recommendations to the institutes staff regarding funding priorities, and advise the institute on scientific policy as it relates to the funding process. In general, awards can only be considered after having received the council's concurrence with IRG recommendations.

The final step is initiated when the institute's extramural research divisions (e.g., Division of Preclinical Research (NIDA) or Division of Epidemiology and Clinical Applications (NHLBI)) recommend grant applications for awards. In general, the criteria that determine funding are the following: (a) priority score; (b) significance of the project in terms of the institute's research mission; (c) budget requirements (IRG recommended budget); and (d) level of available support (institute's budget).

Receiving an Award

Certainly, the most rewarding step in the grants process comes with the receipt of the "Notice of Grant Award." The applicant must now assume responsibility for conducting the research and for the fiscal management of the project and its personnel. During the life of the grant, most typically three years, the applicant will prepare an annual application for continuation. This non-competitive application summarizes progress to date and provides a proposed budget and workplan for the next funding period.

This mechanism allows the applicant an opportunity to keep the project officer appraised of the progress and to discuss anticipated problems or needs. A final report, due shortly after the completion of the last funding period, summarizes the work supported by the grant award and provides a detailed account of the financial expenditures incurred in the conduct of the research.

In the case where an applicant fails to receive approval or a fundable priority score, the "summary statement" serves as a guide for improving the quality of a subsequent application. Applicants planning on resubmitting a revised application should contact the Executive Secretary and Project Officer and discuss the reasonableness of a resubmission effort.

CRITICAL ELEMENTS IN RESEARCH DESIGN

No study is perfect. A study that requires an institute's investment, however, must be as nearly perfect as possible before any hope of funding is realistic. Researchers should critically assess the quality of each component of their study prior to the submission of the proposal. Although a complete discussion about study design will not be possible in this chapter, the following information is intended to provide the most basic guidelines for individuals who are interested in conducting research. The primary elements of a research project are listed in Table 1. In addition to considering these elements, it must be recognized that all of the components of a research project are inextricably related to one another and should receive a fair amount of attention both as a group and as individual components.

Hypothesis Building

The very foundation of every study, of course, is the hypothesis. If the hypothesis is based on outdated research or generally on faulty reasoning, the value of the study is likely to be minimal. A hypothesis is almost always generated by integrating a conceptual framework with the findings from recent, relevant, and well-designed empirical investigations. Unfortunately, many potential grantees are not able or willing to critically and objectively evaluate their own research plan. Oftentimes prospective researchers do not see obvious flaws in the hypothesis—or in their study design. Therefore, the quality of a project's hypothesis should be tested by obtaining critical reviews from other researchers who are experts in the appropriate area. Ignoring this step may very well result in a missed opportunity to (1) improve the hypothesis to a level at which the chance of funding is increased; or, (2) avoid wasting time in the development of a project that is doomed to fail.

Selecting Subjects

If the hypothesis is acceptable, identification and recruitment of subjects must be made with considerable care since these individuals will provide the data from which generalizations will invariably be made (see Cochran, 1966). A problem is likely to occur when the target population—the group of people in whom the investigator is interested—is not well defined or when rigorous inclusionary criteria (characteristics that make persons eligible for the study) and exclusionary criteria (characteristics that make persons ineligible for the study) are not delineated. Such a rigorous recruitment strategy is necessary to obtain a sample that has the characteristics of interest. However, the researcher must pay some attention to those individuals who refuse to take part in the study and to those people, if the study is longitudinal, who drop out of the study. Usually, people who refuse to take part in or who drop out of a study have characteristics that are quite different from the rest of the study population. Failure to obtain data from these individuals may bias the study's results.

Another consideration related to the study population is that of sample size (Friedman, 1982; Kramer, 1987). Of course, the number of subjects in the sample should be adequate to test the hypothesis of interest. Too few observations in a study increases the possibility that the sample is not representative of the target population. Also, if the sample is small, the magnitude of the relationship must be very large to obtain a statistically significant result. On the other hand, very modest relationships may be found to be statistically significant when the sample is large, and much caution should be used when interpreting such results because the relationship may be so weak that it has no practical value whatsoever. For virtually every study in which grant funding is sought, the results from power calculations should usually be presented in a grant proposal to provide evidence that the proposed sample size is adequate.

Choosing a Design

Researchers must consider the consequences of choosing a particular study design (Cook and Campbell, 1979; Webb, 1966). Retrospective studies are those in which subjects are asked about events or behaviors from months or years in the past, and cross-sectional studies where data are obtained about behaviors, attitudes, or more recent events are usually quick and relatively inexpensive to conduct, depending on the number of subjects in the sample. However, neither retrospective nor cross-sectional studies provide data from which the direction of causality can be inferred. Also, both retrospective and cross-sectional designs may suffer from subjects' providing inaccurate data because of errors in the memory of certain events. In longitudinal studies, data are collected from the same individuals at several points in time until either a predetermined

Table 1

A RESEARCH CHECKLIST

HYPOTHESIS

Has a recent literature search been conducted?
Is the proposed hypothesis the next logical step in that
    area of research?
Has the hypothesis been reviewed by others who are experts
    in the area prior to the submission of the grant?

SUBJECT SELECTION

Has the target population been adequately defined?
Have specific inclusionary and exclusionary criteria been
    identified?
Has some attention been paid to the characteristics of
    nonrespondents or those who will drop out of the study?
Is the sample size adequate?
If differences between subgroups will be assessed, do each
    of the subgroups have an adequate number of subjects?
If the sample size is large, will a distinction have to be
    made about clinical versus statistical significance?

STUDY DESIGN

Will the design impair the ability to make inferences about the direction of causality?

Will the problems inherent in the design make testing the stated hypothesis impossible?

INSTRUMENT SELECTION

Does the measure have ample evidence of reliability and validity particularly with the population to which it will be administered?

If the instrument is self-report, have the items been examined to determine if they are appropriate, given the hypothesis?

DATA MANAGEMENT

Have adequate safeguards been taken to ensure a rate of error in the dataset is kept as low as possible?

DATA ANALYSIS

Have the data been analyzed in the appropriate manner? For example, if the data did not have a normal distribution, were nonparametric tests used?

Also, were potentially confounding variables controlled in multivariate models where appropriate?

time period expires or until a condition of interest occurs. The most negative aspect of a longitudinal study is that it is expensive. In terms of money, the cost per subject is increased due to the cost of maintaining contact with subjects and increase in amount of data that has to be processed as a result of multiple assessments of each subject. In terms of time, longitudinal studies may be very expensive because some conditions of interest, such as addiction, may not develop for years. Moreover, technology advances over time and the instruments used at the beginning of the study may be found to be seriously flawed by the time the study is concluded. Therefore, the findings from the final analysis may be open to question.

Yet, only a longitudinal study can provide causal data. (A relationship is considered potentially causal when conditions present at the first round of data collection are related to the outcome of interest that is subsequently observed. Examples of these outcomes are mortality, morbidity, change in behavior, etc.) Again some caution should be used when suggesting a causal relationship–some variable that received no attention in the study may confound the results. (A confounder is a variable that is not related to the hypothesis, but is causally related to both the independent variable and the outcome of interest.)

Selecting Instruments

Of course, the quality of the measure used to collect data influences the quality of the study itself. Researchers should make every effort to select the best instrument available (see Anastasi, 1982; Carmines, 1979; Nunnally, 1978). For most instruments, evidence for the reliability (e.g., stability) and the validity (e.g., precision) of the measure should be available in previously published studies. Because of the numerous considerations that require attention when developing a new instrument, neophyte investigators, in particular, should avoid constructing scales and measures since very often the construct of interest has already been addressed in the literature and corresponding instruments have been developed (see Oetting, this volume).

Managing Data

One step that is often neglected in the planning portion of the research process is the handling of data. The data can suffer from errors during coding, data entry, and programming. Particularly in grant proposals, researchers may consider providing a sketch of the guidelines that will be used to ensure data integrity. Potential steps that can reduce error include: (1) enter the same data into two separate files–comparing the contents of the files to one another; (2) use a computer program that facilitates data collection by having the subject enter the data directly into a file that can be used for the analysis–thus eliminating coding and data entry errors; and/or, a less desirable means, (3) check frequencies and univariate statistics to identify responses that are not in the expected range.

Analyzing the Data

Only after the data are as nearly perfect as possible can the data analysis process begin. Data that are not analyzed properly will cause the results of the entire study to be in doubt. Investigators should become conversant with the data analytic strategies that are often used in their area of study. For example, knowing when to use a parametric or a nonparametric test is important, but alone is not sufficient. In research that examines human behaviors or attitudes, multivariate methods are almost always needed to partial out the effects of potentially confounding variables (Afifi & Clark, 1984; Morrison, 1976). Selecting the appropriate method of analysis should be based on the hypothesis that is being tested and the type of data (for example, categorical versus continuous) that will be included in the mathematical model (e.g., Press, 1978).

Connecting Research Components

As a final note, the overall and combined quality of all the study's components should be carefully explored. The researcher should ask whether the study as a whole will provide data that will address the hypothesis of interest. When the study is proposed, the persons reviewing the grant must agree that: (1) the area is one that requires further study; (2) the proposed research project is the next critical step in the area; and, (3) the proposed project design is the best means by which to answer the question of interest.

BUDGET PREPARATION STRATEGIES

Funding institutes require a detailed description of costs associated with the proposed work including justifications. These itemized cost estimates are generally required in a standardized budget format. For example, the Public Health Service (PHS) 398 Grant Application Kit provides two budget forms which must be included in the body of the grant application. These budgets must be prepared with a great deal of thoughtfulness, since peer reviewers will be instructed by the funding institute to examine the accuracy, relevance, and appropriateness of costs associated with conducting the proposed research.

Budget preparation can be a very difficult and time consuming process. The budget preparer must be able to identify and accurately estimate all costs necessary to complete the research project. Some organizations have finance departments or offices of sponsored research that provide support in developing the budget. Nevertheless, the principal investigator (PI) is responsible for making sure that the costs outlined in the budget are accurate and are reflected in the research being proposed. While the PI can and should receive assistance from the funding institute's project officer and/or the applicants institute's grant administrators in costing out each of the activities of the research, he or she must understand the research well enough to know what activities are necessary to complete the proposed research. Therefore, the PI must first consider all aspects of the proposed research before a final budget can properly be prepared.

For example:

1. To receive funding for a research proposal, the PI must be able to demonstrate his or her competence to do rigorous

research. This competence is conveyed not only in the aims and significance, background, and experimental methods sections, but also in the budget section of the grant application. PIs who fail to appropriately estimate the costs necessary to complete the research may also fail to convey the level of competence necessary to convince a peer review committee to support the requested budget. For the new researcher, estimating current and future costs may present a problem which can be resolved by talking with a more experienced researcher and with the organization's grants administrator.

2. The requested budget must fall within the fiscal budget of the funding institute. It is not wise, for example, to propose a $2 million research project to an institute with only $1 million available for research in the particular field.

3. Another type of problem may exist if a neophyte researcher were to request $1 million to support the cost of a highly complex project. New researchers should begin with smaller research projects with correspondingly smaller budgets. An established track record of research may be critical for PIs who wish to receive funding for relatively large and complex research projects.

4. Finally, reviewers look for an overall level of consistency throughout the research proposal, including the budget section. There must be a match between the proposed research and the costs outlined in the budget. For example, if the PI describes the testing of 100 patients in the research methods section, the PI must also list testing costs for no more or less than 100 patients in the budget section.

Budget Preparation (PHS 398)

The forms required, as part of the PHS 398 Grant Application, include a detailed budget of the first 12-month period and a summary of the costs for the entire budget period (generally, three years). Proper description and justification of most cost items are also required and may be included on continuation pages. If subsequent budget years differ significantly from first year budget figures, it is recommended that detailed budgets be prepared for all years of the project. This will prove helpful in not only justifying the costs, but also in managing the funds when the research is underway.

In addition, these forms require that the PI itemize and justify direct costs for a number of different cost categories including: personnel, consultant, equipment, supplies, travel, patient care, alternations and renovations, consortium/contractual, and other expenses. The determination of these costs may be quite involved. For example, to determine personnel costs, the PI must not only identify the personnel who will work on the project, but also their roles and responsibilities on the project; salaries and fringe benefits; types of appointment; levels of effort on the project; and finally, the PI should anticipate any future salary increases or personnel changes. Most of the administrative information (salaries and fringe benefits) may be obtained from the organization's grants administrator. The use of consultants should also be very carefully considered since failure to provide coverage for missing expertise on the part of the proposed research team may negatively affect the review outcome. On the other hand, if a significant proportion of work is performed by consultants, reviewers may question the overall competence of the PI and the research team.

All other direct costs must be arranged into the cost categories on the budget forms (see Resource list). The costs must also be allowable. For example, some costs, such as depreciation, may not be allowable as direct costs. For a definition of possible project costs and a discussion of allowable and unallowable costs the PI should consult the PHS Grants Policy Statement.

The PHS Grants Policy Statement also provides advice on indirect costs and how to establish the indirect cost rate. Indirect costs are costs which cannot be identified specifically for individual projects or programs. These costs are entered onto the Checklist page of the PHS 398 Grant Application and may include such things as facilities operation and administrative expenses. The PI's organization incurs these costs and must have negotiated an indirect cost rate with the particular Federal agency for which the grant is submitted. A discussion with the applicant institute's grant officer is recommended.

Use of Spreadsheets to Complete Budgets

If a researcher always knew the exact costs of the proposed research; never had to add or delete a cost item; and could always accurately anticipate the future costs of the research, there would be no need for anything but paper and pencil when preparing the budget. However, research plans invariably change and many versions of the budget are likely to be developed during the course of proposal preparation. Each time a cost item is changed the subtotals and totals in the budget must be recomputed. Moreover, attempting to find the right combination of costs to bring about a desired total budget amount might be an overwhelming task with paper and pencil.

Electronic spreadsheet packages were developed to improve the accuracy and efficiency with which financial statements, including budgets, could be created and implemented. Spreadsheets are a series of cells into which the user may enter text, numbers, formulas, or for advanced users, small programs called macros. Spreadsheet packages including Lotus 123, Excel, and QuattroPro, operate on almost any personal computer and allow the user to replicate the desired budget, line item by line item on the computer screen. By using the different types of cells the user can produce a computerized budget which automatically recalculates subtotals and totals, prints out the budget, and even performs error checking.

The budget produced on an electronic spreadsheet may be as simple or complicated as the budget it is representing. In the simplest case, single line items for each cost figure may be summed by the spreadsheet to obtain subtotals and grand totals. However, most cost items acceptable on the PHS 398 grant application are not single items but are the sum or product of additional more detailed cost items. For example, total domestic travel costs are computed by adding travel costs and per diem costs. Travel costs are computed by multiplying the number of round trips by the cost per trip by the number of people traveling on each trip. Per diem costs may be computed by multiplying the number of days per trip by the number of people traveling by the per diem rate. Thus, total domestic travel costs cannot be completely represented by a single line item.

In this case, the budget preparer may create a smaller worksheet within the spreadsheet which would perform all of the detailed cost computations. By linking the final number computed in the smaller worksheet to the corresponding line item in the budget, changes made to the number of trips or the cost per trip, for example, would automatically be reflected in the budget line items. The spreadsheet would also allow the PI to quickly and accurately test the effects of different cost scenarios on the budget totals and print out draft copies of the budget forms.

The advantages of electronic spreadsheets are very appealing but may be enhanced when the spreadsheet is linked to an intelligent system which provides information on budget preparation, customized error checking, high quality replication of the budget forms for direct submission, and linkage to an electronic form submission mechanism. One such system, known as Grant Ware, will be described in the final section of this paper.

DEVELOPING A POWERFUL PRESENTATION STYLE

The importance of good writing skills in the research development process cannot be overemphasized. Too often, otherwise good research proposals go unfunded because the language of the proposal failed to convince the peer review committee of the significance and feasibility of the proposed work. Moreover, sometimes the language simply gets in the way, resulting in an unclear, imprecise, or incorrect document. The result is that the intended audience for the proposed research is likely to reach the unfortunate conclusion that if not enough care and skill went into the writing and editing processes, then perhaps equally shoddy work might be manifest in the science itself.

This leads to the general question of whether or not the writing skills and related competencies of researchers can be improved and how one goes about this difficult task. Experience with the research development process suggests that use of the following three critical skills appears to enhance the presentation of research applications. These skills include: analyzing audiences, organizing information, and improving language and readability.

Audience Analysis

Contrary to what many might believe, there is more than one intended reader or audience for a research application. In fact, at least six audiences exist:

- Project Officers
- Division of Research Grant's staff
- Executive Secretaries
- Members of the Peer Review Committees
- Members of the national advisory councils
- Other senior officials of the funding institute

These diverse readers will, of course, be looking for different things in a proposal, have varying backgrounds, play different roles within the grants process, and have very different biases and beliefs based on their work experiences and responsibilities. All, however, will read the research application and contribute to the grant process, so in a sense they are all potential audiences and they must be taken into account. Taking audiences into account means being generally aware of their expectations, classifying them according to priority, and then engaging in a thoughtful audience analysis technique. Having completed such a process, the researcher cannot help but better target the intended readers and provide measures to evaluate the appropriateness of the language used in the finished product. A useful general audience analysis heuristic involves the following steps:

1. Identify potential audience such as the list cited above;
2. Classify the audiences according to priorities, often targeting peer reviewers and key institute officials; and,
3. Develop the following picture of the audience to get a better sense of audience expectation including:

    a. BACKGROUND (including education, experience, and familiarity with your proposed research);
    b. ROLE (include title/position, duties/responsibilities, and functions with respect to your research application; and

    c. PERSPECTIVE (include biases, special interests, perspective).

Organization of Information

The organization of information contained in a grant application is crucial to its success. Moreover, ideas and facts pertaining to original research usually have to be arranged for clarity and effect before being written into a grant application. One way to begin this task of arrangement is to order the gathered material to meet the reader's needs and expectations. For example, one important factor that can influence the order in which the information will be presented is referencing past research in detail. By developing a research proposal according to this organizational scheme, the resulting document will not only appear to build on prior work, but convey a more compelling argument in support of the proposed research. In other instances, a "cause/effect" ordering principle may be used. Once an organizational pattern is established, the researcher can then develop an outline, which will serve as the basis for multiple drafts of the document.

Language and Readability Issues

Preparation of a grant application is, in many ways, never done. Researchers can always find ways to improve their writing. This is why they find themselves constructing many drafts of the same document and revising a great deal as they go. A better word here, a better way of making the point there–they write and re-write until they have a final draft that meets their needs and suits the intended audience. Drafting, then, is not something that should be seen as only one step in the grant application process. Rather, it is part of an on-going process that involves revision as well.

After a draft of the grant application has been written and, if possible, laid aside for a period of time, it can then be reconsidered for content and language through a set of directed questions:

* Is the organization of the grant application sections effective and conducive to understanding?

- Is there a sufficient amount of detail within each section?
- Is the material contained in the grant application unified and coherent?

Once these structural issues are attended to, the research proposal must then be evaluated and revised for readability and correctness. If the prose is not conducive to understanding or if the researcher consistently fails to accede to language conventions, then the effectiveness of the grant application can be undermined. Moreover, good "writing style" within grant application generally means readability and correctness. If a grant application is "readable," it therefore contains active verbs, is very concise, includes language that is clear and precise, and contains sentences with lengths appropriate to the intended readers. If a grant application is "correct" linguistically, then the conventions of language such as punctuation, grammar, mechanics, spelling, and usage have been given careful attention.

USING MICROCOMPUTERS
FOR RESEARCH DEVELOPMENT

Microcomputers have had a profound impact on social science research (Anderson and Brent, 1989). The advantages and limitations of microcomputers for research purposes have been widely discussed (Carpenter, 1987). Garson (1989) lists a number of reasons why microcomputing has changed the nature of social science research including: (1) convenience and user friendliness; (2) greater technological diffusion; (3) telecommunications; (4) data archiving, simulation, numeric and text analysis through graphics; and, (5) statistical packages and expert systems software with research applications.

Given these characteristics, it is probable that microcomputers and newly emerging software can assist scientists with the research development process from conceptualization of the problem through selection of research designs, data collection strategies, sampling procedures, methods of measurement, diagnosis, and analysis, to presentation of results with graphic analytic techniques. Critiques that will assist the new users are published in many academic publications and computer magazines (for example, Social Science Microcomputer Review, Duke University).

One such prototype software program, Grant Ware,[1] is being designed to assist the under-represented scholar in the development of RO1 grants applications suitable for submission to PHS. The authors are among the senior developers of this program which is to be available in June of this year.

Grant Ware provides the users with the following features:

1. A smart-form version of the PHS 398 Grant Application Form with error checking, hypertext help, and interlinkage to other program/systems;
2. Valuable information that is both institutionally and scientifically significant;
3. Specific checklists that cut across most aspects of the research process;
4. An optimized filing system known as Grant Builder that allows the user to create and retrieve files that can be worked into the emerging grant application;
5. Integrated software for special purpose functions (e.g., statistical mentoring);
6. An evaluation/assessment instrument capable of providing the user with a profile of strengths and weaknesses relative to education, experience, and knowledge of the grants process;
7. An extensive hypertext-linked bibliography on the grant process from preproposal through submission and review to award or resubmission;
8. Strategies for improving the writing process (including audience analysis, organization, revision, and correctness);
9. A set of budget macros for data interchange between the smart form and spreadsheets including budget development consultation;
10. Links to other research software such as SPSS, Harvard Graphics, WordPerfect, Lotus 123, etc.

---

1. Grant Ware is based on earlier work, i.e., HUGO and BACCHUS.

"Grant Ware pulls diverse technologies together under one umbrella, which is Windows" (ComputerWorld, 1991). Grant Ware is intended to reduce the cost and complexity of the grant application process, by ·providing a set of tools which aid in all aspects of research development. Grant Ware includes three distinct sub-systems: (1) an Information System, which includes PHS-specific facts and guidelines; (2) a Mentoring System that includes five discrete modules aimed at enhancing research skills; and (3) a Production System, offering help in filling out the PHS 398 form.

CONCLUSION

To be competitive in today's research environment, scholars need to develop new strategies to improve the probability that research proposals are approved and awarded. Successful researchers report that scientific knowledge is only one element of the grants process. Additional expertise will be required to meet the challenges of increased competition and decreased availability of research funds. Understanding the process including review, strengthening the language of a proposal, presenting well justified budgets, as well as presenting a compelling scientific argument are all requisite research development skills. New and emerging tools, such as computers and research software, make it possible for researchers to adopt an electronic desktop approach for research development, where each step of the process is enhanced by special purpose programs.

INFORMATION SOURCES

The Catalogue of Federal Domestic Assistance. Superintendent of Documents, Government Printing Office, Washington, D.C. 20402.
Commerce Business Daily, Superintendent of Documents, Government Printing Office, Washington, D.C. 20402.
Federal Register, Superintendent of Documents, Government Printing Office, Washington, D.C. 20402.
FEDIX, An On-line Information Service for Universities and Other Research Organizations, User's Guide, September, 1990, Version 3.0, Release 1.0. Available through NTIS, U.S. Department of Commerce, Springfield, VA 22161.
Guide to Research Support, APA, 1200 17th Street, Washington, D.C. 20036.

NIH Guide to Grants and Contracts, Distribution Center, NIH, Room B4-N-08, Building 31, Bethesda, Maryland 20892.

PHS Grant Policy Statement, U.S. DHHS, Publication No. (OASH) 90-50,000 (Rev.) October 1, 1990.

U.S. DHHS, PHS, *Grant Application Form 398*, Rev. 10/88, Reprinted 9/89. NIDA, Office of Grants Management, Rm 8-A54, 5600 Fishers Lane, Rockville, Maryland 20857.

REFERENCES

ADAMHA Handbook on Review of Grant Applications, ADAMHA Management Manual, Program Management Instruction 40-1-1, April, 1987.

Afifi, A.A., and V. Clark. *Computer-Assisted Multivariate Analysis*. Belmont, CA: Lifetime Learning Publications, 1984.

Anastasi, A. *Psychological Testing*. (5th ed.), New York: Macmillan Publishing Co., Inc., 1982.

Carpenter, E.H. The Evolving Statistics and Research Process Using Microcomputers Statistical Software, *Social Science Microcomputer Review*, 5(4), 1987.

Cochran, W.G. *Sampling Techniques* (2nd ed.). New York: Wiley, 1966.

ComputerWorld, March 4, 1991, " Special Report: The Windows Payoff".

Cook, T. and D. Campbell. *Quasi-Experimentation Design and Analysis Issues for Field Settings*. Chicago: Rand McNally College Publishing Co., 1979.

Friedman, H. Simplified determinations of statistical power, magnitude of effect and research samples sizes. *Educational and Psychological Measurements*, 42, 521-526, 1982.

Garson, G. David. Microcomputers and Social Science Research. *Advances in Social Science and Computers*, JAI Press, Inc., Volume 1, 1989.

Kramer, H.C., and S. Thiemann. *Statistical Power Analysis in Research*. Beverly Hills, CA: Sage, 1987.

Nunnally, J.C. *Psychometric Theory*. (2nd ed.), New York: McGraw-Hill Book Co., 1978.

Press, S.J., and S. Wilson. Choosing between logistic regression and discriminant function analysis. *Journal of American Statistical Association*, 73:699, 1978.

Webb, E.J., D.T. Campbell, R.D. Schwartz, and L. Sechrest. *Unobtrusive Measures: Nonreactive Research in the Social Sciences*. Chicago: Rand McNally College Publishing Co., 1966.

Alcohol and Drug Use
Among American Minorities

Howard Rebach

INTRODUCTION

For a variety of social and political reasons, the 1980s saw an increased research on drugs and alcohol. Substance use and abuse among American minorities also received increased attention. Several earlier reviews have examined the subject of drug and alcohol use among minorities (Lex, 1987; Tucker, 1985; Long & Sherl, 1984). This paper grew out of an attempt by the present author, under the direction of the Special Populations Branch of the National Institute on Drug Abuse (NIDA), to prepare a comprehensive annotated bibliography and evaluation of published materials on substance use among minorities. The purpose here is briefly to review the literature, present some examples from the annotated bibliography, and provide an analysis of the literature.

The materials in the larger collection (Rebach et al.) were obtained through searches of three on-line data bases and a direct search of *Sociological Abstracts, Psychological Abstracts*, and *Social Science Index*. In addition, bibliographies of articles were examined for relevant material.

The articles in the collection have been categorized along 4 dimensions:

1. *Ethnic group*: Black, Hispanic, Asian, or Native American;
2. *Age group*: Youth or adults, subdivided by gender where relevant;

Howard Rebach is affiliated with the Department of Social Science at the University of Maryland Eastern Shore.

3. *Topic*: Consequences of use, Epidemiology, Etiology, Diagnosis, Treatment, and Prevention;
4. *Substance covered*: alcohol, drugs, or both (see Appendix for a list of the articles described along the 4 dimensions).

There are several types of articles in the collection. One type, empirical studies, were either of general population samples, school based samples, or clinical reports or studies of persons in alcohol or drug treatment programs. A second type was literature reviews and the third type was labelled "think pieces" which included editorials as well as commentaries either on the state of the field or the state of the literature.

The annotations included evaluations of the research with most attention given to the empirical studies. Evaluation criteria were: (1) Internal validity, (2) external validity, (3) Data analysis, (4) values of findings or other comments, and (5) specific problems. Internal validity refers to the extent to which outcome or criterion measures could be attributed to predictor or independent variables. External validity refers to the generalizability of results beyond the sample studied. For discussions of these concepts including threats to validity, readers are referred to standard works such as Campbell and Stanley (1963) or Babbie (1988). Data analysis techniques were also evaluated where appropriate.

By value of findings I mean whether the findings of the study or the insights of the review or commentary add significantly to our understanding of substance use among minorities. I also mean whether or not the study provides fruitful avenues for further research. Finally, articles were evaluated for specific problems that seemed unique to a particular paper. Examples include sampling issues, logical or conceptual problems, specific measurement problems, definitional problems, and issues of reductionism or ecological fallacy.

In this report I will first briefly summarize what the body of literature shows with regard to the topic area. This will be followed by some examples from the larger annotated bibliography. Finally, I will present a brief analysis and critique of the literature.

WHAT THE LITERATURE SHOWS REGARDING MINORITY SUBSTANCE USE

The four major minority groups covered by this body of literature are Asian-Americans, Blacks, Hispanics, and American Indians or Native Americans. This summary will cover the broad topic areas suggested by the literature.

Consequences to Minorities of Substance Use

One major consequence of substance use is health risk. Alcoholism deaths occur at three times the rate among Blacks as among whites (Gary, 1986). For example, the esophageal cancer death rate among Black men was found to be higher than the rate in the general population with 81% of cases attributable to alcohol use (Pottern et al., 1981; Rogers et al., 1982).

Cirrhosis of the liver is another health problem frequently associated with alcohol use. Herd (1985) cited data showing that cirrhosis rates of Black men between 25 and 34 years old, in seven major cities, was ten times the rate for same-aged white men and, overall, the cirrhosis death rate for Blacks was about twice the rate for whites. While poor nutrition, infectious inflammation of the liver, and other consequences of poverty are associated with the disease, Herd pointed out that "studies of liver morbidity and mortality specify alcohol use as the principle etiological agent in acute liver disease." Herd went on to argue that:

> . . . true cirrhosis is rare in youthful populations. However, the increasing rates of acute liver disease among young black males cannot account for the general increase in liver cirrhosis mortality among non-whites since it is the high rates of mortality in middle aged and older adults which contribute the most to overall death rates.

Lengthy duration of heavy alcohol use was found to be the major risk factor in cirrhosis mortality. These findings are not confined to Blacks. The American Indian mortality rate for cirrhosis was four and a half times the rate of the general population (Beauvais & LeBoeff, 1985). For both American Indians and Blacks, low socioeconomic status may interact with poor nutrition and other disease factors, but alcohol use exacerbates the problem and contributes to morbidity and mortality. Alcohol use was found to be one of the best predictors of health problems among Blacks, either as direct cause or exacerbating or preventing treatment of other conditions (Miller & Miller, 1988; Rogers et al., 1982).

Cognitive impairment was also found to be a direct consequence of drinking in about half of American Indian, white, Black (McShane & Willenbring, 1984) and Puerto Rican (Castanada & Galanter, 1988) patients in studies of detoxification patients and heroin addicts were found to have impaired visual memory (Penk et al., 1981).

Health problems among American Indians occurred at rates 2.5 to 5 times that of the general population. One study found the rate of fetal alcohol effects among Plains tribes to be higher than any other reported in the world (May et al., 1983). Alcohol and other drugs were implicated in 5 of the 10 leading causes of American Indian death. Overall, mortality for American Indians in the 36-44 age group was reported to be 3 to 6 times that of the general population (May, 1986; Young, 1988).

May (1986), citing data from government sources showed that American Indian motor vehicle death rates were 2.5-5.5 times higher than the general population; alcoholism death rates about 5.5 times higher; cirrhosis death rates 2.6-3.5 times higher; suicide 1.2-2.3 times higher; and homicide rates 1.7-2.3 times higher. Among American Indians, 50-65% of motor vehicle deaths, 85% of liver cirrhosis deaths, and a large proportion, more than half, of suicides and homicides are "directly related to alcohol" (Beauvais & LeBoeff, 1985; May, 1982; May, 1986). Young (1988) reported that 80% of suicides and 90% of homicides had alcohol as a factor. Young also reported that "Perhaps the single most disturbing statistic is that 75 percent of all Native American deaths can be traced to alcohol in some way."

Arrests and crimes of violence are another major consequence of substance use. Again studies show that minority members are at higher risk for arrest, for being victims, or for committing violent crimes. For example, studies report that Black men were 5 times more likely to die from homicide than white men and between 40 and 60% of the victims and between 50 and 85% of homicide offenders had been drinking at the time of the homicide (Petersen et al., 1978; Gary, 1986; Harvey, 1985; Primm & Wesley, 1985).

Epidemiology–Extent of Use Among Minorities

Most of the studies reported on alcohol use and abuse. Very little research is available detailing the extent of other drug use. Moreover, the research tends to focus on substance use among minorities as it compares to members of the dominant culture, white Anglos.

The strong finding coming from this research is that whites generally tend to use alcohol and most drugs at higher rates than Blacks, Hispanics or Asians. For example, studies of youth have found whites and American Indians have the highest rates of lifetime and annual prevalence and the highest rates of heavy use of alcohol. By contrast, Black youth have the highest rates of abstention from alcohol. About 2/3 of Hispanic youth and about half of Asian youth were also found to use alcohol. Black youth had the lowest rate of drinkers and heavy drinkers and significantly less use of illicit drugs. Black and Hispanic youth also begin marijuana use at a later age than whites and are less likely to become heavy users (Barnes & Welte, 1986; Welte & Barnes, 1987; Zabin, 1986; Maddahian, NewComb & Bentler, 1985, 1986; Kaplan et al., 1986; Chavez et al., 1986; Thompson & Wilsnack, 1987). However, one study suggested that small town Hispanic youth may use substances at rates higher than national averages (Chavez et al., 1986).

Half to 90% of American Indian youth, depending on tribe, were found to have experimented with alcohol, 40-60% with marijuana (May, 1986). Use of inhalants among American Indian youth is also problematic. Inhalants are the first drug used (Young, 1987). Data from a national sample showed a range of lifetime prevalence from 22% to 33% with about 1/4 continuing to use inhalants. Studies also showed a trend of increasing use of alcohol, marijuana, inhalants, and stimulants among American Indian youth from 1975 to 1983 (Beauvais, Oetting & Edwards, 1985; May, 1986).

School data may underestimate actual rates of use since it is likely that those who have dropped out of school may be heavier users.

Studies of adults mirror those reported above for adolescents. However, the diversity of American Indians, Hispanics, Blacks, and Asian-Americans makes generalization to subgroups within these ethnicities difficult. For example, there are about 300 different tribes of American Indians with distinctive cultures. Generalization about American Indians is tenuous and studies show a wide range of use patterns. For example, annual prevalence for alcohol is estimated to be from 30-80% compared to the national rate of 67%, and rates have generally been found to be higher among urban American Indians than rural or reservation American Indians (Young, 1988; Beauvais & LeBoeff, 1985).

Results from several national surveys show that alcohol abstention rates are lowest among white Anglos, followed by Hispanics, then Blacks. Rates of frequent heavier drinking is highest among whites with Hispanics next, and lowest among Blacks, though Hispanics had the highest rate of heaviest drinking (Caetano, 1984). Herd (1988) studied a national probability sample of about 2300 women, black and white. She discovered that race, independent of other variables, was the strongest predictor of abstention and heavy drinking: Black women were more likely to be abstainers and less likely to be heavy drinkers. Blacks generally show high abstinence rates (between 30 and 40%) and less alcohol use compared to other ethnic groups (Lex, 1987; Hubbard et al., 1986; Caetano, 1984; Neff, 1986; Castanada & Galanter, 1988; Fernandez-Pol et al., 1986; Zager & Megargee, 1981).

Asian Americans generally show alcohol use rates lower than those of whites, Hispanics or American Indians. Among the Asian groups the Japanese Americans, Hawaiians, and persons with one Asian and one Caucasian parent approach the alcohol use rates of whites while Koreans, Chinese, and Filipinos show significantly lower rates. Compared to whites, Asian groups also showed generally lower rates of lifetime prevalence for 11 drugs studied (Kitano, Lubben, & Chi, 1988; Towle, 1988; Johnson et al., 1985; McLaughlin et al., 1987; Sue, 1987).

Gender, age, and degree of acculturation (assimilation into the American culture) are related to rates of substance use. Across ethnic groups, men tend to use alcohol and drugs at significantly higher rates than women (Caetano & Herd, 1984; Caetano, 1984, 1987a, 1987b, 1987d; Sutker et al., 1978; Hser et al., 1987; Mendes de Leon & Markides, 1986; McLaughlin et al., 1987; Kitano et al., 1988). Younger persons across ethnic groups also use drugs and alcohol at higher rates than older persons (Sue, 1987; Kitano et al., 1988; Mendes de Leon & Markides, 1986; Caetano & Herd, 1984; Caetano, 1984, 1987a, 1987c; McLaughlin et al., 1987). Use rates generally vary inversely with age. However, Black men in their 30s showed higher drinking rates than Black men in their 20s, with sharp declines in drinking rates for Black men in their 40s and older (Caetano & Herd, 1984; Caetano, 1984). Abstention rates increase with age across ethnic groups with a larger increase among Black and Hispanic males than white males (Caetano, 1984). On average, Blacks and Hispanics start use of alcohol and other drugs at older ages than do whites (Kaplan et al., 1986; Hser et al., 1987). White drug users, compared to Blacks were found to be younger at the time of first opiate use and used more different drugs (Sutker et al., 1978).

The more acculturated Hispanics and Asian-Americans tend to approach the use pattern of the general U. S. population, and go to bars and clubs and parties more often than less acculturated persons (Kitano et al., 1988; Sue, 1987; Caetano, 1987a, 1987b, 1987c, 1987d; Mendes de Leon & Markides, 1986). The differential rates between males and females is heightened when the level of acculturation is considered. That is, the difference between males and females is greater among the less acculturated than the acculturated. While white women show considerably higher rates of use and problem use than do minority women, the more acculturated Hispanic and Asian women tend to use more alcohol than their less acculturated counterparts (Sue, 1987; McLaughlin et al., 1987; Caetano, 1986, 1987a, 1987b, 1987d; Mendes de Leon, 1986; Kitano, Lubben, & Chi, 1988).

Etiology–Factors Related to Substance Use
Among Minorities

The search for variables that explain drug and alcohol use among minorities range from personality types to macro-sociological influences. Most studies are cross sectional, including studies of patient groups. It is difficult to establish the time order—what is antecedant and what is consequence—in these types of studies. The general interpretation is that drug and alcohol use can generally be seen as a response to environmental stress, experienced by greater segments of minority than majority people.

Socio-Cultural Influences: The conflict between the dominant culture and the cultures of various minorities may be an underlying causative factor in substance use. For example, the accumulation of wealth, competitiveness, and family mobility conflict with American Indian ways. Individual success is not valued because it disrupts social harmony. These values are at odds with the dominant culture but influence the economic and personal well being of American Indian people (Beauvais & LeBoueff, 1985). Values conflict and culture conflict have also been suggested as characterizing substance use among Blacks, Hispanics, and Asians (Harvey, 1985; Wurzman et al., 1982; Yee & Thu, 1987).

Macro-level studies have found rates of alcoholism related to factors that create tension in society, to cultural attitudes toward drinking, and availability of functional alternatives to alcohol for stress reduction. Indicators of stress within social systems—e.g., unemployment rates, family dissolution rates, measures of status integration, and ease of entry to the opportunity structure—were found associated with indices of alcohol use such as cirrhosis death rates, consumption rates, and other alcohol death rates, with high rates associated with minority status (Linsky, Straus & Colby, 1985; Heien & Pompelli, 1987; Query, 1985). These stressors are experienced by greater proportions of minority members and are significant stimuli to subsequent drug and alcohol use. The conditions for the onset of substance abuse may not be much different between majority and minority members, but the conditions of minority life may create the conditions for more people.

Social-Historical studies have also shown the increase in Black drinking in the 20th century to be related to changes in race relations and migration to northern cities among Blacks (Cruz, 1988; Herd, 1985). Alcohol use among Blacks may be an attempt to cope with stress from unemployment, poverty, inadequate housing, family problems, and discrimination, all of which are interrelated (Gary, 1986; Harvey, 1985; Thompson & Carter, 1988). The same may be said for American Indians (Beauvais & LeBoueff, 1985) and Indo-Chinese refugees (Yee & Thu, 1987).

Moreover, these groups are not well integrated into the economic opprortunity structure. Low levels of education, job training and skills characterized Blacks (Harvey, 1985), American Indian (Guyette, 1982), and Hispanic (Wurzman et al., 1982-83) substance users. American Indians have the lowest aggregate and per capita income. The urban environment was the most likely context for first alcohol and drug use for American Indians; 3/4 said they felt they did not belong (Guyette, 1982; Harvey, 1985; Wurzman et al., 1982; Query, 1985).

Elements of traditional culture can also stimulate substance use. The idea of Machismo includes the ability to hold a lot of alcohol (Arredondo et al., 1987). Evidence also suggests that integration can act as a brake on substance use. For example, American Indians who were better integrated into both American Indian and modern systems–had meaningful roles in each culture–were less susceptible to substance abuse (May, 1986). The culture of a traditional society can also act as a brake. Among Asians, those more assimilated, especially women, were more likely to drink while traditional norms stress moderation combining alcohol with family celebration (Chi, Kitano, & Lubben, 1988).

Social Influences: Among the strongest predictors of substance use among both youth and adult members of minority groups was peer use (Dawkins, 1986; Kaplan et al., 1986; Brook et al., 1986; Kleinman & Lukoff, 1978; Jessor, Chase, & Donovan, 1980; Barnes & Welte, 1986; Kaplan et al., 1986) and possibly the ease of acquisition and the availability of drugs and alcohol from friends. Black youth were found to have less availability from friends which made it harder for Black youth to get alcohol and drugs except marijuana from friends compared to whites, Hispanics, and Asians (Maddahian, Newcomb, & Bentler, 1986).

Family models and relationships were also found related to alcohol and drug use. For youth, where parents provided models for substance use or may have been the source of alcohol or drugs, youth are more likely to drink and use drugs. Parental permissiveness and parent-child conflict were also found associated with initiation of use by youth, across ethnic groups (Barnes & Welte, 1986;

Brook et al., 1986; Dawkins, 1986; Jessor, Chase, & Donovan, 1980; Kaplan et al., 1986; Thompson & Wilsnack, 1987; Guyette, 1982). There is also evidence that when youth are taught responsible alcohol use in a family context, they are less prone to abuse (Chi, Kitano, & Lubben, 1988; Valliant, 1986). They are also less likely to initiate use if there is low maternal rejection and permissiveness and high identification with parents (Brook et al., 1986).

Attitude toward use was also found to have a strong association to use. Those who approved of use and saw benefits from use also showed higher levels of use (Caetano 1984, Atkins et al., 1987; Connors et al., 1988; Fernandez-Pol et al., 1986). For example, a group of Black women in treatment attibuted fewer negative consequences to alcohol use than other groups (Amaro, Beckman, & Mays, 1987). Acceptance of substance use was also found inversely related to measures of racial consciousness among Blacks; those who use may be more accepting of use but lower on racial consciousness (Gary & Berry, 1985).

Individual Characteristics: Drug and alcohol use by youth, across minority groups, has been found associated with rejection of conventional values (Kaplan et al., 1986), low orientation to work, higher tolerance for deviance, and perception of self as deviant (Brook et al., 1986; Kleinman & Lukoff, 1978). Poor grades, low school achievement, and school misconduct and low compatibility with family and friends were also associated with use (Barnes & Welte, 1986; Jessor, Chase, & Donovan, 1980). Additionally, experience of stress was associated with initiation to marijuana use and escalation of use across groups, possibly for the relief of stress (Kaplan et al., 1986).

American Indian youth who were inhalant users scored lower on measures of socially desirable physical and psychological assets than non-users. The non-users scored better on tests of academic achievement and evaluated themselves more positively. As inhalant use increased, self appraisal went lower (Wingert & Fifield, 1985).

Black adults in a treatment program were reported to have less psychopathology, depression, and hysteria than white patients. (Penk et al., 1981, Penk et al., 1982). Another study, however, found Black drinkers in a general population sample scored higher on a measure of depression compared to whites and Hispanics.

Across groups, drinkers scored higher on the depression measure than abstainers (Neff, 1986).

Depression was also associated with drinking by Hispanic women (Caetano, 1987c). More Black women in treatment were heavy escape drinkers and reported stronger feelings of social isolation than white women (Amaro, Beckman, & Mays, 1987). And stressors such as divorce and widowhood were found associated with depression and substance use among Asian women (McLaughlin et al., 1987).

Compared to white alcoholics, Black alcoholics perceived their families and families of origin as less disturbed than white alcoholics (Patterson et al., 1981) and Black opiate addicts were found less alienated from society and had greater concern for conventionality, valued equal opportunity, reasonable affluence and ambition. White addicts were more concerned with self and not with conventional achievement roles.

Though some have argued that personality differences make minor contributions to use and show no differences across minority groups (Jessor, Chase & Donovan, 1980, Patterson et al., 1981), others have found such differences. White drug abusers scored higher than Black or Hispanic drug abusers on measures of thrill seeking or sensation seeking. As a result, whites were more likely to use hallucinogens and stimulants than Blacks or Hispanics who also began drug use and opiate use later. Sensation seeking was associated with greater use and use of a wider variety of drugs (Sutker et al., 1978; Galizio & Stein, 1983).

Lewis et al., (1985) reported a study of a cohort of Black men who were in elementary school between 1930 and 1934. They found that those with an anti-social personality disorder had 4 times the rate of alcholism and 18 times the rate of drug abuse compared to non-anti-social men. But anti-social men did not start drinking earlier than non-anti-social men and the former were as likely as the latter to have a first degree relative who was a problem drinker. The anti-social men left home, had sex, were arrested and used drugs earlier than the non-anti-social men. They were also less affiliated with organized religion, had lower education, more school problems, lower occupational status, and were generally more irritable.

Genetics and Physiology: Some studies have examined genetic and physiological differences among ethnic groups with particular attention to the flushing response of Asians and possible differences in the metabolism of alcohol. The flushing response refers to the tendency of Asians to show visible changes in skin color and have a subjective feeling of warmth and tingling skin in response to drinking alcohol. Racial differences have been found in absorption rates and metabolism rates between whites and American Indians, in enzymes that help metabolize alcohol, and in facial flushing and cardiovascular responses between Caucasians and Orientals (Reed, 1985).

Studies of flushers compared to non-flushers found that Japanese Americans who flushed reported lower frequency and quantity of alcohol use and lower frequency of drunkenness, but 3/4 of flushers reported continuing to drink even though flushing (Towle, 1988). Non-flushers drank more per occasion were more likely to drink at home while flushers tended to drink primarily at social settings. Flushers tended to get sleepy from drink and have more unpleasant autonomic responses while non-flushers were more likely to get violent (Suwaki & Ohara, 1985).

These findings should be considered with caution, however, when it is noted that the rate of flushers among Japanese, Chinese, Eskimo, and American Indians is about the same (and at a high rate) but that the drinking habits of these groups are vastly different (Sue, 1987). Thus, Reed (1985) and Fisher (1987) concluded that genetic differences may be a factor in different responses to alcohol, but there is no clear cut evidence for a role of heredity in alcohol abuse. The within group variance is greater than the between group variance in use patterns.

Diagnosis, Treatment, and Prevention Programming with Minorities

The literature on treatment and prevention is very general, largely speculative and polemical. Most writers call for cultural sensitivity as part of treatment and prevention programming in minority groups. But there is a shortage of actual models that operationally specify how clinicians or prevention staff should proceed and a shortage of follow-up studies that indicate the relative success of interventions. There is a clear need for the systematic development and testing of both treatment and prevention programs.

Diagnosis: Attempts have been made to study the diagnosis of substance abuse disorders among minority members using MMPI scales. The evidence suggests the possibility of racial bias in use of these scales with Black alcohol and drug abusers. Two popular scales, labelled the "Ah" scale and the "MAC" scale and made up of selected MMPI items, showed no validity for whites or Blacks though the ICAS scale was found useful (Zager & Megargee, 1981; Snyder, Kline, & Podany, 1985; Patterson et al., 1981; Penk et al., 1981; Penk et al., 1982).

Bell et al. (1985) were more concerned with misdiagnosis of alcohol related disorders contributing to the number of Black patients inappropriately labelled schizophrenic, which in turn has dysfunctional results in treatment. They showed that while Black alcoholism may have the positive signs of schizophrenia–e.g., hallucinations–it does not have the negative signs of emotional withdrawal and blunted affect. Bell et al. presented a convincing body of evidence to show that Black alcoholics have a high rate of misdiagnosis. Evidence also shows that clinicians' lack of understanding of cultural differences in drinking practices and culturally biased diagnostic criteria (the DSM-III) account for the misdiagnosis. Racial stereotyping and clinician-patient cultural differences are also involved.

Knox (1985) argued that spirituality is a tool in the treatment of Black alcoholics and their family and should be included in the assessment. Clinicians should explore sources of hope and strength, the meaning of spirituality, and the diversity of beliefs and practices among Black patients.

The attitude toward substance use may also differ cross culturally. Among Hispanic men, alcohol use defines virility and when drinkers report use levels, they may have different meanings for "light use" or "moderate use" than an Anglo might have. The suggestion is to determine the meaning of the terms that these individuals use. In addition, while acculturated Hispanics may accept the disease concept of alcoholism, less acculturated persons may attribute the problem to externals such as God's will or to witchcraft. Assessment should pay close attention to the patient's explanation for the problem which may be culturally influenced (Arredondo et al., 1987).

Treatment: Minority persons are less likely to seek treatment and less likely to complete treatment once begun (Arredondo et al., 1987; Anglin, Hser, & Booth, 1987; Flores, 1986; Rogan, 1986; Savage & Simpson, 1980; Sue, 1987). Asians are very unlikely to enter treatment. This is true for Asian populations overseas as well as Asian Americans (Sue, 1987).

Minority persons who do receive treatment may enter non-voluntarily. But voluntarily or not, they may enter treatment later in their substance abuse careers which makes positive treatment outcomes less likely.

One explanation for the general finding is based on the cultures of minority groups. For example, in Hispanic cultures, men are expected to be drinkers, to be able "to hold their liquor" and provide for their families. Women are to be protected and cared for. Both are expected to fulfill their familial roles. Men and women are also required not to bring shame to their families. When they have alcohol or drug problems the family will move to prevent shame and try to prevent outsiders from discovering the drug or alcohol problem. This is not the same as "denial" but does limit early identification and treatment. Seeking treatment brings shame (Arredondo et al., 1987; Wurzman et al., 1982). A similar suggestion about family shame and protection was recorded regarding Black women and Japanese-Americans (family members enable by protecting and supporting) (Thornton & Carter, 1988; Brisbane & Stuart, 1985; Sue, 1987).

Cultural values may also influence treatment. The confrontation model may not be appropriate with Hispanics, especially Hispanic men. Because of the Machismo value, confrontation may threaten a man's authority. On the other hand, treatment that emphasizes being better able to fulfill male role requirements and draws heavily on family support, religion, and folk healers or curanderos, may be more effective (Arredondo et al., 1987; Wurzman et al., 1982).

Additional explanations include structural features of the treatment system. Compared to white females, Black women were found to be more likely to get treatment at publicly funded programs.

Their income averaged 1/2 to 1/3 that of the white women alcoholics. The white women were more aware of services and were 10 times more likely to have insurance that covered private alcohol treatment. White women were also more likely to be employed. Since employment was associated with positive treatment outcomes, Black women were thought to be at higher risk for poor outcomes both because of receiving treatment at public programs and because of employment status (Amaro, Beckman, & Mays, 1987).

Another issue is that programs are run by professionals from the white Anglo culture which may cause minority persons to avoid treatment (Rogan, 1986; Arredondo et al., 1987; Savage & Simpson, 1980; Ziter, 1987; Thornton & Carter, 1988). Maypole (1983) elaborated on this theme suggesting that the lack of similarity between Black clients and white professionals, separated by race, wealth, power, education, and status, led to lack of trust and to high drop out rates.

The treatment programs are said to lack and to need an understanding of and sensitivity to ethnic cultures to be effective with minority persons. While many writers call for cultural sensitivity, not much specificity has been provided as to how culturally sensitive treatment would proceed. The most frequent suggestion is that programs be staffed by members of the minority group to be served.

For example, Flores (1986) found that treatment staff and American Indian patients had different value systems and stereotyped each other. Even well educated American Indian staff members could not predict American Indian patients' values. Flores argued that a shared world view is essential to treatment success and that value differences may explain why American Indian patients drop out.

One suggestion regarding culturally sensitive treatment for Blacks has been to link Black patients with the Black community (Maypole, 1983; Amaro, Beckman, & Mays, 1987; Harvey, 1985; Thornton & Carter, 1988; Ziter, 1987). Maypole attributed success to one program because it was less formal and patients could drop in, chat, have coffee, etc.–the program was an integral part of their community rather than part of the dominant culture.

Spirituality seemed to one key to the meaning of cultural sensitivity in treatment. Since spirituality varies by culture, treatment should consider what spirituality means for each culture rather than impose a meaning based on the dominant culture (Knox, 1985; Slagle & Weibel-Orlando, 1986; Hall, 1985). Ziter (1987) added the suggestion that culturally sensitive treatment required a family approach and a bicultural approach–that minority persons must live in two worlds. the one that provides for their economic needs and the one that meets their emotional and spiritual needs. The latter is their own ethnic culture while the former is generally the majority culture. Treatment should empower individuals in both these worlds.

Studies of treatment success are few and far between. What there is has not reported a great deal of success. Studies generally compared minority members in treatment to outcomes for white Anglos. Whites generally showed somewhat higher rates of positive outcome, but most reports show limited success generally (Anglin et al., 1987; Query, 1985; Savage & Simpson, 1980; Joe et al., 1983; Brunswick & Messeri, 1985; Barrett, Simpson, & Lehman, 1988; Comas-Diaz, 1986; Costello, 1987).

Prevention: Prevention must also deal with cultural as well as social and political issues. For example, there are more liquor stores and advertisements in Black communities. This is a form of economic exploitation that results in easy availability of alcohol in these neighborhoods (Gary, 1986; Primm & Westley, 1985; Harvey, 1985; Thornton & Carter, 1988).

Various writers point out the need for culturally specific prevention programming (Maypole & Anderson, 1987; Womble & Bakeman, 1986; Schinke et al., 1985; Murphy & DeBlassie, 1984; May, 1986; Gilchrist et al., 1987; Bobo et al., 1988). The greatest strides in this direction have been made with American Indian youth.

The issue of prevention programming was a social and political issue. Tribes saw programs as being imposed by outsiders (Beauvais & LeBoueff, 1985). Reports from one group indicate limited success to date, but also show promise and a step by step systematic development of programs (Bobo et al., 1988; Gilchrist, 1987; Schinke et al., 1985; Schinke et al., 1988). The first step required that the intervention agents gain acceptance from community members and legitimizers and include local people in the preparation and presentation of materials to be used in prevention programs. Intervention had as a goal increasing coping skills, self-esteem, and reducing substance use.

A GENERAL CRITIQUE OF THE LITERATURE ON MINORITIES AND SUBSTANCE USE AND ABUSE

We must begin this critique with the statement that the extant literature has provided needed information and has served to open the way to understanding. This critique is not to demean the work of the various researchers and commentators but to suggest directions for expanding knowledge and building on the present base. This critique will consider methodological and conceptual issues.

Methodology: One major methodological problem has been the sampling problem. Sue's remark (1987) regarding the research on Asian-Americans could well stand for all research on minorities: "few . . . studies exist and most information is derived from small or select samples that may or may not be representative. . . . " Too often samples are limited when minorities are studied.

Also, too often studies are based on student or patient groups. But minorities are less likely to seek treatment and are more likely to drop out of school. There is a need to know more about the people who do not fall into these groups. It is highly likely that they are significantly different in their rates of use and use patterns than those who do fall into these study groups and whose results get reported. Patient studies are particularly problematic. Most cannot be generalized beyond the specific group of patients studied.

There is some trend in this direction with the National Household Surveys but there is still a need for more well constructed samples that focus on minority groups in more detail, especially groups that are hard to get at such as American Indians, Asian, as well as drop outs and persons without fixed addresses.

A second methodological problem concerns measurement and conceptual and operational definition of terms such as "alcohol or drug abuse," "alcoholism," etc. For studies and findings to be comparable terms like "heavier drinking" and "heavy drinking" need to be replaced with more carefully defined terms. One important step has been the development of quantity frequency indices which represent the best approach to date. Throughout all the research, investigators need to pay more attention to the psychometric properties of their measurement instruments such as reliability and validity.

Third, there is a need for designs that control the time order. It is vital in the understanding of the etiology, treatment, and prevention of substance abuse that what are antecedent conditions and what are consequences be carefully controlled. Cross-sectional studies that use recall data may be assessing the results of selective recall that helps the person justify present behavior. These studies may also be assessing as predictor variables, those variables that are a consequence of earlier substance use. For example, a finding that adolescent users have conflicted relationships with their parents can either be a cause of substance use, an effect of substance use, or both may be a consequent of some unstudied factor.

Fourth, there is a need for more use of ethnographic studies. One apparent omission in the research is the discovery of the meanings that members of ethnic minorities have for the substances they use and for substance use generally. Functional analysis would also help here: what functions are served for whom by the use of substances within minority groups.

Finally, there is a need for more theory-driven research. By and large the research on substance use among minorities has been atheoretical. It is time for developing and testing explanatory theory. Two candidates that have received a little attention have been the ideas of stress, Merton's anomie theory and variations thereof, and social learning theory. Such theoretical development has obvious practical value for both treatment and prevention.

Conceptual: The subject of substance use and abuse among ethnic minority groups suggests that ethnic membership is a variable for study. This is a conceptual error. Ethnicity is not a variable but a marker for a host of variables. As an area of study, it is necessary for investigators to "unpack" the concepts of ethnicity and minority. Ethnic group differences are often found in family arrangements, styles of child rearing, male-female relations, and on and on, covering many lifestyle issues including the place of alcohol and drug use.

Minority group status in America also carries with it a host of meanings related to socioeconomic status, access to life chances, and entry into the opportunity structure. Studies that control for SES, education, etc., often control out what being a minority member means within the context of American society.

Minority status usually means a specific relationship to the ownership of the means of production, to political power, and the power to self-determination. These macro sociological issues cannot be divorced from the study of alcohol and drug use among minorities as they usually are. These issues translate themselves into the everyday lives of individuals and the things that provide stresses that may prompt "self medication" to find relief through the use of alcohol or drugs.

Closely related to this idea is Fisher's idea (1987) regarding the medicalization and reification of alcoholism. Fisher noted that characterizing alcoholism as a disease has resulted in its being applied cross culturally in ways similar to broken bones or measles. Among other things, Fisher concludes that this approach is a gross oversimplification of alcoholism and that clinicians view it as a single entity. It makes it an individual phenomenon apart from the environment of the individual and the environment of the group that the individual belongs to. As a disease, it is something the individual "has." Fisher asserts that alcoholism cannot be understood or dealt with apart from the socio-cultural context.

King (1983) also wrote that the research is based on an epistemology that treats political issues as "some immutable genetic-type unfolding outside of the concrete social activity." It over geneticizes and psychologizes social problems in the Black community. Thus based, research cannot guide treatment in any community, especially the Black community. It fails to represent the context–economic and historic relations–in which alcoholism occurs. But explanation of alcohol abuse must be grounded in the analysis of "the concrete reality of both the economic (material) and historic (symbolic) relations of the person/group being studied in the society."

While we suggest unpacking the concept of ethnicity, it is important to also note that generic terms like "Black," "American Indian," "Hispanic," and "Asian-American" do not refer to simple homogeneous entities. As noted there are about 300 tribal groups of American Indians, and about 200 languages and dialects. Each has a unique culture and, very likely, different norms regarding substance use and related matters. Likewise, Hispanics come from Puerto Rico, Mexico, Cuba, as well as Spain and all the countries of Central and South America. Again, there is likely to be diversity between and within these groups related to when they came to the U. S., why they came, what their status was in their countries of origin, the circumstances of their adjustment to U. S. society and their level of acculturation. The same may be said for Asians who also come from a variety of cultures–Japanese, Korean, Indo-Chinese, Chinese, Pacific Islands, etc.

The research also needs to focus more on the sources of within group variance. The evidence suggests that the within group variance among minorities is greater than the between group variance. Studies that compare ethnic minorities to the dominant culture miss the phenomenon in a major way. The diversity of Blacks in America, for example, suggests that it is unlikely that there will be a general principle explaining substance use among all Blacks. It is important that the diversity within groups be studied in its own right.

Conceptually, it may also be useful for research to understand the concept of equifinality. It means that there are many paths to a similar outcome. The medical influence on research on substance use and the application of the disease concept is misleading in another way than that mentioned by Fisher. Most diseases have an identifiable "cause," as those diseases that result from infectious agents. However, on the individual level of analysis, it is unlikely that alcoholism, and other drug abuse by extension, has a cause or course that is followed by all those "who contract the disease." More likely, there are multiple paths to the outcome of substance abuse disorders.

Moreover, researchers need to expand the conceptualization of substance use. Not all use is abuse. The likelihood of a drug and alcohol free society is virtually zero. Intoxicants have been a feature of all recorded societies. But many cultures teach responsible use and define what responsible use is. Problematic use, however, becomes a social problem and needs to be approached as such by researchers in the field. That is, researchers need to depart from the individual focus and investigate problematic use as a social problem.

Closely related to the above, it should be noted that substance abuse is not an isolable phenomenon but is a bit of behavior within a cluster of behaviors. The findings show that substance abuse is associated with other deviant behaviors. Yet treating it as an individual problem and as a disease divorces the study of substance abuse from the general realm of the study of behavior. Most theorists suggest that deviant behaviors are shaped in a social context much like normative behaviors are shaped. Thus, substance abuse needs to be studied as a behavior not a disease.

REFERENCES

Amaro, H., Beckman, L.J., & Mays, V.M.; 1987. A comparison of Black and white women entering alcoholism treatment. *Journal of Studies on Alcohol.* 48:220-228.

Anglin, M.D., Hser, Y., & Booth, M.W.; 1987. Sex differences in addict careers. 4. Treatment. *American Journal of Drug and Alcohol Abuse.* 13:253-280.

Arredondo, R., Weddige, R.L., Justice, C.L., & Fitz, J.; 1987. Alcoholism in Mexican-Americans: Intervention and Treatment. *Hospital and Community Psychiatry.* 38:180-183.

Atkins, B.J., Klein, M.A., & Mosley, B.; 1987. Black adolescents' attitudes toward and use of alcohol and other drugs. *International Journal of the Addictions.* 22:1201-1211.

Bailey, D.N.; 1987. Phencyclidine detection during toxicology testing at a University medical center patient population. *Clinical Toxicology.* 25:517-526.

Barnes, G.M., & Welte, J.W.; 1986. Patterns and predictors of alcohol use among 7-12th grade students in New York State. *Journal of Studies on Alcohol.* 47:53-61.

Barrett, M.E., Simpson, D.D., & Lehman, W.E.K.; 1988. Behavioral changes of adolescents in drug abuse intervention programs. *Journal of Clinical Psychology.* 44:461-473.

Beauvais, F., & LaBoueff, S.; 1985. Drug and alcohol abuse intervention in American American Indian communities. *The International Journal of the Addictions.* 20:139-171.

Beauvais, F., Oetting, E.R., & Edwards, R.W.; 1985. Trends in Drug use of

American Indian adolescents living on reservations: 1975-1983. *American Journal of Drug & Alcohol Abuse. 11*:209-229.

Bell, C.C., Thompson, J.P., Lewis, D., Redd, J., Shears, M., & Thompson, B.; 1985. Misdiagnosis of alcohol-related organic brain syndromes: Implications for treatment. *Alcoholism Treatment Quarterly. 2*:45-65.

Bobo, J.K., Gilchrist, L.D., Cvetkovich, G.T., Trimble, J.E., & Schinke, S.P.; 1988. Cross-cultural service delivery to minority communities. *Journal of Community Psychology. 16*:263-272.

Bobo, J.K., Snow, W.H., Gilchrist, L.D., & Schinke, S.P.; 1985. Assessment of refusal skill in minority youth. *Psychological Reports. 57*:1187-1191.

Boscarino, J.; 1980. Alcoholism in VA inpatient facilities: Some implications of the VA patient census. *American Journal of Drug and Alcohol Abuse. 7*:237-250.

Bradstock, K., Forman, M.R., Binkin, N.J., Gentry, E.M., Hogelin, G.C., Williamson, D.F. & Trowbridge, F.L.; 1988. Alcohol use and health behavior lifestyles among U.S. Women: The Behavioral Risk Factor Surveys. *Addictive Behaviors. 13*:61-71.

Brisbane, F.L. & Stuart, B.L.; 1985. A self-help model for working with Black women of alcoholic parents. *Alcoholism Treatment Quarterly. 2*:199-219.

Brook, J.S., Whiteman, M., Gordon, A.S., Nomura, C., & Brook, D.W.; 1986. Onset of adolescent drinking: A longitudinal study of intrapersonal and interpersonal antecedents. *Alcohol and Substance Abuse in Women and Children.* 91-109.

Brunswick, A.F., & Messeri, P.; 1985. Timing of first drug treatment: A longitudinal study of urban Black youth. *Contemporary Drug Problems. 2*:401-418.

Brunswick, A.F., & Messeri, P.A.; 1986a. Pathways to Heroin Abstinence: A longitudinal study of urban Black youth. *Advances in Alcohol and substance Abuse. 5*:111-135.

Brunswick, A.F., & Messeri, P.; 1986. Drugs, lifestyle, and health: A longitudinal study of urban Black youth. *American Journal of Public Health. 76*:52-57.

Caetano, R.; 1984. Ethnicity and drinking in Northern California: a comparison among whites, Blacks, and Hispanics. *Alcohol and Alcoholism. 19*:31-44.

Caetano, R.; 1986. Alternative definitions of Hispanics: Consequences in an alcohol survey. *Hispanic Journal of Behavioral Sciences. 8*:331-344.

Caetano, Raul. 1987a. Acculturation and drinking patterns among U.S. Hispanics. *British Journal of Addiction. 82*:789-799.

Caetano, R.; 1987b. Acculturation, drinking, and social settings among U.S. Hispanics. *Drug and Alcohol Dependence. 19*:215-226.

Caetano, R.; 1987c. Alcohol use and depression among U.S. Hispanics. *British Journal of Addiction. 82*:1245-1251.

Caetano, R.; 1987d. Acculturation and attitudes toward appropriate drinking among U.S. Hispanics. *Alcohol and Alcoholism. 22*:427-435.

Caetano, R. & Herd, D.; 1984. Black drinking practices in Northern California. *American Journal of Drug and Alcohol Abuse. 10*:571-587.

Capel, W.C., & Peppers, L.G.; 1978. The aging addict: a longitudinal study of known abusers. *Addictive Diseases. 3*:389-403.

Caracci, G., Migone, P., & Dornbush, R.; 1983. Phencyclidine in an East Harlem psychiatric population. *Journal of the National Medical Association.* 75:869-874.

Carter, J.H.; 1982. Alcoholism in Black Vietnam veterans: Symptoms of posttraumatic stress disorder. *Journal of the National Medical Association.* 74:655-660.

Castaneda, R. & Galanter, M.; 1988. Ethnic differences in drinking practices and cognitive impairment among detoxifying alcoholics. *Journal of Studies on Alcohol.* 49:335-339.

Chavez, E., Beauvais, F., & Oetting, E.R.; 1986. Drug use by small town Mexican American youth: A pilot study. *Hispanic Journal of Behavioral Science.* 8:243-258.

Chi, I., Kitano, H.H.L., & Lubben, J.E.; 1988. Male Chinese drinking behavior in Los Angeles. *Journal of Studies on Alcohol.* 49:21-25.

Cohen, A.; 1986. A psychosocial typology of drug addicts and implications for treatment. *International Journal of the Addictions.* 21:147-154.

Comas-Diaz, L.; 1986. Puerto Rican Alcoholic women: Treatment considerations. *Alcoholism Treatment Quarterly.* 3:47-57.

Combs-Orme, T., Taylor, J.R., & Robins, L.N.; 1985. Occupational prestige and mortality in Black and white alcoholics. *Journal of Studies on Alcohol.* 45:443-446.

Connors, G.J., Maisto, S.A., & Watson, D.W.; 1988. Racial factors influencing college students' ratings of alcohol's usefulness. *Drug and Alcohol Dependence.* 21:247-252.

Costello, R.M.; 1987. Hispanic alcoholic treatment considerations. *Hispanic Journal of Behavioral Sciences.* 9:83-89.

Craig, R.J., & Olsen, R.E.; 1988. Differences in psychological need hierarchies between Black and white drug addicts. *Journal of Clinical Psychology.* 44:82-86.

Cruz, J.D.; 1988. Booze and blues: alcohol and Black popular music, 1920-1930. *Contemporary Drug Problems.* 149-186.

Curtis, R.L.; 1975. Adolescent orientations toward parents and peers: variations by sex, age, and socioeconomic status. *Adolescence.* 10:482-494.

Dawkins, M.P.; 1986. Social correlates of alcohol and other drug use among youthful Blacks in an urban setting. *Journal of Alcohol and Drug Education.* 32: 15-28.

Dawkins, M.P., & Harper, F.D.; 1983. Alcoholism among women: A comparison of Black and white problem drinkers. *The International Journal of the Addictions.* 18:333-349.

Dignan, M.B., Steckler, A., Block, G.D., Howard, G., & Cosby, M.; 1986. Prevalence of high risk behaviors among seventh grade students in North Carolina. *Southern Medical Journal.* 79:295-.

Fawzy, F.I., Coombs, R.H., Simon, J.M., & Bowman-Terrell, M.; 1987. Family composition, socioeconomic status, and adolescent substance use. *Addictive Behaviors.* 12:79-83.

Fernandez-Pol, B., Bluestone, H., Missouri, C., Morales, G., & Mizruchi, M.S.;

1986. Drinking patterns of inner-city Black Americans and Puerto Ricans. *Journal of Studies on Alcohol.* 47:156-160.

Fisher, A.D.; 1987. Alcoholism and race: The misapplication of both concepts to North American American Indians. *Canadian Review of Sociology and Anthropology.* 24:81-98.

Flores, P.J.; 1986. Alcoholism treatment and the relationship of Native American cultural values to recovery. *The International Journal of the Addictions.* 20:1707-1726.

Foster, S.W.; 1985. The decision to really stop: from the life of a Black woman alcoholic. *Sage.* 2:40-42.

Galizio, M., & Stein, F.S.; 1983. Sensation seeking & drug choice. *The International Journal of the Addictions.* 18:1039-1048.

Gary, L.E.; 1985. Drinking, Homicide, and the Black male. *Journal of Black Studies.* 17:15-31.

Gary, L.E., & Berry, G.L.; 1985. Predicting attitudes toward substance use in a Black community: implications for prevention. *Community Mental Health Journal.* 21:42-51.

Gilchrist, L.D., Schinke, S.P., Trimble, J.E., & Cvetkovich, G.T.; 1987. Skills enhancement to prevent substance abuse among American American Indian adolescents. *International Journal of the Addictions.* 22:869-879.

Guyette, S.; 1982. Selected characteristics of American American Indian substance abusers. *The International Journal of the Addictions.* 17:1001-1014.

Hall, R.; 1985. Distribution of the sweat lodge in alcohol treatment programs. *Current Anthropology.* 26:134-135.

Harvey, W.B.; 1985. Alcohol abuse and the Black community: A contemporary analysis. *Journal of Drug Issues.* 15:81-91.

Heien, D., & Pompelli, G.; 1987. Stress, ethnic, and distribution factors in a dichotomous response model of alcohol abuse. *Journal of Studies on Alcohol.* 48:450-455.

Herd, D.; 1985. Migration, cultural transformation, and the rise of Black liver cirrhosis. *British Journal of Addiction.* 80:397-410.

Herd, D.; 1987. Rethinking Black drinking. *British Journal of Addiction.* 82:219-223.

Herd, D.; 1988. Drinking by Black and white women: Results from a national survey. *Social Problems.* 35:493-505.

Hser, Y., Anglin, M.D., & McGlothlin, W.; 1987. Sex differences in addict careers. 1. Initiation of use. *American Journal of Drug & Alcohol Abuse.* 13:33-57.

Hubbard, R.L., Schlenger, W.E., Rachal, J.V., Bray, R.M., Craddock, S.G., Cavanaugh, E.R., & Ginzberg, H.M.; 1986. Patterns of alcohol and drug abuse in drug treatment clients from different ethnic backgrounds. *Annals of the New York Academy of Science.* 472:60-74.

Humm-Delgado, D., & Delgado, M.; 1983. Hispanic adolescents and substance abuse: Issues for the 1980s. *Child and Youth Services.* 6:71-87.

Humphrey, J.A., & Friedman, J.; 1986. The onset of drinking and intoxication among university students. *Journal of Studies on Alcohol. 47*:455-458.

Icard, L. & Traunstein, D.M.; 1987. Black, Gay, & Alcoholic men: Their character and treatment. *Social Casework. 68*:267-272.

Inciardi, J.A., Pottieger, A.E., & Faupel, C.E.; 1982. Black women, heroin & crime. *Journal of Drug Issues. 12*:241-250.

Jacobs, D., & Fuller, M.; 1986. The social construction of drunken driving: Modeling the organizational processing of DWI defendants. *Social Science Quarterly.* __:785-802.

Jessor, R., Chase, J.A., & Donovan, J.E.; 1980. Psychosocial correlates of marijuana use and problem drinking in a national sample of adolescents. *American Journal of Public Health. 70*:604-613.

Joe, G.W., Lloyd, M.R., Simpson, D.D., & Singh, B.K.; 1983. Recidivism among opioid addicts after drug treatment: An analysis by race & tenure in treatment. *American Journal of Drug & Alcohol Abuse. 9*:371-382.

Johnson, B., Anderson, K., & Wish, E.D.; 1988. A day in the life of 105 drug addicts and abusers: Crimes committed and how the money was spent. *SSR. 72*:185-191.

Johnson, E.H., & Broman, C.; 1987. The relationship of anger expression to health problems among Black Americans in a national survey. *Journal of Behavioral Medicine. 10*:103-116.

Johnson, R.C., Schwitters, S.Y., Wilson, J.R., Nagoshi, C.T., & McClearn, G.E.; 1985. A cross-ethnic comparison of reasons given for using alcohol, not using alcohol, or ceasing to use alcohol. *Journal of Studies on Alcohol. 46*:283-288.

Johnson, R.L.; 1985. Black adolescents: issues critical to their survival. *Journal of the National Medical Association. 77*:447-8.

Kaplan, H.B., Martin, S.S., Johnson, R.J. & Robbins, C.A.; 1986. Escalation of marijuana use: Application of a general theory of deviant behavior. *Journal of Health & Social Behavior. 27*:44-61.

King, L.M.; 1983. Research on alcohol abuse barriers to treatment research and action regarding Black Americans. *Journal of Psychiatric Treatment and Evaluation. 5*:505-513.

Kitano, H.H.L., Lubben, J.E., & Chi, I.; 1988. Predicting Japanese American drinking behavior. *The International Journal of the Addictions. 23*:417-428.

Kleinman, P.H. & Lukoff, I.F.; 1978. Ethnic differences in factors related to drug use. *Journal of Health & Social Behavior. 19*:190-99.

Knox, D.H.; 1985. Spirituality: A tool in the assessment and treatment of Black alcoholics and their families. *Alcoholism Treatment Quarterly. 2*:31-44.

Kosten, T.R., Gawin, F.H., Rounsaville, B.J., & Kleber, H.D.; 1986. Cocaine abuse among opioid addicts: demographic & diagnostic factors in treatment. *American Journal of Drug & Alcohol Abuse. 12*:1-16.

Kosten, T.R., Rounsaville, B.J., & Kleber, H.D.; 1985. Ethnic and gender differences among opiate addicts. *The International Journal of the Addictions. 20*:1143-1162.

Lewis, C.E., Robins, L., & Rice, J.; 1985. Association of alcoholism with antisocial personality in urban men. *Journal of Nervous and Mental Disease. 173*: 166-174.

Lex, B.W.; 1987. Review of alcohol problems in ethnic minority groups. *Journal of Consulting and Clinical Psychology. 55*:293-300.

Linsky, A.S., Straus, M.A., & Colby, J.P.; 1985. Stressful events, stressful conditions, and alcohol problems in the United States: A partial test of Bales's theory. *Journal of Studies on Alcohol. 46*: 72-80.

Lubben, J.E., Chi, I., & Kitano, H.H.L.; 1988. Exploring Filipino American drinking behavior. *Journal of Studies on Alcohol. 49*:26-29.

Luepnitz, R.R., Randolph, D.L., & Gutsch, K.U.; 1982. Race and socio-economic status as confounding variables in the accurate diagnosis of alcoholism. *Journal of Clinical Psychology. 38*:665-669.

Maddahian, E., Newcomb, M.D., & Bentler, P.M.; 1986. Adolescents' substance use: impact of ethnicity, income, & availability. *Advances in Alcohol & Substance Abuse. 5*:63-78.

Maddahian, E., Newcomb, M.D., & Bentler, P.M.; 1985. Single and multiple patterns of adolescent use: Longitudinal comparisons of four ethnic groups. *Journal of Drug Education. 15*:311-326.

Martinez, J.; Minorities and alcohol/drug abuse. 1976. *American Journal of Drug and Alcohol Abuse. 3*:185-187.

May, P.A.; 1982. Substance abuse and American American Indians: Prevalence and susceptibility. *The International Journal of the Addictions. 17*:1185-1209.

May, P.A.: 1986. Alcohol and Drug misuse prevention programs for American American Indians: Needs and opportunities. *Journal of Studies on Alcohol. 47*:187-195.

May, P.A., Hymbaugh, K.J., Aase, J.M., & Samet, J.M.; 1983. Epidemiology of fetal alcohol syndrome among American American Indians in the Southwest. *Social Biology. 30*:374-387.

May, P.A., & Smith, M.B.; 1988. Some Navajo American Indian opinions about alcohol abuse and prohibition: A survey and recommendations for policy. *Journal of Studies on Alcohol. 49*:324-334.

Maypole, D.E., & Anderson, R.B.; 1987 Culture-specific substance abuse prevention for Blacks. *Community Mental Health Journal. 23*:135-139.

Maypole, D.E., & Anderson, R.; 1983. Minority alcoholism programs: Issues in service delivery models. *The International Journal of the Addictions.* 18:987-1001.

McLaughlin, D.G., Raymond, J.S., Murakami, S.R., & Goebert, D. 1987. Drug use among Asian Americans in Hawaii. *Journal of Psychoactive Drugs. 19*:85-94.

McShane, D., & Willenbring, M.L.; 1984. Differences in cerebral asymmetries related to drinking history and ethnicity: A computerized axial tomography (CAT) Scan study. *The Journal of Nervous & Mental Disease. 172*:529-532.

Mendes de Leon, C.F., & Markides, K.S.; 1986. Alcohol consumption and physical symptoms in a Mexican American population. *Drug and Alcohol Dependence. 16*:369-379.

Miller, J.S., Sensenig, J., Stocker, R.B., & Campbell, R.; 1973. Value patterns of drug addicts as a function of race & sex. *The International Journal of the Addictions. 8*:589-598.

Miller, J.M., & Miller, J.M.; 1988. Alcoholism in a Black urban area. *Journal of the National Medical Association. 80*:621-623.

Murphy, S. & DeBlassie, R.R.; 1984. Substance abuse and the Native American student. *Journal of Drug Education. 14* (4):315-321.

Nail, R.L., Gunderson, E., & Arthur, R.J.; 1974. Black-white differences in social background & military drug abuse patterns. *American Journal of Psychiatry. 131*:1097-1102.

Neff, J.A.; 1986. Alcohol consumption and psychological distress among U.S. Anglos, Hispanics, and Blacks. *Alcohol and Alcoholism. 21*:111-119.

Nurco, D.N., Kinlock, T.W., Hanlon, T.E., & Ball, J.C.; 1988. Nonnarcotic drug use over an addiction career–A study of Heroin Addicts in Baltimore and New York City. *Comprehensive Psychiatry. 29*:450-459.

Nurco, D.N., Ball, J.C., Shaffer, J.W., Kinlock,T.W., & Langrod, J.; 1986. A comparison by race/ethnicity of narcotic addict crime rates in Baltimore, New York, and Philadelphia. *American Journal of Drug and Alcohol Abuse. 12*:297-307.

Nurco, D.N., Ball, J.C., Schaffer, J.W., Kinlock, T.W., & Langrod, J.; 1986. A comparison by race/ethnicity of narcotic addict crime rates in Baltimore, New York, & Philadelphia. *American Journal of Drug & Alcohol Abuse. 12*:297-307.

Nurco, D.N., Bonito, A.J., Lerner, M., & Balter, M.B.; 1975. Studying addicts over time: Methodology and preliminary findings. *American Journal of Drug and Alcohol Abuse. 2*:183-196.

Patterson, E.T., Charles, H.L., Woodward, W.A., Roberts, W.R., and Penk, W.E.; 1981. Differences in measures of personality and family environment among Black and white alcoholics. *Journal of Consulting & Clinical Psychology. 49*:1-9.

Penk,W.E., Brown, A.S., Roberts, W.R., Dolan, M.P., Atkins, H.G., & Robinowitz, R.; 1981. Visual memory of Black & white male heroin and nonheroin users. *Journal of Abnormal Psychology. 90*: 486-489.

Penk, W.E., Roberts, W.R., Robinowitz, R., Dolan, M.P., Atkins, H.G., & Woodward, W.A.; 1982. MMPI Differences of Black & white male polydrug abusers seeking treatment. *Journal of Consulting and Clinical Psychology. 50*: 463-465.

Petersen, D.M., Schwirian, K.P., & Bleda, S.E.; 1978. The drug arrest: Empirical observations on the age, sex, & race of drug offenders in a Midwestern city. *Drug Forum. 6*:371-386.

Pottern, L.M., Morris, L.E., Blot, W.J., Ziegler, R.G., & Fraumeni, J.F.; 1981. Esophageal Cancer among Black men in Washington D.C. I. Alcohol, tobacco & other risk factors. *Journal of the National Cancer Institute. 67*:777-783.

Primm, B.J., & Wesley, J.E.; 1985. Treating the multiply addicted Black alcoholic. *Alcoholism Treatment Quarterly.* 2:151-178.

Query, J.M.N.; 1985. Comparative admission and follow-up study of American American Indians and whites in a youth chemical dependency unit on the North Central Plains. *The International Journal of the Addictions.* 20:489-502.

Rebach, Howard, Bolek, Catherine S., Williams, Katherine L., Russell, Robert. Substance abuse among ethnic minorities in America: A critical annotated bibliography, Gariano Press, 1992.

Reed, T.E.; 1985. Ethnic differences in alcohol use, abuse and sensitivity: A review with genetic interpretation. *Social Biology.* 32:195-209.

Reed, T.E., & Hanna, J.M.; 1986. Between- and within-race variation in acute cardiovascular responses to alcohol: Evidence for genetic determination in normal males in three races. *Behavior Genetics.* 16:585-598.

Rogan, A.; 1986. Recovery from alcoholism: Issues for Black & Native American alcoholics. *Alcohol Health & Research World.* 11:42-44.

Rogers, E.L., Goldkind, L., & Goldkind, S.F.; 1982. Increasing frequency of esophageal cancer among Black male veterans. *Cancer.* 49:610-617.

Savage, L.J., & Simpson, D.D.; 1980. Post-treatment outcomes of sex and ethnic groups treated in methadone maintenance during 1969-1972. *Journal of Psychedelic Drugs.* 12:55-64.

Schinke, S.P., Schilling, R.F., Gilchrist, L.D., Barth, R.P., Bobo, J.K., Trimble, J.E., & Cvetkovich, G.T.; 1985. Preventing substance abuse with American American Indian Youth. *Social Casework.* 66:213-217.

Schinke, S.P., Schilling, R.F., & Gilchrist, L.D.; 1986. Prevention of drug and alcohol abuse in American American Indian Youths. *Social Work Research and Abstracts.* Winter:18-19.

Schinke, S.P., Orlandi, M.A., Botvin, G.J., Gilchrist, L.D., Trimble, J.E., & Locklear, V.S.; 1988. Preventing substance abuse among American American Indian adolescents: A bicultural competence skills approach. *Journal of Counseling Psychology.* 35:87-90.

Segal, B.; 1983. Alcohol and alcoholism in Alaska: Research in a multicultural and transitional society. *The International Journal of the Addictions.* 18:379-392.

Shaffer, J.W., Nurco, D.N., Ball, J.C., & Kinlock, T.W.; 1986. Patterns of non-narcotic drug use among male narcotic addicts. *Journal of Drug Issues.* 16:435-442.

Slagle, A.L. & Weibel-Orlando, J.; 1986. The American Indian Shaker Church and Alcoholics Anonymous: Revitalistic Curing Cults. *Human Organization.* 45:310-319.

Snyder, D.K., Kline, R.B., & Podany, E.C.; 1985. Comparison of external correlates of MMPI substance abuse scales across sex & race. *Journal of Consulting & Clinical Psychology.* 53:520-525.

Sue, D.; 1987. Use and abuse of alcohol by Asian Americans. *Journal of Psychoactive Drugs.* 19:57-66.

Sutker, P.B., Archer, R.P., & Allain, A.N.; 1978. Drug abuse patterns, personality characteristics, and relationships with sex, race, and sensation seeking. *Journal of Consulting & Clinical Psychology.* 46:1374-1378.

Suwaki, H. & Ohara, H.; 1985. Alcohol induced facial flushing and drinking behavior in Japanese men. *Journal of Studies on Alcohol.* 46:196-198.

Thompson, K.M., & Wilsnack, R.W.; 1987. Parental influence on adolescent drinking: Modeling, attitudes, or conflict? *Youth & Society.* 19:22-43.

Thornton, C.I. & Carter, J.H.; 1988. Treating the Black female alcoholic: Clinical observations of Black therapists. *Journal of the National Medical Association.* 80:644-647.

Towle, L.H.; 1988. Japanese-American drinking: Some results from the joint Japanese-U.S. alcohol epidemiology project. *Alcohol Health & Research World.*12:217-223.

Trimble, J.E.; 1984. Drug abuse prevention research among American Indians and Alaskan Natives. *White Cloud Journal.* 3:22-34.

Tucker, M.B.; 1985. U.S. ethnic minorities and drug abuse: An assessment of the science and practice. *The International Journal of the Addictions.* 20:1021-1047.

Vaillant, G.: 1986. Cultural factors in the etiology of alcoholism: A prospective study. *Annals of the New York Academy of Science.* 472:142-148.

Watts, T.D., & Wright, R.; 1987. Some comments on research, policy, and practice issues in Black alcoholism. *Journal of Alcohol and Drug Education.* 32:13-18.

Welte, John W. & Barnes, G.M.; 1985. Alcohol: The gateway to other drug use among secondary school students. *Journal of Youth and Adolescence.* 14:487-498.

Welte, J.W., & Barnes, G.M.; 1987. Alcohol use among adolescent minority groups. *Journal of Studies on Alcohol.* 48:329-336.

Wingert, J.L., & Fifield, M.G.; 1985. Characteristics of Native American users of inhalants. *The International Journal of the Addictions.* 20:1575-1582.

Womble, M. & Bakeman, V.V.; 1986. A comprehensive culturally specific approach to drunk driving for Blacks. *Alcoholism Treatment Quarterly.* 3:103-113.

Wurzman, I., Rounsaville, B.J., & Kleber; 1982. Cultural values of Puerto Rican opiate addicts: An exploratory study. *American Journal of Drug and Alcohol Abuse.* 9:141-153.

Yee, B.W.K., & Thu, N.D.; 1987. Correlates of drug use and abuse among Indochinese refugees: Mental health implications. *Journal of Psychoactive Drugs.* 19:77-83.

Young, T.J.; 1987. Inhalant use among American Indian youth. *Clinical Psychiatry and Human Development.* 18:36-46.

Young, T.J., 1988. Substance abuse among Native Americans. *Clinical Psychology Review.* 8:125-138.

Zabin, L.S., Hardy, J.B., Smith, E.A., & Hursch, M.B.; 1986. Substance use & its relation to sexual activity among inner city adolescents. *Journal of Adolescent Health Care.* 7:320-331.

Zager, L.D., & Megargee, E.I.; 1981. Seven MMPI alcohol and drug abuse scales. An empirical investigation of their interrelationships, convergent and discriminant validity and degree of racial bias. *Journal of Personality & Social Psychology. 40*:532-544.

Ziter, M.L.P.; 1987. Culturally sensitive treatment of Black alcoholic families. *Social Work. 32*:130-135.111.

APPENDIX I

LISTING OF ARTICLES ALONG 4 DIMENSIONS

Reference	Ethnic	Age Group	Topic	Substance
1. Amaro et al., 1987	B & W	adult women	treatment	alcohol
2. Anglin et al., 1987	H & W	adults	treatment	opiates
3. Arredondo et al., 1987	Mex.	adults	treatment	alcohol
4. Atkins et al., 1987	Blacks	youth	prevention	D & A*
5. Bailey, 1987	B-W-H	adults	epidemiology	PCP
6. Barnes & Welte,1986	general	youth	epidemiology	alcohol
7. Barrett et al., 1988	Mex.	youth	treatmeant	D & A
8. Beauvais & LeBoueff, 1985	Nat. Amer.	general	general	D & A
9. Beauvais et al., 1985	Nat. Amer.	youth	epidemiology	drugs
10. Bell et al., 1985	Blacks	adults	Dx & Tx	alcohol
11. Bobo et al., 1988	Nat. Amer.	youth	prevention	D & A
12. Bobo et al.,	Nat. Amer.	youth	prevention	D & A
13. Bradstock et al., 1988	B-W	adult women	epidemiology	alcohol
14. Brisbane & Stuart, 1985	Blacks	adult women	treatment	alcohol
15. Brook et al., 1986	B-W	youth	etiology	alcohol
16. Brunswick & Messeri, 1986	Blacks	youth	treatment outcome	heroin
17. Brunswick & Messeri, 1986b	Blacks	adults	etiology	drugs
18. Brunswick & Messeri, 1985	Blacks	youth	treatment	heroin
19. Caetano, 1986	Hispanic	adults	epidemiology	alcohol
20. Caetano, 1987a	Hispanic	adults	epidemiology	alcohol
21. Caetano, 1987b	Hispanic	adults	epidemiology	alcohol

22. Caetano, 1987c	Hispanic	adults	epidemiology	alcohol
23. Caetano, 1987d	Hispanic	adults	epidemiology	alcohol
24. Caetano, 1984	B-W-H	adults	epidemiology	alcohol
25. Caetano & Herd, 1984	Blacks	adults	epidemiology	alcohol
26. Capel & Peppers, 1978	B-W	adults	Tx:course	opiates
27. Caracci et al., 1983	Blacks	youth & adults	epid./etiol.	PCP
28. Carter, 1982	Blacks	adult	Dx & Tx	alcohol
29. Castanada & Galanter, 1988	B-W-H	adult men	consequences & treatment	alcohol
30. Chavez et al., 1986	Mex.	youth	epidemiology	D & A
31. Chi et al., 1988	Chinese	adult men	epidemiology	alcohol
32. Cohen, 1986	B & W	adults	epidemiology & etiology	heroin
33. Comas-Diaz, 1986	Puerto Rican	adult women	treatment	alcohol
34. Combs-Orme et al., 1985	B & W	adults*	treatment outcome	alcohol
35. Conners et al., 1988	B & W	youth	etiology	alcohol
36. Costello, 1987	Hisp & Anglo	adult men	treatment outcome	alcohol
37. Craig & Olsen, 1988	B & W	adults	etiology	drugs
38. Cruz, 1988	Blacks	adults	etiology	alcohol
39. Curtis, 1975	general	youth	etiology	D & A
40. Dawkins, 1986	Blacks	youth	etiology	D & A
41. Dawkins & Harper, 1983	B & W	adult women	epidemiology & treatment	alcohol
42. Dignan et al., 1986	B & W	youth	epidemiology	alcohol
43. Fawzy et al., 1987	Hisp/Angl	youth	etiology	drugs
44. Fernandez-Pol et al., 1986	Black/Hisp	adults*	epidemiology	alcohol
45. Fisher, 1987	Nat. Amer.	adults	etiol & diag.	alcohol
46. Flores, 1986	Nat. Amer. & Whites	adults*	treatment	alcohol
47. Foster, 1985	Blacks	adult women	treatment	alcohol
48. Galizio & Stein, 1983	B & W	adult men*	etiology	alcohol
49. Gary, 1986	Blacks	adult men	consequences	alcohol
50. Gary & Berry, 1985	Blacks	adults	etiology	D & A
51. Gilchrist et al., 1987	Nat. Amer.	youth	prevention	D & A

52. Guyette, 1982	Nat. Amer.	adults*	epidemiology & treatment	D & A
53. Hall, 1985	Nat. Amer.	adults*	treatment	alcohol
54. Harvey, 1985	Blacks	adults	prevention & treatment	alcohol
55. Heien & Pompelli, 1987	general	adults	etiology	alcohol
56. Herd, 1985	Blacks	adults	epidemiology	alcohol
57. Herd, 1987	Blacks	adults	etiology	alcohol
58. Herd, 1988	B & W	adult women	epidemiology & etiology	alcohol
59. Hser et al., 1987	Mex/Angl	adults*	etiology	opiates
60. Hubbard et al., 1986	Black/white/ Hispanic	adults*	epidemiology & etiology	D & A
61. Humm-Delgado & Delgado, 1983	Hispanic	youth	general	D & A
62. Humphrey & Friedman, 1986	Black/white	youth	epidemiology	alcohol
63. Icard & Traunstein, 1987	Black	adult(gay) men	treatment	alcohol
64. Inciardi et al., 1982	Black	adult women	consequences	opiates
65. Jacobs & Fuller, 1986	general	adults	treatment	alcohol
66. Jessor et al., 1980	general	youth	etiology	D & A
67. Joe et al., 1983	B & W	adult men*	treatment outcomes	opiates
68. Johnson, B. et al., 1988	Black & Hispanic	adult men	consequences: crime	drugs
69. Johnson, E., & Broman, 1987	Blacks	adults	consequences: health	alcohol
70. Johnson, R.L., 1985	Blacks	youth	consequences	D & A
71. Johnson, R.C. et al., 1985	general	adults	epidemiology & etiology	alcohol
72. Kaplan et al., 1986	B-W-H	youth	etiology	marijuana
73. King, 1983	Blacks	general	general	alcohol
74. Kitano et al., 1988	Japanese	adults	epidemiology	alcohol
75. Kleinman & Lukoff, 1978	B,W, Oth.	adults	etiology	drugs
76. Knox, 1985	Blacks	adults	diagnosis & treatment	alcohol
77. Kosten et al., 1986	B & W	adults*	diagnosis & treatment	drugs
78. Kosten et al., 1985	B-W-H	adults*	epidemiology & etiology	opiates

79. Lewis et al., 1985	Blacks	adult men	etiology	alcohol
80. Lex, 1987	general	general	general	alcohol
81. Linsky et al., 1985	general	general	etiology	alcohol
82. Lubben et al., 1988	Asian	adults	epidemiology	alcohol
83. Luepnitz et al., 1982	B & W	adults	diagnosis	alcohol
84. Maddahian et al., 1986	Black/white/ Hisp/Asian	youth	epidemiology & etiology	D & A
85. Maddahian et al., 1985	Black/white/ Hisp/Asian	youth	epidemiology & etiology	D & A
86. Martinez, 1976	Puerto Rican	general	treatment	D & A
87. May, 1986	Nat. Amer.	general	general	D & A
88. May et al., 1983	Nat. Amer.	adult women*	epidemiology	alcohol
89. May & Smith, 1988	Nat. Amer.	adults	epidemiology	alcohol
90. May, 1982	Nat. Amer.	general	epidemiology & etiology	alcohol
91. Maypole & Anderson, 1987	Blacks	youth & families	prevention	D & A
92. Maypole & Anderson, 1983	Blacks	adults	treatment	alcohol
93. McLaughlin et al., 1987	Asians	adults	epidemiology	D & A
94. McShane & Willenbring, 1984	Black/white/ Nat. Amer.	adults*	consequences/ diagnosis	alcohol
95. Mendes de Leon & Markides, 1986	Mexicans	adults	consequences/ epidemiology	alcohol
96. Miller & Miller, 1988	Blacks	adults*	epidemiology	alcohol
97. Miller et al., 1973	Black/white	adults*	epidemiology	opiates
98. Murphy & DeBlassie, 1984	Nat. Amer.	youth	prevention & treatment	D & A
99. Nail et al., 1974	Black/ white	adult men*	epidemiology & etiology	drugs
100. Neff, 1986	Black/white/ Hispanic	adults	etiology	alcohol
101. Nurco et al., 1986a	Black/white /Hispanic	adults, men*	consequences, crime	opiates
102. Nurco et al., 1975	Black/white /Hispanic	adults, men*	consequences crime	opiates
103. Nurco et al., 1988	Black/white	adults, men*	consequences, crime	opiates
104. Patterson et al., 1981	Black/white	adults*	diagnosis, etiology	alcohol

105. Penk et al., 1981	Black/white	adults, men*	diagnosis consequences	heroin
106. Penk et al., 1982	Black/white	adults, men*	etiology & diagnosis	polydrug
107. Petersen et al., 1978	Black/white	adults	consequences, crime	polydrug
108. Pottern et al., 1981	Blacks	adults, men	consequences, health	alcohol
109. Primm & Wesley, 1985	Blacks	adults	etiology & treatment	D & A
110. Query, 1985	white/ Nat. Am.	youth*	treatment, outcomes	D & A
111. Reed, 1985	general	adults	etiology	alcohol
112. Rogan, 1986	Black/ Nat. Am.	adults	treatment	alcohol
113. Rogers et al., 1982	Blacks	adults, men*	etiology & consequences	alcohol
114. Savage & Simpson, 1980	Black/ white	adults*	treatment outcomes	opiates
115. Schinke et al., 1985	Nat. Amer.	youth	prevention	D & A
116. Segal 1983	Nat. Amer.	general	epidemiology	alcohol
117. Snyder et al., 1985	Black/ white	adults*	diagnosis	D & A
118. Shaffer et al., 1986	Black/ white	adults	epidemiology	drugs
119. Sutker et al., 1978	Black/ white	adults*	epidemiology, etiology	drugs
120. Suwaki & Ohara	Asians	adults	epidemiology & etiology	alcohol
121. Slagle & Weibel-Orlando, 1986	Nat. Amer.	adults	treatment	alcohol
122. Thompson & Wilsnack, 1987	Black/white/ Hispanic	youth	epidemiology & etiology	alcohol
123. Thornton & Carter, 1988	Blacks	adults, women	treatment	alcohol
124. Towle, 1988	Japanese/ white	adults	epidemiology	alcohol
125. Trimble, 1984	Nat. Amer.	adults	prevention	D & A
126. Tucker, 1984	general	general	general	drugs
127. Vaillant, 1986	white ethnics	adults	etiology	alcohol
128. Watts & Wright	Blacks	general	general	alcohol
129. Welte & Barnes, 1987	general	youth	epidemiology	alcohol

130. Welte & Barnes, 1985	general	youth	epidemiology	D & A
131. Wingert & Fifield, 1985	Nat. Amer.	youth	epidemiology	inhalant
132. Womble & Bakeman, 1986	Blacks	adults	prevention & treatment	alcohol
133. Wurzman et al., 1982	Black/white/ Puerto Rican	adults*	treatment	opiates
134. Yee & Thu, 1987	Asians	adults	etiology	D & A
135. Zabin et al., 1986	Black/ white	youth	epidemiology	D & A
136. Zager & Megargee	Black/ white	adults, men*	diagnosis	D & A
137. Ziter, 1987	Blacks	adults, women	treatment	alcohol

*D & A = Drugs and alcohol

Methodological Issues in Conducting Substance Abuse Research on Ethnic Minority Populations

R. Lorraine Collins

SUMMARY. Common methodological problems in substance abuse research in ethnic minority populations, and issues related to research design, are described. These issues include sampling, the failure to acknowledge sources of heterogeneity within ethnic groups, and the need for common definitions of constructs. It is suggested that attention to these issues will lead to improvements in the design and conduct of quantitative research on substance abuse. Improvements in methodology will result in advances in knowledge concerning substance abuse in ethnic minorities.

The ideal context for conducting research is one in which a program of research is designed and conducted within a conceptual framework that guides the generation of hypotheses, the specification of variables and the interpretation of results. In such a situation, the conceptual framework provides a guide for selecting variables from a vast array of potentially important factors. Results of particular studies are used to refine the conceptual framework and add to the accumulation of knowledge.

The state of the art of conducting research on substance use/ abuse among minority populations is very far from this idealized state (Tucker, 1985). Thus the forthcoming discussion of methodological issues and problems makes no assumptions as to the framework within which research occurs. Discussion of the resolution of the host of conceptual issues related to research on substance use/

R. Lorraine Collins is affiliated with the Research Institute on Alcoholism.

59

abuse among minorities, is beyond the purview of this chapter. Rather, we will focus on common methodological issues and problems in quantitative research on substance abuse among minority populations.

The methodological issues to be outlined exist in all of the domains in which research on substance use/abuse is conducted: prevalence, etiology, prevention, and treatment. For example, racial/cultural factors impact on our assessment of research on existent models of etiology. The question being whether these models are specific to majority culture, can be modified to consider minority populations, or whether models specific to minority populations are necessary. Similar questions arise in the areas of prevention and treatment where strategies for increasing identification with aspects of minority culture (e.g., the language, ethnic identity of intervener) have been proposed for enhancing the efficacy of programs. Methodological issues common to the different domains of quantitative research now will be described.

COMMON METHODOLOGICAL PROBLEMS

Representative Sampling
and Generalization of Results

The fact that an individual or subgroup can be identified as being a member of a particular ethnic/racial group does not mean that the individual or subgroup is representative of all members of that ethnic/racial group. Without representative sampling, generalization to the larger group is untenable. Even so, results from nonrepresentative samples have been interpreted as indicating the functioning of the entire ethnic/racial group. For example, Fenna, Mix, Schaefer and Gilbert (1971) reported that whites metabolized alcohol at a significantly faster rate than Native Americans, and generalized this finding to all Native Americans, thereby scientifically substantiating the notion that Native Americans were biologically unsuited to using alcohol. A methodological flaw of this study was the fact that hospitalized Native Americans had been compared to healthy whites. When this flaw was rectified via use of more comparable subjects, Native American and white subjects were found to have similar rates of alcohol metabolism (Bennion & Li, 1976; Rex, Bosron, Smialek, & Li, 1985). The foregoing example illustrates that comparative studies must be careful to select subjects who are comparable on dimensions (e.g., health status) that may be of importance to the question(s) being asked. In addition, unless a sample is carefully selected to be representative of a particular ethnic/racial group, generalization of results to all members of the ethnic/racial group should not occur. Ponterotto's (1988) critique of racial/ethnic minority research in counseling psychology reported that 83.6% of the samples described in published research between 1976 and 1986 focused on student samples. Students are hardly representative of all members of minority populations, yet the results of such research are often generalized to entire groups.

Issues of representativeness can be raised for studies of prevalence. Lex (1987) has pointed out that in prevalence research on drug abuse "community surveys may have oversampled persons living in fixed places of residence and may have undercounted individuals estranged from their families or individuals who are institutionalized or homeless" (p. 294). This may be a particular problem for surveys of use of illicit substances because illicit substance use is sometimes linked to transient or criminal lifestyles. Similarly, surveys of adolescent drug use can be faulted for focusing on convenient samples of high school students while ignoring adolescents who have dropped out of school and who may be at greatest risk for substance use/abuse. The results of these surveys cannot be seen as representative of adolescent drug use but only as representative of adolescents currently attending school.

Obviously, representative samples are not always possible and the nature of the research to some extent may dictate whether a representative sample is possible or necessary. Thus, studies of the prevalence of substance use/abuse should make a more stringent effort to select random and/or representative samples, while a representative sample may be less crucial for a small pilot project designed to demonstrate the efficacy of an innovative treatment technique. If a sample is not representative, then this limitation should be central to interpretation of the results and generalization of the findings must be cautioned.

The "Myth of Homogeneity"

While many researchers acknowledge the heterogeneity among minority populations, recognition of heterogeneity within specific minority groups has only recently begun to be incorporated into research designs, and is not acknowledged in many descriptions of study samples. Trimble (1990-91) has described this failure to acknowledge heterogeneity within ethnic groups as involving the use of "ethnic glosses." The use of such glosses is relatively common. For example, Ponterotto (1988) reported that only 28.6% of 49 studies involving racial/ethnic minorities included controls for differences within groups. Heterogeneity within ethnic/racial groups includes variables such as socioeconomic status, education, acculturation, gender, age, and country of origin; many of which may interact. If not specifically acknowledged or measured, each source of diversity can become a source of measurement error, which can obscure significant differences among groups. In addition, acknowledgement of diversity within groups can impose appropriate limits on the generalization of results and can serve to negate stereotypes. The dilemma then is to acknowledge heterogeneity within groups without having to rely on the use of single subject designs in order to capture within group diversity.

Certain factors that denote diversity within groups have been predictably linked to substance use/abuse. Age and gender in particular are commonly cited and assessed as sources of diversity in substance use/abuse behavior within minority groups. For example, female members of minority groups tend to drink less alcohol and to use fewer drugs than their male counterparts (National Institute on Alcohol Abuse and Alcoholism, 1987). However, variations in use patterns have been identified among different groups of minority females, as have variations within female members of a particular ethnic group (Leland, 1984). Even with an extensive body of research suggesting age and gender differences in various aspects of substance use, research in which these differences are disregarded (thereby confounding the pattern of results) can still be found. The situation for other, seemingly less obvious, sources of diversity is even more acute. Some of these will now be described.

Socioeconomic status (SES). In the U. S., historical and social events have combined to create a situation in which a large proportion of members of minority populations are found in the lower social classes. In some cases this has resulted in a tendency for minority group behaviors related to the preponderance of low SES members to be generalized to the entire group. An added complication is the fact that criteria for SES categories developed for majority culture may not directly apply to SES categories within minority cultures (Gordon, 1973). Thus SES serves as an important, yet complex source of diversity in research on minorities.

Drinking and substance use norms and behavior have been found to vary across social classes. SES as a source of diversity may be overlooked in research on minority populations because of the tendency to confound race/ethnicity with class. For example, in the area of psychological functioning, early research reported that African Americans were more psychologically distressed than European Americans (e.g., Warheit, Holzer, & Arey, 1975). These assertions were refuted in later research in which controls (based on the assumption that race and class had additive influences) for the impact of social class were implemented. In these better controlled studies, race differences in distress were attenuated (e.g., Neff & Husani, 1980). The most recent studies in this area report that rather than having an additive effect, SES and race have an interactive effect on psychological distress, such that race differences were more pronounced in lower class blacks (Kessler & Neighbors, 1986; Ulbrich, Warheit, & Zimmerman, 1989). Controversies such as these highlight the fact that care must be taken not only in consideration of the role of SES in substance use/abuse but also in approaches to controlling for the impact of these effects.

National origin and acculturation. Many of the minority groups in the U.S. are made up of individuals who are relatively recent emigrants from other countries. An example of the role of country of origin is the designation "Hispanic." In the U. S. the primary constituents of the Hispanic group are individuals of Mexican, Puerto Rican, and Cuban heritage. However, new patterns of immigration are leading to increased numbers of Hispanics from Central America and South America. Even given a common heritage and language, the norms and practices regarding substance use vary among Hispanics. For example, a survey of substance use among

Hispanics found general similarities in the drug use patterns of Mexican-Americans and Puerto Ricans, and differences between these two groups and Cuban-Americans (National Institute on Drug Abuse, 1987). Consistent with findings regarding acculturation, Mexican-Americans born in the U. S. were twice as likely to be past or current drug users than were those born in Mexico. Similarly, De La Rosa, Khalsa and Rouse (1990) reported differences in the use of illicit drugs among Mexican-Americans, Cubans, and Puerto Ricans as well as differences within each group. Within group differences were related to variables such as age, gender, and degree of acculturation.

Welte and Barnes (1987) distinguished between African Americans and West Indians of African heritage in their study of alcohol and drug use in adolescent members of minority groups. Although there were similarities in the drinking behavior of these two groups, West Indians reported fewer problems related to alcohol use, possibly related to their being generally more middle class than the African Americans in the sample.

"Acculturation refers to the complex process whereby the behaviors and attitudes of the migrant change toward the dominant group as a result of exposure to a cultural system that is significantly different" (Rogler, Malgady, Constantino, & Blumenthal, 1987; p. 567). Evidence is accumulating to suggest that level of identification with majority culture may be related to substance use/abuse. Lukoff and Brook (1974) reported differences in contact with heroin users among migrants to the United States, first generation, and second generation offspring of migrants, suggesting a trend for increases in such contacts with increased acculturation. Caetano and Mora (1988) assessed acculturation, drinking and drinking-related problems in Mexican-Americans and Mexicans. Although both groups shared a common heritage, Mexican men drank larger amounts of alcohol, but drank more infrequently, than did Mexican-American men. Mexican-American women drank more heavily and had a lower rate of abstention than did Mexican women. Changes in men's drinking behavior occurred relatively early (< 5 years) after moving to the United States. In a comparison of Japan-born and American-born Japanese, Japan-born males were reported to be heavier drinkers and the levels of heavy drinking in the American-born sample was similar to that of other Californians (Kitano, Hatanaka, Yeung, & Sue, 1985).

Failure to acculturate was linked to increased opium use among Hmong refugees in the United States (Westermeyer, Lyfoung, & Neider, 1989). In a report on somatic symptoms of Mexican Americans and Puerto Ricans, Angel and Guarnaccia (1989) found that persons who completed the interview in Spanish reported poorer health. Among the explanations for this finding was the possibility that those who took the interview in Spanish were "more culturally Mexican or Puerto Rican" suggesting the possibility of a "culturally-conditioned response pattern in addition to actual poorer overall health" (p. 1234). These examples illustrate that acculturation can play a role in various aspects of behavior. At minimum, some assessment of generational status of members of immigrant groups should be collected (cf. Markides, Krause, & Mendes de Leon, 1988).

While far from comprehensive, the foregoing discussion was designed to illustrate factors that may render general designations of samples as "African American" or "Hispanic American" noninformative. Not only does the lack of acknowledgement of heterogeneity within groups signal a lack of knowledge of and insensitivity to diversity, it can also create problems for analysis of data and interpretation of findings (cf., Anderson, 1989).

Stereotypes as a Source of Bias

Stereotypes of the substance use/abuse patterns of minority groups can become reified in research. These stereotypes can range from the "drunken Indian" (Leland, 1976) to the "macho" drinking of Hispanic men. As with all stereotypes, these images can serve to undermine a specific group's position in comparison to other groups and/or lead to individual members of a group being perceived as carrying a particular set of characteristics or engaging in particular behaviors, even if such is not the case. Since substance use/abuse is not valued by the larger society, negative stereotypes concerning drug use by members of a particular group can be very damaging to all members of the stereotyped group.

The effects of stereotypes are insidious. To the extent that members of stereotyped groups come to identify with their stereotypes, they can become self-fulfilling prophecies. For example, while many researchers acknowledge the diversity in the drinking behavior of Native Americans (Young, 1988), many Native Americans subscribe to stereotypes about Indian drinking. May and Smith (1988) reported that in their survey of alcohol-related knowledge and attitudes in Navajo Indians, the majority of responses conformed to the scientifically unsubstantiated "drunken Indian" stereotype, which suggests that Indians have a physical problem with alcohol and cannot help drinking. Even small amounts of alcohol consumption were seen as negative and community policies and efforts to control alcohol consumption were often based on this stereotype. Acknowledging the self-fulfilling nature of this attitude, the researchers suggested the need to address this stereotype through education.

Other seemingly more positive stereotypes such as the notion that Asians do not become alcoholics (Chi, Kitano, & Lubben, 1988) can also create problems for the group. For example, individual members of this group may engage in excessive drinking on the assumption that they have "immunity" from alcohol problems, thereby setting themselves at risk for alcoholism. Clearly then, researchers need to be sensitive to issues concerning the role of stereotypes in studies of minority substance use/abuse. Selective, unrepresentative sampling, the nature of the questions asked and the generalization of results beyond the purview of the research questions are all modes of creating and/or reifying stereotypes.

The Need for Care in Selecting and/or Developing Measures

The quality of data is related to the psychometric rigor of the instrument used to collect it. If the instrument is not rigorous then findings based on the data are likely to be questionable. Some basic indicants of psychometric rigor include reliability (test-retest, inter-rater, internal consistency), and validity (face, concurrent, discriminant) and factor structure. Descriptions of these constructs and other aspects of test construction are beyond the purview of this chapter, but the interested reader is referred to books by Anastasi (1982),

Cronbach (1960), and Nunnally (1967). In the present chapter we will focus on issues concerning the cultural specificity of measures.

In surveys of prevalence of substance use/abuse and research on prevention there is a tendency to rely heavily on self-report measures. Although self-reports concerning substance use have been shown to be reliable under certain circumstances (Polich, 1982; Sobell et al., 1988), issues of concern include the possibility that respondents will provide socially desirable responses or will not be able to provide accurate retrospective reports of behavior. Some of these problems can be minimized via assuring anonymity of responses or providing structured questionnaires in which subjects report use of substances for short and discrete units of time (e.g., past week or month).

Even if the limitations of self-report are addressed, for the researcher conducting studies on minority populations the dilemma of the need for culturally sensitive measures and the need to use instruments that possess high levels of psychometric rigor is likely to arise. Whenever possible, instruments that possess both of these criteria should be used. However, in many cases the researcher is faced with the choice of either investing in a costly and intensive program of scale development to create a new culturally sensitive measure or modifying (the less the better) an existent instrument developed on a majority population for use with a specific minority group. Even if the existent measure has proven psychometric rigor on the general population for which it was developed, the psychometric features of the modified measure must be assessed for the minority population.

A modification as seemingly straightforward as a translation of an instrument can change its features. Angel and Guarnaccia (1989) discussed differences in the meanings of different ratings of health in a survey conducted in English and Spanish as possibly accounting for statistically significant differences in the health ratings of acculturated versus unacculturated Mexican Americans and Puerto Ricans. Less acculturated individuals, who took the survey in Spanish, tended to rate their health as "buena" (good) and "regular" (fair/poor) while more acculturated individuals, who took the survey in English, tended to rate their general health as "very good" or "good." Angel and Guarnaccia speculate that less acculturated individuals may see their responses as appropriate for describing normal health (analogous to the English phrase "Just fine") while those who made ratings in English used more favorable terms as appropriate for describing normal health.

Some of the limitations of questionnaires can be overcome by use of more objective measures. Ponterotto (1988) among others has cited the over reliance on self-report measures in research on minorities. He found that only eight of 49 studies (16.3%) he reviewed used behavioral measures as dependent variables. Thus, where applicable, use of objective behavioral or physiological measures could also enhance the quality of data on substance use/abuse.

The Need for Common Definitions of Constructs

As with research within majority samples, terms such as "problem drinking" and "drug abuse" are often not objectively defined and thereby are less than informative. The lack of objective definitions of terms and/or the lack of similar definitions of terms create problems for attempts to replicate findings or make comparisons across studies. In such cases direct comparisons between studies focused on a particular minority group and/or detailed comparisons of findings between different groups cannot easily be made (between group comparisons where "Whites" serve as the normative standard are often counterproductive). Along with detailed and specific definitions of terms, the use of common measures will enhance the potential for replication and/or comparison of results across studies.

RESEARCH DESIGN

Issues of heterogeneity within and among different ethnic/racial groups and conceptualizations of substance use as being multiply determined combine to suggest the need for more complex approaches to research design and data analysis. Much of the research to date on minority populations is not methodologically rigorous but rather focuses on descriptions of small, nonrepresentative samples

(Ponterotto, 1988). While the relative paucity of research on minority populations leaves an important role for descriptive and observational research, the variety of factors related to substance use/abuse suggests the need for more sophisticated, multimethod and/or multidisciplinary approaches to research. The integration of ethnographic and survey methods for research on ethnic minority groups has been recommended (Lex, 1987) and each can be applied to research in areas such as prevalence. In addition, advances in knowledge are more likely to occur with the use of experimental designs and hypothesis testing as well as application of more sophisticated multivariate data analytic techniques. At a more comprehensive level, testing of hypothetical models of relationships among variables via approaches such as path analysis and causal modeling (e.g., LISREL) can be used to capture the complexity of relationships among predictive variables as well as between predictor variables and dependent variables such as amount or type of drug consumption (cf. Windle, Barnes, & Welte, 1989).

Correlational Designs

Many studies (particularly prevalence studies) of minority substance use/abuse employ correlational designs in which self-reports of substance use are categorized according to demographic characteristics and correlated to measures of social or psychological functioning. Correlational designs allow assessment of the relationships among variables, particularly when no clear specification of cause/effect relationships is possible. They also serve as the basis for more sophisticated data analytic strategies such as multiple regression, path analyses, and causal modeling. The use of these more sophisticated strategies enhances identification of variables that are of more central importance. For example, techniques such as multiple regression allow the relative predictive power of variables to be evaluated.

Correlational designs contain limitations that are often overlooked in making interpretations of their results. Three common and oft cited problems are directionality, the third variable problem, and multicollinearity. The problem of directionality involves the trite but true adage that correlation does not equal causation. In essence finding a correlational relationship between two variables does not tell us whether a variable causes a particular effect. Causal relationships are best tested in experimental designs which will be described later. The third variable problem involves the possibility that a third (unmeasured) variable mediates the correlational relationship between the two variables that have been assessed. Lastly, multicollinearity refers to the high intercorrelation among variables, which may account for some of the significant relationships found. For example, a group of independent variables may account for the same variance of each independent variable to the dependent variable. Thus, as the possibility of multicollinearity becomes greater, researchers should move to strategies that control for these interrelationships among variables.

Experimental Designs: Issues in Research on Prevention and Treatment

A major problem for research on prevention and treatment is definition/selection of the sample. While diagnosis in treatment research has become more sophisticated, thorough assessments of individuals are often not conducted. Such assessment might include specific patterns of substance use (amounts, frequency, dose/potency as indicated by levels of substance in blood, etc.), signs of physical dependence (e.g., withdrawal symptoms) and tolerance as well as behavioral indicants (e.g., body sway) of addiction. Issues of reliability and validity of assessment instruments and/or diagnostic criteria and typologies of substance use are also important, but rarely cited.

Having selected the population for the intervention, a comparison or control group is necessary. In prevention research, traditional control groups such as placebo controls, waiting-list controls and/or no-treatment control groups can be used if care is taken to minimize contact between groups, thereby minimizing contamination of control conditions. In addition, the intervention program should be made available to these groups following the completion of the study. In the area of substance abuse treatment, traditional control groups are seen as practically and ethically disadvantageous since some subjects must continue to experience the negative effects of drug use while participating in research. Basham (1986) has suggested the use of comparative designs in which "one compares two or more treatments without conceptualizing either as being a formal control group" (p. 90). In such a design, the differences between two treatments are compared in relative terms involving questions such as "Which works best?" and "How do they differ?" rather than the absolute question, "Does it work?" implicit in most control group designs" (p. 90). These designs are particularly useful in situations where a treatment package cannot be easily divided into components. The need to incorporate multiple elements in designing effective treatments for minority populations often may preclude the breakdown of treatments into specific components each of which can be compared.

Assignment to conditions. In addition to the use of comparative designs and appropriate subject selection, sound methods for assignment to treatment are important tenets of good research methodology. Random assignment to treatment assumes that sources of error are randomly distributed among conditions. Subject matching involves assessment of subject characteristics of potential importance (e.g., age, SES, acculturation, motivation for treatment, referral source) and assignment of subjects to treatment conditions in such a way as to equate the impact of these characteristics. Without the use of techniques such as these, sources of bias related to subject characteristics cannot be ruled out and the reasons for the differential efficacy of treatments cannot clearly be identified (Kazdin, 1980).

Therapist/client matching. Sources of bias related to the person conducting the intervention can also exist in research on prevention and treatment. One potential source of bias in research with minority populations is the ethnic/racial identity of the therapist/experimenter. The results of research concerning the need for a match between therapist and client are inconsistent. Generally these results suggest that members of minority groups express a preference for working with minority therapists, yet the treatment outcomes are similar for minority client/majority therapist pairings and minority client/minority therapist pairings (Sue, 1988). Even with this inconsistency, selecting therapists with sensitivity to sociocultural factors and minority concerns as well as skills (e.g., fluency in the client's language) that facilitate treatment should enhance efficacy (Collins & McNair, 1986). Obviously treatment specific therapist characteristics (e.g., level of training, experience, orientation) should also be equalized when comparative designs are used.

Attrition. Attrition may be a problem for research on treatment and prevention. Research suggests that ethnic minority clients tend to drop out of treatment at higher rates than do Whites (Sue, 1977). In addition, subjects who complete treatment may not be easy to locate for follow-up. Attrition becomes even more of a problem if an extensive follow-up of participants is planned. Since the efficacy of a prevention or treatment program is best evaluated over extensive periods of time this issue can be extremely important. Generally, a conservative and sound approach to the issue of how to categorize subjects lost to follow-up is to treat all such persons as treatment failures (Nathan & Lansky, 1978). However, it is best to plan research by structuring methods for minimizing problems related to attrition (cf. Kazdin, 1980).

Clinical versus Statistical Significance

Having employed the correct design and methodology, it is often the case that one can achieve results that are statistically significant. The results of many experimental and correlational studies are based on analysis of group data. Application of appropriate data analytic techniques yield indicants of significant differences between groups and/or changes over time. However, the statistical significance achieved may be indicative of change in the means of groups, but is not indicative of individual change or change with regard to normative standards that may be of interest in applied settings (Jacobson & Truax, 1991). This latter type of change relates to the ''clinical'' significance of findings.

In research on minority populations, issues related to whether tests of statistical significance (based on group data) are of value in clinical and other applied settings often arise, particularly with reference to the ethical responsibility to provide feedback to minority research participants and their communities (Gordon, 1973; Ponterotto, 1988).

Assessment of the clinical significance of findings is often thorny, because the most readily available traditional statistical techniques tend to emphasize group data and because the nature of clinical significance may vary with the nature of the problem. Indicants of clinical significance such as change in individuals and/or proportion of subjects in a group, the use of normative standards, and social validation of behavior change may provide valuable adjuncts and/or alternatives to reliance on the statistical significance of results in some contexts. This is particularly true in situations where new or innovative techniques designed for a specific minority group are being tested in a pilot study. For example, if assessing the efficacy of two different treatments (e.g., Treatments X and Y for cocaine abuse) then comparison of mean posttreatment levels of use between the groups would offer a statistical basis for determining efficacy. In addition, indicants of the proportion of change in the different treatments or descriptions of intersubject variability within a specific treatment group could provide information that allows for assessment of the clinical significance of the differences between the two treatments. The greatest mean decrease in cocaine use may have occurred with Treatment X, but if this decrease occurred because a small proportion of the persons in the group abstained from cocaine use, while Treatment Y had a significantly lower mean decrease in cocaine use, but this decrease was experienced by all members of the group, it may be best to suggest using Treatment Y for most cocaine abusers (cf. Hugdahl & Ost, 1981). A within group look at the highly successful versus the less successful participants in Treatment X could also be instructive when making clinical decisions. On the other hand, assessment of the clinical significance of a public education campaign to prevent smoking would occur at the level of behavior change in various high risk groups rather than at the individual level.

Social validation can also serve as an indicant of clinically significant change (Kazdin, 1977). Two aspects of social validation are social comparison and subjective evaluation. Social comparison involves making comparisons between the target individual or group and other similar individuals or groups who already possess appropriate levels of the behavior. The comparison group serves as a normative standard. The question being: Does the behavior that has been targeted for change correspond to that of the comparison group? There are some limitations of using normative standards and appropriate comparison groups. They include problems of defining the normative level if no satisfactory norm exists and difficulties in defining the normative group. However, use of social comparison provides opportunities for researchers and communities to select reference groups of relevance to their particular group.

Subjective evaluation involves having judgments as to the "quality" of the change being made by expert judges or others who interact with the individuals targeted for change. For example, in working with adolescent drug abusers, ratings from teachers or probation officers might serve as indicants of change over time. Whatever the source of information concerning clinical significance, its determination is likely to enhance the use of research findings in minority communities.

CONCLUSION

Having been exposed to some of the methodological issues in research on substance use/abuse in minority populations, the researcher might feel that the factors that must be considered when conducting research place an additional burden on working in an already difficult area of research. The issues raised in this chapter should not be seen as constraining research on minority populations, but rather as a means of increasing the quality of research on these understudied groups. Consideration of the aforementioned issues is important if the nature and quality of the knowledge base on substance use/abuse in minority populations is to improve. Many of the issues raised in this chapter are of relevance to research on substance abuse regardless of the population being studied, but clearly extra attention to these issues is needed when conducting research on minority groups.

REFERENCES

Anastasi, A. (1982). *Psychological testing* (5th ed.). New York: Macmillan.
Angel, R., & Guarnaccia, P. J. (1989). Mind, body and culture: Somatization among Hispanics. *Social Sciences Medicine, 28*, 1229-1238.
Anderson, N. B. (1989). Racial differences in stress-induced cardiovascular reac-

tivity and hypertension: Current status and substantive issues. *Psychological Bulletin, 105*, 89-105.

Basham, R. B. (1986). Scientific and practical advantages of comparative design in psychotherapy outcome research. *Journal of Consulting and Clinical Psychology, 54*, 88-94.

Bennion, L., & Li, T.-K., (1976). Alcohol metabolism in American Indians and Whites. *New England Journal of Medicine, 294*, 9-13.

Caetano, R., & Mora, M. E. M. (1988). Acculturation and drinking among people of Mexican descent in Mexico and the United States. *Journal of Studies on Alcohol, 49*, 462-471.

Chi, I., Kitano, H. H., & Lubben, J. E. (1988). Male Chinese drinking behavior in Los Angeles. *Journal of Studies on Alcohol, 49*, 21-25.

Collins, R. L., & McNair, L. D. (1986). Black women and behavior therapy: Exploring the biases. *the Behavior Therapist, 9*, 7-10.

Cronbach, L. J. (1960). *Essentials of psychological testing* (Revised). New York: Harper & Row.

De La Rosa, M., Khalsa, J. H., & Rouse, B. A. (1990). Hispanics and illicit drug use: A review of recent findings. *International Journal of the Addictions, 25*, 665-691.

Fenna, D., Mix, L., Schaefer, O., & Gilbert, J. A. L. (1971). Ethanol metabolism in various racial groups. *Canadian Medical Journal, 105*, 472-475.

Gordon, T. (1973). Notes on White and Black psychology. *Journal of Social Issues, 29*, 87-95.

Hugdahl, K., & Ost, L-G. (1981). On the difference between statistical and clinical significance. *Behavioral Assessment, 3*, 289-295.

Jacobson, N. S., & Truax, P. (1991). Clinical significance: A statistical approach to defining meaningful change in psychotherapy research. *Journal of Consulting and Clinical Psychology, 59*, 12-19.

Kazdin, A. E. (1977). Assessing the clinical or applied importance of behavior change through social validation. *Behavior Modification, 1*, 427-451.

Kazdin, A. E. (1980). *Research design in clinical psychology*. New York: Harper & Row.

Kessler, R. C., & Neighbors, H. W. (1986). A new perspective on the relationships among race, social class, and psychological distress. *Journal of Health and Social Behavior, 27*, 107-115.

Kitano, H. H. L., Hatanaka, H., Yeung, W. T., & Sue, S. (1985). Japanese-American drinking patterns. In L. A. Bennett & G. M. Ames (Eds.), *The American experience with alcohol: Contrasting cultural perspectives* (pp. 335-357). New York: Plenum.

Leland, J. (1976). *Firewater myths*. New Brunswick, NJ: Rutgers Center of Alcohol Studies.

Leland, J. (1984). Alcohol use and abuse in ethnic minority women. In S. C. Wilsnack & L. J. Beckman (Eds.), *Alcohol problems in women* (pp. 66-96). New York: Guilford.

Lex, B. W. (1987). Review of alcohol problems in ethnic minority groups. *Journal of Consulting and Clinical Psychology, 55*, 293-300.

Lukoff, I. F., & Brook, J. S. (1974). A socio-cultural exploration of reported heroin use. In C. Winick (Ed.), *Sociological aspects of drug dependence* (pp. 35-56). Boca Raton, FL: CRC Press.

Markides, K. S., Krause, N., & Mendes de Leon, C. F. (1988). Acculturation and alcohol consumption among Mexican-Americans: A three-generation study. *American Journal of Public Health, 78,* 1178-1181.

May, P. A., & Smith, M. B. (1988). Some Navajo Indian opinions about alcohol abuse and prohibition: A survey and recommendations for policy. *Journal of Studies on Alcohol, 49,* 324-334.

Nathan, P. E., & Lansky, D. (1978). Common methodological problems in research on the addictions. *Journal of Consulting and Clinical Psychology, 46,* 713-726.

National Institute on Alcohol Abuse and Alcoholism. (1987). *Alcohol and health: Sixth special report to the U. S. Congress* (DHHS Publication No. ADM 87-1519). Washington, DC: U.S. Government Printing Office.

National Institute on Drug Abuse. (1987). *Use of selected drugs among Hispanics: Mexican-Americans, Puerto Ricans, Cuban-Americans* (DHHS Publication No. ADM 87-1527). Washington, DC: U.S. Government Printing Office.

Neff, J. A., & Husani, B. A. (1980). Race, socioeconomic status and psychiatric impairment: A research note. *Journal of Community Psychology, 8,* 16-19.

Nunnally, J. C. (1978). *Psychometric theory* (2nd ed.). New York: McGraw Hill.

Polich, J. M. (1982). The validity of self-reports in alcoholism research. *Addictive Behaviors, 7,* 123-132.

Ponterotto, J. G. (1988). Racial/ethnic minority research in the *Journal of Counseling Psychology*: A content analysis and methodological critique. *Journal of Counseling Psychology, 35,* 410-418.

Rex, D. K., Bosron, W. F., Smialek, J. E., & Li, T.-K. (1985). Alcohol and aldehyde dehydrogenase isoenzymes in North American Indians. *Alcoholism: Clinical and Experimental Research, 9,* 147-152.

Rogler, L. H., Malgady, R. G., Constantino, G., & Blumenthal, R. (1987). What do culturally sensitive mental health services mean?: The case of Hispanics. *American Psychologist, 42,* 565-570.

Sobell, L. C., Sobell, M. B., Riley, D. M., Schuller, R., Pavan, D. S., Cancilla, A., Klajner, F., & Leo, G. I. (1988). The reliability of alcohol abusers' self-reports of drinking and life events that occurred in the distant past. *Journal of Studies on Alcohol, 49,* 225-232.

Sue, S. (1977). Community mental health services to minority groups: Some optimism, some pessimism. *American Psychologist, 32,* 616-624.

Sue, S. (1988). Psychotherapeutic services for ethnic minorities: Two decades of research findings. *American Psychologist, 43,* 301-308.

Sue, S., & Zane, N. (1987). The role of culture and cultural techniques in psychotherapy. *American Psychologist, 42,* 37-45.

Trimble, J. (1990-91). Ethnic specification, validation prospects, and the future of drug use research. *International Journal of the Addictions, 25,* 149-170.

Tucker, M. B. (1985). U. S. ethnic minorities and drug abuse: An assessment of the science and practice. *The International Journal of the Addictions*, 20, 1021-1047.

Ulbrich, P. M., Warheit, G. J., & Zimmerman, R. S. (1989). Race, socioeconomic status, and psychological distress: An examination of differential vulnerability. *Journal of Health and Social Behavior, 30*, 131-146.

Warheit, G., Holzer, C. E., & Arey, S. S. (1975). Race and mental illness: An epidemiological update. *Journal of Health and Social Behavior, 16*, 243-256.

Welte, J. W., & Barnes, G. M. (1987). Alcohol use among adolescent minority groups. *Journal of Studies on Alcohol, 48*, 329-336.

Westermeyer, J., Lyfoung, T., & Neider, J. (1989). An epidemic of opium dependence among Asian refugees in Minnesota: Characteristics and causes. *British Journal of Addiction, 84*, 785-789.

Windle, M., Barnes, G. M., & Welte, J. (1989). Causal models of adolescent substance use: An examination of gender differences using distribution free estimators. *Journal of Personality and Social Psychology, 56*, 132-142.

Young, T. J. (1988). Substance use and abuse among Native Americans. *Clinical Psychology Review, 8*, 125-138.

Psychosocial Predictors
of Substance Use Among
Urban Black Male Adolescents

Kenneth I. Maton
Marc A. Zimmerman

SUMMARY. Three sets of variables–Lifestyle, Social Support/Stress, and Well Being–were used to predict frequency of alcohol, marijuana, and hard drug use among urban African-American male adolescents. A sample of 150 adolescents, most of whom had dropped out of school, participated in an initial 90-minute interview and a follow-up interview six months later. The prevalence rates for illicit substance use among this sample of Black males were higher than the National average. Using a hierarchical regression approach, different psychosocial variables were found to predict use of different substances. Lifestyle was a significant predictor of marijuana and hard drug use at both measurement points, and a predictor of alcohol use at one of two measurement points. Support/Stress explained significant variance in alcohol use at both measurement points, and in marijuana use at one of two measurement points. Among individual predictor variables, in cross-sectional analyses (with all predictor variables entered) independent variance in substance use was explained by in-school status (alcohol and marijuana use), spirituality (marijuana and hard drug use), and life event stress (marijuana use). In longitudinal analyses with Time One substance use controlled, Time Two in-school status and life event stress each explained sig-

Kenneth I. Maton is affiliated with the University of Maryland, Baltimore County.

Marc A. Zimmerman is affiliated with the University of Michigan.

This research was supported by the National Institute on Drug Abuse, Grant No. RO1DA04766, and the U.S. Department of Justice, Office of Juvenile Justice and Delinquency Prevention, Grant No. 87JNCX0010.

Correspondence should be addressed to Kenneth I. Maton, Department of Psychology, University of Maryland, Baltimore County, Baltimore, MD 21228.

nificant variance in alcohol use, while Time Two parent support was related to marijuana use. Finally, in prospective analyses with Time One substance use controlled, low self-esteem at Time One predicted to increased marijuana use six months later. Suggestions for future research and implications for preventive intervention are discussed.

INTRODUCTION

Research on the etiology of substance use among adolescents has generated a diverse set of empirical predictors and theoretical explanations (Bennett, 1982; Hawkins, Lishner, & Catalano, 1985; Murray & Perry, 1985; Newcomb & Bentler, 1989). However, the vast majority of researchers have studied middle class, in-school youth. Especially glaring has been the absence of research on urban, minority adolescent samples (Prendergast, Austin, Maton, & Baker, 1989). This is unfortunate since urban minority adolescents represent a group that is particularly at high risk for various problem behaviors, including substance use. A large number of minority youth drop out of school and are unemployed, and available research suggests that unemployed, school dropouts have substantially higher rates of substance use than in-school or employed peers (Bachman, O'Malley & Johnson, 1978; Kandel, 1980; Johnston & O'Malley, 1986). In one of the few research studies focused explicitly on urban minority teenagers, Brunswick, Merzel, and Messeri (1985) reported higher rates of substance abuse among urban Black adolescents than in the general population (NIDA, 1988). Clearly, an understanding of the psychosocial factors predictive of drug abuse among high-risk African-American teenagers is a high priority for drug use researchers.

Several psychosocial paradigms have been proposed to explain substance use and abuse for general samples of adolescents. Perhaps most support exists for the lifestyle paradigm, which posits that substance use results when adolescents lack conventional aspirations, engage in a socially deviant lifestyle, and lack the psychosocial controls which follow from daily involvement in meaningful activity (Hawkins & Weis, 1984; Jessor, Chase, & Donovan, 1980). School involvement and religiosity appear especially important as meaningful activities which may buffer adolescents from a non-conventional lifestyle, and the accompanying high levels of drug use (Jessor & Jessor, 1977; Donovan & Jessor, 1978; Selnow, 1985).

A second, social support/stress model focuses on the etiological role of low quality social relationships, and high levels of stress, leading to psychosocial problems, including substance use. Low quality support relationships are those lacking in the provision of love, acceptance, emotional support, advice, and tangible help (cf. Cohen & Wills, 1985). Perhaps most important in terms of substance use is the quality of the adolescent's support relationships with parents, as poor quality family relationships are generally considered to constitute a risk factor for adolescent substance use (Maddahian, Newcomb, & Bentler, 1988). High levels of stress (e.g., experiencing multiple negative life events) may lead to substance abuse because the individual feels overwhelmed by environmental demands (Brown, 1989; Newcomb, Maddahian, & Bentler, 1986; Wills, 1986).

A third, psychological well-being paradigm views substance use as the consequence of impaired psychological well being (cf. Cox, 1982). In this model, substance abuse is viewed neither as a way of life nor as a function of inadequate support systems and high levels of life stress. Rather, it is viewed as reflecting an underlying, intra-psychological deficiency. In adolescent substance use research, psychological symptoms (e.g., depression, anxiety) and self-esteem are representative of the well-being variables studied (cf. Murray & Perry, 1985). To date, the psychological well-being model has received only mixed support (e.g., Jessor, 1981; Wingard, Huba, & Bentler, 1980) in general samples of adolescents.

Few researchers have tested all three of these models–lifestyle, support/stress, and psychological well being–in the same study. Furthermore, as noted above, most previous research on adolescents has included only in-school samples, has not focused on high-risk, minority populations, and has been cross-sectional in nature. The current research represents one of the few (short-term) longitudinal studies of psychosocial predictors of substance use among a high-risk minority sample–urban, male Black adolescents, most of whom have dropped out of school and are unemployed. Lifestyle, social support/stress, and well-being measures were used as predictor variables. The findings from the research will hopefully help to guide policy makers and professionals in developing preventive intervention programs which are specifically tailored to this most important youth population.

METHOD

Research Participants

The sample contains 150 Black male adolescents from inner-city Baltimore who completed both Time One and Time Two interviews. Four additional youth who completed both sets of interviews were not included due to the perceived invalidity of their data (see below). An additional 66 youth completed Time One interviews but did not complete Time Two interviews (30% of the initial sample). Analyses indicated that non-completers did not differ significantly from completers on age, recruitment source (see below), eight of nine predictor variables, and two of three substance use measures (Time One). However, non-completers did report somewhat higher levels than completers of stressful events, r (215) = .14, p < .05, and marijuana use, r (215) = .14, p < .05.

At Time One, the average age of the 150 youth in the final sample was 17.2 (range from 15 through 19). At Time One, 107 of the youth (71%) in the final sample reported they were not attending school. At Time Two (six months later), 88 youth (59%) reported they were not attending school; 19 youth had returned to school. Among youth not attending school at Time One, the last grade completed ranged from 7th to 11th (median = 9th); furthermore, about half had been out of school 6 or fewer months, while the other half had been out from 7 months to 48 months (median = 6 months). Ninety-one youth (61%) reported that their father was employed (43 did not know), and 113 (75%) said their mother was employed (5 did not know). Sixty-six of the youths (44%) said they did not spend any time with their father, and only 29 (19%) reported spending more than 10 hours per week with their father.

Procedure

Four recruitment strategies were used to solicit youth involvement in the study: mail solicitations to previous year school dropouts whose names were provided by a large, urban school district (48 dropouts; 6 re-enrolled in-school); on-the-street recruitment by peer recruiters who were paid to recruit youth in their neighborhood (42 dropouts; 25 in-school); referrals from agencies such as the Urban League and Urban Services (6 dropouts; 6 in-school); and solicitation through media, posters and flyers (11 dropouts; 6 in-school). In all cases, special emphasis was placed on recruiting youth who had dropped out of school. For all youth, only those who were currently unemployed (defined as working less than 10 hours per week) were included in the study. Chi-square analyses indicated that significantly different proportions of school drop-outs were recruited across the four recruitment methods, $X^2 (3) = 12.82$, $p < .01$.

All youth were informed that the purpose of the research was to learn about the life stresses, daily activities, and well being of male teenagers, and that some questions focused on drug use. Participants were informed that all information was confidential, and that the confidentiality of information about drug use was legally protected by a federal certificate (described below). The youth were paid $15 for an initial 90-minute interview, and $35 for a six-month follow-up. The measures used in the current study were verbally administered by trained interviewers (following which a 45-minute semi-structured interview was administered). Along with written consent from participants, parental written consent was obtained for all non-emancipated youth under the age of 18. Nine trained student interviewers, both blacks and whites and males and females, performed the interviews. The interviewers ranged in age from 21 to 40, and included both advanced undergraduates and graduate students. Interviewers and interviewees were matched on gender or race only in those occasional instances when a youth indicated a gender or race preference in response to a question about whether they had a preference. Analyses did not indicate any effects of interviewer ethnicity or gender on reported levels of alcohol, marijuana, or hard drug use at either measurement point.

Measures

Independent Variables. The three Lifestyle predictor variables were school status, spirituality, and self-perceived participation in meaningful activities. School status was dummy coded into in-school and drop-out categories. Spirituality was assessed with a three item measure, which had achieved good reliability and expected relationships with criterion variables in previous research (Maton, 1989). The three items are: "I experience a personal, close relationship with God"; "I experience God's love and caring on a regular basis"; and "My religious faith helps me to cope during times of difficulty." The items were completed on a 5-point Likert type scale (ranging from "not at all accurate" to "completely accurate"). The alpha reliability of the measure in the current research (Time One) was .80. The meaningful activities measure included six items, and had achieved acceptable reliability and expected relationships with criterion variables in previous research (Maton, 1990). The items assess frequency of involvement in the past week in activities related to goal achievement, contributing to others, and the use of valued skills. The items were completed on a 5-point Likert type scale (ranging from "not at all" to "very often"). In the current research, the alpha reliability of the measure (Time One) was .73.

The three Support/Stress predictor variables were perceived social support from parents, perceived social support from friends, and total negative, uncontrollable life events. Parent support and friend support were assessed with shortened forms of Procidano and Heller's (1983) parents and friends scales, derived by factor analysis (Maton, Gouze, & Keating, 1987). The items were completed on a 5-point Likert type scale (ranging from "not at all accurate" to "completely accurate"). An example of an item from the 12-item parent support scale was "I rely on my parents for emotional support." An example of an item from the 10-item friend support scale was "I rely on my friends for emotional support." The alpha reliabilities for parent support and friend support (Time One) were .91

and .78, respectively. The life stress measure included 35 events, primarily focused on death, illness and injury which happened during the past 6 months to family members and friends.

The three Well-Being predictor variables were symptoms, self-esteem, and life satisfaction. The 12-item symptoms measure combined the 6-item Depression and 6-item Anxiety scales from the Brief Symptom Inventory (Derogatis & Spencer, 1982), and assessed the extent to which various symptoms were experienced during the past week. (The two scales were combined to provide a general measure of distress, and to maintain the same number of Well-being as Lifestyle and Support/Stress predictors.) The items were completed on a 5-point Likert type scale (ranging from "not at all" to "extremely"). Self-esteem was assessed with Rosenberg's (1979) 10-item scale. Life satisfaction was assessed with Diener, Emmons, Larsen, and Griffin's (1985) 5-item scale. The self-esteem and life satisfaction items were completed on a 5-point Likert type scale (ranging from "not at all accurate" to "completely accurate"). Each of the well-being measures has established reliability and validity. In the current sample, the alpha reliabilities for symptoms, self-esteem, and life satisfaction (Time One) were .78, .75, and .81, respectively.

Demographic Variables. Age was calculated from the date of birth information provided at the time of each interview. The variable "Father present while growing up" was dummy coded from the respondent's response to the question, "Was your father living with you while you were growing up." Unfortunately, a measure of socioeconomic status (SES) could not be constructed given the large amount of missing data and the lack of detailed information youth were able to report about both mother's and fathers's education and occupation.

Dependent Variables. Measures of alcohol use, marijuana use, and hard drug use were designed for this research, based upon measures used by Newcomb and Harlow (1986). Each measure asked youth to indicate the frequency of use over the past six months, using the same 6-point scale (0 = not at all; 1 = once or twice; 2 = a few times; 3 = once a month; 4 = once a week; 5 = once a day; 6 = more than once a day).

Alcohol use was assessed by summing the frequency ratings for beer and hard liquor consumption. Marijuana use was assessed by a single item assessing the frequency of use over the past six months. Hard drug use was assessed by summing the frequency ratings for cocaine/crack, hallucinogens, heroin, stimulants, depressants, and phencyclidine (PCP). The correlations of the alcohol, marijuana, and hard drug use measures with a social desirability scale (from Jackson's Personality Research Form, Jackson, 1967) were not significant at either Time One or Time Two, providing some assurance that the levels of use reported were not simply a function of social desirability. Additional possible concerns about the quality of the data are discussed below.

Quality of the Data

The truthfulness of the respondents' answers is of concern because the interview included questions about unlawful behavior (i.e., illicit substance use) and because disenfranchised minority adolescents are not expected to be completely truthful to university researchers. We employed several strategies to help ensure that we were obtaining accurate data. However, it is still possible that our data underestimate substance use.

One strategy was to build youths' trust by guaranteeing confidentiality. We assured the interviewees that we would not use the data for any purpose other than the current research, and that name and address information were collected only so we could contact them for the follow-up interview. We also obtained a federal "Confidentiality Certificate" (i.e., subpoena protection) from one of our granting agencies (National Institute of Drug Abuse) and presented it to the youths at the first interview.

We also trained our interviewers to work on building rapport with the youths so they might be more likely to trust our intentions. As part of the training, each interviewer observed an interview, and then conducted a number of practice interviews before they were sent out to conduct actual interviews. The practice interviews were done with male Black adolescents who were paid for taking part, and who were involved in a community program designed to help them obtain their GED (i.e., high school equivalency degree) and develop job skills. The practice interviews were observed and/or tape recorded, and each interviewer received feedback about their style and the interview process.

We also asked for feedback from the youths when the practice interview was completed. We spoke to them about the issues of accuracy, content and relevance of the interview, and possible problems with white or female interviewers. They agreed that the gender or ethnicity of the interviewer was less important than the rapport that is developed. They also suggested that this rapport was the best strategy for ensuring truthful responses. In addition, they indicated that the content of the interview would be acceptable and relevant for their peers. As noted above, for both Time One and Time Two data, neither sex nor ethnicity of interviewer were significantly related to any of the dependent measures.

Finally, to help ensure that the data collected in the study were useful and valid, interviewers rated every interview in the research for consistency of response, comprehension of the questions, flow or ease of the interview, youth's attention, and youth's overall attitude about the interview. They used a three point scale (1 = good; 2 = neutral; 3 = bad). They also rated their impression of the validity of the data for each measure in the interview. They indicated whether or not they thought the responses were valid, questionable, or invalid. These ratings were partly based on the interviewers' overall impressions, and in part on responses to interviewer probing about items, especially those which were reverse coded. Any respondent who had more than four invalid or bad ratings was eliminated (four individuals).

RESULTS

The percentages of youth reporting at least some use of substances during the past six months (Time One) were 61% for alcohol, 39% for marijuana, and 16% for hard drugs (most often used were cocaine, by 10%; smack, by 7%; and depressants, by 5%). The National Household Survey of Drug Abuse (NIDA, 1988) indicated lower rates of use during the past 12 months among black 12-17 year old males: 38% for alcohol, 18% for marijuana and 4% for cocaine (comparable data on other hard drugs was not reported). The three substance use criterion variables were moderately and nificantly correlated: among Time One criteria the correlations ranged from .36 (alcohol and hard drugs) to .47 (alcohol and marijuana), and among Time Two criteria from .32 (alcohol and marijuana) to .55 (marijuana and hard drugs).

The correlations among the predictor variables are reported in Table 1. In general, the pattern of correlations among life style, support/stress, and well-being variables were consistent in magnitude and direction with that reported in the empirical literature, supporting the general validity of the data set (for instance, lifestyle variables were significantly related to well-being variables in expected directions). Since the highest intercorrelation among variables was only $r = -.53$ (symptoms and self-esteem), multicollinearity does not appear to be a problem. The Time One-Time Two intercorrelations (not shown in Table 1) averaged $r = .58$ for the nine psychosocial predictor variables, with a range from .38 to .74. (Interestingly, the three lowest Time One-Time Two intercorrelations, $r = .38$ for Meaningful Activity, $r = .46$ for Stress, and $r = .53$ for Symptoms, were for the three scales which asked individuals to focus on a specified, recent, time period–e.g., the past week–when responding to the items.)

Primary Analyses

The data analytic strategy involved first carrying out multivariate multiple regression analyses, to test for the overall significance of the relationship between predictor variables and all three substance use criteria. If significant, then separate regression analyses were carried out for the alcohol, marijuana and hard drug use criteria. For each criterion variable, four analyses were carried out: Time One predictors and Time One substance use criterion (Cross-sectional Analysis); Time Two predictors and Time Two substance use criterion (Cross-sectional Analysis); Time One predictors and Time Two substance use criterion, with Time One substance use controlled (Prospective Analysis); and Time Two predictors and Time Two substance use criterion, with Time One substance use controlled (Longitudinal Analysis).

For the Cross-sectional Analyses, the following hierarchical procedure was used: first, age and/or father in household when growing up were entered into the equation only if a significant amount of variance were explained; second, the three Lifestyle independent variables were entered as a set; third, the three Support/Stress variables were entered as a set; and fourth, the three Well-Being predictors were entered as a set. Lifestyle was entered before the other predictor sets because it has consistently been found in adolescent research to be related to substance use (e.g., Donovan & Jessor, 1985; Hundleby, 1987; Jessor & Jessor, 1977). Support/Stress was entered next because of the central importance of current social relationships and life stress to adolescent well being (e.g., Compas, 1987; Newcomb & Bentler, 1988). Well-Being was entered last since a large body of theory and research suggests that it may be directly caused by levels of Social Support/Stress (e.g., Cohen & Wills, 1985; Vaux, 1988). For each analysis, the percent of variance accounted for by the predictor set is presented in the tables, as well as the standardized beta from the final equation, reflecting the contribution of each variable to the criterion independent of every other entered variable. Finally, the zero-order correlations of all variables are reported.

Two modifications were made when carrying out the Prospective (Time One predictors) and Longitudinal (Time Two predictors) Analyses. First, Time One substance use was entered as a covariate (the other covariates were next entered only if they explained additional variance). Second, the predictor variables within each predictor set were made available for entrance in step-wise (i.e., "forward") fashion, so that only the variable(s) that explained a significant amount of remaining variance was entered. This procedure, rather than forced entry of all three variables in a set was followed to reduce the probability that predictors in a set with overlapping variance would all drop below significance following entrance (given the relatively smaller amount of variance remaining to be explained in the criterion following the entrance of Time One substance use). First, the three Lifestyle predictors were made available for entrance, in step-wise fashion, next the three Support/Stress predictors, in step-wise fashion, and finally the three Well-Being predictors, in step-wise fashion. In all analyses reported below, the minimum tolerance level of any predictor variable was .69, indicating the absence of multicollinearity among predictors.

Table 1

Correlation Matrix of Predictor Variables (Time One Above Diagonal; Time Two Below Diagonal)

	1	2	3	4	5	6	7	8	9	10	11
1 Age		.03	-.41ᶜ	-.09	-.10	-.15	-.08	.05	.08	-.02	-.18ᵃ
2 Father Growing Up	.05		.08	-.03	.09	.17	-.07	-.09	-.19ᵃ	.11	.11
3 In School	-.36ᶜ	.08		.25ᵇ	.16ᵃ	.18ᵃ	.09	-.22ᵇ	-.01	.12	.34ᶜ
4 Spiritual	-.14	.02	.10		.37ᶜ	.28ᶜ	.10	-.05	.08	.15	.24ᵇ
5 Activity	-.05	.01	.14	.31ᶜ		.32ᶜ	.28ᶜ	.07	-.03	.26ᵇ	.30ᶠ
6 Parent Support	-.12	.01	.18ᵃ	.34ᶜ	.32ᶜ		.08	-.23ᵇ	-.22ᵇ	.35ᶜ	.42ᶜ

	1	2	3	4	5	6	7	8	9	10	11
7 Friend Support	-.12	-.10	-.01	.13	.32[c]	.24[b]		.01	-.01	.20[a]	.09
8 Stress	.06	.04	-.14	.02	.03	-.12	.11		.26[c]	-.20[a]	-.31[c]
9 Symptoms	.11	-.16	-.01	-.02	-.17[a]	-.19[a]	-.03	.19[a]		-.53[c]	-.26[c]
10 Self-Esteem	.03	.15	.13	.15	.30[c]	.22[b]	.22[b]	-.10	-.42[c]		.48[c]
11 Life Satisfaction	-.25[b]	.11	.27[c]	.27[c]	.31[c]	.38[c]	.17[a]	-.09	-.20[a]	.30[c]	

[a] p < .05

[b] p < .01

[c] p < .001

Missing data on the independent variables were replaced through means substitutions. Among Time One predictors, two predictor variables were missing three cases, and five were missing one case. Among Time Two predictors, one variable was missing seven cases, one variable was missing two cases, and two variables were missing one case. The results were generally similar when analyses without means substitution were compared with those reported below.

Multivariate Multiple Regression Analyses. The multivariate tests of significance of the predictor variables on the three criteria were highly significant (all less than $p < .01$) for the Time One, Time Two, Prospective, and Longitudinal analyses. The results of the separate regression analyses for each criterion variable are reported below.

Alcohol Use. Table 2 reports the results for the cross-sectional multiple regression analyses with alcohol consumption as the criterion. When entered first in the equation, in both Time One and Time Two analyses age was positively and significantly related to alcohol use (explaining 7.4% and 5.5% of the variance, respectively). In the Time One analysis, independent of age the Support/Stress variables explained an additional, significant amount of variance (7.8%). In the Time Two analysis, Lifestyle (7.8%) and Support/Stress (4.5%) each explained significant amounts of variance. The Multiple R for the final Time One equation (.452) represents a significant 20.4% of the variance in alcohol use accounted for by predictors, $F (10,139) = 3.56, p < .01$. The Multiple R for Time Two (.447) indicates a comparable, significant 20.0% of variance accounted for, $F (10,139) = 3.47, p < .001$.

With all variables entered into the equation, only in school status, $\beta = -.25, p < .05$, for Time Two, remained significantly related to alcohol use. Specifically, independently of all other factors, youth who were still attending school reported lower levels of alcohol use.

Table 3 reports the results for the prospective and longitudinal analyses with alcohol consumption (Time Two) as the criterion. Although four of the psychosocial predictors from Time One had significant zero-order correlations with Time Two alcohol use, none explained significant variance beyond that accounted for by Time One alcohol use (which itself explained 27.3% of variance). In the longitudinal analysis, however, both Time Two in-school status, ß = –.15, p < .05, and Time Two life event stress, ß = .14, p < .05, were significantly related to alcohol use in expected directions, independent of Time One alcohol use. Thus, youth who were not attending school at Time Two, and youth reporting a higher number of stressful life events during the preceding six months each were more likely to report increased drinking compared to six months earlier.

Marijuana Use. Table 4 reports the results of the cross-sectional analyses for marijuana use, which were similar in some but not all regards to the findings for alcohol use. As with alcohol use, age was positively related to marijuana use, explaining a significant 4.9% of variance at Time One and 3.5% of variance at Time Two. Lifestyle explained a large 17.5% of variance at Time One, and 10.3% of variance at Time Two. Support/Stress explained a significant 4.5% of variance in marijuana use, at Time One only. The Multiple R for the final Time One equation (.536) represents a significant 28.7% of the variance in marijuana use accounted for by predictors, F (10,139) = 5.60, p < .001. The comparable Multiple R for Time Two (.415) was smaller in magnitude, indicating 17.2% of variance was accounted for, F (10,139) = 2.88, p < .01.

With all variables entered into the equation, in school status, ß = –.19, p < .05, and spirituality, ß = –.32, p < .001, were inversely and significantly related to marijuana use at Time One, while life event stress, ß = .17, p < .05, was positively and significantly related. Only in school status, ß = –.20, p < .05, was significantly related to marijuana use at Time Two, with all variables entered.

Table 5 reports the results for the prospective and longitudinal analyses with marijuana use (Time Two) as the criterion. Although five of the psychosocial predictors from Time One had significant zero-order correlations with Time Two marijuana use, only self-esteem, ß = –.16, p < .05, explained significant variance beyond that accounted for by Time One marijuana use (which itself explained 27.3% of variance). Thus, youth with lower levels of self-esteem at Time One were more likely to report increased levels of marijuana use six months later. In the longitudinal analysis, only parent support, ß = –.15, p < .05, was significantly related to marijuana use independent of Time One use. Thus, youth who reported lower levels of parent support at Time Two were more likely to

Table 2

Zero-Order Correlations and Multiple Regression Results for Alcohol Use: Time One (Predictors and Criterion) and Time Two (Predictors and Criterion) Cross-Sectional Analyses

Predictor Set	Time One		Time Two	
	r	Final Beta	r	Final Beta
Covariates				
Age	.27[c]	.16	.24[b]	.09
Father Growing Up	-.01		-.05	
Step R^2 change		.074[c]		.055[b]
Lifestyle				
In School	-.27[c]	-.12	-.32[c]	-.25[b]
Spirituality	-.05	.04	-.14	-.09
Meaningful Activity	-.05	.04	.01	.10

Step R^2 change	.028		.078[b]	
Support/Stress				
Parent Support	-.25[b]	-.13	-.23[b]	-.16
Friend Support	-.12	-.11	.06	.07
Life Event Stress	.28[c]	.15	.16[a]	.08
Step R^2 change	.078[b]		.045[a]	
Well Being				
Symptoms	.20[a]	.14	.11	.11
Self-Esteem	-.13	.10	.04	.15
Life Satisfaction	-.27[c]	-.13	-.20[a]	-.08
Step R^2 change	.023		.021	

Note. For both analyses, the Predictor Sets were entered in the order listed above. The variables within the Covariate Set were made available for entrance in stepwise fashion; the variables within the other three Sets were entered simultaneously. The betas listed are the standardized betas from the final equation, i.e., with all entered variables.

a $p < .05$ b $p < .01$ c $p < .001$

Table 3

Zero-Order Correlations and Multiple Regression Results for Alcohol Use: Prospective (Time One Predictors, Time Two Criterion) and Longitudinal (Time Two Predictors, Time Two Criterion) Analyses

Predictor Set	Prospective		Longitudinal	
	r	Final Beta	r	Final Beta
Covariates				
Time One Alcohol Use	.52[c]	.52[c]	.52[c]	.48[c]
Age	.24[b]		.24[b]	
Father Growing Up	-.13		-.05	
Step R^2 change		.273[c]		.273[c]
Lifestyle				
In School	-.25[b]		-.32[c]	-.15[a]
Spirituality	-.12		-.14	
Meaningful Activity	-.00		.01	

Step R² change			.026ᵃ
Support/Stress			
Parent Support	-.20ᵃ	-.23ᵇ	
Friend Support	.05	.06	
Life Event Stress	.19ᵃ	.16ᵃ	.14ᵃ
Step R² change			.020ᵃ
Well Being			
Symptoms	.08	.11	
Self-Esteem	-.04	.04	
Life Satisfaction	-.22ᵇ	-.20ᵃ	
Step R² change			

Note. For both analyses, Time One Alcohol Use was entered first. Then, Age and Father in Home were made available for entrance in stepwise fashion. Finally, the variables within the other three Sets were simultaneously made available for entrance, in stepwise fashion. The betas listed are the standardized betas from the final equation, i.e., with all entered variables.

a $p < .05$ b $p < .01$ c $p < .001$

Table 4

Zero-Order Correlations and Multiple Regression Results for Marijuana Use: Time One (Predictors and Criterion) and Time Two (Predictors and Criterion) Cross-Sectional Analyses

Predictor Set	Time One		Time Two	
	r	Final Beta	r	Final Beta
Covariates				
Age	.22[b]	.09	.19[a]	.04
Father Growing Up	-.09		-.15	
Step R^2 change		.049[b]		.035[a]
Lifestyle				
In School	-.37[c]	-.19[a]	-.28[c]	-.20[a]
Spirituality	-.35[c]	-.32[c]	-.25[b]	-.16
Meaningful Activity	-.05	.13	-.16[a]	.00

<u>Step R² change</u>	.175c		.103c	
Support/Stress				
Parent Support	-.12	.08	-.26c	-.11
Friend Support	-.10	-.08	-.10	-.03
Life Event Stress	.27c	.17a	.01	-.05
<u>Step R² change</u>	.043a		.019	
Well Being				
Symptoms	.08	.07	.09	.05
Self-Esteem	-.10	.07	-.11	.02
Life Satisfaction	-.29c	-.16	-.28c	-.13
<u>Step R² change</u>	.020		.015	

<u>Note</u>. For both analyses, the Predictor Sets were entered in the order listed above. The variables within the Covariate Set were made available for entrance in stepwise fashion; the variables within the other three Sets were entered simultaneously. The betas listed are the standardized betas from the final equation, i.e., with all entered variables.

a $p < .05$ b $p < .01$ c $p < .001$

Table 5

Zero-Order Correlations and Multiple Regression Results for Marijuana Use: Prospective (Time One Predictors, Time Two Criterion) and Longitudinal (Time Two Predictors, Time Two Criterion) Analyses

Predictor Set	Prospective		Longitudinal	
	r	Final Beta	r	Final Beta
Covariates				
Time One Marijuana Use	.58c	.56c	.58c	.55c
Age	.19a		.19a	
Father Growing Up	-.14		-.15	
Step R^2 change		.332c		.331a
Lifestyle				
In School	-.23b		-.28c	
Spirituality	-.24b		-.25b	
Meaningful Activity	-.10		-.16a	

Step R^2 change

Support/Stress

Parent Support	-.17[a]		-.26[c]	-.15[a]
Friend Support	-.09		-.10	
Life Event Stress	.13		.01	
Step R^2 change			.022[a]	

Well Being

Symptoms	.12		.09	
Self-Esteem	-.21[b]	-.16[a]	-.11	
Life Satisfaction	-.27[c]		-.28[c]	
Step R^2 change		.025[a]		

<u>Note</u>. For both analyses, Time One Marijuana Use was entered first. Then, Age and Father in Home were made available for entrance in stepwise fashion. Finally, the variables within the other three Sets were simultaneously made available for entrance, in stepwise fashion. The betas listed are the standardized betas from the final equation, i.e., with all entered variables.

a $p < .05$ b $p < .01$ c $p < .001$

have had increased levels of marijuana use over the preceding six months.

Hard Drug Use. Table 6 reports the results of the cross-sectional analyses for hard drug use. Only Lifestyle was significantly related to hard drug use, explaining 7.7% of the variance at Time One and 5.5% at Time Two. Interestingly, age, which had been significantly related in each of the previous analyses, was not significantly related to level of hard drug use. The Multiple R for the final Time One equation (.403) represents a significant 16.2% of the variance in hard drug use accounted for by the predictors, F (9,140) = 3.01, $p < .01$. With all variables entered, the comparable Multiple R for Time Two (.309) indicates a non-significant 9.6% of variance accounted for, F (9,140) = 1.64, $p < .11$.

Table 7 reports the results for the prospective and longitudinal analyses with hard drug use (Time Two) as the criterion. Although six of nine predictors from Time One had significant zero-order correlations with Time Two hard drug use, only spirituality, ß = − .24, $p < .01$, explained significant variance beyond that accounted for by Time One hard drug use. Thus, youth who reported lower levels of spirituality at Time One were more likely to report increased levels of hard drug use six months later. Concerning the longitudinal analysis, although spirituality and two other Time Two predictors had significant zero-order correlations with Time Two hard drug use, none of the three explained significant variance beyond Time One hard drug use (which itself explained 41.5% of variance).

DISCUSSION

The current research provides new information about the psychosocial correlates of substance abuse among male, urban, African-American adolescents, and supports contentions that this sample is at higher risk than the general population. The higher rates of illicit drug use in the present sample than in national samples were expected, since the sample included a large number of individuals who did not complete high school and who were unemployed. hese characteristics have been identified as risk factors for substance use (Kandel, 1980).

The pattern of results for the regression analyses suggests that Lifestyle is a substantive and consistent predictor of marijuana and hard drug use, in both Time One and Time Two analyses. Specifically, leaving school before graduating was associated with greater marijuana use at both points in time, while spirituality was associated with less marijuana and hard drug use, independent of all other variables in Time One analyses. In addition, in a longitudinal analysis, leaving school before graduating (assessed at Time Two) was predictive of increased levels of alcohol consumption from Time One to Time Two. Several investigators have found similar patterns of results for involvement in conventional activities (Hawkins & Weiss, 1984; Jessor et al., 1980) and for religious commitment (Donovan & Jessor, 1978; Selnow, 1985) for more heterogeneous samples. Our research extends these results to a sample of high-risk, urban male Black adolescents.

The Support/Stress variables, as a set, predicted to level of alcohol use at both measurement points, and to level of marijuana use at one of two measurement points. In terms of specific predictor variables, with all other variables entered, higher levels of life event stress were related to higher levels of marijuana use, at Time One. In addition, in a longitudinal analysis, higher levels of life event stress (reported at Time Two) were predictive of increased levels of alcohol use from Time One to Time Two. Finally, in a prospective analysis, lower levels of parent support (reported at Time One) were predictive of increased levels of marijuana use, six months later. Interestingly, the variable friend support was not a significant correlate of substance use. The lack of significant findings for friend support may reflect the mixed role of the peer group for adolescents–serving both to encourage, or discourage, substance use depending on the nature of the peer's own usage and values.

As a set, the Well-Being variables did not explain a significant amount of variance in any of the cross-sectional analyses. Furthermore, with all variables entered into the cross-sectional equations, individual well-being variables did not explain independent variance, even though eight of eighteen possible zero-correlations were significant. Interestingly, however, in the prospective analysis of marijuana use, lower self-esteem (reported at Time One) was predictive of higher levels of marijuana use, six months later. The

Table 6

Zero-Order Correlations and Multiple Regression Results for Hard Drug Use: Time One (Predictors and Criterion) and Time Two (Predictors and Criterion) Cross-Sectional Analyses

Predictor Set	Time One		Time Two	
	r	Final Beta	r	Final Beta
Covariates				
Age	.06		.04	
Father Growing Up	-.13		-.13	
Step R^2 change				
Lifestyle				
In School	-.14	-.01	-.19[a]	-.14
Spirituality	-.27[c]	-.24[b]	-.16[a]	-.13
Meaningful Activity	-.08	.07	-.06	.02

Step R² change	.055ᵃ		.077ᵇ	
Support/Stress				
Parent Support	-.06	-.15	-.05	-.21ᵇ
Friend Support	.05	.04	.07	.03
Life Event Stress	.15	.19ᵃ	.06	.19ᵃ
Step R² change	.036		.039	
Well Being				
Symptoms	.07	.10	.09	.18ᵃ
Self-Esteem	.04	-.05	-.09	-.24ᵇ
Life Satisfaction	-.04	-.14	-.15	-.28ᶜ
Step R² change	.005		.046	

Note. For both analyses, the Predictor Sets were entered in the order listed above. The variables within the Covariate Set were made available for entrance in stepwise fashion; the variables within the other three Sets were entered simultaneously. The betas listed are the standardized betas from the final equation, i.e., with all entered variables.

a $p < .05$ b $p < .01$ c $p < .001$

Table 7

Zero-Order Correlations and Multiple Regression Results for Hard Drug Use: Prospective (Time One Predictors, Time Two Criterion) and Longitudinal (Time Two Predictors, Time Two Criterion) Analyses

Predictor Set	Prospective		Longitudinal	
	r	Final Beta	r	Final Beta
Covariates				
Time One Hard Drug Use	.64^c	.64^c	.64^c	.64^c
Age	.04		.04	
Father Growing Up	-.13		-.13	
Step R^2 change		.414^c		.414^c
Lifestyle				
In School	-.12		-.19^a	
Spirituality	-.13		-.16^a	
Meaningful Activity	-.07		-.06	

Step R² change

Support/Stress

Parent Support	-.04	-.15
Friend Support	-.03	.04
Life Event Stress	.12	.19[a]

Step R² change

Well Being

Symptoms	.11	.10
Self-Esteem	-.09	-.05
Life Satisfaction	-.14	-.14

Step R² change

Note. For both analyses, Time One Hard Drug Use was entered first. Then, Age and Father in Home were made available for entrance in stepwise fashion. Finally, the variables within the other three Sets were simultaneously made available for entrance, in stepwise fashion. The betas listed are the standardized betas from the final equation, i.e., with all entered variables.

a $p < .05$ b $p < .01$ c $p < .001$

general lack of significant relationships between substance use and the distress and self-esteem variables is contrary to some previous research (e.g., Newcomb & Harlow, 1986). It may be due in part to the fact that previous researchers did not examine the contribution of these variables after Lifestyle and Support/Stress variables were already entered. Interestingly, the well-being variable which most consistently achieved significant zero-order relationships with substance use criteria was life satisfaction, both in terms of cross-sectional (five of six) and across-time (Time-One-Time Two, both directions; five of six) correlations. Previous substance use theory and research with adolescents has not generally included life satisfaction as a variable of interest. The consistent zero-order relationships obtained in the current study, however, suggest the value of including life satisfaction as a possible antecedent, intervening, or outcome variable in future theoretical and empirical work.

The current research is one of the few studies that has examined predictors of substance use among high risk urban Black youths. Other studies that included some information on minority substance use typically included samples of in school youth (Newcomb, Maddahian, & Bentler, 1986; Johnston & O'Malley, 1985). A notable exception is the longitudinal research on black Harlem youth carried out by Brunswick; however, Brunswick's program of research primarily focused on substance use as a predictor of health status (e.g., Brunswick & Messeri, 1986). Overall, the findings of the current research indicate that various psychosocial predictor variables and models each explain some variance in substance use. This finding suggests that the multiple psychosocial risk-factor approach proposed for etiological research on adolescents in general (cf. Newcomb & Bentler, 1989) may also be suited for research on high-risk minority youth.

The truthfulness of the youths' responses regarding substance use is an important issue when asking interviewees about unlawful behaviors. The youths may have under-reported their substance use, although the relative levels of use reported across youth may have been veridical. The fact that substance use rates from our sample are similar to those from other studies (e.g., Brunswick et al., 1985) with comparable samples provides some confidence in the data. It is quite likely, however, that respondents are under-reporting drug use in all of these studies. Under-reporting may partly explain why the univariate correlations between the predictors and substance use are generally small (though significant).

A limitation of this research is the absence of follow-up data over a longer time period. Ideally, longitudinal designs in which high-risk, inner city samples are assessed before they commence drug use, and for an extensive period of time afterwards, are necessary to more fully examine the psychosocial factors involved in use. The Time Two completion rate of 70% in the current study suggests that longitudinal research is possible for inner city, high risk minority samples. In future research, a larger and more representative sample of inner city youth is also desirable. While diverse recruitment methods were used, it is not clear if an adequate cross-section of inner city youth was obtained. A larger sample would contribute to more confidence in the robustness of the findings; it might also contribute to more variance in the criterion measures, especially hard drug use, which in turn may lead to a greater predictive power of the psychosocial variables.

A final limitation of the study is that we did not distinguish between substance use and abuse. An occasional substance user may not have a high risk lifestyle, low social support, or experience a diminishment in well-being to the same extent as a youthful drug abuser. This is not to say that substance use is warranted or might not be dysfunctional for adolescents. In fact both substance use and abuse during adolescence are associated with delinquency, precocious sexual behavior, deviant attitudes, and school dropout (Newcomb & Bentler, 1989). The point is, however, that occasional users may have a different pattern of psychosocial predictors than abusers. Future research needs to develop and employ measures to distinguish between substance use and abuse.

Implications for Intervention

The results suggest possible intervention approaches to prevent and reduce substance use among young urban African-American males. The results on in-school status, for instance, suggest that interventions aimed at keeping Black male adolescents in school may have the added benefit of reducing substance use for the "gateway" drugs. One way to reduce substance use in urban settings may be to improve the structure and quality of schools, so they can be more relevant, interesting, and responsive to the concerns and issues of its students. It is not coincidental that public concerns about substance use is highest in the same communities (i.e., large urban areas) where the school systems have received the most criticism, and appear to have the fewest resources. Additionally, interventions to maintain church and family involvements which contribute to personal spirituality, if carefully and sensitively developed, represent another intervention implication of the findings (Maton & Pargament, 1987).

Interventions designed to enhance the support skills and relationships among family members, especially parents, may be an effective strategy for combatting substance use among this high risk group. Bowman (1984) asserts that social alienation and a lack of a social identity may be central factors leading to substance abuse. Innovative family interventions which bring youth and parents together in engaging and meaningful activities, and, equally important, which link the family to community support resources and support networks may simultaneously enhance the support and skills of parents and of youth.

These intervention strategies avoid the problems of more traditional approaches that focus only on the drug culture. Bangert-Drowns (1988) conducted a meta-analysis of school-based drug education programs that focused on educating youths about the effects of the drugs, the social culture surrounding drug use, and the problems associated with the individual drug user. Bangert-Drowns concludes that the benefits of interventions with these approaches are limited. In a similar analysis of 143 adolescent prevention programs, Tobler (1986) found that the most effective interventions for the most high risk populations were programs promoting alternative activities. These approaches targeted both the individual user and environmental factors to help the adolescent develop personal skills (e.g., leadership) and participate in community and leisure activities. Interventions that focus on social and behavioral factors that are associated with substance use, but are not specifically targeted on drugs and drug related behaviors may be more effective in reducing substance use than more traditional programs that focus on the drug culture and drug attitudes.

This research provides a first step in understanding the psychosocial predictors of substance use among a group that is particularly vulnerable to the deleterious effects of substance use (Prendergast, Austin, Maton, & Baker, 1989). Future research should continue to focus on minority populations, extending focus to other minority groups that are known to have both high and low rates of substance use. The long term goal for research in this area must be to develop viable, multi-faceted interventions and public policies designed to lessen the negative impact that drugs and associated problems have on youth and the urban minority community.

REFERENCES

Bachman, J.G., O'Malley, P.M., & Johnston, J. (1978). *Youth in Transition: Adolescence to Adulthood–Change and Stability in the Lives of Young Men* (Volume Six). Ann Arbor, MI.: Institute of Social Research.

Bangert-Drowns, R.L. (1988). The effects of school-based substance abuse education: A meta-analysis. *Journal of Drug Education, 18*, 243-264.

Bennett, G. (1982). Youthful substance abuse. In G. Bennett, C. Vourakis & D.S. Wolf (Eds.), *Substance Abuse: Pharmacologic, Developmental, and Clinical Perspectives*. John Wiley & Sons: N.Y.

Bowman, P.J. (1984). A discouragement-centered approach to studying unemployment among black youth: Hopelessness, attributions, and psychological distress. *International Journal of Mental Health, 13*, 68-91.

Brown, S.A. (1989). Life events of adolescents in relation to personal and parental substance abuse. *American Journal of Psychiatry, 146*, 484-489.

Brunswick, A.F., & Messeri, P.A. (1986). Drugs, lifestyle, and health: A longitudinal study of urban Black youth. *American Journal of Public Health, 76*, 52-57.

Brunswick, A.F., Merzel, C.R., & Messeri, P.A. (1985). Drug use initiation among urban Black youth: A seven-year follow-up of developmental and secular influences. *Youth and Society, 17*, 189-216.

Cohen, S., & Wills, T.A. (1985). Stress, social support, and the buffering hypothesis. *Psychological Bulletin, 98*, 310-357.

Compas, B.E. (1987). Coping with stress during childhood and adolescence. *Psychological Bulletin, 101*, 393-403.

Cox, W.M. (1982). Personality correlates of substance abuse. In M. Galizio & S.A. Maistro, (Eds.), *Determinants of Substance Abuse: Biological, Psychological, and Environmental Factors*. New York: Plenum.

Derogatis, L.R., & Spencer, P.M. (1982). *The Brief Symptom Inventory (BSI): Administration, Scoring and Procedures.*

Diener, E., Emmons, R.A., Larsen, R.J., & Griffin. S. (1985). The Satisfaction With Life Scale. *Journal of Personality Assessment, 49*, 71-75.

Donovan, J.E., & Jessor, R. (1978). Adolescent problem drinking- Psychosocial correlates in a national sample study. *Journal of Studies in Alcohol, 39*, 1506-1524.

Donovan, J.E. & Jessor, R. (1978). Structure of problem behavior in adolescence and young adulthood. *Journal of Consulting and Clinical Psychology, 53*, 890-904.

Hawkins, J.D., Lishner, D., & Catalano, R.F. Jr. (1985). Childhood predictors and the prevention of adolescent substance abuse. In C.R. Jones & R.J. Battjes (Eds.), *Etiology of Drug Abuse: Implications for Prevention*, NIDA Monograph no. 56, Rockville, MD.

Hawkins, J., & Weiss, J.G. (1984). The social development model: An integrated approach to delinquency prevention. *Journal of Primary Prevention, 5*, 21-36.

Hundleby, J.D. (1987). Adolescent drug use in a behavioral matrix: A confirmation and comparison of the sexes. *Addictive Behaviors, 12*, 103-112.

Jackson, D.N. (1967). *Personality Research Form Manual*. Goshen, N.Y.: Research Psychologists Press.

Jessor, R. (1981). Critical issues in research on health promotion. In D. Coates (Ed.), *Promoting Adolescent Health: A Dialogue on Research and Practice*. New York: Academic Press (pp. 447-465).

Jessor, R., Chase, J.A., & Donovan, J.E. (1980). Psychosocial correlates of marijuana use and problem drinking in a national sample of adolescents. *American Journal of Public Health, 70*, 604-613.

Jessor, R., & Jessor, S.L. (1977). *Problem Behavior and Psychosocial Development: A Longitudinal Study of Youth*. Academic Press: New York.

Johnston, L.D., & O'Malley, P.M. (1986). Why do the nation's students use drugs and alcohol: Self-reported reasons from nine national surveys. *Journal of Drug Issues, 16*, 29-66.

Kandel, D.B. (1980). Drug and drinking behavior among youth. *Annual Review of Sociology, 6*, 235-285.

Maddahian, E., Newcomb, M.D., & Bentler, P.M. (1988). Risk factors for substance use: Differences among adolescents. *Journal of Substance Abuse, 1*, 11-23.

Maton, K.I. (1989). The stress-buffering role of spiritual support: Cross-sectional and prospective investigations. *Journal for the Scientific Study of Religion, 28*, 310-323.

Maton, K.I. (1990). Meaningful involvement in instrumental activity and well-being: Studies of older adolescents and at-risk inner-city teenagers. *American Journal of Community Psychology, 18*, 297-320.

Maton, K.I., Gouze, K.R., & Keating, D.P. (1988). *Social support directionality in friendship and mutual help-group contexts: Direct and stress-buffering relationships to well-being*. Unpublished manuscript.

Maton, K.I., & Pargament, K.I. (1987). Roles of religion in prevention and promotion. In L.A. Jason, R.D. Felner, R. Hess, & J.N. Mortisugu, (Eds.), *Prevention: Toward a Multidisciplinary Approach*. New York: The Haworth Press, Inc. (pp. 161-206).

Murray, D.M. & Perry, C.L. (1985). The prevention of adolescent drug abuse: Implications of etiological, developmental, behavioral, and environmental models. In C.R. Jones, & R.J. Battjes, (Eds.), *Etiology of Drug Abuse: Implications for Prevention.* NIDA Monograph no. 56, Rockville, Md.

Newcomb, M.D., & Bentler, P.M. (1988). Impact of adolescent drug use and social support on problems of young adults: A longitudinal study. *Journal of Abnormal Psychology, 97,* 64-75.

Newcomb, M.D., & Bentler, P.M. (1989). Substance use and abuse among children and teenagers. *American Psychologist, 44,* 242-248.

Newcomb, M.D., & Harlow, L.L. (1986). Life events and substance use among adolescents: Mediating effects of perceived loss of control and meaningfulness in life. *Journal of Personality and Social Psychology, 51,* 564-577.

Newcomb, M.D., Maddahian, E., & Bentler, P.M. (1986). Risk factors for drug use among adolescents: Concurrent and longitudinal analyses. *American Journal of Public Health, 76,* 525-531.

NIDA [National Institute on Drug Abuse]. (1988). *National Household Survey on Drug Abuse: Main Findings 1985.* DHHS Publication No. (ADM)88-1565. Washington, D.C.: U.S. Government Printing Office.

Prendergast, M.L., Austin, G.A., Maton, K.I., & Baker, R. (1989). *Substance Use among Black Youth.* Prevention Research Update 3, Spring. Los Alamitos, CA: Western Center for Drug-Free Schools and Communities.

Procidano, M.E., & Heller, K. (1983). Measures of perceived social support from friends and from family: Three validation studies. *American Journal of Community Psychology, 11,* 1-24.

Rosenberg, M. (1979). *Conceiving the Self.* New York: Basic Books.

Selnow, G.W. (1985). Using a stratified approach in substance intervention and prevention programs among adolescents: An empirical analysis. *Journal of Drug Education, 15,* 327-341.

Tobler, N.S. (1986). Meta-analysis of 143 adolescent drug prevention programs: Quantitative outcome results of program participants compared to a control or comparison group. *Journal of Drug Issues, 16,* 537-568.

Vaux, A. (1988). *Social Support: Theory, Research and Intervention.* New York: Praeger.

Wills, T.A. (1986). Stress and coping in early adolescence: Relationships to substance use in urban school samples. *Health Psychology, 5,* 503-529.

Wingard, J.A., Huba, G.J., & Bentler, P.N. (1980). A longitudinal analysis of personality structure and adolescent substance use. *Personality and Individual Differences, 1,* 259-272.

Illicit Drug and Alcohol Use Among Homeless Black Adults in Shelters

Norweeta G. Milburn
Jacqueline A. Booth

INTRODUCTION

Alcohol abuse has always been a significant problem in the homeless population; in particular when it consisted of a large, older male, skid row population (for example, see Bahr, 1969a; 1969b). However, with the declining age of this population (Jones, Goldstein & Gray, 1984; Lamb, 1982; Seigal & Inciardi, 1982; Stark, 1985), other drug abuse seems to be occurring increasingly (Mulkern & Spence, 1984).

The prevalence of drug abuse among homeless people has not been tapped by the large surveys of drug use conducted by the National Institute on Drug Abuse such as the Household Survey (i.e., Abelson et al., 1977). Furthermore, there is very little empirical data on just how much the abuse of drugs other than alcohol occurs among homeless people, and whether drug abuse is truly

Norweeta G. Milburn is affiliated with the Department of Psychology, Hofstra University, Hempstead, NY 11550.

Jacqueline A. Booth is affiliated with the Institute for Urban Affairs and Research, Howard University, Washington, DC 20008.

This research was supported by a grant (5-R01-DA04513) from the National Institute on Drug Abuse, Alcohol, Drug Abuse and Mental Health Administration, Public Health Service, Department of Health and Human Services. The authors appreciate the assistance of Shari Miles who helped prepare the tables.

more prevalent in this population than it is among the general population.

Recent studies suggest that drug abuse does occur with some degree of frequency (Arce et al., 1983; Bassuk et al., 1984; Roth et al., 1985; Hoffman et al., 1982; Lindelius & Salum, 1976). However, the prevalence and incidence of drug abuse among homeless people has not been systematically documented in the studies that have been done on homeless people (Fisher & Breakey, 1985).

Typically, researchers have noted that drug abuse is a problem, but, little attempt has been made to identify, using an epidemiologic approach, the characteristics of homeless people who are likely to use drugs. Very few studies have attempted to document drug abuse among homeless people in conjunction with demographic and homeless state characteristics, such as age, gender and the duration of homelessness. The exceptions are studies by Morse and Calyson (1985) and Fischer (1984).

This paper attempts to further this research by exploring the nature and extent of illicit drug and alcohol use in one subgroup of the homeless population, Black adults who use shelters in Washington, DC. These adults were selected for this investigation for several reasons. As in other studies of drug use, previous studies on homeless people suggest that those who use drugs are more likely to be members of minority groups (Braucht et al., 1973; Ladner et al., 1986; Mulkern & Spence, 1984; Rosnow et al., 1985). Moreover, minority people seem to be overrepresented in the homeless population, and intra-group differences among minority homeless people have not been explored (Martin, 1985). The lifetime, annual and current prevalence of illicit drug and alcohol use among homeless Black adults will be examined and compared to prevalence estimates for non-homeless Black adults from the general population. In addition, the relationship of demographic characteristics and homeless state characteristics to the prevalence of illicit drug and alcohol use will be determined. Illicit drug use will be viewed as the use of any controlled substance such as marijuana, cocaine, and non-medically prescribed psychotherapeutic drugs. Illicit drug use will be referred to as drug abuse.

NATURE AND PREVALENCE OF DRUG ABUSE IN GENERAL AND HOMELESS POPULATIONS

General Black Population

The large, nationwide surveys of drug abuse continue to indicate that it is a national problem even though the use of many classes of drugs, excluding cocaine is declining (Johnston et al., 1986; Miller et al., 1983; National Institute on Drug Abuse, 1988). Table 1 provides an overview of the prevalence estimates for the general Black population for drug use by classes of drugs from the 1985 Household Survey. The estimates for the lifetime use of any illicit drug, however, are for the total general population which includes Blacks, Whites, Hispanics and others. Sixty-four (64) percent of young adults, age 18 to 25 years, have used illicit drugs in their lifetimes. Among older adults, those 35 and older, the lifetime prevalence for the use of illicit drugs is 20 percent.

Marijuana and cocaine are the illicit drugs that have been used the most often among non-homeless Black adults, with the highest prevalence for lifetime use among both younger and older Black adults. Alcohol is the licit drug that has been used the most often by non-homeless Black adults.

These findings suggest that marijuana will be the most frequently used illicit drug among homeless Black adults and that alcohol will be the most frequently used licit drug. Furthermore, we expect the lifetime, annual and current prevalence estimates for marijuana, cocaine and alcohol use to be higher for homeless Black adults than those for non-homeless Black adults in the same age categories.

Homeless Population

Researchers have documented varying prevalence estimates for drug abuse, which is often referred to as substance abuse and usually reflects the use of alcohol and other drugs, among homeless people (Arce et al., 1983; Fisher et al., 1984; 1986). When drug abuse and alcohol abuse are assessed separately in homeless samples, usually alcohol abuse is more prevalent but this is true for the

Table 1

Percent Reporting Illicit Drug and Alcohol Use among the General Black
Non-Homeless Population by Age

Drug	Age Groups 1		
	18-25	26-34	35+
Illicit:			
All Drugs2			
(Lifetime)	64	62	20
Marijuana			
(Lifetime)	50	54	21
(Annual)	33	28	8
(Current)	24	23	6
Stimulants, sedatives tranquilizers & analgesics			
(Lifetime)	15	14	8
(Annual)			
(Current)	4	3	2

Cocaine			
(Lifetime)	13	17	8
(Annual)	11	10	4
(Current)	6	5	2
PCP			
(Lifetime)	1	3	1
(Annual)			
(Current)			
Heroin			
(Lifetime)	2	2	2
(Annual)			
(Current)			
Alcohol			
(Lifetime)	80	87	80
(Annual)	73	78	53
(Current)	57	66	44

1. These percentages are for a weighted sample.
2. This is for the total population including Blacks, Whites, Hispanics and others.

Note: All figures have been rounded to the nearest whole number.

general population as well. Nonetheless, other drug abuse is a problem even among homeless people who are alcohol abusers (Bassuk et al., 1984; Corrigan & Anderson, 1984).

Looking at drugs other than alcohol, researchers have found diverse estimates of drug abuse. For example, Hoffman et al., (1982) found in a sample of shelter users that 26 percent had a drug abuse problem and 5 percent probably had a drug abuse problem. Lipton et al. (1983), found through case record review that only 4 percent of a homeless sample had a drug or alcohol problem. Jones et al. (1983), found in a sample of homeless people that 38 percent had taken drugs and 48 percent drank heavily.

Table 2 presents an overview of prevalence estimates that can be gleaned from these studies. The first eight studies are from a critical review of the literature by Mulkern and Spence (1984). Overall, the prevalence estimates for drug use vary across these studies, in part, because drug abuse is defined in a number of different ways. For example, estimates tend to be lower when drug abuse is defined as "drug dependence." Estimates of drug use also vary widely depending upon the inclusion or exclusion of alcohol as a drug. Estimates tend to be higher when alcohol is included. Despite this variability some cautious generalizations about the prevalence of drug use among homeless people can be made from these studies. The prevalence estimates for lifetime drug use range from 3 to 71 percent. Prevalence estimates for annual drug use range from 31 to 55 percent. The estimates for current drug use range from 10 to 31 percent. For daily drug use, the range is 3 to 11 percent.

RELATIONSHIP OF DEMOGRAPHIC
AND HOMELESS STATE CHARACTERISTICS
TO ILLICIT DRUG AND ALCOHOL USE

Demographic Characteristics

Most studies with data on drug abuse among homeless people do not report on the characteristics of homeless drug users. Those that do suggest that homeless people who are male, have some income, and are under age 40 will be more likely than their counterparts to use illicit drugs (Division of Substance Abuse Services, 1983; Ladner et al., 1986; Mulkern & Spence, 1984; Roth et al., 1985; Rosnow et al., 1985).

These findings are consistent with other studies of drug use patterns. For example, men and women have been found to differ in their drug use patterns; with women more likely than men to use tranquilizers (Bell et al., 1984). However, men are more likely than women to abuse all other classes of drugs including alcohol (Boscarino, 1981; Bell et al., 1984; Cahalan, 1970; Cahalan et al., 1969). Age has a curvilinear relationship with alcohol use and younger adults tend to use drugs other than alcohol, such as marijuana and cocaine, more than older adults (Cahalan et al., 1969; Johnston et al., 1986; National Institute on Drug Abuse, 1988).

The findings on income and its relationship to drug abuse have been inconclusive. Some research has suggested that drug abuse occurs more often in low-income segments of the population (Braucht et al., 1973) but recent findings indicate that drug abuse, when within impoverished populations, is more likely to occur among those with more income (Lukoff, 1980). Alcohol abuse seems to increase with income, except among women (Cahalan et al., 1969).

The relationship of other demographic characteristics such as marital status and educational attainment to drug abuse has not been explored in the literature and remains to be determined. Data on alcohol abuse suggest some possible relationships (Cahalan et al., 1969). Looking at marital status, alcohol abuse occurs more often among those who are single and divorced/separated. With regard to educational attainment, among men, alcohol abuse occurs more often among those who have finished high school; while among women, it occurs more often among those who have finished college.

These findings suggest that the prevalence estimates for illicit drug and alcohol use will vary among Black homeless adults as a function of demographic characteristics. The lifetime, annual and current prevalence estimates for drug abuse will be higher among younger homeless adults than those who are older, and will be higher among men than among women. The lifetime, annual, and

Table 2

Prevalence of Drug and Alcohol Abuse Among Homeless People
from Previous Research

Study	Prevalence
Brown, C., et al. 1982	32% alcohol daily/regularly 3% drugs daily/regularly
Crystal, S. 1982	21% alcohol regularly 6% drugs regularly
Stark, L. 1983	38% alcohol 1-2 days per week 26% alcohol > 3 days per week 18% drugs 1-9 days per week 4% drugs > 20 days per week
DSAS 1983	55% drugs within last 6 months 31% serious drug use
Robinson, P. 1982	35% alcohol 13% 1 or more drugs

Wynne, J. 1984	32% "drinking problem" 44% drugs within 90 days
SSD 1984	35% alcohol daily 14% alcohol 2 times per week 11% drugs daily 4% drugs > 2 times per month
Mulkern, V. & Spence, R. 1984	30% shelter drug use 27% street drug use 20% shelter drug use at least once per week 25% street drug use at least once per week
Hoffman, S., et al. 1982	26% drug abuse problem
Lipton, F., et al. 1983	41% alcohol, drug or alcohol and drug use 4% alcohol or drug dependence
Arce, A., et al. 1983	3% drug use
Jones, B., et al. 1984	38% drug use
Bassuk, E., et al. 1984	1% drug dependence
Ball, J. & Havassy, B. 1984	9% drug dependence problem

Table 2 (continued)

Study	Prevalence
Corrigan, E. & Anderson, S. (1984)	58% drug use
Roth, D., et al. 1985	32% drug use (includes medication)
Morse, G., et al. 1985	21% drug use/current 6% drug use/daily 4% drug abuse problem
Fisher, P., et al. 1985	20% alcohol or drug abuse and dependence/current 31% alcohol or drug abuse and dependence/annual 71% alcohol or drug abuse and dependence/lifetim
Ladner, S., et al. 1986	17% drug abuse
Parr, R., et al. 1986	10% drug abuse and dependence/current 31% drug abuse and dependence/lifetime
Mowbray, C., et al. 1986	38% shelter drug abuse problem 44% hospital drug use/current or former 31% shelter drug use/current

current prevalence estimates for alcohol use will be higher for homeless men than for homeless women. Drug abuse will be more prevalent among homeless adults with some income than among those with little or no income. The lifetime prevalence estimates for alcohol use will be higher for homeless adults who are divorced/separated or never married than those who are married or widowed. The lifetime prevalence estimate for alcohol use will be higher for homeless individuals with more education than those with less education.

Homeless State Characteristics

Categories of homelessness derived from the characteristics of the nature of individuals' homeless experiences have only recently been considered in the research literature. Some researchers have developed definitions of homelessness that include variables such as the duration of an individual's homeless state (Arce et al., 1983; Hoffman et al., 1982; Rooney, 1980). Duration has been found to be related to the prevalence of alcohol abuse but not the abuse of other drugs (Hoffman, 1982; Roth & Bean, 1985).

There is evidence which suggests that illicit drug use may be linked to other homeless state characteristics such as psychiatric status and previous hospitalization. For example, Farr et al. (1986) found homeless drug users had symptoms of other mental disorders. In other studies, alcohol and illicit drug use have been found to be a secondary psychiatric diagnosis among homeless people who suffer from mental disorders. Arce et al. (1983) found 18 percent of their sample had a secondary diagnosis of alcohol and drug abuse.

We expect that the lifetime prevalence estimates for illicit drug and alcohol use in homeless Black adults will vary as a function of homeless state characteristics. Homeless adults with psychological problems will have higher lifetime prevalence estimates for drug abuse than will those without psychological problems. Homeless adults who have been hospitalized will have higher lifetime prevalence estimates for alcohol use than will individuals who have not been previously hospitalized. Lifetime prevalence estimates for alcohol use will be higher among those adults who have been chronically homeless than their counterparts who have been intermittently or temporarily homeless.

METHOD

Sample

A random, stratified probability-based sample of 414 homeless people, 261 men and 153 women, who used shelters in Washington, DC in the winter of 1988 (January-April) participated in the study.[1] Eighty-seven (87) percent of these respondents were Black. The respondents were interviewed with a structured interview face-to-face by trained interviewers at shelter sites throughout the city. All of the instrument items were pretested with homeless people who were shelter users to insure that they were understandable and appropriate for a face-to-face interview.[2]

The findings that will be described are based upon the 358 Black respondents. Males comprise about two-thirds of this group. Most of these adults (81%) were over age 25, the median age was 31.5 years. Sixty-five (65) percent of these adults had completed at least 12 years of schooling, and some (19%) had attended college. The majority of these respondents were not currently married; 56 percent had never married. Sixty (60) percent of these adults had annual incomes of less than $7,000 per year; consequently, many lived below the poverty level (56%).

Measures

Drug use. Several measures were used to assess the respondents' use of illicit drugs and alcohol. Illicit drug use or drug abuse was tapped by items from the "Monitoring the Future" survey developed by Johnston and his colleagues (1979). These items assessed the lifetime, annual and current prevalence of drug abuse across the main classes of drugs other than alcohol. The drug categories surveyed included marijuana, LSD, PCP, cocaine/crack, psychedelics, heroin, other narcotics, inhalants, psychotherapeutic drugs, and other drugs. Prevalence estimates for illicit drug use were combined to include the use of any of these drugs. Items from the Household Survey developed by Miller and her colleagues (1983) were used to ascertain the lifetime, annual and current prevalence of alcohol use.

To determine the lifetime use of each substance, respondents were asked to indicate how many different times they had used it in their lifetimes; for annual use, how often in the past 12 months; and for current use, how often during the past 30 days. The response categories for each time period ranged from "0 times" to "40 or more times." However, for this paper, use was defined as using the substance at least one time during the specified time period.

Demographic characteristics. A number of demographic characteristics were also assessed. Specific items ascertained the sex, age, educational level, and marital status of respondents. Age was grouped into three categories: 18 to 25 years, 26 to 34 years and 35 years or older. Personal income was ascertained for the year preceding the study, 1987. Four income categories were used: less than $3,000, $3,000-$6,999, $7,000-$11,999, and $12,000 or more. Education was categorized into four levels: 0 to 11 years (less than high school), 12 years (high school graduate), 13 to 15 years (some college or vocational school) and 16 or more years (college graduate or higher). Four categories were used for marital status: married, widowed, divorced/separated and never married. The categories for age and education levels are the same as those used in the Household Survey.

Homeless state characteristics. Items referring to homeless state characteristics assessed psychological problems, history of psychiatric hospitalization and duration of homelessness.

Psychological problems were measured using the Center for Epidemiologic Studies Depression Scale or the CES-D (Radloff, 1977). The CES-D was a 20-item scale which assessed the recent occurrence of depressive symptoms. The scale included items that tapped depressed mood, feelings of guilt and worthlessness, feelings of helplessness and hopelessness, loss of appetite, psychomotor retardation and sleep disturbance. Respondents were asked to indicate how often they had experienced such states in the past week. Responses for each item ranged from "0," rarely or never, to "3," most of the time. The final CES-D score was derived for each respondent by summing across the 20 items. A score of 16 or greater is generally considered to be indicative of a depressed state. This sample of homeless Black adults were classified as depressed or non-depressed based upon this criterion.

Previous psychiatric hospitalization was ascertained by asking respondents if they had ever spent time in a hospital for a mental problem or a problem with their nerves. Responses were recorded as "yes" or "no."

The duration of homelessness was derived from the number of homeless episodes and the recency or length of the current episode of homelessness. Two items were used to determine the number of periods the respondent had been without permanent housing. The first was, "Since the first time you were homeless, how many times have you lived in your own room, apartment or house for a month or more?" The second question was, "Since you were first homeless, how many times have you lived with family or friends for a month or more?" The number of homeless episodes was computed as the number of times the respondent had been housed either in his own home or that of a family member or friend for at least one month since first becoming homeless, plus the current episode of homelessness. Responses to these two items were summed for each respondent and a "1" was added to reflect the present homeless period. This figure resulted in the number of homeless episodes. The "episodes" variable was grouped into 3 categories: 1 episode, 2 to 5 episodes and 6 or more episodes.

Recency or length of the current homeless episode was determined using the two previously described items and follow-up questions. The follow-up questions asked respondents to indicate the last time they had been in each situation; lived in their own home or with family and/or friends for a month or more since becoming homeless. The response categories were: "0", currently; "1," 1 to 6 months ago; "2," 7 to 12 months ago; "3," 13 to 18 months ago; "4," 19 to 24 months ago; and "5," more than 24 months ago. The most current of these two circumstances (i.e., living in own home for at least a month or living with family/friends for at least a month since first being homeless) was the variable that was used to determine recency. For respondents who indicated that they had not been housed in their own home or that of family/friends for at least one month, the length of the present episode of homelessness was considered to be the difference between the age at which the respondent first became homeless and his/her present age. For individuals who indicated they had been housed in their own home or that of family/friends for at least one month, the length of the present episode of homelessness was the minimum amount of time they had been housed in their own home or with family/friends. Recency was categorized as less than 6 months ago, 7 to 12 months ago, 13 to 24 months ago, and more than 24 months ago.

The duration of homelessness encompassed the recency of the current homeless episode as well as the number of episodes of homelessness. Duration classified respondents into three groups: the newly homeless, the intermittently homeless and the chronically homeless. Respondents who were newly homeless had become homeless within the last six months and were homeless for the first time. Respondents designated as intermittently homeless had experienced more than one episode of homelessness; recency among this group varied from within the last 6 months to over 2 years. The chronic homeless had endured only one period of homelessness ever, and this period had begun in the past 7 months to more than 2 years ago.

Data Analysis

The prevalence estimates that are reported here are the percentage of respondents who had used illicit drugs or alcohol one or more times during the specified period. Frequencies, chi-square analysis and multiple classification analysis (MCA) were used to examine the data. MCA was used to estimate the singular and relative relationship of demographic and homeless state characteristics to illicit drug and alcohol use. In MCA, eta assesses the singular relationship of a variable to another variable and beta assesses the relative relationship; the relationship of other variables are accounted for (Andrews et al., 1973).

RESULTS: COMPARISON OF ILLICIT DRUG
AND ALCOHOL USE AMONG HOMELESS
AND NON-HOMELESS BLACK ADULTS

Sixty-two (62) percent of this sample of homeless Black adults reported that they had used illicit drugs in their lifetimes; 38 percent had used drugs within the past year and 26 percent were currently using drugs. As expected, marijuana (17%), and cocaine (16%) were the illicit drugs that were reported most frequently as being used currently. Eighty-six (86) percent had used alcohol in their lifetimes; 74 percent had used alcohol within the past year and 59 percent were currently using alcohol. (All of these percentages were significantly different from zero at p < .001 using a chi-square one-sample test.)

As can be seen in Table 3, 73 percent of those age 18 to 25, 67 percent, age 26 to 34, and 50 percent, age 35 and older, had used illicit drugs in their lifetimes. These figures are somewhat higher than those for the total general population (see Table 1) but the greatest difference occurs among older adults, those 35 years and older. Older homeless Black adults have a lifetime estimate for illicit drug use that is 2.5 times higher than the figure for older non-homeless adults in the total general population.

Comparing the prevalence estimates for illicit drugs among homeless and non-homeless Black adults, revealed a number of differences. For marijuana, homeless Black adults were more likely than non-homeless Black adults to have used it in their lifetimes across all age categories (18-25, $X^2 = 5.89$, df = 1, p ≤ .05; 26-34, $X^2 = 5.03$, df = 1, p ≤ .05; 35+, $X^2 = 24.9$, df = 1, p ≤ .001). The differences in annual and current use were not statistically significant.

Looking at the non-medical use of psychotherapeutic drugs, only homeless Black adults who were older were more likely than non-homeless Black adults who were older to have used these drugs in their lifetimes ($X^2 = 24.4$, df = 1, p ≤ .001). The differences among other age cohorts for lifetime, annual and current use were not significant. Nor were differences in annual and current use among older adults.

Differences in cocaine use were significant across all age categories for lifetime, annual and current use. Younger, mid-aged and older homeless Black adults were more likely than their non-homeless counterparts to have used cocaine in their lifetimes ($X^2 = 32.9$, df = 1, p ≤ .001; $X^2 = 44.3$, df = 1, p ≤ .001; $X^2 = 47.9$, df = 1, p ≤ .001, respectively), and during the past year ($X^2 = 31.3$, df = 1, p ≤ .001; $X^2 = 85.2$, df = 1, p ≤ .001, $X^2 = 40.8$, df = 1, p ≤ .001, respectively). Younger and mid-aged homeless Black adults were more likely than non-homeless younger and mid-aged Black adults to be currently using cocaine ($X^2 = 21.5$, df = 1, p ≤ .001; $X^2 = 110.7$, df = 1, p ≤ .001, respectively).

Homeless Black adults were more likely than non-homeless Black adults to have used PCP in their lifetimes across all age categories (18-25, $X^2 = 536.9$, df = 1, p ≤ .001; 26-34, $X^2 = 381.9$, df = 1, p ≤ .001; 35+, $X^2 = 363.9$, df = 1, p ≤ .001). Mid-aged and older homeless adults were more likely than their non-homeless counterparts to have used heroin in their lifetimes ($X2 = 66.6$, df = 1, p < .001; $X2 = 123.2$, df = 1, p < .001, respectively).

Looking at the use of alcohol, only older homeless Black adults were more likely than their non-homeless counterparts to have used alcohol in their lifetimes, during the past year and within the past month ($X^2 = 12.8$, df = 1, p ≤ .001; $X^2 = 35.0$, df = 1, p ≤ .001; $X^2 = 21.9$, df = 1, p ≤ .001, respectively). Mid-aged homeless Black adults were less likely than their non-homeless counterparts to be currently using alcohol ($X^2 = 4.1$, df = 1, p ≤ .05).

DEMOGRAPHICS, HOMELESS STATE CHARACTERISTICS AND DRUG ABUSE

Demographic and homeless state characteristics were significantly related to illicit drug use in this sample of homeless Black adults but not always as we anticipated that they would be. Tables 4 through 6 present these findings.

Overall, gender was significantly related to the lifetime, annual, and current use of illicit drugs. Men had used illicit drugs more than women within their lifetimes (eta = .10, p = .022), within the past year (eta = .11, p = .019), and within the past month (eta = .11, p = .003).

Table 3

Percent Reporting Illicit Drug and Alcohol Use Among
Sheltered Homeless Black Adults by Age

Drugs	Age Groups		
	18-25	26-34	35+
	(68)	(158)	(128)
All Drugs* (Lifetime)	73	67	50
Marijuana			
(Lifetime)	65	63	39
(Annual)	38	33	12
(Current)	27	22	6
Stimulants, sedatives, tranquilizers & analgesics			
(Lifetime)	15	15	20
(Annual)	6	6	3
(Current)	0	3	2

Cocaine			
(Lifetime)	37	37	25
(Annual)	31	32	15
(Current)	19	23	6
PCP			
(Lifetime)	35	30	16
(Annual)	18	20	6
(Current)	10	10	
Heroin			
(Lifetime)	3	11	17
(Annual)	2	6	8
(Current)	0	4	3
Alcohol			
(Lifetime)	77	85	93
(Annual)	68	74	79
(Current)	50	58	65

*Excluding alcohol.

Table 4

Relationship of Demographic and Homeless State Characteristics
to Lifetime Drug Abuse Among Homeless Black Adults:
Multiple Classification Analysis

Demographics	Class Mean	Beta	Beta 2	Eta	Eta 2	N
Gender						
Men	.65	.13	.02	.10	.01	227
Women	.55					115
Age						
18-25	.73	.20	.04	.20	.04	67
26-34	.67					151
35+	.49					124
Income						
Less than $3,000	.49	.23	.05	.23	.05	116
$3,000-$6,999	.58					89
$7,000-$11,999	.71					65
$12,000 or more	.78					72

Education		.08	.01	.08	.01	
0 – 11 years	.59					152
12 years	.63					125
13 to 15 years	.69					52
16 years or more	.54					13
Marital Status		.09	.01	.14	.02	
Married	.55					33
Divorced/Separated	.63					106
Widowed	.31					13
Never Married	.54					190
Homeless State Characteristics						
Duration of Homelessness		.10	.01	.11	.01	
Newly	.60					91
Intermittently	.69					110
Chronically	.57					141
Previous Psychiatric Hospitalization		.07	.00	.02	.00	
Not hospitalized	.61					305
Hospitalized	.65					37

Table 4 (continued)

	Class Mean	Beta	Beta^2	Eta	Eta^2	N
Demographics						
Psychotic Symptoms						
No sumptoms	.61	.05	.00	.05	.00	290
Symptoms	.67					52
Depression						
Not depressed	.59	.00	.00	.04	.00	105
Depressed	.63					237

R 2 = 13
N = 358

As expected, age was significantly related to lifetime, annual and current use of illicit drugs. Young adults, those age 18 to 25 years, had used drugs more than adults, age 25 to 34 and 35 and older, within their lifetimes (eta = .20, p = .055), within the past year (eta = .22, p = .005), and within the past month (eta = .28, p = .001).

Education and marital status were not significantly related to the lifetime, annual or current use of illicit drugs.

As expected, income was significantly related to lifetime, annual and current use of illicit drugs. Individuals with the highest incomes had used illicit drugs more than those with the lowest incomes in their lifetimes (eta = .23, p = .002), within the past year (eta = .27, p = .001), and currently (eta = .25, p = .001).

None of the homeless state characteristics were significantly related to the lifetime use of illicit drugs. We had hypothesized that previous hospitalization and the two measures of psychological problems, psychotic symptoms and depressive symptoms, would be. However, duration of homelessness was significantly related to the annual and current use of illicit drugs. Individuals who were intermittently homeless had used illicit drugs more than those who were chronically or newly homeless in the past year (eta = .21, p = .001) and within the past month (eta = .19, p = .01).

The relationships of age, gender, income, and duration of homelessness held when the relationships of other variables were accounted for. (See Tables 3-5.)

Age Cohorts

Additional analysis was conducted to determine whether the pattern of relationships for this set of demographic and homeless state characteristics was consistent across age cohorts.

Among those age 18 to 25, this particular set of demographic and homeless state characteristics was not significantly related to lifetime, annual or current drug abuse. Only duration of homelessness was significantly related to lifetime drug abuse (eta = .36, p ≤ .019). Individuals who were 18 to 25 and were intermittently homeless had used drugs in their lifetimes more than those who were chronically or newly homeless.

Table 5

Relationship of Demographics and Homeless State Characteristics to
Annual Drug Abuse Among Homeless Black Adults:
Multiple Classification Analysis

Demographics	Class Mean	Beta	Beta^2	Eta	Eta^2	N
Gender		.13	.02	.11	.01	
Men	.41					227
Women	.30					115
Age		.19	.04	.22	.05	
18-25	.49					67
26-34	.42					151
35+	.23					124
Income		.29	.08	.27	.07	
Less than $3,000	.25					116
$3,000-$6,999	.31					89
$7,000-$11,999	.40					65
$12,000 or more	.60					72

						N
Education		.10	.01	.06	.00	
0 to 11 years	.35					152
12 years	.38					125
13 to 15 years	.42					52
16 years or more	.31					13
Marital Status		.10	.01	.15	.02	
Married	.24					33
Divorced/Separated	.38					106
Widowed	.08					13
Never married	.41					190
Homeless Characteristics						
Duration of Homelessness		.20	.04	.21	.04	
Newly	.35					91
Intermittently	.51					110
Chronically	.27					141

Table 5 (continued)

	Class Mean	Beta	Beta ^{2}	Eta	Eta ^{2}	N
Previous Psychiatric Hospitalization						
Not Hospitalization	.37	.04	.00	.01	.00	305
Hospitalized	.38					37
Psychotic Symptoms						
No symptoms	.34	.04	.00	.01	.00	305
Symptoms	.38					37
Depression						
Not Depressed	.37	.05	.00	.00	.00	105
Depressed	.37					237

R = 20
N = 358

Among those age 26 to 34, this set of demographic and homeless state characteristics was significantly related to lifetime, annual and current drug abuse (F = 2.64, df = 15, p ≤ .002; F = 3.23, df = 15, p ≤ .001; F = 2.97, df = 15, p ≤ .001, respectively). Looking at lifetime use, gender (beta = .36, p ≤ .001) and income (beta = .27, p ≤ .018) had the greatest influences. Mid-aged men had used illicit drugs more than mid-aged women in their lifetimes (eta = .27, p ≤ .001) and mid-aged individuals who had the highest incomes had used illicit drugs more than those with the lowest incomes in their lifetimes (eta = .30, p ≤ .018).

Looking at annual use, income (beta = .29, p ≤ .011) and gender (beta = .21, p ≤ .013), again, had the greatest influences along with duration of homelessness (beta = .31, p ≤ .001). Mid-aged individuals with the highest income had also used drugs within the past year more than those with the lowest incomes (eta = .27, p ≤ .011) and mid-aged men had used illicit drugs within the past year more than mid-aged women (eta = .19, p ≤ .013). Mid-aged individuals who were intermittently homeless had also used illicit drugs in the past year more than their chronically or newly homeless counterparts (eta = .29, p ≤ .001).

Looking at current use, income (beta = .26, p ≤ .001), gender (beta = .19, p ≤ .027), education (beta = .26, p ≤ .018) and duration of homelessness (beta = .24, p ≤ .009) had the greatest influences. Mid-aged individuals with the highest income had used drugs currently more than mid-aged individuals with the lowest income (eta = .30, p ≤ .001); mid-aged individuals who were college graduates had used drugs currently more than mid-aged individuals with less education (eta = .09, p ≤ .018); mid-aged men had currently used drugs more than mid-aged women (eta = .18, p ≤ .027); and mid-aged adults who were intermittently homeless had currently used drugs more than those who were chronically or newly homeless (eta = .23, p ≤ .009).

Among those 35 and older, this set of variables was not significantly related to lifetime or current illicit drug abuse. Only previous hospitalization was related to current drug abuse (eta = .14, p ≤ .03). Older individuals who had never been hospitalized for a psychiatric problem currently used drugs more than those who had been hospitalized. These variables were, however, significantly

Table 6

Relationship of Demographics and Homeless State Characteristics to Current Drug Abuse Among Homeless Black Adults: Multiple Classification Analysis

Demographics	Class Mean	Beta	Beta ^{2}	Eta	Eta ^{2}	N
Gender						
Men	.29	.16	.03	.11	.01	227
Women	.18					115
Age						
18-25	.36	.25	.06	.28	.08	67
26-34	.34					151
35+	.09					124
Income						
Less than $3,000	.16	.25	.06	.25	.06	116
$3,000-$6,999	.19					89
$7,000-$11,999	.31					65
$12,000 or more	.43					72

Education						
0 to 11 years	.23	.13	.02	.10	.01	152
12 years	.27					125
13 to 15 years	.31					52
16 years or more	.08					13
Marital Status						
Married	.18	.04	.00	.12	.01	33
Divorced/Separated	.23					106
Widowed	.08					13
Never married	.29					190
Homeless State Characteristics						
Duration of Homelessness						
Newly	.26	.16	.03	.19	.04	91
Intermitently	.35					110
Chronically	.16					141
Previous Psychiatric Hospitalization						
Not Hospitalized	.48	.01	.00	.03	.00	305
Hospitalized	.55					37
Psychotic Symptoms						
No Symptoms	.23	.11	.01	.11	.01	290
Symptoms	.37					52
Depression						
Not depressed	.21	.06	.00	.01	.00	105
Depressed	.27					237

related to annual drug abuse (F = 2.49, df = 15, p ≤ .003). Income and marital status had the greatest influences. Older individuals with the highest incomes (eta = .33, p ≤ .002) and older individuals who had never married (eta = 26, p ≤ .02) had used drugs more within the past year than their counterparts.

DEMOGRAPHICS, HOMELESS STATE CHARACTERISTICS AND ALCOHOL USE

As expected, demographic characteristics were also related to alcohol use. Gender was significantly related to lifetime, annual and current alcohol use. Men were more likely than women to have used alcohol in their lifetimes (X^2 = 10.87, df = 1, p < .001); within the last year (X^2 = 22.03, df = 1, p < .001); and to be using it currently (X^2 = 20.7, df = 1, p < .001).

Education, marital status and income were not significantly related to lifetime, annual or current use of alcohol. We had anticipated that marital status and educational attainment would be significantly related to alcohol use.

Previous hospitalization and duration of homelessness were not significantly related to the lifetime, annual or current use of alcohol. We had expected that duration would be significantly related to lifetime use of alcohol. Psychological state was significantly related to the annual use of alcohol. Individuals who were depressed were more likely than individuals who were not depressed to have used alcohol within the past year (X^2 = 3.91, df = 1, p < .05).

Gender was the only demographic characteristic related to lifetime, annual or current alcohol use controlling for age. None of the other demographic characteristics was related to lifetime use while controlling for age. (See Tables 7-9.)[3] Among those 18 to 25, men were more likely than women to have used alcohol during their lifetimes (X^2 = 4.32, df = 1, p ≤ .05). Among those 18 to 25 and 35 or older, men were more likely than women to have used alcohol within the past year (X^2 = 10.49, df = 1, p ≤ .01 and X^2 = 5.61, df = 1, p ≤ .05, respectively). Again, among those 18 to 25 and those 35 and older, gender was significantly related to current use of alcohol–men were more likely to be currently using alcohol than women ($X^2 = 7.22$, df = 1, p ≤ .01 and $X^2 = 6.09$, df = 1, p ≤ .05, respectively).

Age Cohorts

Psychological state was related to lifetime use of alcohol controlling for age. Among those 26 to 34 those who were depressed were more likely than those who were not depressed to have used alcohol in their lifetimes ($X^2 = 4.32$, df = 1, p ≤ .05).

Duration of homelessness was not significantly related to the lifetime, annual or current use of alcohol within any age cohort. (See Tables 7-9.) However, for the youngest age group, there was a trend such that intermittently homeless individuals were the most likely to have used alcohol ($X^2 = 5.03$, df = 2, p = .08).

DISCUSSION AND CONCLUSION

Drug abuse seems to be more of a problem among homeless Black adults in shelters than it is among non-homeless Black adults in the general population. For example, lifetime illicit drug use is more prevalent among homeless Black adults than non-homeless adults in the general population; in particular, among those who are 35 and older. Surprisingly, there is not much difference between homeless and non-homeless Black adults in their lifetime, annual and current use of marijuana. There are very startling differences, though, in the use of cocaine. Homeless Black adults in shelters are more likely than non-homeless Black adults to have used cocaine in their lifetimes, to have used it within the past year and to be currently using it; in particular, those who are under the age of 35. Homeless Black adults in shelters are also more likely than their non-homeless counterparts to have used PCP in their lifetimes, and homeless Black adults who are over 25 are more likely to have used heroin in their lifetimes than their non-homeless counterparts.

Looking at the patterns of drug use by demographic and homeless state characteristics revealed findings that are somewhat congruent with previous research on drug abuse (Cahalan et al., 1969; Johnston et al., 1986; Lukoff, 1980; National Institute on Drug

Table 7

Percent Reporting Lifetime Use of Alcohol Among Sheltered Homeless
Black Adults by Age, Demographic and Homeless State Characteristics

Demographic Characteristics	18-25	Age Group 26-35	35+
Total	77	85	93
Gender			
Male	90*	83	94
Female	66	78	89
Educational Level			
Less than high school	81	83	92
High school graduate	71	84	93
Some college	70	92	94
College graduate		67	100
Marital Status			
Married	80	92	93
Divorced/Separated	83	85	93
Widowed		83	86
Never married	75	83	93

Income			
Less than $3,000	87	85	92
$3,000–$6,999	65	82	97
$7,000–$11,999	86	81	87
$12,000 or more	64	92	95
Homeless State Characteristics			
Duration of Homelessness			
Newly	64	81	90
Intermittently	88	89	100
Chronically	73	81	87
Previous Hospitalization			
Not hospitalized	76	84	91
Hospitalized	100	88	100
Psychological State			
Not depressed	67	89*	91
Depressed	79	74	96

* $p < .05$
** $p < .01$

147

Table 8

Percent Reporting Annual Use of Alcohol Among Sheltered Homeless
Black Adults by Age, Demographic and Homeless State Characteristics

Demographic Characteristic	Age Group		
	18-25	26-34	35+
Total	68	74	79
Gender			
Male	90**	79	84*
Female	50	66	60
Educational Level			
Less than high school	73	73	76
High school graduate	62	73	84
Some college	60	81	77
College graduate		67	86
Marital Status			
Married	80	92	80
Divorced/Separated	67	71	78
Widowed		67	71
Never married	67	74	81

Income level			
Less than $3,000	74	70	77
$3,000-$6,999	60	73	81
$7,000-$11,999	71	73	80
$12,000 or more	64	82	86
Homeless State Characteristic			
Duration of Homelessness			
Newly	55	66	77
Intermittently	76	84	78
Chronically	67	76	79
Previous Hospitalization			
Not hospitalized	67	73	77
Hospitalized	100	82	90
Psychological State			
Not depressed	53	65	74
Depressed	72	78	83

* p < .05
** p < .01

Table 9

Percent Reporting Current Use of Alcohol Among Sheltered Homeless
Black Adults by Age, Demographic and Homeless State Characteristics

Demographic Characteristics	18-25	Age Group 26-34	35+
Total	50	58	65
Gender			
Male	70**	64	71*
Female	34	47	42
Educational Level			
Less than high school	62	65	58
High school graduate	43	55	74
Some college	20	54	65
College graduate		50	67
Marital Status			
Married	60	62	57
Divorced/Separated	50	59	70
Widowed		50	43
Never married	49	58	64

Homeless State Characteristic			
Income level			
Less than $3,000	61	57	60
$3,000–$6,999	45	55	71
$7,000–$11,999	50	54	60
$12,000 or more	36	68	70
Duration of Homelessness			
Newly	32	56	63
Intermittently	52	63	63
Chronically	60	62	70
Previous Hospitalization			
Not hospitalized	50	58	67
Hospitalized	50	59	52
Psychological State			
Not depressed	40	44	60
Depressed	53	63	67

* $p < .05$
** $p < .01$

Abuse, 1988). Income seems to have the most consistent relationship with drug abuse or the use of illicit drugs among these homeless Black adults. Income was related to lifetime, annual and current prevalence estimates of illicit drug use overall and across age categories; in particular, among those age 26 to 34. Homeless Black adults who have higher incomes are more likely to use drugs than those with lower incomes. Illicit drug use among homeless Black adults is clearly tied to having some financial means to purchase drugs.

Duration of homelessness seems to be the only homeless state characteristic that is consistently related to drug abuse. For the overall sample, those who are intermittently homeless, that is they seem to be cycling in and out of being housed, are more likely than those who are chronically and newly homeless to use drugs. This finding was also consistent across age categories. For example, among those 26 to 34 years, the intermittently homeless are more likely than the chronically or newly homeless to have used drugs at some point in their lifetimes ($X^2 = 8.5$, df = 2, p < .014).

Overall, the prevalence estimate for current illicit drug use in this sample, 26 percent, was slightly higher than some studies of homeless people (i.e., Morse, 1985), however, this was not unexpected because of increasing drug problems in the District of Columbia where the data were collected. Moreover, other studies that have looked at current use have assessed drug dependence which is often lower than drug use (e.g., Farr et al., 1986). Our figure does fall well within the wide range of estimates from previous research on current drug use of 10 to 30 percent.

Lifetime alcohol use is only more prevalent among homeless Black adults than among non-homeless Black adults in older adults. Lifetime alcohol use is not higher among the other age cohorts. This is somewhat surprising. However, previous studies of homeless people have found alcohol abuse is more prevalent among older homeless people (e.g., Ladner et al., 1986). Younger and mid-aged homeless Black adults do not seem to use alcohol anymore than their non-homeless counterparts. Among older adults, those 35 and older, annual and current use of alcohol is also higher among homeless Black adults than among non-homeless Black adults.

As expected, Black homeless men are more likely than Black homeless women to use alcohol across all the time periods. This is similar to findings in the general Black non-homeless population (National Institute on Drug Abuse, 1988). However, among those who are older and younger, the gender differences in the pattern of alcohol use are more striking than they are in the general non-homeless Black population (National Institute on Drug Abuse, 1988). For example, 90 percent of homeless Black men in shelters who are 18 to 25 use alcohol annually compared to 50 percent of homeless Black women in shelters. In the general Black population, it is 76 percent versus 70 percent. Findings for the relationship of other demographic characteristics to alcohol use were not as expected but these findings focus on use and not abuse. Previous research that has found relationships between demographic characteristics such as marital status and alcohol use has focused on alcohol abuse (e.g., Cahalan et al., 1969).

The homeless state characteristic, duration, was not related to alcohol use. Previous research had suggested that it would be (Hoffman, 1982; Roth & Bean, 1985). We found that chronic homeless Black adults in shelters are not more likely than those who are newly or intermittently homeless to use alcohol. This may be attributable to differences in our duration measure and the nature of our sample. The duration measure took into account the length of time homeless and number of times homeless. Previous research did not take the number of episodes into account. In addition, our investigation focused on Black homeless adults who may have alcohol use patterns that differ from the other homeless people just as Blacks and Whites differ in their alcohol use patterns in the general population (National Institute on Drug Abuse, 1988).

The results from findings from indirect comparisons such as those found in this paper should be considered with some caution. However, these findings emphasize differences in drug use patterns between the homeless and non-homeless populations as well as intra-group differences among homeless adults; in this instance, homeless Black adults. Some of the findings suggest that treatment for drug abuse is necessary for homeless Black adults who are young men, under age 35, or intermittently homeless. However, other findings on the types of drugs that are abused, such as cocaine which is highly addictive, and findings that use seems to begin prior to homelessness suggest prevention activities targeted at young Black men, in particular, may be one long-term solution to homelessness and drug abuse.

NOTES

1. The stratification was based upon the type of shelter (stay for one night or more than one night) and the gender of the residents (male or female including families who were usually mothers and their children).

2. Double-counting (i.e., interviewing the same respondent in different shelters on subsequent days) was avoided as much as possible by gathering data on respondents' age, race, gender and mother's maiden name. Interview duplication was checked using these data during the data collection period. Duplicate interviews were not included in the sample. In addition, interviews were conducted in one section of the city at a time during as short a time period as possible. Despite these precautions, one duplicate interview was discovered during the preliminary data analysis and the respondent was eliminated from all subsequent analyses.

3. The p values in these tables are from comparisons within age groups of lifetime, annual and current alcohol abuse by demographic and homeless state characteristics.

REFERENCES

Abelson, H.T. et al. (1977). *National survey on drug abuse: 1977–A nationwide study–Youth, adults and older people* (DHEW Publication No. (ADM) 78-618). Washington, DC: U.S. Government Printing Office.

Andrews, F.M., Morgan, J.N., Sonquist, J.A., & Klem, L. (1973). *Multiple classification analysis: A report on a computer program for multiple regression using categorical predictors.* Ann Arbor, MI: University of Michigan, Institute for Social Research, Survey Research Center.

Arce, A.A. et al. (1983). A psychiatric profile of street people admitted to an emergency shelter. *Hospital and Community Psychiatry, 34*(9), 812-816.

Bahr, H.M. (1969a). Family size and stability as antecedents of homelessness and excessive drinking. *Journal of Marriage and the Family, 31*(3), 477-483.

Bahr, H.M. (1969b). Lifetime affiliation patterns of early and late onset heavy drinkers on skid row. *Quarterly Journal of Studies on Alcohol, 30*(3), 645-656.

Bassuk, E.L. et al. (1984). Is homelessness a mental health problem? *American Journal of Psychiatry, 141*, 1546-1550.

Hoffman, S. et al. (1982). *Who are the homeless? A study of randomly selected men who use the New York city shelters.* New York, NY: New York State Office of Mental Health.

Johnston, L. et al. (1979). *1979 Highlights: Nation's high school students, five year trends.* (DHEW Publication No. (ADM) 81-930). Washington, DC: U.S. Government Printing Office.

Jones, B. et al. (1984, May). *Psychodynamic profiles of the urban homeless.* Paper presented at the 137th annual meeting of the American Psychiatric Association, Los Angeles, CA.

Lamb, R.H. (1982). Young adult chronic patients: The new drifters. *Hospital and Community Psychiatry, 33*(6), 465-468.

Levine, I.S. (1984). Homelessness: Its implications for mental health policy and practice. *Psychosocial Rehabilitation Journal, 13*(1), 6-16.

Miller, J.D. et al. (1983). *National survey on drug abuse: Main findings 1982* (DHHS Publications No. (ADM) 84-1263). Washington, DC: U. S. Government Printing Office.

Mulkern, V. & Spence, R. (1984). *Illicit drug use among homeless persons: A review of the literature.* (Report prepared for the National Institute on Drug Abuse.) Boston, MA: Human Services Research Institute.

Radloff, L.S. (1977). The CES-D Scale: A self-report depression scale for research in the general population. *Applied Psychological Measurement, 3*, 385-401.

Roth, D. et al. (1985). *Homelessness in Ohio: A study of people in need.* Columbus, OH: Ohio Department of Mental Health.

Siegal, H.A. & Inciardi, J.A. (1982). The demise of skid row. *Society*, January/February, 39-45.

Stark, L.R. (1985). Strangers in a strange land: The chronically mentally ill homeless. *International Journal of Mental Health, 14*(4), 95-111.

Cultural Sensitivity in Drug Treatment Research with African American Males

Jose M. Pena
Joan D. Koss-Chioino

INTRODUCTION

An interesting finding of recent reviews of the substance abuse treatment literature is the degree to which our current knowledge is based on an assumption of generalizability that ignores ethnic group membership as a salient issue. Investigations which do attempt to account for ethnic factors frequently rely on general ethnic labels such as "Hispanic American," "African American" or "Asian American," with little explanation of the label's specific meaning or validity for the subjects of the particular study (Trimble, 1990; Trimble and Bolek, 1988; Tucker, 1985; Hanson, 1985; Iiyama, Matsunaga and Johnson, 1976). A majority of treatment effectiveness studies ignore the issue of ethnicity altogether and do not address its potential influence on the interpretation of results or their applicability to other groups and settings. Therefore, little is known about the degree to which such investigations are "culture bound" in the sense of being applicable to one or many culturally distinct groups or populations.

This paper is based on the notion that substance abuse treatment

Jose M. Pena is affiliated with the Department of Psychiatry and Neurology, Tulane University Medical School.

Joan D. Koss-Chioino is affiliated with the Department of Anthropology, Arizona State University, Tempe, AZ 85287.

Address all correspondence and requests for reprints to Jose M. Pena, M.D., Tulane University School of Medicine, Department of Psychiatry, 1430 Tulane Avenue, New Orleans, LA 70112.

157

studies which do not specifically assess and take into account the cultural characteristics of the subject population, are open to serious criticism regarding their internal validity and generalizability. Furthermore, even a careful operationalization of ethnic labels, such as "Hispanic American" or "Asian American," may not be sufficient. Culturally sensitive research can only be achieved through a careful adaptation of the design and procedures of the particular research endeavor to the ethno-cultural characteristics of the subjects. In this we agree with Rogler that culturally sensitive mental health research must involve an ". . . open-ended series of substantive and methodological insertions and adaptations designed to mesh the process of inquiry with the cultural characteristics of the groups being studied" (1989, p. 296). This in turn can only be accomplished if the researcher explicitly considers how the ethnic composition of the subject population influences the validity of each step in the research protocol, from choice of assessments and instruments through analysis and interpretation of results.

The methodological advantages of a technology model of psychotherapy research for cocaine abuse have recently been discussed by Carroll and Rounsaville (1990). They consider the capacity to address threats to the internal validity of the investigation to be a significant strength of this approach and specifically discuss the difficulties presented by heterogeneity in subject populations, selection pressures, attrition, and subject expectancies. Given the large body of literature indicating that ethnicity can influence such things as patient expectancy, engagement in treatment, attrition, validity of assessment instruments, utilization of services and selection bias, the lack of consideration of ethnic factors in discussions of state-of-the-art substance abuse treatment research methodologies is striking (Brown et al., 1985; Neale Query, 1985; Battjes, 1982-83; Greene, 1987; Yamamoto et al., 1968; Acosta et al., 1982; Yamamoto et al., 1967; Kleinman and Lukoff, 1978). In our perspective the internal validity of treatment efficacy studies can be insured only if culturally sensitive adaptations of the research protocol address the specific characteristics of the subject population.

Cultural sensitivity is also necessary to address concerns about the generalizability of results. Carroll and Rounsaville (1990) point out the dichotomy (and perhaps inherent conflict) between techniques which protect against threats to the internal and external validity of a study. We would add that adequate description of the characteristics of a subject population facilitates attempts by other investigators (or clinicians) to assess the potential validity and replicability of a given finding for their particular setting and patient population. Again, given great variability in the ethnic composition of patient populations at different treatment and research sites, the lack of attention, in treatment efficacy studies, devoted to detailed descriptions of subjects' ethno-cultural characteristics is remarkable.

Over the last decade substance abuse research has moved away from reductionistic models of the addictions which focus on single factors as either causes or effects of addictive behavior (Donovan and Marlatt, 1988). Treatment research now assesses multiple domains of patient functioning and adjustment as both predictors and measures of outcome. In their seminal work on the psychotherapeutic treatment of opiate users, Woody et al. (1987) measured patient improvement by assessing change in patient legal status, employment, levels of psychopathology and drug use. They found differential response in each of these areas to different treatments, with the two psychotherapy conditions, Supportive-Expressive and Cognitive-Behavioral, yielding greater improvement compared to drug counseling. In a study of alcoholic subtypes Donovan et al. (1986) discuss the shift in the research literature away from a priori subtyping as a method of predicting response to treatment. They describe the more recent use of a statistical model utilizing pretreatment patient evaluation in multiple domains and cluster analysis to identify five alcoholic subtypes on an a posteriori basis. These subtypes were predictive of, and validated against, treatment outcome.

The development of integrative models such as these, which view addiction as the result of complex interactions between multiple biological and social factors, provides an avenue for integrating the cultural dimension into research designs by including culturally relevant adaptations in research procedures, as well as culturally relevant variables and instruments in the domains of assessment.

The discussion which follows describes our attempts to adapt a technological research model of psychotherapy treatment for cocaine abuse to our particular treatment setting and population at the

New Orleans, Veterans Administration Hospital-Drug Dependency Treatment Unit (NOVA-DDTU). Specific attention is given to the ethno-cultural context and characteristics of the setting and subject population.

PRELIMINARY CONSIDERATIONS

The Cocaine Epidemic

The seriousness of the cocaine epidemic in the 1980's was perhaps best reflected in the statistic that cocaine-related deaths increased from 554 to 2,496 between 1985 and 1989; an increase of 450% (NIDA, 1990). Moreover, the high cost to society could be seen in the use of cocaine as part of a deviant life style (Robbins, 1980) and an unhealthy life pattern, resulting in demands for extensive health and other resources (Castro et al., 1987). Although recent indicators suggest a leveling off of cocaine use nationwide (NIDA, 1990), rates of cocaine use will probably continue at endemic levels. Although cocaine has replaced heroin use by some older addicts, cocaine users are increasingly young, male, urban, poor and more likely to be unemployed (Herridge and Gold, 1988). Cocaine also became a substance of choice for African Americans and other minority drug users in the eighties. National figures for 1988 indicated that cocaine was the most frequently mentioned drug in drug related emergency room visits. Of these 57% were by Afican Americans and 67% by males. Although comparison between sites is difficult several studies show inner-city African American substance use rates to be significantly higher (up to three times) than rates for white substance use (Brunswick, 1988).

In 1988 in New Orleans, cocaine was the most frequently mentioned drug in emergency room visits and medical examiner deaths. Eighty-four per cent of cocaine related emergency room visits were made by African Americans and 78% by males. By 1989, 90% of patients admitted to the Drug Dependency Treatment Unit of the New Orleans Veterans Administration Hospital were identifying cocaine as the primary drug of abuse. Of these primary cocaine users, 57% and 36% respectively smoked Crack, or injected as the preferred route of administration. Moreover, 85% of admissions in 1989 were persons of African American ethnicity. Ninety-eight percent of admissions were males. Our unit was witnessing the severe impact of the cocaine and Crack epidemic on African American males in New Orleans.

Psychiatric Co-Morbidity

Numerous studies have demonstrated the prevalence of psychiatric problems among substance abusers (see for example, Ross et al., 1988; Rounsaville et al., 1991). Advocates of the self-medication hypothesis suggest that drug users choose specific drugs of abuse in order to self-treat underlying dysphoria (Khantzian, 1985; Khantzian et al., 1974). Studies have suggested that individuals with mood disturbances are particularly susceptible to cocaine addiction because of the drug's stimulant and euphoric effects (Gawin et al., 1988). Gawin and Kleber (1986) found a 50% prevalence of affective disorders in cocaine abusers in treatment. Weiss et al., (1986) originally found a similar prevalence (53%) in their inpatient sample. However, in a later study, Weiss et al., (1988) found a significant decrease (21%) in rates of affective disorder. The authors conclude that over the last five years, premorbid psychopathology had become a less important risk factor for cocaine abuse (Weiss et al., 1988). Some authors propose that specific social-environmental factors such as dysfunctional families, lack of educational and employment opportunities, racist attitudes, and a drug-filled environment, are more salient as explanations of drug use than individual or personality attributes such as rebelliousness or depression (Brunswick, 1988; Taylor, 1986/87).

Studies on our own unit have examined the extent to which personality disorders and associated symptom criteria were found among cocaine and opiate dependent men undergoing inpatient treatment (Malow et al., 1989). Cocaine users showed lower rates of borderline and antisocial personality disorders and reported less subjective distress than opiate addicts. It was also found that opiate addicts were characterized by significantly greater problems with anxiety, depression and adjustment in contrast to cocaine users. Utilizing the Adjustment Problem Check List, items pertaining to tension and anxiety showed significant differences between the opiate and cocaine groups, the latter had lower levels of pathology (Malow et al., 1990). These data are consistent with other researchers' findings that show less psychopathology among cocaine compared to opiate users (Spotts and Shontz, 1983).

It is to be especially noted that our studies showed opiate and cocaine groups to significantly differ in age and ethnicity. Cocaine users were significantly younger, and significantly more white men reported opiate use than African American men. These data, though only applicable to our treatment unit, suggest that younger, African American male cocaine users in general may have less psychopathology than older white men who use cocaine.

African American Males: Social and Cultural Factors

The recent vivid portrait of young, urban, African American, lower-class males by a number of authors in Gibbs et al., (1988) confirms herself descriptors of them as "endangered," "embittered" and "embattled." Gibbs herself carefully describes the facts behind the poverty and powerlessness experienced by African American youth–high rates of unemployment, undereducation, unemployability, delinquency, and criminality. She traces the historical, economic and political factors that underlie the current situation. To these must be added the enormously complicating factor of drug use as both cause and outcome (Brunswick, 1988). Other studies, cited in Griffith and Bell (1989), point out the high rates of suicide and homicide among young African American men. They suggest the association of these rates with family and media violence, and discuss the view that homicidal behavior is an adaptation to poverty and a racist environment.

Brunswick (1988) is clear that explanations for problem drug use that only emphasize personality attributes are inadequate for the case of the African American, urban male. A social-situational model must be added, one that considers different norms and values, developmental needs and community opportunities and constraints. She particularly notes how drugs can serve occupational needs for this group along with recreational ones. Moreover, she emphasizes that cocaine and marijuana users are more likely to be employed than are heroin addicts–which may relate to the observations that cocaine abusers have less severe psychopathology than heroin abusers.

To this litany of societal and social problems must be added the extreme difficulty in achieving satisfactory levels of personal adjustment as a African American male fulfilling social roles. Casenave (1980) describes the African American male's "quest for manhood" and the limited positive opportunities for masculine attainment that make crime, violence and rebellion seem rewarding alternatives. He points out however, that the white working class standard of the patriarch-provider is not applicable to the lower-class African American male. The competitive-achiever male model may also have limited salience in the economically-beleaguered, lower-class African American male world.

Ethnicity and Treatment Outcome in Cocaine Abuse

Despite burgeoning interest in cocaine abuse treatment, there is little consensus regarding the best treatment strategies (Carroll et al., 1987). Strategies that have been advocated as potentially most effective are pharmacological (Gawin, Kleber et al., 1989) and cognitive-behavioral (Donovan and Marlatt, 1988). Others proposed that individual psychotherapy in its supportive and psychodynamic forms may be of greater benefit (Carroll et al., 1987; Kleber and Gawin, 1986; Rounsaville et al., 1985). Carroll et al., (1987) point specifically to the potential of Supportive-Expressive (SE) psychotherapy (Luborsky, 1984). They show how the exploration of core conflicts in relationships, while at the same time supporting important aspects of the patient's personality is a "here and now" way to bring the cocaine abuse under the patient's control. Family therapy has also been suggested as potentially beneficial (Spitz and Spitz, 1987). However, there are no controlled prospective studies of family therapy for cocaine abuse.

The relationship between ethnicity of drug abusers (opiate, cocaine or others) and treatment outcome has not been clearly established. Matching treatment to the characteristics of a particular ethnic group has been suggested but not yet studied. Systematic evaluations of treatment for cocaine abuse among ethnic minority patients are few. Rounsaville and his colleagues have a study in progress that includes African American subjects (described in Rounsaville, Gawin and Kleber, 1985) but they have not yet published results. Several authors note the importance of service delivery and treatment outcome for ethnic minorities, yet studies of outcome that have included African American male subjects have not considered racial/ethnic factors as features of the research design (Tucker, 1985; Trimble and Bolek, 1988).

Therefore, there is lack of consensus about the best treatment strategies for cocaine abuse and an overall lack of knowledge regarding the relationships between ethnicity, psychopathology and treatment outcome.

TREATMENT OUTCOME STUDIES: DRUG COUNSELING/PSYCHOTHERAPY FOR OPIATE USERS

The discussion that follows begins with a review of the current literature on treatment outcome and ends by describing how the choice of treatment models and assessments can be guided by the ethnic characteristics of the patient population.

Rounsaville and Kleber (1985) provide a review of drug counseling outcome studies in drug-free methadone and naltrexone programs for opiate abusers. In comparing counseling with psychotherapeutic modalities the latter appears to have greater benefits in most, but not all cases. However, these studies suffer methodological problems such as lack of random assignment. In one investigation of drug counseling, Resnick et al. (1980) utilized random assignment and found that street addicts showed greater improvement over post-methadone patients.

Studies of outcome of drug treatment focusing on counselor characteristics show no significant differences based on level of formal education or previous history of addiction among counselors (McLellan et al., 1988). Recent studies by the University of Pennsylvania group have used drug counseling as a comparison group with psychotherapy and have found that adding psychotherapy with qualified professionals does improve outcome. Psychotherapy differs from counseling in its focus on changing psychological processes.

A brief overview of early studies of psychotherapy for opiate-dependence can be found in Woody et al. (1983). Woody, McLellan, Luborsky and O'Brien have been central figures in recent treatment outcome studies of psychotherapy compared to drug counseling with methadone-maintained heroin abusers (Luborsky et al., 1982; Woody et al., 1983; Luborsky et al., 1985; Woody et al., 1987; and McLellan et al., 1988). They conclude that adding individual psychotherapy (specifically Supportive-Expressive therapy, Luborsky, 1988) to a program of drug counseling brought added benefits in terms of improved psychological function, decreased need for medication, decreased illicit drug use and more employment.

In a review of outcome studies of psychotherapy for opiate addicts, Rounsaville and Kleber (1985) evaluate its use in three different treatment settings and suggest that it is beneficial to some individuals across programs. In the studies reviewed, including those of the University of Pennsylvania, psychotherapy in the context of a methadone maintenance program seems of greatest benefit for patients with relatively severe levels of psychiatric symptoms.

Psychotherapy as Treatment for Cocaine Users

Kleber and Gawin (1986) review psychotherapeutic approaches, dividing their discussion along three dimensions, behavioral, psychodynamic and supportive techniques, a combination of these being the most common clinical approach. Carroll et al., (1987) note that despite the rapid development of programs to treat cocaine abuse there is no agreement as to optimal treatment strategies. Much systematic work is needed to evaluate outcomes. Moreover, reports of treatment outcome are mainly based on clinical observations rather than controlled trials. Rounsaville et al., (1985) describe a study adapting Interpersonal Psychotherapy (IPT) to cocaine abusers in combination with trials of several medications. Study results are in the form of typical case histories rather than data derived from an experimental design. Carroll et al., (1987) review individual and group approaches and provide key clinical guidelines. However, they fail to cite any controlled studies of cocaine abusers. As noted earlier, Supportive-Expressive psychotherapy is discussed in detail as beneficial for certain types of psychopathology, particularly persons with narcissistic issues as well as those with personality disorders. Moreover, Supportive-Expressive psychotherapy (in common with other psychodynamic approaches) deals with the quality of the alliance with the therapist and transference reactions, factors not dealt with in drug counseling. We argue below that this type of treatment could be effective for low-income, African American substance abusers.

To our knowledge the only comparison psychotherapy study of cocaine abuse in the literature was recently published by Kang et al. The authors compared the efficacy of once a week family therapy, psychotherapy and group therapy. They found no significant relationships between improvement in any area, including drug use, and the type of treatment. Although subject population was predominately male and non-white, the potential contribution or significance of ethnicity for the results was not specifically discussed (Kang et al., 1991).

Psychotherapy for African American Male
Cocaine Users

Given the multiple sources of social/personal problems, especially evident in the population of young, African American men who respond by abusing cocaine (or other substances), we propose that a psychotherapeutic intervention that deals with psychic processes underlying conflictual interpersonal relationships has a high potential for empowering these men to control abuse of drugs. This approach is different from those which suggest that low SES and African American ethnicity are negative predictors for success in insight-oriented psychotherapies. (See Jones, 1985 for a review of the issue.) It considers that among African American males there appears to be a more complicated relationship between psychopathology and treatment outcome than has been found by previous studies that do not specifically take ethnicity into account.

Jones (1985), discussing the literature that says that African American clients achieve less successful outcomes in expressive therapies, notes the confusion between low SES and ethnicity (see also Sue, 1988). Some studies have shown that lower SES and ethnic clients are actually better risks for psychodynamic therapies (Jones and Matsumoto, 1982). Several authors have commented on the degree to which conceptualization and approach to treatment issues have been affected by unfavorable stereotypes about lower-class and ethnic persons (often the same; see Jackson, 1983). Although the controversy continues as to whether ethnic minority persons are likely to benefit from psychotherapeutic treatment, Sue (1988) shows that available research findings fail to demonstrate that ethnic minority patients achieve differential outcomes from white patients.

Supportive-Expressive psychotherapy has been shown to be clinically significant for substance abusers with various levels of severity of psychopathology, even though high severity of psychopathology was found to be a statistically significant predictor of psychotherapy success (Woody et al., 1987). Paralleling the discussion by Carroll et al., (1987) on types of psychopathology common to cocaine abusers, we suggest that African American male cocaine abusers are as (or more) likely to have problems with low self-esteem and a narcissistic self concept. The origin of these difficulties can readily be seen in the ways African American families become dysfunctional in response to societal constraints in their social environments (Boyd-Franklin, 1989). Clinical observations on our unit suggest that Stanton and Todd's (1982) formulations about male substance abusers' family experience generally apply to many African American cocaine abusers. However, intrapsychic problems, such as separation fears, overdependence, escapism and low self-esteem, must be reassessed within a psychosocial etiology that examines scapegoating, enmeshment, co-dependence, family violence and negative racial identity. In this perspective, Supportive-Expressive therapy's capacity to develop awareness of and solutions to interpersonal problems, has good potential for aiding the African American substance abuser in his quest for abstinence.

For psychotherapeutic techniques to be successful with a particular ethnic group, specific attention must also be given to the therapeutic alliance. Derived from Freudian concepts regarding transference in psychoanalytic work, the therapeutic or helping alliance is now identified as a central factor in the success of psychotherapy and other interventions. Several studies (Aiken et al., 1984; LoScuito et al., 1984; and Brown et al., 1973) look at paraprofessional compared with professional drug counselors and conclude that there are no significant differences in how patients perform with each type of counselor. In fact, those without professional education are reported to do significantly better in some cases. However, McLellan et al., (1988) found significant differences in the effectiveness of *individual* drug counselors, regardless of formal education. This finding paralleled Luborsky et al.'s, findings (1983; 1985; 1986) of individual differences in the effectiveness of psychotherapists. These and other studies demonstrate the pivotal contribution of the helping relationship to outcomes of both drug counseling and psychotherapy.

With regard to ethnic factors in the therapeutic alliance, recent reviews report a lack of evidence that African American patients do better with African American therapists or counselors. There is almost no evidence for therapist-patient matching for substance abuse treatment and, in fact, Sue (1988) shows how this issue is confused with other factors such as therapist competence. However, given the lack of objective data on this issue, it is our impression that the most conservative approach for current studies is to match therapist and counselors on ethnic lines. Our reasons are as follows: (1) clinical experience suggests that the therapeutic alliance is particularly important in treating substance abusers because lack of trust is a prominent problem; (2) given potential problems in racial identity, a African American therapist is not as likely to be rejected; (3) particularly for short term interventions, a therapeutic alliance must be established quickly; and (4) in research efforts (as in clinical reality) the initial stages of treatment (and especially engagement) is crucial to successful outcome and diminished attrition.

Family Treatment as an Alternative Choice

Family therapy, especially systems-derived models, is considered an important treatment approach for substance abuse (Stanton and Todd, 1984; Kaufman, 1984; Spitz and Spitz, 1987; Szapocznik and

Kurtines, 1989) and is widely utilized. With the exception of Stanton's and Szapocznik's studies the efficacy of family interventions has not been systematically investigated. Stanton's study population consisted of heroin abusers. Szapocznik studied marijuana and suspected other drug use in Hispanic youth. There are no controlled studies of family therapy for cocaine abusers or any studies that are concerned with African American ethnicity as a clinical factor.

The regular presence of family members is itself an indicator of treatment success. Kosten et al., (1983) found that those opiate addicts in their naltrexone program who lived with family members had better outcomes *if* family members were supportive of attempts to be clean. These researchers also found that addicts who denied their condition in the presence of family members had poor prognoses. Moreover, it is widely agreed that family support is essential to the prevention of relapse. Stanton and Todd (1982) summarize the outcome of their four treatment conditions in a study of opiate abusers: Paid family therapy showed a clear superiority (measured by attendance and clean urines) over Movie and Non-family treatments. The outcomes of Unpaid family therapy were somewhat but not significantly inferior to Paid family therapy. Payment appeared to ensure attendance and heighten therapeutic effect.

Family Treatment of Cocaine Abuse for African Americans

Family therapy for cocaine abuse as reviewed by Spitz and Spitz (1987) focuses on the perspective of the family in dynamic equilibrium. Factors of importance are family boundaries, triangulation leading to dysfunction, scapegoating, over-involvement and detachment between family members. Systems-derived techniques and treatment flexibility which responds to a symptom as unpredictable as cocaine use appear especially helpful. Boyd-Franklin (1989) suggests ways of adapting family therapy for African American families. She demonstrates the necessity of considering specific cultural values and also the social/cultural context of family life. In particular, she describes African American families in terms of normative household family patterns that may include grandmothers, aunts, cousins or stepparents. Extended family patterns may include all the above and also neighbors, ministers or close friends as pseudo-kin.

Boyd-Franklin (1989) explains how role flexibility is normative in African American families but can lead to confusion and family dysfunction. She describes the importance of considering religion and spirituality in working with African American families. Her approach is the latest in a series of works advocating a cultural perspective in family therapy (Falicov, 1983; McGoldrick et al., 1982) and complements other discussions of the African American family such as McAdoo (1980) and Staples (1981).

Unfortunately, Boyd-Franklin does not discuss families and substance abuse. A few papers do describe "culturally-sensitive" alcohol treatment for African Americans (Ziter, 1987), treatment models for multiply-addicted substance abusers considering both social context and African American culture (Okpaku, 1985) and innovative programs for preventing substance abuse using churches and public schools (Maypole and Anderson, 1987). However, Boyd-Franklin's formulations regarding therapists' roles and a multisystems approach to family therapy with African Americans are concrete suggestions for tailoring family therapy to lower-class African American families of cocaine abusers. In addition, her chapter on racial identification in the family context, related both to family dynamics and individual self-esteem, are important factors in both carrying out family therapy and measuring its outcome. Similarly Jackson et al., (1988) discuss the importance of understanding the relationship between psychological health, and personal and group identity in African American families. The role of racial identity in the etiology of substance abuse and as a factor in planning treatment and relapse prevention has not to our knowledge been investigated.

Operationalizing Family Treatment

The type of family unit targeted for a family intervention should reflect the patient's description of the relatives with whom they are most closely bonded. The reality of African American families in the United States is that these relatives may not reside with the patient. In order to explore this issue in our own patient population of African American males we examined "family of origin"–those relationships that the patient described as important during childhood and adolescence. For the majority of our patients both biological parents were identified as important, mother more frequently than father (99% and 89% respectively). Stepfathers were mentioned more often than stepmothers (21% and 12%). Stepfathers frequently appeared to replace fathers in these families of origin. In most cases, the biological father had left the family while the patient was a child. This was true whether or not the patient mentioned biological father as important and present during their childhood. This was also the case with biological grandmothers and grandfathers, the former being significantly more important than the latter. Siblings, aunts and uncles were also frequently mentioned as important during childhood and adolescence. These data tended to confirm the observations made in the family literature of the importance of a three-generation pattern in the African American child rearing family (Boyd-Franklin, 1989).

We also examined the presence or absence of alcohol or drug abuse in families of origin. As expected, in all relationship categories male relatives were much more likely to have substance abuse problems. This was true for stepparents as well as biological parents, suggesting that role modeling in the family is important to the initiation of substance abuse for our patient population.

A second investigation on our unit focused on current family relationships. Patients' "current family" was defined as relatives and nonrelatives the patient thought affectively important at the time of admission to the unit. Parental bonds appeared to be most important, with mother identified twice as frequently as father (63% and 31%). Stepfathers were mentioned twice as frequently as stepmothers (7% and 3%). A majority of patients (64%) had a spouse, mate or girlfriend. Siblings were mentioned as important approximately 33% of the time. Children were mentioned as part of the current family by 75% of the patients, whether or not they resided with them. These data confirm the expected, that the most important roles of African American males on our unit were, concurrently, son, spouse and father. When we specifically assessed the proportion of patients who reported a "typical" family pattern, consisting of spouses and children in a nuclear family, we found that only

15% conformed to that pattern. These data suggest that the definition of "current family" for African American men should not be limited to the nuclear family or those individuals living in the household. Rather it should be defined as a functional unit including those relatives who are mentioned as affectively important or who provide support. It may also include nonrelatives such as ministers, neighbors or friends (see also Boyd-Franklin, 1989).

Which Family Treatment Model?

Strategic Family Therapy (Szapocznik and Kurtines, 1989) assumes that individual family members' behavior needs to be understood from an interactive and interdependent standpoint. This implies that individual behavior is different when viewed in one-to-one situations as opposed to being viewed within the systems context. Treatment is problem-focused, meaning that the chief complaint, such as the use of cocaine, is the context through which the family is engaged. Therapy is time limited with a recommended total of 8-15 sessions. This model has several advantages which make it suitable for adaptation to our setting and patients: (1) there is an operationalized treatment guide and manual; (2) it was specifically developed for treatment of substance abuse and has demonstrated success in that area; (3) the manual includes scales to measure therapist conformity to technical guidelines; and (4) there are specific strategies for engaging families that diminish drop-out from treatment (Szapocznik et al., 1988). This model can also be adapted to the ethnic characteristics of the African American family, by defining the family unit in a manner that reflects the patient's description of the relatives with whom he/she is most closely bonded, whether they reside with the patient or not. This flexible definition of the family reflects the extended kinship reality of many African American families, including those of the patients on our unit.

THE CULTURAL DIMENSION IN ASSESSMENT

Choosing a treatment modality is only one aspect of integrating cultural sensitivity into research design. Types of assessments must also be considered in efforts to make research on our unit ethnically relevant. For example, we have begun to measure racial identity as a predictor of treatment outcome.

In the last two decades there have been a number of studies that identify the need to examine how group (racial/ethnic) identity and self-esteem are related. Boyd-Franklin (1989) discusses the phenomenon of intrafamilial color prejudice in African American families viewing it as the projection of societal racial attitudes onto selected children. The struggle for a positive racial identity, made more difficult by the reality of color prejudice in white society, appears to be an important factor in the low self-esteem exhibited by African American cocaine abusers.

Although some investigations have studied the relationship between positive and negative racial identity, social adjustment and self-esteem, hardly anyone has systematically considered this factor in relation to substance abuse. An exception to this, Gary and Berry (1985), examined attitudes towards substance abuse in a African American community. They found that racial consciousness (defined as a positive racial identity plus awareness of racial oppression) strongly correlated with negative substance use attitudes.

Current studies on our unit include the Racial Identity Attitude Scale (IRAS) as a predictor measure of treatment outcome. This scale was developed by Parham and Helms (1981) to measure individual racial identity attitudes. It allows scoring of the respondent's stage of racial consciousness. It is based on Cross' (1971; 1978) model of psychological "nigrescence" and self actualization (Helms, 1990). Validity studies have shown good correlations with other measures of racial identity and African American consciousness (Grace, 1984; Parham and Helms, 1981, 1985).

CONCLUSION

Kleinman (1988; pg. 12) comments that "validity is the negotiated outcome of (a) transforming interaction between concept and experience in a particular context. Thus, validity can be regarded as a type of ethnographic understanding of the meaning of an observation in a local cultural field." This describes an attitude we consider essential for culturally-aware substance abuse research; that judgments about the validity of a particular research protocol must include consideration both of the ethnic context within which the research is being conducted and the ethnicity of its subjects. Studies which do not consider the potential influence of ethnicity at each stage of the investigative process, risk serious threats to their internal validity.

In this brief discussion we have focused on two aspects of the research–choice of treatment interventions and assessments. The degree to which the adaptations we suggest are applicable to other treatments, settings and populations can only be evaluated on an individual basis. Assumptions about the generalizability of our recommendations should be made with caution and only within the context of particular settings. However, it is our position that if ethno-specific adaptations in the protocol create threats to the external validity of a particular study or finding, they can be addressed through explicit descriptions of the adaptations as part of the interpretation of results. On the other hand the validity of a study or how relevant its results are to other settings and patient populations, is much more open to question if culturaly sensitive adaptations are not included in the research design, or if the ethnic dimension of data collection and treatment is ignored or left undefined.

LITERATURE CITED

Aiken, L.S., LoScuito, L.A., Ausetts, M.A., & Brown, B.A. (1984). Paraprofessional Versus Professional Drug Counseling: The Progress of Clients in Treatment. *Int J Addict*, 19:383-401.

Battjes, R.J. (1982-83). Similarity of Clients and Treatment Outcome in Outpatient Drug-Free Programs. *Am J Drug Alcohol Abuse*, 9(3), 263-279.

Boyd-Franklin, N. (1989). *Black Families in Therapy: A Multisystems Approach.* New York: Guilford.

Brown, B.S., Joe, G.W. & Thompson, P. (1985). Minority group status and treatment retention. *Int J Addict*, 20:2, 319-335.

Brunswick, A.F. (1988). Young black males and substance use. In J.T. Gibbs (Ed.), *Young, Black and Male in America.* (166-187). MA: Auburn House.

Carroll, K.M., Keller, D.S., Fenton, L.R. & Gawin, F. (1987). Psychotherapy for Cocaine Abusers. *The Cocaine Crisis*, D. Allen (Ed.) (75-105). New York: Plenum Press.

Carroll, K., Rounsaville, B. (1990). Can a Technology Model of Psychotherapy Research be Applied to Cocaine Abuse Treatment? *National Institute on Drug*

Abuse Research Monograph Series 104. Psychotherapy and Counseling in the Treatment of Drug Abuse. (pp. 91-104), U.S. Department of Health and Human Services Public Health Service Alcohol, Drug Abuse, and Mental Health Administration.

Castro, F.G., Newcomb, M.D. & Cadish, K. (1987). *J Drug Educ,* 17:89-111.

Cazenave, N. (1980). Black Men in America: The Quest for Manhood. In *Black families,* H.P. McAdoo (Ed.), 2nd ed., (176-185). California: Sage Publications.

Cross, W.E. (1971). The Negro-to-Black Conversion Experience: Towards a Psychology of Black Liberation. *Black World,* 20: 13-37.

Cross, W.E. (1978). The Cross and Thomas Models of Psychological Nigrescence. *J Black Psychology,* 5:13-19.

Donovan, D.M., Kivlahan, D.R. & Walker, R.D. (1986). Alcoholic subtypes based on multiple assessment domains: Validation against treatment outcome. In M. Galanter, (ed.), *Recent Developments in Alcoholism.* (Volume 4, pp. 207-222). New York, NY: Plenum.

Donovan, D.M. & Marlatt, G.A. (1988). *Assessment of Addictive Behaviors.* New York, NY: Guilford.

Gary, L.E., & Berry, G.L. (1985). Predicting Attitudes Toward Substance Use in a Black Community: Implications for Prevention. *Community Mental Health J,* 21: 42-51.

Gawin, F.H., & Kleber, H.D. (1986). Abstinence Symptomatology and Psychiatric Diagnosis in Cocaine Abusers: Clinical Observations. *Arch Gen Psychiatry,* Vol. 43, 107-113.

Gawin, F.H., & Ellinwood, E.H. (1988). Cocaine and Other Stimulants: Actions, Abuse and Treatment. *New England J of Med,* Vol. 318, No. 18, 1173-1182.

Gawin F.H., Kleber, H.D., Byck, R., Rounsaville, B.J., Kosten, T.R., Jatlow, P.I., & Morgan, C. (1989). Desipramine Fascilitation of Initial Cocaine Abstinence. *Arch Gen Psychiatry* 46:117-121.

Gibbs, J.T., Brunswick, A.F., Connor, M.E., Dembo, R., Larson, T.E., Reed, R.J., and Solomon, B. (1988). *Young, Black and Male in America.* Mass: Auburn House Publishing Co.

Greene, R.L. (1987). Ethnicity and MMPI Performance: A review. *J of Consulting and Clinical Psych,* Vol. 55, No. 4, 497-512.

Griffith, E.E.H., & Bell, C.C. (1989). Recent Trends in Suicide and Homocide Among Blacks. *J American Med Assoc.* 262: 2265-2269.

Hanson, B. (1985). Drug Treatment Effectiveness: The Case of Racial and Ethnic minorities in America–Some Research Questions and Proposals. *Int J Addicts,* 20:1, 99-137.

Helms, J.E. (1990 in press). An Overview of Black Racial Identity Theory, *Black and White Racial Identity: Theory Research and Practice.* chapter 2, Greenwood Press.

Herridge, P., & Gold, M.S. (September 1988). The New User of Cocaine: Evidence from 800-COCAINE. *Psychiatric Annals,* Vol. 18, No. 9, 521-522.

Iiyama, P., Nishi, Matsunaga, S., & Johnson, B.D. (1976). *Drug Use and Abuse*

Among U.S. Minorities: An Annotated Bibliography. New York, NY: Praeger Press.

Jackson, A.M. (1983). Treatment Issues for Black Patients. *Psychotherapy: Theory, research and practice,* 20: 143-151.

Jackson, J.S., McCullough, W.R., & Gurin, G. (1988). Group Identity Development Within Black Families. *Black Families,* 17:252-263. In H.P. McAdoo (Ed.), 2nd ed., California: Sage Publications.

Jones, E.E. (1985). Psychotherapy and Counseling With Black Patients. In *Handbook of Cross-Cultural Counseling and Therapy,* 173-180. Pedersen, P., ed., Conn: Greenwood Press.

Jones, E.E., & Matsumoto, D.R. (1982). Psychotherapy with the Underserved: Recent Developments . . . in . . . *Reaching the underserved: Mental health needs of neglected populations.* Sbowden, L. R., Ed., California: Sage.

Kang, S.Y, Kleinman, P.H., Woody, G.E., Millman, R.B., Todd, T.C., Kemp, J., Lipton, D.S. (1991). Outcomes for Cocaine Abusers After Once-a-Week Psychosocial Therapy. *Am J Psychiatry,* 148: 630-635.

Kaufman, E. (1984). *Substance abuse and family therapy.* New York: Grune & Stratton.

Khantzian, E.J., Mack, J.E., & Schatzberg, A.F. (1974). Heroin Use as an Attempt to Cope: Clinical Observations. *Am J Psychiatry,* 131: 160-164.

Khantzian, E.J. & Treece, C. (1985). DSM-III Psychiatric Diagnosis of Narcotic Addicts. *Arch of Gen Psych,* 42, 1067-1071.

Kleber, H.D., & Gawin, F.H. (1986). Cocaine. *Am Psychiatric Association Annual Review,* Chapter 5:160-185.

Kleinman, A. (1988). *Rethinking Psychiatry: From Cultural Category to Personal Experience.* New York, NY: Macmillan.

Kleinman, P.H., & Lukoff, I.F. (1978). Ethnic Differences in Factors Related to Drug Use. *J of Health and Social Behavior,* Vol. 19, pp. 190-199.

Kosten, T.R., Rounsaville, B.J., & Kleber, H.D. (1983). Concurrent Validity of the Addiction Severity Index. *The J Nervous and Mental Disease,* 171: 606-610.

LoScuito, L., Aiken, L.S., Ausetts, M.A., & Brown, B.S. (1984). Paraprofessional versus Professional Drug Abuse Counselors: Attitudes and Expectations of the Counselors and Their Clients. *Int J Addict,* 19:232-252.

Luborsky, L. (1984). Do Therapists Vary in Their Effectiveness? Findings from Four Outcome Studies. *Principles of Psychoanalytic Psychotherapy: A Manual for Supportive-Expressive Treatment.* New York, NY: Basic Books.

Luborsky, L., Crits-Christoph, P., Alexander, L., Margolis, M., & Cohen, M. (1983). Two Helping Alliance Methods for Predicting Outcomes of Psychotherapy: A Counting Signs vs. a Global Rating Method. *Nervous and Mental Disease,* 171: 480-491.

Luborsky, L., McLellan, T., Woody, G.E., O'Brien, C.P., & Auerback, A. (1985). Therapist Success and Its Determinants. *Arch Gen Psychiatry,* 42: 602-611.

Luborsky, L., Woody, G.E., McLellan, T., & O'Brien, C.P. (1982). Can Independent Judges Recognize Different Psychotherapies? An Experience with Manual Guided Therapies. *J Consulting Clinical Psychology,* 50: 49-62.

McAdoo, H.P. (1988). *Black Families.* Newbury Park, California: Sage Publications.

McLellan, A.T., Woody, G.E., Luborsky, L. & Goehl, L. (1988). Is the Counselor an Active Ingredient in Substance Abuse Rehabilitation? *J Nerv Ment Dis,* 76:7, 423-430.

Malow, R.M., West, J.A., Pena, J.M., & Lott, C.W. (1991). Affective Disorders and Adjustment Problems in Cocaine and Opioid Addicts. *Psychology of Addictive Behaviors.* Vol. 6 pp. 4-11.

Malow, R., West, J., Williams, J., & Sutker, P. (1989). Personality Disorder Classification and Symptoms among Cocaine and Heroin Abusers. *J of Cons and Clinical Psych,* 57, 765-767.

Maypole, D.E., & Anderson, R.B. (1987). Culture Specific Substance Abuse Prevention for Blacks. *Community Mental Health J,* 23: 135-139.

Neale-Query, J.M.N. (1985). Comparative Admission and Follow-up Study of American Indians and Whites in a Youth Chemical Dependency Unit on the North Central Plains. *International J of the Addictions,* 20(3): 489-502.

Okpaku, S.O. (1985). State of the Art on the Multiply Addicted–Treatment Models for Blacks. *Alcoholism Treatment Quarterly,* 2: 141-154.

Parham, T.A., & Helms, J.E. (1981). The Influence of Black Student's Racial Identity Attitudes on Preference for Counselor's Race. *J Couns Psychology,* 28: 250-257.

Parham, Thomas A. & Helms, Janet E. (1985). Relation of Racial Identity Attitudes to Self-Actualization and Affective States of Black Students. *J Couns Psychol,* 32:3, 431-40.

Resnick, R.B., Washton, A.M., Stone-Washton, N., et al. (1981). *Problems of Drug Dependence: 1980,* (109-115). N.I.D.A. Harris, L.C., ed., DHHS Pub. No. (ADM) 81-1058 U.S. Govt. Print. Off., Washington, D.C.

Robbins, L.N. (1980). Theories on Drug Abuse: Selected Contemporary Perspectives, N.I.D.A. Research Monograph 30, DHHS publication No. (ADM) 80-967. U.S. Govt. Print. Off., Washington, D.C.

Rogler, L.H. (1989). The Meaning of Culturally Sensitive Research in Mental Health. *Am J Psychiatry,* 146:3, 296-303.

Ross, H.E., Glaser, F.B., and Germanson, T. (1988). The prevalence of Psychiatric Disorders in Patients with Alcohol and other Drug Problems. *Arch Gen Psychiatry,* 45: 1023-1031.

Rounsaville, B., Anton, S.F., Carroll, K.M., Budde, D., Prusoff, B.A., & Gawin, F. (1991). Psychiatric Diagnoses of Treatment-Seeking Cocaine Abusers. *Arch Gen Psychiatry,* Vol. 48, pp. 43-51.

Rounsaville, B.J., Gawin, F., & Kleber, H. (1985). Interpersonal Psychotherapy Adapted for Ambulatory Cocaine Abusers. *Am J Drug Alcohol Abuse,* 11: 171-191.

Rounsaville, B.J., & Kleber, H.D. (1985). Psychotherapy/ Counseling for Opiate

Addicts Strategies for Use in Different Treatment Settings. *International J Addictions*, 20: 869-696.

Sobel, K.H. (1990). Cocaine Related Hospital Emergency Room Visits Drop 30 Percent. *NIDA NOTES*, Vol. 5, No. 4.

Spitz, H.I., & Spitz, S.T. (1987). Family Therapy of Cocaine Abuse. *Cocaine abuse: New directions in treatment and research*, Spitz, H., Roselah, J., 8:202-232.

Spotts, J.V., & Shontz, F.C. (1983). Psychopathology and Chronic Drug Use: A Methodological Paradigm. *Inter J of the Addictions*, 18, 633-680.

Stanton, M.D. & Todd, T.C. (1981). Engaging Resistant Families in Treatment. *Family Process*, 20, 261-293.

Staples, R. (1981). The Black American Family. *Ethnic families in America patterns and variations*, Mindel, C.H., and Habenstein, R.W. (Ed.), 2nd ed., New York: Elsevier Science Publishing Co. chapter 10: 217-244.

Sue, S. (1988). Psychotherapeutic Services for Ethnic Minorities. *Am Psychol*, 43:4, 301-308.

Szapocznik, J. (1989). *Breakthroughs in Family Therapy with Hispanics*. Paper presented at the annual meeting of the Association of Hispanic Mental Health Professionals. New York, October 22.

Szapocznik, J., Kurtines, W., Santisteban, D.A. & Rio, A.T. (in press). The Interplay of Advances Among Theory, Research and Application in Treatment Interventions Aimed at Behavior Problem Children and Adolescents. *J Consult and Clin Psychol*.

Taylor, R.L. (1986/1987). Black Youth in Crisis. *Humboldt J Soc Relat*, 14: 106-133.

Trimble, J.E., (1990; in press). Ethnic Specification, Validation Prospects and the Future of Substance Abuse Research. *Int J Addict*.

Trimble, J.E. & Bolek, C.S. (1988). *Ethnic minority substance abuse research perspectives: A literature Review with commentary*. Presented at National Institute on Drug Abuse meeting, Rockville, Maryland, May 1-2.

Tucker, M.B. (1985). U.S. Ethnic Minorities and Drug Abuse: An Assessment of the Science and Practice. *Int J Addict*, 20: 6&7, 1020-2047.

Weiss, R.D., Mirin, S.M., Michael, J.L., & Sollogub, A.C. (1986). Psychopathology in Chronic Cocaine Abusers. *Am J Drug Alcohol Abuse*, 12 (1&2), pp. 17-29.

Weiss, R.D., Mirin, S.M., Griffin, M.L., & Michael, J.L. (1988). Psychopathology in Cocaine Abusers: Changing Trends, *J of Nervous and Mental Disease*, Vol. 176, No.12, 719-725.

Woody, G.E., McLellan, A.T., Luborsky, L., & O'Brien, C.P. (1985). Sociopathy and Psychotherapy Outcome. *Arch Gen Psychiatry*, 42: 1081-1086.

Woody, G.E., Luborsky, L., McLellan, A.T., O'Brien, C.P., Beck, A.T., Blaine, J., Herman, I., & Hole, A. (1983). Psychotherapy for Opiate Addicts: Does It Help? *Arch Gen Psychiatry*, 40: 639-645.

Woody, G. (1987). Twelve month follow-up of psychotherapy for opiate dependence. *Am J Psychiatry*, 144:5, 590-596.

Yamamoto, J., James, Z.C., Bloombaum, M., & Hattem, J. (1967). Racial Factors in Patient Selection. *Amer. J. Psych*, 124:5, 84-90.

Yamamoto, J., James, Q.C., Palley, N. (1968). Cultural Problems in Psychiatric Therapy. *Arch Gen Psych*. Vol. 19, pp. 45-49.

Ziter, M.L.P. (1987; March-April). Culturally Sensitive Treatment of Black Alcoholic Families. *Social Work*, 130-135.

Research on Drug Abuse
Among Asian Pacific Americans

Nolan Zane
Toshiaki Sasao

There is increasing interest in the relationship between ethnicity and substance-abuse behavior in the United States, but the lack of empirical information limits our understanding of Asian Pacific Americans and their particular patterns of substance abuse (Austin, Prendergast, & Lee, 1989; Johnson & Nishi, 1976; Trimble, Padilla, & Bell, 1987). The research literature provides mixed findings about the nature and extent of substance use problems among Asian Pacific Americans. For example, a number of survey studies have found that Asian Pacific American groups do not seem to abuse illicit substances as frequently as other non-Asian Pacific groups. In contrast, clinical and anecdotal evidence suggests that serious substance abuse problems exist for certain Asian Pacific populations (Nakashima, 1986). There is an obvious need for more empirical work on Asian Pacifics that can facilitate effective prevention and treatment of substance abuse problems in these communities.

The purpose of this chapter is to provide a critical review of the

Nolan Zane is Assistant Professor of Counseling Psychology and Asian American Studies at the University of California, Santa Barbara.

Toshiaki Sasao is Research Psychologist and Project Director for California Statewide Asian Drug Service Needs Assessment at the National Research Center on Asian American Mental Health, Department of Psychology, University of California at Los Angeles.

The preparation of this paper was supported in part by Grant #R01 MH44331 from the National Institute on Mental Health and by a contract grant from California State Department of Alcohol and Drug Programs. The authors thank Julie Lee for her bibliographic assistance.

181

selected literature on substance abuse among Asian Pacific Ameri
cans, with a focus on (1) patterns of substance use and abuse, (2) the
conceptual models that may be applicable in explaining the substance
abuse patterns for this ethnic minority population, and (3) the effec
tiveness of prevention and treatment programs in serving these com
munities. We conclude each section by discussing some research
issues and strategies that may prove helpful for advancing research
on substance abuse within the larger context of Asian Pacific Amer
ican health and mental health.

EXTENT OF SUBSTANCE ABUSE
AMONG ASIAN PACIFIC AMERICANS

The majority of the literature consistently suggests that Asian
Pacifics use and abuse substances of any kind less frequently than
non-Asian Pacific individuals (e.g., Iiyama, Nishi, & Johnson, 1976
Tucker, 1985; Mclaughlin, Raymond, Murakami, & Goebert, 1987
Johnson, Nagoshi, Ahern, Wilson, & Yuen, 1987; Sue, Zane & Ito
1979; Sue & Morishima, 1982; Trimble, Padilla, & Bell, 1987)
However, given the limitations of the research, acceptance of this
general finding would be premature. Most of these studies have
focused on the larger and more acculturated Asian Pacific groups
such as Chinese and Japanese, used primarily student samples
rarely examined Asian Pacific groups who may be at greatest risk
for substance abuse problems (e.g., refugees, recent immigrants
adolescents), relied on disproportionately small sample sizes, seldom controlled for socioeconomic and other demographic differences that may be confounded with ethnicity, failed to use bilingual
measures, administered translated measures without evaluating
conceptual equivalence, and not accounted for cultural differences
that may affect self-report or self-disclosure with respect to substance use and abuse.

Estimates from Untreated Cases

Much of the evidence for infrequent abuse or the relatively lower
use of substances among Asian Pacifics has been documented in

surveys of untreated cases from community samples. Most studies have compared various ethnic groups, but specific Asian Pacific groups have not been identified or differentiated from one another. This makes it difficult to determine if the findings can truly be generalized to the various Asian Pacific populations. In a study comparing Asian Pacific with non-Asian Pacific students, Sue, Zane and Ito found (1979) that Asian Pacific students consumed less alcohol, had more negative attitudes toward drinking and used fewer cues in the regulation of their own drinking than non-Asian Pacific counterparts. It was suggested that with assimilation into American culture came more lenient and positive attitudes toward alcohol consumption, including the possibility of alcohol abuse. More recent surveys of students (Newcomb, Maddahian, Skager, & Bentler, 1987; McCarthy, Newcomb, Maddahian, & Skager, 1986; Maddahian, Newcomb, & Bentler, 1985, 1986) also have revealed that the Asian Pacific respondents tend to report lower levels of substance use of cigarettes, alcohol, marijuana, cocaine, and other hard drugs when compared to other ethnic groups, particularly Whites. For example, in the Newcomb et al. (1987) study data were collected anonymously in 1985 from 2,926 7th, 9th, and 11th graders in Ventura County, California. The study assessed substance abuse frequency, perceived harmfulness of marijuana, perceived parental attitudes toward drug use, and mood state measures. When the risk factors (e.g., emotional distress, low educational aspirations, and poor psychological adjustment) were constructed for different groups, the Asians also showed the lowest level of risk for future substance abuse. As with other previous research, specific Asian Pacific groups were not differentiated; the small sample size ($n =$ 77) may limit the generalizability of the findings; and the study did not examine many socio-cultural variables that reflect important individual differences among Asian Pacific Americans (e.g., acculturation level).

Adlaf, Smart, and Tan (1989) compared drug use patterns across eight ethnic groups in Ontario, Canada. This study sought to examine inter-ethnic differences, but their operationalization of the ethnicity varied from other studies. Ethnic group affiliation was designated as the ethnicity of participant's "ancestors on the male side on coming to this continent." Based on this definition, presumably participants of mixed ethnicity were included in the various ethnic samples. After controlling for certain demographic variables such as level of acculturation, religion, age, provincial region, and gender, the Asian Pacific group (Chinese and Japanese, $n = 102$) had the lowest use of tobacco, alcohol, and cannabis.

The survey studies appear to present convergent evidence of relatively lower substance use among Asian Pacifics from different geographical regions. However, these comparisons with other ethnic groups may be difficult to interpret because the Asian Pacific sample sizes were extremely small in both an absolute and relative sense. In each comparative study, the Asian or Asian Pacific group constituted less than three percent of the total survey sample. The actual number of respondents studied ranged from 63 to 117.

The few studies that have included sizeable samples of Asian Pacifics have been conducted in either California or Hawaii. Two studies conducted in Los Angeles on 7th and 8th graders (Projects SMART & SHARP, John Graham, personal communication, 1988) indicated that the lifetime use of cigarettes, marijuana, and alcohol was lower for Asian Pacifics compared to Blacks, Hispanics, or Whites. Similar patterns of use were found in a state-wide survey of drug and alcohol use among students in grades 7, 9, and 11 (Skager, Fisher, & Maddahian, 1986; Skager, Frith, & Maddahian, 1989). One of the few studies to examine inter-Asian Pacific differences in substance use was conducted as part of a state-wide alcohol, drug, and mental health survey in Hawaii (McLaughlin, Raymond, Murakami, & Gilbert, 1987). Using face-to-face interviews, the relative prevalence of alcohol and other drug use was determined among Chinese Americans, Japanese Americans, Filipino Americans, Native Hawaiians, and White Americans. Native Hawaiians and Whites reported a higher level of use for various drugs (e.g., barbiturates, tranquilizers, alcohol, and pain drugs) than the other three Asian Pacific American groups. Few ethnic differences existed in the relative frequency with which tranquilizers, marijuana/hashish, pain drugs, or cocaine were chosen as the respondent's primary substance of choice. However, alcohol was cited far less frequently by the Chinese, Japanese, and Filipinos than by Whites and Native Hawaiians. While the results underscore the importance of examining inter-Asian Pacific differences in substance use, it is unclear if the differences observed can be generalized to non-Hawaiian Asian communities. A number of investigators have noted how Hawaiian Asian groups may be quite different from their mainland counterparts in terms of their non-minority status, acculturation, English language proficiency, community cohesiveness, social-political identification, etc. (Sue & Morishima, 1982; Kitano & Daniels, 1988).

A bilingual telephone survey (n = 127) of a predominantly Japanese community in southern California was conducted to assess the community perception of substance abuse prevalence and use of cigarettes, alcohol, and marijuana (Sasao, 1989). The results indicated that substance abuse is perceived as a significant social issue in this community. Respondents reported levels of lifetime alcohol use (73%) and cigarette use (55%) that were comparable to or greater than levels found for the American general public. Further analysis of 30-day prevalence revealed that 55% of all lifetime cigarettes users and 61% of all lifetime alcohol users used the substance in the last month. The use of the telephone as a mode of data collection has been criticized with respect to biased sampling due to low survey cooperation, reliability/validity problems, and anonymity/confidentiality issues. However, in this phone survey the interview completion rate was high (82%). Important differences occurred between American-born and Japan-born Japanese. Compared to the former, the latter had a higher rate of refusing to participate and exhibited less knowledge and social concern over substance abuse. The majority of the Japan-born respondents were housewives of Japanese businessmen, who tended to reside in the United States for only a short period of time. There also appeared to be a difference in the manner by which the two subgroups defined "substance abuse." Japanese-born respondents tended to reserve this term for hard drugs such as marijuana, LSD, and heroin and did not include alcohol use and cigarette use as potential substance abuse problems. The American-born definition of substance abuse was more inclusive involving both the use of alcohol or cigarettes. This difference may have important implications for prevention work with Japanese of different generations.

In a number of studies focused only on alcohol drinking patterns among Asian Pacifics, Kitano and his colleagues questioned the myth of Asian Pacific Americans as non-drinkers (Chi, Lubben, & Kitano, 1988, 1989; Kitano & Chi, 1985; Kitano, Lubben & Chi, 1988; Lubben, Chi, & Kitano, 1989). Surnames of Chinese, Japanese, and Korean respondents were drawn from Los Angeles phone directories, in proportion to the Los Angeles population of each group. For the Filipino respondents, the "snowball" sampling technique was used. Initial interviews with Filipinos from known organizations were followed by referral to other potential Filipino respondents. The final sample included 298 Chinese, 295 Japanese, 280 Koreans, and 230 Filipinos. The demographic characteristics indicate that most of these respondents were married men between the ages of 30 to 60 years. Results indicated that the alcohol drinking patterns of young Asian Pacific males are very similar to that found for a national sample of young adult male respondents (Cahalan & Cisin, 1976) and that certain Asian Pacific groups had a high proportion of heavy drinkers. The Japanese (25.4%) and Filipinos (19.6%) had the highest percentage of heavy drinkers followed by the Koreans (14.6%) and the Chinese (10.4%). Analyses of attitude items corroborated Sue et al.'s (1979) findings in which more permissive attitudes associated with greater acculturation were related to heavier alcohol consumption. It appears that, at least in the case of alcohol consumption, Asian Pacific substance use has been underestimated (cf. D. Sue, 1987). In a related finding, Maddahian et al. (1985) found that Asians were the largest group that tried *only* alcohol and no other substances.

Kitano has explained that the diversity and variability among various Asian Pacifics in their drinking patterns can be attributed to the cultural patterns brought over by their ancestors. His study was one of the first large sample surveys conducted to determine the alcohol drinking practices of various Asian Pacific groups. However, the sampling methodology which involved household interviews based on the phone directories, may have omitted certain individuals in the Asian Pacific population considered at highest risk for alcohol problems (e.g., single, recent immigrant males living alone or in crowded communal arrangements with no private phones).

Another large epidemiological survey of alcohol use among Chinese, Japanese, Whites, and Asian-Whites (mixed parentage) was conducted in Hawaii (Wilson, McClearn, & Johnson, 1978). This survey was designed to control for the effects of certain socio-demographic variables (e.g., social class, gender). Whites tended to drink more and flush less than either the Chinese or Japanese, whereas the two Asian Pacific groups did not differ from one another in drinking or flushing. Individuals of mixed Asian-White ancestry had mean alcohol consumption levels that were very similar to those of the White group and considerably higher than those of the Asian Pacific groups. However, Asian-Whites resembled Asian Pacifics more than Whites in their tendency to flush. The results suggest that cultural variables such as assimilation (in this case, marital assimilation) into American mainstream culture have an important influence on the extent of alcohol use.

Given the diversity of the Asian Pacific population, it would be especially important to examine the substance use patterns of Asian Pacific groups considered at high risk for health and/or mental health problems. Yee and Thu (1987) reported on the prevalence and nature of the substance use problems among one such group, Southeast Asian refugees. Their study sampled 840 refugees, mainly Vietnamese, residing in Houston, Texas, and several cities in Louisiana and employed household interviews to assess drug use and mental health status. Approximately 45% of the sample reported problems involving alcohol and/or tobacco use although the use of other drugs was not seen as problematic. A significant number of the respondents viewed alcohol and smoking as acceptable ways for directly coping with stressful situations, and for alleviating personal problems resulting from stress.

Wong (1985) investigated substance use among Chinese youth in a community associated with high-risk indicators, San Francisco's Chinatown. Using a non-random sampling of 123 Chinese youths, ages 13-19 years, Wong estimated that the prevalence of substance abuse among these youth was higher than that found among other youth in the previous study conducted in San Francisco with the same methodology (Feldman, 1984). The lifetime use of cigarettes, marijuana, cocaine, and valium by the Chinese sample was similar to that reported by the non-Asian Pacific samples (Whites, Blacks, Hispanics). The Chinese sample tended to use Quaaludes more frequently than the other groups.

Estimates from Treated Cases

The use of treated cases or utilization data to estimate prevalence is a hazardous venture fraught with selection biases due to socioeconomic, administrative, and other nosocomial factors (Kramer & Zane, 1984). Nevertheless, this approach provides an alternative source for examining Asian Pacific substance use and abuse. Over the recent years in both San Francisco and Los Angeles, Asian Pacifics using drug abuse treatment services have been consistently underrepresented with respect to their respective proportions in the local populations. This has commonly been interpreted as reflecting service underutilization (cf. Murase, 1977) rather than a lesser need for services related to lower levels of substance abuse.

Asian, Inc. (1978) used a key informant approach and estimated that the substance use of Chinese and Filipinos is lower than that of the general population whereas the level of use for Japanese is similar to that found in the general San Francisco population. In a national study of drug abuse programs, Phin and Phillips (1978) found that Asian Pacifics (55%) and Whites (63-67%) were primarily admitted for heroin abuse. As for drug abuse patterns, Asian Pacifics relative to Whites indicated a greater involvement with barbiturates (45% to 11%, respectively). Using the information collected from a large ambulatory population using the Kaiser-Permanente Medical Care Program in Oakland and San Francisco, Klatsky, Friedman, Siegelaub & Gerard (1977) reported that when compared to Whites, Blacks, and Others, Asian Pacific males and females (n = 4,319) had the highest level of abstinence from alcohol. Namkung (1976) found that of the Asian Pacifics in the California prison population, 95% were incarcerated for drug-related reasons. These studies have suffered from the same limitations as the untreated case studies by not distinguishing between different Asian Pacific groups, using relatively small samples, not controlling for important demographic variations, and assuming cultural equivalence among the self-report measures and interview procedures.

The state of California has one of the largest databases of treated cases, the California Drug Abuse Data System (CAL-DADS), which many local agencies and governments use to make policy decisions. CAL-DADS replaced the Client Oriented Data Acquisition Process (CODAP) system in July 1, 1982 when National Institute on Drug Abuse discontinued this system. The CAL-DADS admission data for Los Angeles and San Francisco counties indicate that the relative use of drugs (mainly heroin, marijuana, and cocaine) among different ethnic groups has been fairly stable from 1982 to 1989 (Sasao, 1990). Asian Pacifics had the lowest admission rates to county or federal treatment facilities. Again, this appears to reflect underutilization rather than a lower need for services on the part of Asian Pacifics.

In summary, on the basis of research on either untreated or treated cases it is difficult to obtain good estimates of the level of substance use and abuse for the various Asian Pacific populations. Nevertheless, certain tentative conclusions can be formed. First, it appears that alcohol use has been underestimated, particularly for certain Asian Pacific groups such as Japanese males and Filipino males. Second, there is some evidence which suggests that a major substance abuse problem for older Asian Pacific groups may involve the use of barbiturates, tranquilizers, and pain drugs. Third, cultural factors appear to play an important role in limiting and, at other times, enhancing substance use among certain Asian Pacific groups. Fourth, the past research has not been very informative because it is usually unclear which Asian Pacific groups are being studied. This is a serious methodological shortcoming because the Asian Pacific groups which appear at highest risk for developing substance abuse problems have seldom been studied or have not been separately identified in previous research. Finally, it is likely that the estimates provided by these data will soon be outdated and will grossly underestimate because many of the groups with the highest risk factors (i.e., Southeast Asian refugees, Koreans, and Filipinos) also are the fastest growing groups in the Asian Pacific population. Whereas the Japanese and Chinese constituted the largest groups in 1970, it is estimated that by the year 2000 Filipinos will be the largest group followed by the Chinese, Vietnamese, Koreans, and Japanese. In the near future as significant changes in the socio-demographic and ethnic profile of the general Asian Pacific population occur, these undoubtedly will be associated with certain changes in substance use and abuse patterns.

EXPLANATORY MODELS OF ASIAN PACIFIC SUBSTANCE ABUSE

An impressive array of theories and associated empirical work have been developed to understand the etiology of substance abuse. Explanatory models have highlighted family relationships (e.g., Clayton & Lacey, 1982), peer relationships (e.g., Oetting & Beauvais, 1987), stressful life events (e.g., Labouvie, 1986), and psychological distress (e.g., Kaplan, 1985). In contrast, most of the work on Asian Pacific substance abuse has been atheoretical and, more importantly, not linked to mainstream substance abuse research. The one exception has been in the area of alcohol research.

Models of Asian Pacific Alcohol Use and Abstinence

The low level of alcoholism among Asian Pacific Americans has been usually attributed to ethnic differences in physiological reactions (e.g., flushing, rapid heart rate, drop in blood pressure) to ethanol which are accompanied by objective and subjective symptoms of discomfort (Ewing et al. 1974; Goodwin, 1979). This dysphoria is directly linked to the higher accumulation of acetaldehyde in flushing subjects most likely as a result of less-active liver enzyme, aldehyde dehydrogenase isozyme (ALDHI) in metabolizing acetaldehyde (Agarwal, Eckey, Harada, & Goedde, 1984). While it appears that the higher alcohol-related sensitivity in Asian Pacifics can reduce alcohol consumption, Chan (1986) concluded in his review of the biochemical research that socio-cultural and environmental factors must also be considered. The results of research comparing Asian Pacifics with non-Asian Pacifics generally support the idea that there are significant racial differences in social and physiological reactions to various substances, including alcohol. However, as noted by Trimble et al. (1987), such results must be interpreted with caution because they are usually based on restricted student samples, examine "heterogeneous" Asian Pacific groups, use culturally inappropriate instruments, and erroneously assume the "context-free" nature of pharmacological research. In addition, Johnson and Nagoshi (1990) have noted that the physiological model of Asian Pacific alcohol use cannot account for the wide variation in alcohol use across different periods of Chinese history, the substantial increase in alcohol use among various Asian Pacific American groups over time, marked differences in alcohol consumption among Asian countries, and consistent sex differences in alcohol use within Asian Pacific groups. They indicate that sociopsychological and cultural factors are probably more important determinants of Asian Pacific alcohol use.

The physiological model of alcohol consumption could still account for the variations observed by Johnson and Nagoshi by positing that these were due to differences in chronic tolerance to the flushing response. However, Newlin (1989) directly examined the relationship between the flushing response and the development of alcohol tolerance and found no support for this explanation. In a comparison of Asian flushers and non-flushers he found significant cardiovascular changes in response to alcohol between the two groups but no differential development of tolerance. There were also no differences in self-reported mood between flushers and non-flushers after alcohol consumption.

Sue and Nakamura (1984) have proposed a reciprocity model to explain the alcohol consumption of Asian Pacifics. They note that previous studies comparing ethnic groups in alcohol use usually have confounded physiological differences in alcohol-related sensitivity with differences on socio-cultural factors such as acculturation. They suggest that physiological reactivity, socio-cultural factors, and alcohol consumption have mutual influences on each other. In a partial test of this model, Akutsu, Sue, Zane, and Nakamura (1989) found that both socio-cultural factors and physiological reactivity were related to drinking but not general acculturation variables.

The Akutsu et al. study has several important implications for research focused on understanding Asian Pacific substance use and abuse. First, it is important to clearly delineate how ethnic differences translate into differences on variables which have been found to be *empirically linked* to substance use. In the preceding case, familial attitudes and physiological reactivity were examined because both have been directly related to alcohol consumption among Asian Pacifics (Kitano, Lubben, & Chi, 1988; Lubben, Chi, & Kitano, 1989; Chan, 1986). Too often studies have focused on cultural variables (e.g., family size, percent of Asian Pacific friends) that are quite distal to the substance-related behavior of interest. Second, cultural variables must be on the same level of specificity as other predictors for the study to adequately test the relative effects of cultural influences. In the Akutsu et al. study no relationship was found between acculturation, as measured by generation, and drinking. However, a relationship may have been found if the acculturation variable had been operationalized to reflect a continuum of traditional to acculturated values with specific reference to drinking.

Future Emphases

There is a great need for the work on Asian Pacific substance abuse to converge with previous research which has identified important predictors of substance use. In this way, socio-cultural variables can be examined in terms of how their effects on substance use and abuse are mediated by certain common socio-psychological processes (e.g., loss of control, peer cluster relationships). Substance abuse research on Asian Pacifics has tended to be descriptive and atheoretical in nature. There needs to be stronger links between this research and empirically-supported etiological theories of substance abuse. Given the current research emphases in Asian Pacific American health and mental health, it appears that some promising areas of convergence would be in research on stressful life events involving issues of cultural adjustment, social skills deficits, motives for use, family cohesion, and peer relationships.

Stressful Life Events

Stressful life events, such as death in the family and a transition to a new environment or culture, often enhance the use of various substances as a means for coping with the pain and disruption caused by these events (Dohrenwend & Dohrenwend, 1981; Smith, 1985; Tolan & Thomas, 1987; Willis & Shiffman, 1985). Past research has identified several categories of stressors such as major life events, "daily hassles," life transitions, and developmental changes. However, it is unclear which stressors are related to substance use for Asian Pacifics or if the impact of these stressors is similarly experienced by Asian Pacific individuals differing in acculturation level, country of origin, etc. There may be important differences among Asian Pacific groups in the exposure to and appraisal of these stressors. For example, recent immigrant children and adolescents may be at greater risk for developing substance abuse problems because they must cope with multiple stressors, associated with cultural adjustment (e.g., demands to fit in with peers and family members, parental pressure for high academic achievement) in addition to the stress resulting from normal developmental issues involving puberty and strivings for personal autonomy. These events may affect decisions to initiate or increase substance use among new immigrant youth. Future investigations into the etiology of substance abuse among Asian Pacifics also could assess culturally acceptable and unacceptable coping strategies for different stressful events.

Social Skill Deficits

Successful outcomes in the prevention or reduction of substance abuse have occurred in programs that enhance or maximize the ability of youth to interact effectively with others (Botvin & Willis, 1985; Rhodes & Jason, 1988). There may be important cultural and ethnic differences in the development of social skills. Western-oriented social skills often emphasize open self-expression, assertiveness, and individualism that can directly conflict with traditional Asian Pacific values and role expectations held by Asian Pacific parents. For Asian Pacific youth the development and application of these skills may be adaptable outside of the family but not reinforced or even discouraged within the family. A study of Vietnamese adolescents illustrates this cultural dilemma (Charron & Ness, 1983). Youth who did not form friendships with American-born peers were more prone to develop emotional problems, but youth who had such school-based friendships were more at risk for conflicts with parents. The acquisition of adequate social skills may be especially important for refugees and other recent immigrant Asian Pacifics because such skill deficits often are the source of social discrimination and interpersonal conflict at school or home (Beiser, Turner, & Ganesan, 1989; Cohon, 1981). However, it is still unclear how applicable or appropriate various social skill programs are for Asian Pacific individuals. For example, Zane, Sue, Hu, and Kwon (in press) have raised several concerns about the use of certain anxiety management treatments for Asian Pacifics with assertion difficulties.

Motives for Use

With the increasing use of cognitive-behavioral and community education programs, substance abuse intervention and prevention efforts have adopted a strong cognitive emphasis to changing drug-using habits and behaviors. The assessment of the perceived reasons for using drugs can serve to better target such interventions. In a study of cognitive motivations for using alcohol and marijuana Newcomb et al. (1988) found important gender and age differences in the perceived reasons for using these drugs. Similar studies may be helpful in determining if different Asian Pacific groups vary in their reasons for substance use. Such research may also yield important acculturation differences in motivations for use.

Family Cohesion

The family system is of central importance to the psychosocial functioning of Asian Pacific individuals (Sue & Morishima, 1982). Asian Pacific families and extended kinship networks have often been cited as an important protective factor against many health and mental health problems (Hsu, 1973). On the other hand, others have noted that Asian Pacific families can become a significant source of stress for the individual as evidenced by intergenerational and family role conflicts (Lee, 1982). More empirical work is needed to determine which aspects of Asian Pacific families and their extended networks prevent or facilitate drug use.

Peer Relationships

In a path analysis study, Oetting and Beauvais (1987) found that socialization factors such as family strength, family sanctions against drugs, school adjustment, and religious involvement only indirectly influence drug use. It appears that these influences are mediated through their effects on peer cluster associations which, in turn, directly affect drug use. Peer clusters are not synonymous with peer groups but instead refer to small, close-knit groups in which members share very similar attitudes, values, and lifestyles. The peer model of substance abuse suggests that most socialization experiences affect the formation of certain types of peer relationships which either facilitate or discourage drug use. Research is needed to determine if this causal model is generalizable to Asian Pacific individuals. Given the great emphasis placed on family and kinship involvement, it is possible that a more direct influence on drug use may be found for the family socialization experiences of Asian Pacifics. Such differences in the causal pathways would have important implications for the development of substance abuse prevention programs for Asian Pacific communities.

METHODOLOGICAL ISSUES IN RESEARCH ON ASIAN PACIFIC SUBSTANCE ABUSE

Research in any of the previously mentioned areas would greatly enhance our understanding of substance abuse among Asian Pacifics, but such empirical work must consider certain methodological issues that are particularly relevant when examining this population. What follows are specific methodological caveats that can facilitate substance abuse research on Asian Pacifics.

Population Heterogeneity

Any examination of Asian Pacific American substance use and abuse patterns must address the wide range of diversity among different Asian Pacific groups. The immediate implication is that most research cannot assume that Asian Pacifics can be aggregated into a single population entity. Often this inter-group diversity has gone unrecognized or underappreciated. More than 20 Asian Pacific groups have been identified by the U.S. Bureau of the Census. The three largest in descending order are Chinese, Filipino, and Japanese. The diverse nature of the population is evident in a number of demographic characteristics. The vast majority of Vietnamese, Koreans, Asian Indians, Filipinos, and Chinese in the United States were born overseas. However, Samoans, Japanese, Guamanians, and Hawaiians were largely born in the United States (U.S. Bureau of the Census, 1989). Considerable age differences can be seen within the Asian Pacific American population, with Japanese and Asian Indians having median ages that exceed the national average and with other Asian Pacific groups having median ages lower than the national average. In terms of economic indices, the median family income of Japanese Americans ($27,400) was substantially higher than that of Vietnamese Americans ($12,800). Great variation also exists among Asian Pacific groups in educational attainment and achievement. The drop-out rates for Filipinos are much higher compared with other Asian Pacific groups and White Americans. It is possible that the level of specific risk factors such as drop-out rate may be quite different depending on the Asian Pacific group examined. Finally, concomitant with this inter-group diversity are important within group differences in terms of acculturation, ethnic identity, primary language dialect, country of origin, etc. Some of these variables may be important predictors of substance use for a particular Asian Pacific population. For example, a number of studies have found that acculturation is a strong predictor of alcohol consumption for certain Asian Pacific groups such as the Chinese and Japanese.

Cultural Differences versus Ethnic Differences

Too often substance abuse research on Asian Pacific Americans has been focused at a descriptive level in which ethnic differences are examined. The distinction between ethnic and cultural differences is an important one to make because it appears that the latter constitutes the more proximal determinants of substance use and abuse. Ethnic differences refer to variations on those personal-social characteristics (e.g., social class) which an individual tends to have simply by being a member of a certain ethnic group. Cultural differences, on the other hand, imply certain differences in attitudes, values, and perceptual constructs as a result of different cultural experiences. Whereas the former simply involves group membership, the latter constitutes a host of socio-psychological variables which are linked to different cultural lifestyles and perspectives. Ethnicity implies cultural differences but often these socio-psychological variables have not been directly assessed in substance abuse research. That Chinese Americans drink less than White Americans does not contribute much to our understanding of substance use in Asian Pacific communities. However, if it was found that this difference in drinking is related to variant cultural attitudes toward drunken behavior, this information would have important implications for prevention and intervention efforts with Chinese. At a minimum, research on cultural differences must achieve two empirical tasks. First, a study must demonstrate that differences exist on a socio-cultural variable. Second, there must be some evidence that there is a functional link or relationship between these differences and the behavior of interest, in this case, substance abuse. In previous research, studies either have simply described ethnic differences in drug consumption or have examined cultural differences but not linked these differences to differential substance use. Clearly, studies that do both are needed.

Measure Development and Application

There have been excellent reviews (Sue & Sue, 1987; Hui & Triandis, 1985) of the problems and methodological issues that must be addressed in the development of reliable measures that are conceptually equivalent and possess construct validity for culturally-diverse populations. The purpose of this section is to highlight only those issues that may be particularly relevant for research on substance problems within Asian Pacific American communities. Many of the measures utilized in substance abuse research rely on self-report. A number of problems can occur when using self-report measures with certain Asian Pacific populations. First, many Asian Pacifics whose primary language is not English may have difficulty in responding to items that have very little context in terms of time, place, and person. Most East Asian languages are very contextualized in that the context often establishes the tense, status of the person, etc. For example, in attempting to respond to the item, "I have difficulty making decisions," an Asian Pacific respondent may want to know the time period involved (e.g., during the past month) and the type of decisions considered (e.g., financial, career, or family) before an appropriate response can be made.

Second, there is often significant stigma and shame associated with having personal problems such as substance abuse that impair a person's ability to fulfill role responsibilities and obligations to the family or community group. Consequently, self-report responses may vary greatly depending on the public or private nature of the measure's administration. Many self-report measures need be administered under highly public conditions because many Asian Pacifics are non-English speaking and, thus, require bilingual interviewers who can translate the questionnaire. In these cases, the public nature of the administration may seriously compromise open self-disclosure of sensitive problems such as substance abuse. Special efforts must be made to move the report of substance abuse problems into a more private context to minimize shame and loss of face on the part of Asian Pacific respondents. In our study of Chinese elderly at a health clinic at first no elderly reported having suicidal thoughts in response to an interview-based questionnaire (Zane, 1982). Only when we administered the questionnaire by means of a tape recorder in which participants could respond without the interviewer present were we able to obtain some variance on this item.

Finally, it may be wise to reappraise the measurement of acculturation and cultural identity variables. These variables constitute one of the most important domains of individual differences within Asian Pacific groups. Previous research has assumed that acculturation and cultural identity development reflect a bipolar model. This model posits that as people become more acculturated or identified with Western culture they become less acculturated or identified with their particular Asian Pacific culture. In other words, to be highly acculturated in Western culture presumes low acculturation in East Asian or Pacific Islander culture. Oetting and Beauvais (1989) have raised the possibility that acculturation and changes in cultural identity may not proceed according to the bipolar model. They suggest that a person's identification with one culture is independent or orthogonal to his or her identification with another culture. Oetting and Beauvais found empirical support for the model in their study of American Indian and Mexican American youth. If applicable to Asian Pacific acculturation and cultural identity, this orthogonal model of cultural identity implies a change in how acculturation variables are measured. It may be necessary to assess acculturation in two cultures, American culture and the respondent's specific Asian Pacific culture. On the basis of this model, a number of interesting comparisons can be made. For instance, the substance abuse and use patterns of mono-cultural individuals (highly acculturated in one culture but lowly acculturated in the other culture) can be compared to bicultural individuals (highly acculturated in both cultures) as well as "alienated" individuals (lowly acculturated in both cultures).

TREATMENT OF ASIAN PACIFIC SUBSTANCE ABUSE

To date, few studies have directly examined the outcomes (in terms of decreased drug use) of Asian Pacific clients in substance abuse treatment. Phin and Phillips (1978) compared the treatment of outcomes of Asian Pacifics and Whites using retention in treatment, drug use patterns, change in employment, and legal status as indices of treatment outcome. Asian Pacific clients reported that treatment had positive effects on living conditions and/or health and led to decreased drug use. Compared to Whites, Asian Pacific clients stayed in therapy longer but had higher rates of continuing drug abuse. These outcome data are difficult to interpret because the Asian Pacific and White samples were not comparable in age or drug abuse patterns at admission to treatment.

Culturally-Responsive Services and Programs

Given that Asian Pacifics tend to underutilize substance abuse treatment programs, it is not surprising that relatively more emphasis has been placed on developing programs which are responsive to the specific needs of Asian Pacific communities and their youth. Various strategies and solutions have been proposed to develop effective services for Asian Pacifics. Murase (1977) has identified the following structural and organizational characteristics that facilitate the provision of culturally relevant services to Asian Pacific American communities: (1) location of delivery site within the community itself; (2) involvement of a broad cross-section of the community in decisions concerning the service programs; (3) employment of full bilingual and bicultural staff; (4) cultivation and utilization of existing indigenous formal and informal community care/support systems; and, (5) development of innovative intervention methods. Specifically, such treatment approaches should recognize the family as an integral part of treatment, establish an active, highly personalized therapeutic relationship, focus on survival-related tasks to facilitate the engagement process, address the possible conflict between the cultural dynamic of "loss of face" and the confessional character of psychotherapy, differentiate between cultural behavioral propensities and pathology, reevaluate the self-determination construct, permit flexibility in session scheduling and duration, and recognize the ameliorative effect of a familiar and predictable cultural milieu.

In terms of program development, Sue (1977) has proposed three alternative strategies for implementing such changes: (1) train personnel from existing agencies to be culturally-sensitive, (2) develop independent but parallel services (i.e., service units or programs which are operationally and, at times, physically separate from mainstream agencies but remain similar in function and organizational structure) or (3) establish new, nonparallel service programs and agencies that do have comparable entities in the conventional service delivery system (Sue, 1977). As Uba (1982) indicated, research has not determined the relative merit of the various alternative forms of service delivery. However, in the related area of mental health treatment, it has been demonstrated that when services are provided by bilingual, bicultural personnel working from community-based agencies, such services are utilized by Asian Pacific American clients. In Seattle, an Asian Pacific American counseling and referral service served as many Asian Pacific Americans in one year as were served by 18 other community mental health centers over a three-year period (Sue & McKinney, 1975). True (1975) found that in Oakland a county out-patient and emergency mental health facility served only 3 Chinese Americans from a total of 500 clients. During that same year, an Asian Pacific American community-based agency initiated operations and served 131 Chinese Americans. A community-supported mental health center in San Francisco saw more Asian Pacific American clients in its first three months of operation than the total number of Asian Pacific Americans served in that catchment area during the previous five years (Wong, 1977). Zane (1989) found that the premature termination problem often found for Asian Pacifics using mental health services was reduced to such an extent at a parallel service agency that no differences in premature termination were evident between Asian Pacific and White clients.

Despite these encouraging signs, the question of whether culturally responsive and appropriate substance abuse treatments have been developed for Asian Pacifics remains unanswered. The development of parallel service substance abuse programs in areas where Asian Pacifics have concentrated (e.g., San Francisco, Los Angeles) implies that drug abuse treatment may require modification in some way to make it effective and culturally responsive to the needs of Asian Pacific clients. There is an obvious need to conduct studies that determine if treatment equity in effectiveness has been achieved for Asian Pacific clients, but it is also important for outcome research to help identify those aspects of the treatment that make it culturally responsive. Oftentimes, outcome designs comparing ethnic groups have been able to accomplish the former but not the latter.

Identification of Culturally-Responsive Aspects of Treatment

Kiesler (1966) has argued that the traditional process-outcome distinction is not a useful one because outcome research can involve the study of process while process research can investigate outcomes; in essence, they are equivalent. The dichotomy has fostered the misconception that in-treatment client changes are not legitimate variables of interest to outcome researchers. However, the identification of aspects of a treatment that work to make it effective for Asian Pacific clients requires a clear conceptualization of how substance abuse treatment procedures and their impact are related to final targeted outcomes of the program.

Instrumental versus Ultimate Criteria

Dependent measures can be classified as pertaining to either a final goal of treatment (ultimate criteria) or a condition required (instrumental criteria) for attaining this final goal (Fiske et al., 1970). Substance abuse outcome studies typically have focused on assessing ultimate criteria to determine treatment efficacy. It is proposed that treatment studies also incorporate instrumental criteria into the research design. The inclusion of instrumental criteria provides the critical empirical link between treatment procedures and substance abuse outcome needed to identify aspects important for culturally responsive treatment. Figure 1 shows how instrumental criteria are to be included in outcome research designs and the concomitant methodological issues that must be addressed.

Treatment Impact versus Treatment Relevance

In terms of the proposed model, treatment efficacy becomes a multi-faceted issue. Rather than one, at least two questions are involved: Did treatment have the desired impact by achieving its instrumental goals? and was the achievement of these instrumental goals relevant to making it effective for Asian Pacific or other ethnic minority clients? Within the context of program evaluation, Weiss (1972) has distinguished between a program failure as opposed to a theory failure. Programs attempt to activate a "causal process" which then leads to some desired effect. Program failure occurs when the program has not achieved its desired impact such that the "causal process" has been set in motion. Theory failure occurs when the program is successful in producing the intended impact but the resultant "causal process" does not lead to the desired end-goals.

In a similar manner, treatment failure with Asian Pacifics can involve either procedure or theory failure. The treatment may be

FIGURE 1. Model for Outcome Research.

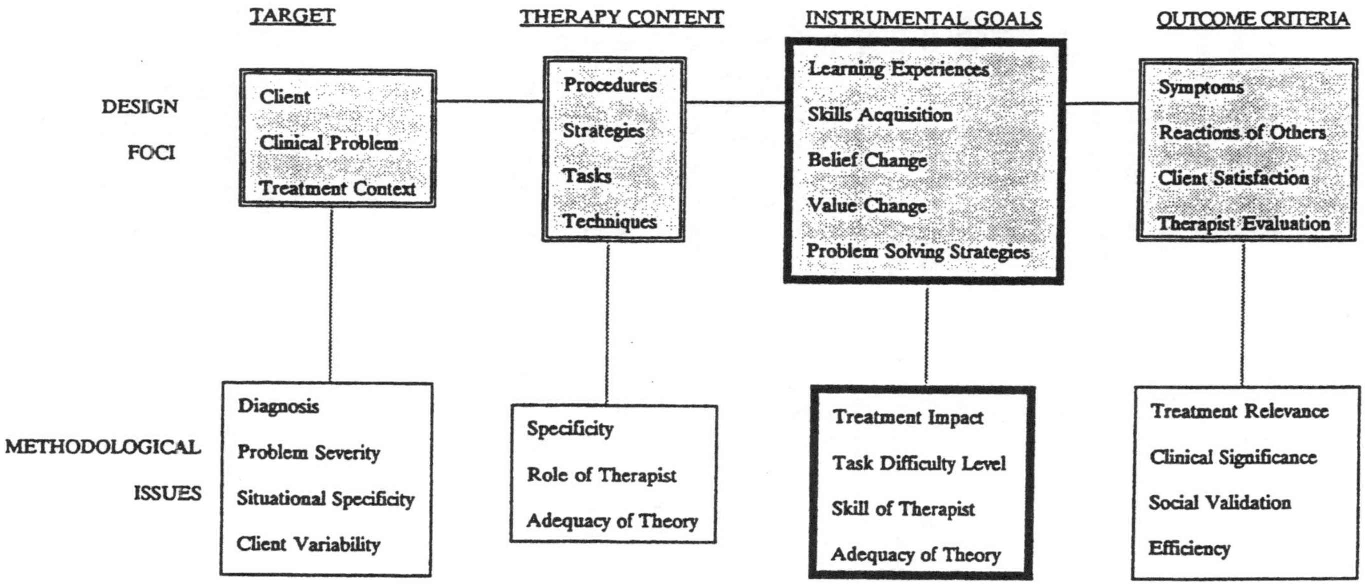

	TARGET	THERAPY CONTENT	INSTRUMENTAL GOALS	OUTCOME CRITERIA

DESIGN
FOCI

Client
Clinical Problem
Treatment Context

Procedures
Strategies
Tasks
Techniques

Learning Experiences
Skills Acquisition
Belief Change
Value Change
Problem Solving Strategies

Symptoms
Reactions of Others
Client Satisfaction
Therapist Evaluation

METHODOLOGICAL
ISSUES

Diagnosis
Problem Severity
Situational Specificity
Client Variability

Specificity
Role of Therapist
Adequacy of Theory

Treatment Impact
Task Difficulty Level
Skill of Therapist
Adequacy of Theory

Treatment Relevance
Clinical Significance
Social Validation
Efficiency

ineffective because its procedures did not have the expected impact; the targeted learning experiences did not occur because the treatment as implemented may have clashed with certain cultural values held by the client or adversely affected certain peer or family relations supporting the client's adaptive behavior. On the other hand, the theory on which the treatment is based may not be that applicable to Asian Pacific communities such that achievement of the desired changes in treatment are not related to the substance abuse problem resulting in little improvement in personal functioning.

The proposed strategy allows for a more refined interpretation of outcome results with respect to cultural influences in treatment. Because the measurement of both instrumental and ultimate goals prevents the confounding of procedure failure with theory failure, researchers can determine which is in need of revision or further development to facilitate its effectiveness with culturally diverse clients. As a result, technique-building is systematically tied to theory development. In addition to impact and relevance, a third issue can be considered when evaluating treatments: How efficient is the treatment? Treatment efficiency essentially involves a cost-effectiveness analysis of the substance abuse treatment. The costs involve the difficulty level of the therapeutic tasks (which is often influenced by the cultural differences between client and therapist) and the level of skill (including cultural sensitivity skills) needed by the therapist to implement these tasks. These costs are weighed against the improvement in the client's substance abuse problem.

CONCLUSION

Many Asian Pacific communities are concerned about substance use and abuse, but the available research has not been adequate in guiding the development of effective and efficient substance prevention and treatment programs for these communities. Clearly, more empirical work is needed to examine substance abuse issues for each separate Asian Pacific group, particularly the Pacific Islanders and the Southeast Asian refugees. There are serious conceptual and methodological issues that require closer scrutiny in future investigations. However, it appears that most of these problems are not insurmountable. Hopefully, the issues and the research strategies discussed in this paper can serve as a preliminary step to the development of empirical efforts that can more successfully capture the etiological underpinnings and substance abuse patterns of various Asian Pacific populations.

REFERENCES

Adlaf, E.M., Smart, R.G., & Tan, S.H. (1989). Ethnicity and drug use: A critical look. *International Journal of the Addictions, 24*(1), 1-18.

Agarwal, D.P., Eckey, R., Harada, S., & Goedde, H.W. (1984). Basis of aldehyde dehydrogenase deficiency in Orientals: Immunochemical studies. *Alcohol, 1,* 111-118.

Akutsu, P.D., Sue, S., Zane, N.W.S., & Nakamura, C.Y. (1989). Ethnic differences in alcohol consumption among Asians and Caucasian in the United States. *Journal of Studies on Alcohol, 50*(3), 261-267.

Austin, G.A., Prendergast, M.L., & Lee, H. (1989). Substance abuse among Asian American youth. *Prevention Research Update, 5,* 1-28.

Beiser, M., Turner, J., & Ganesan, S. (1989). Catastrophic stress and factors affecting its consequences among Southeast refugees. *Social Science & Medicine, 28*(3), 183-195.

Botvin, G.J., & Willis, T.A. (1985). Personal and social skills training: Cognitive-behavioral approaches to substance abuse prevention. In C.S. Bell & R. Battjes (Eds.), *Prevention research: Deterring drug abuse among children and adolescents.* Rockville, MD: National Institute on Drug Abuse, DHEW (ADM) 47.

Cahalan, D., & Cisin, I.H. (1976). Drinking behavior and drinking problems in the United States. In G. Kissin & H. Begleiter (Eds.), *Social aspects of alcoholism* (pp. 77-115). New York: Plenum Press.

Chan, A.W.K. (1986). Racial differences in alcohol sensitivity. *Alcohol and Alcoholism, 21,* 93-104.

Charron, D., & Ness, R. (1983). Emotional distress among Vietnamese adolescents: A statewide study. *Journal of Refugee Resettlement, 1,* 7-15.

Chi, I., Lubben, J.E., & Kitano, H.H.L. (1988). Heavy drinking among young adult Asian males. *International Social Work, 31,* 219-229.

Chi, I., Lubben, J.E., & Kitano, H.H.L. (1989). Differences in drinking behavior among three Asian-American groups. *Journal of Studies on Alcohol, 50*(1), 15-23.

Clayton, R.R., & Lacey, W.B. (1982). Interpersonal influences on male drug use and drug use intentions. *International Journal of the Addictions, 17,* 655-666.

Cohon, D. (1981). Psychological adaptation and dysfunction among refugees. *International Migration Review, 15*(1), 255-275.

Dohrenwend, B.S., & Dohrenwend, B.P. (1981). *Stressful life events and their contexts.* New York: Prodist.

Ewing, J.A., Rouse, B.A., & Aderhold, R.M. (1979). Studies of the mechanism of Oriental hypersensitivity to alcohol. *Currents in Alcoholism*, *5*, (pp. 45-52). New York: Grune & Stratton.

Fiske, D.W., Hunt, H.F., Luborsky, L., Orne, M.T., Parloff, M.B., Reiser, M.F., & Tuma, A.H. (1970). Planning of research on effectiveness of psychotherapy. *American Psychologist*, *25*, 725-737.

Goodwin, D.W. (1979). Protective factors in alcoholism. *Journal of Drug and Alcohol Dependency*, *4*(1/2), 99-100.

Hsu, F.L.K. (1973). Kinship is the key. *Center Magazine*, *6*, 4-14.

Iiyama, P., Nishi, S., & Johnson, B. (1976). *Drug use and abuse among U.S. minorities*. N.Y.: Praeger.

Hui, C.H., & Triandis, H.C. (1985). Measurement in cross-cultural counseling: a review and comparisons of strategies. *Journal of Cross Cultural Psychology*, *16*, 131-152.

Johnson, R.C., & Nagoshi, C.T. (1990). Asians, Asian-Americans, and alcohol. *Journal of Psychoactive Drugs*, *22*, 45-52.

Johnson, R.C., Nagoshi, G.T., Ahern, F.M., Wilson, J.R., & Yuen, S.H.L. (1987). Cultural factors as explanations for ethnic group differences in alcohol use in Hawaii. *Journal of Psychoactive Drugs*, *19*(1), 67-75.

Johnson, B., & Nishi, S. (1976). Myths and realities of drug use by minorities. In P. Iiyama, S. Nishi & B. Johnson (Eds.), *Drug use and abuse among U.S. minorities*. New York: Praeger.

Kaplan, H.B. (1985). Testing a general theory of drug abuse and other deviant adaptations. *Journal of Drug Issues*, *15*, 477-492.

Kiesler, D.J. (1986). Some myths of psychotherapy research and the search for a paradigm. *Psychological Bulletin*, *65*, 110-136.

Kitano, H.L., & Chi, I. (1985). Asian Americans and alcohol: The Chinese, Japanese, Koreans, and Filipinos in Los Angeles. In D. Spiegler, D. Tate, S. Aitken & C. Christian (Eds.), *Alcohol use among U.S. ethnic minorities* (pp. 373-382). Rockville, MD: NIAAA.

Kitano, H.H.L., & Daniels, R. (1988). *Asian Americans: Emerging minorities*. Englewood Hall, New Jersey: Prentice Hall.

Kitano, H.H.L., Lubben, J.E., & Chi, I. (1988). Predicting Japanese American drinking behavior. *International Journal of the Addictions*, *23*(4), 417-428.

Klatsky, A.L., Friedman, G., Siegellaub, A.B., & Gerard, M.J. (1977). Alcohol consumption among White, Black, or Oriental men and women. *American Journal of Epidemiology*, *105*, 311-323.

Kramer, M., & Zane, N. (1984). Projected needs for mental health services. In S. Sue & T. Moore (Eds.), *The pluralistic society: A community mental health perspective* (pp. 47-76). New York: Human Sciences Press.

Labouvie, E.W. (1986). The coping function of adolescent alcohol and drug use. In R.K. Silbereisen, K. Eyferth & G. Rudinger (Eds.), *Development as action in context: Problem behavior and normal youth development* (pp. 229-239). Berlin, FRG: Springer-Verlag.

Lee, E. (1982). A social systems approach to assessment and treatment for Chinese American families. In M. McGoldrick, J.K. Pearce, & J. Giordano (Eds.), *Ethnicity and family therapy.* New York: Guilford.

Lubben, J.E., Chi, I., & Kitano, H.H.L. (1989). The relative influence of selected social factors on Korean drinking behavior in Los Angeles. *Advances in Alcohol and Substance Abuse, 8*(1), 1-17.

Maddahian, E., Newcomb, M.D., & Bentler, P.M. (1985). Single and multiple patterns of adolescent substance use: Longitudinal comparisons of four ethnic groups. *Journal of Drug Education, 15*(4), 311-326.

Maddahian, E., Newcomb, M.D., & Bentler, P.M. (1986). Adolescents' substance use: Impact of ethnicity, income, and availability. *Advances in Alcohol and Substance Abuse, 5*(3), 63-78.

McCarthy, W.J., Newcomb, M.D., Maddahian, E., & Skager, R. (1986). Smokeless tobacco use among adolescents: Demographic differences, other substance use, and psychological correlates. *Journal of Drug Education, 16*(4), 383-402.

McLaughlin, P.G., Raymond, J.S., Murakami, S.R., & Goebert, D. (1987). Drug use among Asian Americans in Hawaii. *Journal of Psychoactive Drugs, 19*(1), 85-94.

Murase, K. (1977). Delivery of social services to Asian Americans. In National Association of Social Workers (Ed.), *The encyclopedia of social work.* New York: Author.

Nakashima, J. (1986). Substance abuse: The dark side of "Nikkei Boulevard." *Rice Paper, 10,* 1-3.

Namkung, P.S. (1976). Asian American drug addiction—the quiet problem. In P. Iiyama, S.M. Nishi & B. Johnson (Eds.), *Drug use and abuse among U.S. minorities.* New York: Praeger.

Newcomb, M.D., Maddahian, E., & Bentler, P.M. (1987). Substance abuse and psychosocial risk factors among teenagers: Associations with sex, age, ethnicity, and type of school. *American Journal of Drug and Alcohol Abuse, 13,* 413-433.

Newlin, D.B. (1989). The skin-flushing response: Autonomic, self-report, and conditioned responses to repeated administrations of alcohol in Asian men. *Journal of Abnormal Psychology, 98,* 421-425.

Newcomb, M.D., Chou, C., Bentler, P.M., & Huba, C.J. (1988). Cognitive motivations for drug use among adolescents: Longitudinal tests of gender differences and predictors of change in drug use. *Journal of Counseling Psychology, 35,* 426-438.

Oetting, E.R., & Beauvais, F. (1987). Peer cluster theory, socialization characteristics, and adolescent drug use: A path analysis. *Journal of Counseling Psychology, 34,* 205-213.

Oetting, E.R., & Beauvais, F. (1989, April). An orthogonal model of cultural identification. Paper presented at National Institute of Drug Abuse workshop on Designing Research to Reduce Drug Abuse among Minority Populations, Washington, D. C.

Phin, J.G., & Phillips, P. (1978). Drug treatment entry patterns and socioeconomic characteristics of Asian American, Native American, and Puerto Rican clients.

In A.J. Schecter (Ed.), *Drug dependence and alcoholism: Vol. 2, Social and Behavioral Issues.* New York: Plenum Press.

Rhodes, J.E., & Jason, L.A. (1988). *Preventing substance abuse among children and adolescents.* New York: Pergamon Press.

Sasao, T. (1989, August). Patterns of substance use and health practices among Japanese Americans in southern California. Paper presented at the third annual conference of Asian American Psychological Association, New Orleans.

Sasao, T. (1990, March). Substance abuse among Asian Pacific Islanders: Current trends and research issues. Paper presented at the conference sponsored by Asian American Recovery Services, "Meeting the Challenge of High-Risk Asian Youth in the 90's," San Francisco, California.

Skager, R., Fisher, D.G., & Maddahian, E. (1986). *A statewide survey of drug and alcohol use among California students in grades 7, 9, and 11.* Sacramento: Office of the Attorney General, Crime Prevention Center.

Skager, R., Frith, S.L., & Maddahian, E. (1989). *Biennial survey of drug and alcohol use among California students in grades 7, 9, and 11: Winter 1987-1988.* Sacramento: Office of the Attorney General, Crime Prevention Center.

Smith, E.M. (1985). Ethnic minorities: Life stress, social support, and mental health issues. *The Counseling Psychologist, 13,* 537-579.

Sue, D. (1987). Use and abuse of alcohol by Asian Americans. *Journal of Psychoactive Drugs, 19*(1), 57-66.

Sue, S. (1977). Community mental health services to minority groups: Some optimism, some pessimism. *American Psychologist, 32,* 616-624.

Sue, S., & Nakamura, C. (1984). An integrative model of physiological and social/psychological factors in alcohol consumption among Chinese and Japanese Americans. *Journal of Drug Issues, 14,* 349-364.

Sue, S., & McKinney, H. (1975). Asian Americans in the community mental health care system. *American Journal of Orthopsychiatry, 45,* 111-118.

Sue, S., & Morishima, J.K. (1982). *The mental health of Asian Americans.* San Francisco: Jossey-Bass.

Sue, D., & Sue, S. (1987). Cultural factors in the clinical assessment of Asian Americans. *Journal of Consulting and Clinical Psychology, 55*(4), 479-495.

Sue, S., Zane, N., & Ito, J. (1979). Alcohol drinking patterns among Asian and Caucasian Americans. *Journal of Cross-Cultural Psychology, 10*(1), 41-56.

Trimble, J.E., Padilla, A., & Bell, C.S. (1987). *Drug abuse among ethnic minorities.* Rockville, MD: National Institute on Drug Abuse.

True, R. (1975). Mental health services in a Chinese American community. In W. Ishikawa & N. Hayashi (Eds.), *Service delivery in Pan Asian Communities.* San Diego: Pacific Asian Coalition.

Tucker, M.B. (1985). U.S. ethnic minorities and drug use: An assessment of the science and practices. *International Journal of the Addictions, 20*(6/7), 1021-1047.

Uba, L. (1982). Meeting the mental health needs of Asian Americans: Mainstream or segregated services. *Professional Psychology, 13,* 215-221.

Weiss, C.H. (1972). *Evaluation research*. Englewood Cliffs, New Jersey: Prentice-Hall.

Willis, T.A., & Shiffman, S. (1985). Coping and substance use: A conceptual framework. In S. Shiffman & T.A. Willis (Eds.), *Coping and substance use*. New York: Academic Press.

Wilson, J.R., McClearn, G.E., & Johnson, R.C. (1978). Ethnic variation in use and effects of alcohol. *Drug & Alcohol Dependence, 3*, 147-151.

Wong, H. (1977, June). Community mental health services and manpower and training concerns of Asian Americans. Paper presented to the President's Commission on Mental Health, San Francisco.

Wong, H.Z. (1985). Substance use and Chinese American youths: Preliminary findings on an interview survey of 123 youths and implications for services and programs. Unpublished Manuscript. S.F.: The Richmond Area Multi-Services, Inc.

Yee, B.E.K., & Thu, N.D. (1987). Correlates of drug use and abuse among Indochinese refugees: Mental health implications. *Journal of Psychoactive Drugs, 19*(1), 77-83.

Zane, N. (1982, August). Methodological problems in the evaluation of indigenous service delivery systems. Papers presented at the American Psychological Association Convention, Washington, D.C.

Zane, N. (1989, August). Parallel services for ethnic minority clients: A review of the evidence. Paper presented at the American Psychological Association Convention, New Orleans.

Zane, N., Sue, S., Hu, L., & Kwon, J.H. (in press). Asian American assertion: A social learning analysis of cultural differences. *Journal of Counseling Psychology*.

Hispanic Substance Use:
Problems in Epidemiology

Ernest L. Chavez
Randall C. Swaim

The Hispanic population of the United States is one of the fastest growing ethnic subpopulations in the country. The 1980 census reported that 14.6 million persons of Hispanic descent reside in the United States, making this group the second largest minority in the country (6.4% of the total population). The U.S. Census Bureau (1987) projects that this population will continue to grow by 45.9% through the year 2000.

Hispanics are also a very heterogeneous population. The composition of the Hispanic population in the U.S. in 1980 was 59.8% Mexican American, 13.8% Puerto Rican, 5.5% Cuban and 20.9% other Hispanic, which includes individuals from Central and South America, and Spain. More current estimates indicate that Mexican Americans account for 62.3% of all U.S. Hispanics (U.S. Census Bureau, 1987). The major Hispanic groups also differ significantly from one another across several demographic characteristics. For example, the median age for Puerto Ricans is 20.7, compared to 23.5 for Mexican Americans, and 33.5 for Cubans. The median age for the white non-Hispanic U.S. population is 32.6 years. The birth rate for various Hispanic groups also differs, with Mexican Americans having 2.9 children per female, Puerto Ricans having 2.1, and Cubans having only 1.3 children per female. The national birth rate for white non-Hispanics is 1.7 children per female and 2.4 for

Ernest L. Chavez and Randall C. Swaim are affiliated with the Tri-Ethnic Center for Prevention Research, Department of Psychology, Colorado State University.

blacks. It is anticipated that by the year 2000 in the southwestern states of Arizona, California, Colorado, New Mexico and Texas, Mexican Americans will constitute a majority of people under the age of 30, and soon thereafter they are expected to become the majority population in the Southwest (WICHE, 1987).

Given the dramatic growth rates and the youthfulness of the Mexican American and Puerto Rican populations, the importance of understanding the drug use and abuse patterns of these groups is self-evident. The need for national epidemiological studies of substance use among the Hispanic population and its subpopulations is high. We will first briefly review general studies of drug use epidemiology, then consider studies specifically devoted to Hispanic substance use, and finally, discuss problems in interpreting Hispanic substance use epidemiology results.

GENERAL STUDIES OF DRUG USE EPIDEMIOLOGY

In a recent article, Oetting, Edwards, and Beauvais (1988) presented a brief history of epidemiological drug studies for the overall population. According to their review, early studies tended to focus on either specific populations of individuals, such as lower class youth, or the use of specific drugs. These early studies fostered a stereotypic impression of the drug user as a member of some deviant group. Prior to the 1960's, substance use *was* a much more deviant form of behavior, and individuals who used drugs were more likely to be generally more deviant. But, the dramatic increase in use among adolescents during the 1960's and 1970's made substance use a more normative, and less deviant behavior. The early stereotypes of the drug user as a lower class, ethnic minority, addicted to opiates no longer applied, even though such attitudes were slow to disappear.

The 1962 White House Conference on Narcotics and Drug Abuse and the Comprehensive Drug Abuse Prevention and Control Act of 1970 initiated early efforts toward data collection of substance use rates on the national level. The first attempts at data collection focused on the medical community with programs such as the Drug

Abuse Warning System (DAWN) and the Client Oriented Data Acquisition Process (CODAP). Minority group members were found to be disproportionately represented in CODAP, with Blacks and Hispanics representing 38.1% of clients seeking substance use treatment, while comprising only 18.1% of the national population. Overrepresentation of minorities was even more dramatic when heroin and PCP use were considered (Schinke, Moncher, Palleja, Zayas, & Schilling, 1988; Tucker, 1985). These early efforts to develop a data base for drug use focused on individuals seeking treatment in public facilities, and therefore, led to biased samples for national epidemiological research.

Minority populations, in general, have been considered to be at higher risk for drug abuse than the general population for well over 100 years (HHS Task Force on Black and Minority Health, 1985). During the 1930's, for example, use of marijuana was associated with the Mexican-American population. This same HHS report cites the conclusions of the 1973 National Commission on Marijuana and Drug Use which stated: "Many observers believe that American minorities, such as the Spanish-speaking, Blacks, and Native Indians have a higher risk potential to drug-dependence in the sense that they are disproportionately poor and have disproportionately higher percentages of drug-dependent persons." However, despite these claims of increased risk for minorities, they were not based on accurate, unbiased estimates of drug use epidemiology among minority populations.

The dramatic socio-cultural changes that swept the country in the 1960's accentuated the need for evaluating the growing use of drugs among youth. One of the key measures of drug use epidemiology among the nation's high school seniors has been the annual Monitoring the Future survey which has been collected since 1976 (Johnston, O'Malley, & Bachman, 1989). Their data show a consistent decline in substance use for several substances over the course of the last decade. Johnston et al.'s survey has included Hispanics, but their numbers have been small, so that no data have been presented for this specific population on an annual basis. Richards (1980) summarized the large number of national studies which were completed in the late 60's and early 70's. Similar to Johnston et al.

(1989), these studies included only very small numbers of Hispanics, making it difficult to accurately evaluate the actual drug use patterns within this population.

HISPANIC SUBSTANCE USE EPIDEMIOLOGY

A number of recent studies have gathered more accurate estimates of substance use epidemiology among the Hispanic population. Unfortunately, the 1982 National Household Survey on Drug Use (NIDA, 1982) provided substance use estimates for only two racial categories, white, and Black and other races. The last two National Household Surveys, (NIDA, 1985; NIDA; 1988), however, have oversampled Blacks and Hispanics to provide more stable estimates for these subpopulations. Each of these surveys indicated that substance use was generally higher among white non-Hispanics compared to Hispanics. The primary exceptions were for cocaine and crack for which use was generally higher among Hispanics.

The Hispanic Health and Nutrition Survey (HHANES, 1987) collected national substance use rates for Hispanics. However, no data were obtained from non-Hispanics for purposes of comparison. Interview data collected between 1982 and 1984 were from 8,021 Hispanics aged 12 to 74. All three major Hispanic subgroups were surveyed: 3,394 Mexican Americans, 1,286 Puerto Ricans, and 555 Cuban Americans. Questions were asked regarding the use of four drugs: marijuana, cocaine, inhalants, and sedatives. Respondents were asked whether they had ever used any of these four drugs; positive responses were followed up with questions about recent use. In general, Cuban Americans were less likely than the other two Hispanic groups to be past or present drug users. Among all Hispanic groups, men were more likely than women to have ever tried drugs. Also, as education level increased, the likelihood of having ever tried drugs also increased. Hispanics who preferred to be interviewed in English were two to three times more likely to have used drugs, and those living at or above the poverty line evidenced higher rates of use. Mexican Americans and Puerto Ricans who were born in the U.S. also reported higher levels of use than those who were born in their native country.

The Texas Commission on Alcohol and Drug Abuse commissioned two large surveys of drug use in the state of Texas (Fredlund, Spence and Maxwell, 1989; Spence, Fredlund and Kavinsky, 1989). The first of these assessed the substance use of 5,156 adults over the age of 18, 1082 of whom were Hispanic. Results from this study indicated that Hispanic adults were the group most likely to report multiple alcohol-related problems. Overall, however, prevalence rates for Hispanics were lower than for whites, but higher than those reported by Blacks. A second Texas study assessed substance use of students in secondary schools with a sample size of 7154 students in grades seven through twelve. Of the entire sample, 2419 were Hispanic. Hispanic students in this study reported the highest rates of use for marijuana and cocaine. However, in another study of Texas high school students (Watts & Wright, 1988), although no significant differences between Hispanics and whites in overall drug use rates were generally found, Hispanic males evidenced higher rates of use for a number of substances.

Oetting and Beauvais (1990) reported on drug survey data collected in classrooms throughout the southwest United States using the American Drug and Alcohol Survey.™ Their sample was comprised of 1512 self-identified Mexican American youth and 446 self-identified Spanish American youth in the eighth through twelfth grades. They concluded that use rates were the same or lower for minority youth when compared to majority youth from this sample. However, those who self-identified as Spanish American reported rates of use more similar to white non-Hispanics, than to Mexican Americans. A recent publication based on data from the National Senior Survey (Bachman, Wallace, O'Malley, Johnston, Kurth, & Neighbors, 1991) presented aggregated data from 1985 to 1989. With the higher number of minority high school seniors from this aggregated sample, comparisons were made between racial/ethnic groups. They concluded that rates of use among Hispanics fell into an intermediate range between Native Americans and whites, whose levels were higher, and Asian Americans and Blacks, for whom rates of use were lower.

RECONCILING CONTRADICTIONS
WITHIN THE LITERATURE

The Hispanic substance use literature cited above contains several contradictory findings. A number of studies indicate that Hispanic substance use is generally lower than use among white non-Hispanic individuals, other studies indicate no differences, and others report that Hispanic use may be higher for some substances. Differences in design or deficiencies in research methodology may partially explain these variations in findings. However, we propose that an alternate explanation for these inconsistent results is that they reflect the inherent complexity of the Hispanic population. The question, "How does Hispanic substance use compare to the use of other population groups?" cannot be answered simply.

The variations and apparent contradictions in much of this literature are due in large part to the cultural diversity and complexity of the Hispanic population. We will identify and discuss key factors that must be taken into account when evaluating reports of Hispanic substance use epidemiology. Failure to consider these factors may lead to misleading and inaccurate conclusions. Key factors that lead to significant variations in substance use epidemiology findings for Hispanics include: (1) gender, (2) Hispanic subgroups, (3) socioeconomic level, (4) community characteristics, (5) educational attainment, and (6) acculturation. The discussion below of each of these factors is not intended to be a comprehensive review for this topic. Rather, we will illustrate how each factor can alter, or even distort findings of Hispanic substance use. (For comprehensive reviews on Hispanic drug use see Austin & Gilbert, 1989; Caetano, 1983; DeLaRosa, Khalsa, & Rouse, 1990; Gilbert & Cervantes, 1986; Morales, 1984; Rouse, 1987; Trimble, Padilla, & Bell, 1987.) The HHANES (1987) study is one of the more comprehensive data sets available for Hispanic drug use, due to its evaluation of multiple factors that are likely to impact substance use differentially. Much of the discussion below will draw examples from this data set.

Gender. A primary finding throughout the Hispanic substance use literature is the disparity in rates of use between males and females. Hispanic males use substances at substantially higher rates than females. This male/female difference is not as pronounced among other ethnic groups. Austin and Gilbert (1989) note in their review, however, that gender disparity in rates of use among Hispanics is not as large among Puerto Ricans, compared to Mexican Americans and Cuban Americans, among youth compared to adults, and for illicit drug use compared to alcohol use.

Results from recent National Household Surveys (NIDA, 1985; NIDA, 1988) and HHANES (1987) support these findings on gender differences, but also demonstrate that interactions with other variables can affect their magnitude. The 1988 National Household Survey (NIDA, 1988) presents drug use epidemiology for whites and individual Hispanic subgroups. Illustrative examples of results on male/female disparity are presented in Table 1. These are combined results for ages 12 to 35 and older. For lifetime prevalence for alcohol use, 87% of Hispanic males reported having ever tried, compared to 72% for females, a male/female disparity of 15%. For whites the gender disparity was 8% (91% males, and 83% females). Gender differences were even more pronounced among Hispanics for last month use of alcohol. A total of 62% of Hispanic males reported last month use compared to 37% of Hispanic females, a 25% disparity. Among whites, 61% of males reported last month use compared to 50% for females, an 11% disparity. The major difference between ethnic groups was accounted for by the lower rate of alcohol use for Hispanic females. Gender disparities for illicit drugs were also larger for Hispanics compared to whites, but these differences were not as great as for alcohol. Gender disparity for lifetime prevalence of marijuana was 5% for whites, compared to 13% for Hispanics. No differences were found in rates for current use of marijuana. Even fewer differences existed for lifetime prevalence and last month use of cocaine.

Data from the HHANES (1987) study show that gender differences are also likely to vary by Hispanic subgroup and type of illicit drug. Rates of use by gender by Hispanic subgroup, taken from HHANES (1987), were compared to rates by gender for the entire U.S. population based on estimates from the 1982 Household Survey (NIDA, 1982). For lifetime prevalence of marijuana use, ever tried rates for each Hispanic subgroup by gender were as follows: Mexican Americans (Males, 54%; Females, 28%), Puerto

Table 1. Gender Disparity in Substance Use Between Whites and Hispanics (National Household Survey, 1988; Ages 12-35+)

Alcohol

	Ever Tried (%)		Used Last Month (%)	
	Whites	Hispanics	Whites	Hispanics
Males	91	87	61	62
Females	83	72	50	37
Gender Disparity (%)	8	15	11	25

Marijuana

	Ever Tried (%)		Used Last Month (%)	
	Whites	Hispanics	Whites	Hispanics
Males	36	34	8	8
Females	31	21	4	4
Gender Disparity (%)	5	13	4	4

Cocaine

	Ever Tried (%)		Used Last Month (%)	
	Whites	Hispanics	Whites	Hispanics
Males	13	14	2	4
Females	9	8	1	2
Gender Disparity (%)	4	6	1	2

Ricans (Males, 52%; Females, 36%), and Cuban Americans (Males 28%; Females 13%). Estimates for the overall U.S. population by gender were 38% for males and 29% for females. For lifetime prevalence of marijuana use, the gender disparity was largest for Mexican Americans (26%), moderate for Puerto Ricans and Cuban Americans (16%, 15%) and least for the overall population (9%). By comparison, gender disparities by Hispanic subgroup were minimal for lifetime prevalence of cocaine. The above results indicate that gender disparities are larger among Hispanics than whites, but that these differences will vary by Hispanic subgroup, type of drug, and measure of drug use.

The results cited above were based on population estimates of subjects age 12 to 35 and older. Gender disparities among Hispanics are likely to be the greatest, however, among older Hispanics. The trend toward greater male/female disparity with increasing age is not only observable when youth and adults are compared; it can also be seen within adolescence. We conducted a three-year study of Mexican American substance use in which a national probability sample of 8th and 12th grade Mexican Americans and white non-Hispanics were surveyed (Chavez & Swaim, submitted for publication). Further analysis of this data set (Swaim, Chavez, Oetting, Beauvais, & Edwards, manuscript in progress) shows that the male/female discrepancy for alcohol use among Mexican Americans increases from 8th grade to 12th grade. Analysis of variance conducted on an alcohol involvement scale yielded a significant Ethnicity X Gender X Grade interaction (F = 17.206; df = 1,8077; p. = .000). Hispanic 8th grade females were similar to Hispanic 8th grade males in their level of alcohol use. However, these two groups were more distinct by the 12th grade, with female use being substantially lower than male use. This effect was not present among white non-Hispanic youth. The three way interaction was not significant for drunk involvement, marijuana involvement, cocaine involvement, or other drug involvement. There appears, then, to be a trend for alcohol use among Mexican Americans, of increasing male/female disparity in rates of use. At the 8th grade level, males and females are similar in use. Gender disparity is more prevalent by 12th grade and reaches the highest level of magnitude when Mexican American adults are compared. It should be noted, however, that this may not be a simple age effect. Rate of school dropout and level of acculturation may partially account for this trend. Also, it is not known what differences may exist among 8th and 12th grade Puerto Rican or Cuban American students.

Hispanic Subgroups. The heterogeneous nature of the Hispanic population within the U.S. demands that drug use epidemiology be conducted separately on each Hispanic subgroup. Differences between groups are sufficiently large that important variations in rates and patterns of use are lost when subgroups are aggregated. For example, we demonstrated above that gender disparities are not uniform across Hispanics, but will vary by subgroup. Results from HHANES (1987) further identify important variations in rates of use by Hispanic subgroup by type of drug use. For the combined sample (ages 12-44), lifetime prevalence rates of marijuana use for Mexican Americans and Puerto Ricans were very similar (42% and 43%), whereas use for Cuban Americans was much lower (20%). The same general pattern emerged for last month marijuana use. A different pattern emerges, however, for cocaine use. Puerto Ricans reported the highest level of lifetime prevalence for cocaine (22%), compared to Mexican Americans and Cuban Americans whose levels of use were similar (11% and 9%). Similar results emerged for current cocaine use.

These data, however, when aggregated for age, disguise important developmental differences in rates of use. A comparison of Mexican American and Puerto Rican lifetime prevalence for marijuana (HHANES, 1987) will illustrate this point. At younger ages (12 to 17), more Mexican Americans have tried marijuana than Puerto Ricans (31% vs. 26%). This trend reverses for older individuals (18 to 34), for whom, Puerto Rican ever tried rates for marijuana are higher. Among the oldest group surveyed (35 to 44), rates of use were more stable and rates of use between Mexican Americans and Puerto Ricans were similar (27% vs. 25%). Developmental patterns, unique to specific Hispanic subgroups as those described above, can help identify key periods of risk for initiation of use. Critical time periods for initiation are useful in the development of prevention efforts. Relevant subgroup differences are invaluable data that can lead to appropriate tailoring of programs based on specific group needs. For example, based on the HHANES data cited above, it appears that marijuana prevention programs might need to begin earlier for Mexican American youth, compared to Puerto Ricans.

Socioeconomic Status. Austin and Gilbert (1989) conclude that the relationship between SES level and rate of substance use is weak and inconsistent. They add, however, that the effect of economic status "is likely dependent on the interaction of multiple factors" (p. 7). We will illustrate how interactions can affect Hispanic drug use epidemiology with data taken again from HHANES (1987). SES by Hispanic Subgroup by Drug by Prevalence Measure of Use will be discussed. Among Mexican Americans, higher SES level is associated with a higher lifetime prevalence for marijuana. For use last month, however, higher SES level is associated with lower prevalence of marijuana. The patterns for Puerto Ricans and Cuban Americans are consistent across both lifetime prevalence and last month use; higher SES level is associated with higher marijuana use. A different pattern emerges for lifetime prevalence of inhalants. Whereas higher SES is related to higher lifetime marijuana use for Mexican Americans, it relates to lower lifetime prevalence for inhalants. For Puerto Ricans, higher SES is associated with higher lifetime inhalant use. The effects of age on these relationships are not available from the HHANES (1987) data set; consideration of this factor would add another layer of complexity to this question.

No generalized relationship exists, then, between SES level and Hispanic substance use. It is likely to vary by Hispanic subgroup, type of drug, and type of drug use measure. Past findings of a weak relationship between SES and substance use are, perhaps, due to the effects of differences occurring in opposite directions which are then disguised when aggregated samples are used for analysis.

Community Characteristics. Drug use has historically been viewed as a big city problem, and past findings from a number of sources have supported this appraisal. Reports during the last few years, however, have indicated that rural areas have become increasingly at risk for substance use levels that approach, or may even exceed rates of use (for some substances) found in large cities (Peters, Beauvais, Edwards, & Oetting, 1989; Swaim, Beauvais, Edwards, & Oetting, 1986). Despite the narrowing of the gap between urban and rural locations, inner city neighborhoods (barrios, ghettos) remain at exceedingly high risk for high rates of drug use (Austin & Gilbert, 1989; Padilla et al., 1979; Perez et al., 1980).

When levels of substance use among youth in the Mexican American barrio are compared to results for the overall Hispanic population (HHANES, 1987), the severity of the substance use problem within the barrio is underscored. Padilla et al. (1979) found lifetime prevalence rates of 42% for marijuana in a barrio in East

Los Angeles. This compared to a rate of 31% for overall Hispanics from HHANES (1987). This difference is sizable, but not extraordinary. Much larger differences were noted, however, for current use of marijuana. HHANES (1987) reported an overall Hispanic use of marijuana in the last month of 10%. This compares to Padilla et al.'s (1979) finding of 27% of barrio youth who reported use of marijuana in the previous week. Padilla et al.'s (1979) use of a more restrictive measure for current use, use in the last week, would normally yield lower rates than a measure of use in last month. Despite the use of this more restrictive measure, rates of marijuana use in the barrio were substantially higher than those reported by overall Hispanic youth. Even greater differences were reported for inhalant use. Lifetime prevalence for inhalants among overall Hispanics was 5% compared to 27% among barrio youth. Current inhalant use rates were 0.7% for overall Hispanics and 13% for barrio youth.

Because of their isolation from other sources of influence, small, rural areas may develop idiosyncratic patterns of substance use, leading to large variations in rates of use from one rural area to another (Swaim, Beauvais, Edwards, & Oetting, 1986). Chavez, Beauvais, & Oetting (1986) found within one rural town in the Southwest that rates of Hispanic substance use (alcohol, marijuana, uppers, downers, tranquilizers) were substantially higher than rates of use for the overall U.S. Population (NIDA, 1982). Given the wide variability in drug use within rural areas, these results should not be generalized to all rural Hispanic drug use. They do reflect, however, that a linear relationship between community size and rate of drug use does not always exist.

Chavez et al. (1986) also compared substance use rates in this small town to those reported by Padilla et al. (1979) in his barrio sample. Lifetime prevalence of alcohol use in the rural sample (85%) was significantly higher than that reported in the barrio sample (51%). Alternatively, lifetime inhalant use was significantly higher in the barrio, compared to the rural sample (27% vs. 13% respectively).

The susceptibility of rural areas to localized epidemics of substance use, sometimes of a single substance, are further illustrated in the Chavez et al. (1986) study. As noted above in the section on gender, Mexican American males tend to use substances (especially alcohol) at substantially higher rates than their female counterparts. Chavez et al. (1986) found, however, that with the exception of alcohol, smokeless tobacco, and inhalants, Mexican American females reported the highest rate of use (including higher rates than male and female anglo students) for 15 different substances. These females' lifetime alcohol use was higher than that of Mexican American males (88% vs. 82%), and second only to white males (95%).

The above set of results illustrate the importance of considering community characteristics in the evaluation of Hispanic substance use. The aggregation of overall Hispanic data will obscure important community differences. It is likely that the highest rates of use will be found in inner city populations. However, specific communities may evidence rates of use, for specific substances, even higher than that among barrio populations. Most study of community characteristics, to date, has been conducted with Mexican Americans. Further study needs to be done on how community characteristics affect drug use among other Hispanic subgroups.

Educational Attainment. Drug use epidemiology conducted on student populations presents a unique set of challenges. One factor that must be taken into account is the underestimate of school-based surveys for the overall school-aged population due to lack of inclusion of school dropouts. Substance use rates have been found to be generally higher for school dropouts than for those who remain in school (Annis & Watson, 1975; Johnston, 1973; Mensch & Kandel, 1988; Winburn & Hayes, 1974). Epidemiology estimates are further confounded when different ethnic groups are compared, since there is often a differential dropout rate between groups. Hispanic youth are at particularly high risk for school dropout. Past reports indicate the rate of dropout to be as high as 45% among Hispanics in some locations (ASPIRA, 1983; Wetzel, 1987; Rumberger, 1983). A recent report from the American Council on Education (?) indicated a dropout rate of 44% for Hispanics. However, there was substantial variation among the three major Hispanic subgroups. The highest rate of school dropout was among Mexican Americans (57%), followed by Puerto Ricans (46%) and Cubans (37%). These rates compare to a dropout rate among whites of 18%. In an ongoing study of Mexican American and white non-Hispanic dropouts, Chavez, Edwards, & Oetting (1989) found substantially higher rates of substance use among dropouts from both ethnic groups, compared to matched controls of students not at academic risk. These were preliminary data from a continuing project, and due to small sample sizes, comparisons could not be made between ethnic groups. However, within ethnicity there was a consistent pattern of higher drug use among dropouts. For example, among Mexican American males, 77% of dropouts reported lifetime usage of marijuana, compared to 57% of controls. Lifetime prevalence of cocaine use was reported by 32% of dropouts, compared to 18% of controls. Results among Mexican American females were even more dramatic. Lifetime marijuana use was reported by 83% of dropouts, compared to 49% of controls. For cocaine, 43% of dropouts reported having ever tried, compared to 13% of controls. Differences between white non-Hispanic dropouts and controls appeared to be of even larger magnitude, with dropout usage substantially higher than controls.

Due to the higher number of Hispanic dropouts, then, school-based surveys are likely to yield estimates of use that seriously underestimate levels of use for all Hispanic youth. This effect will not be as great among white youth, for whom rates of school dropout are substantially lower. An example of this dropout effect can be seen in the Mexican American drug use epidemiology cited above (Chavez & Swaim, submitted for publication). Surveys of drug and alcohol use were conducted with a national probability sample of 8th and 12th grade Mexican American and white non-Hispanic students. Mexican American 8th graders reported generally higher rates of use than white non-Hispanics based on lifetime prevalence, use in last month, and total drug involvement. They also reported higher frequencies of high risk drug behaviors. This pattern was reversed, however, among 12th grade students, for whom white non-Hispanic rates of use were higher. These results could be explained by differing developmental patterns of drug acquisition between these two groups. That is, substance use may begin at an earlier age among Mexican Americans, with white non-Hispanic use subsequently surpassing Mexican American use in later years. However, drug acquisition curves presented by Chavez and

Swaim (submitted for publication) argue against this hypothesis. The most likely explanation for the differences in rates of use between ethnic groups from 8th to 12th grade is the larger percentage of Mexican Americans who drop out of school and who are not reflected in the 12th grade sample. As we learn more about the comparative rates of drug use among dropouts, it may become possible to utilize a dropout correction factor that will account for this effect. Until then, however, evaluation of school-based surveys must consider the effects of this factor.

Acculturation. Numerous studies have identified differences in Hispanic substance use that are associated with varying levels of acculturation (e.g., Amaro, Whitaker, Coleman, & Herrin, 1990; Caetano, 1987a, 1987b; Santisteban & Szapocznik, 1982). Measurement of acculturation has been obtained using both direct and indirect indicators. For example, indirect measures include language (preference for Spanish vs. English), origin of birth (e.g., Mexico vs. U.S.), and number of generations with residence in the U.S. Data from HHANES (1987) indicate that Hispanics who preferred to be interviewed in English were two to three times more likely to have used drugs. Velez and Ungemack (1989) found that adolescents in Puerto Rico were less likely than Puerto Ricans residing in New York to use drugs. Also, the longer their residence in New York, the higher the probability of substance use. Similar findings were reported in HHANES (1987). Mexican Americans and Puerto Ricans born in the U.S. were more likely to have used drugs than those born in their native country.

These external measures based on language usage, place of birth, and so forth, provide an indicator of identification with one's culture. Self report measures have also been used to assess cultural identification. Oetting and Beauvais (in press) have developed a new approach to the measurement of cultural identification, orthogonal cultural identification theory, that allows the subject to independently express identification or lack of identification with several cultures. Rather than higher identification with one culture necessarily lowering identification with another culture, high identification (or low identification) can be endorsed simultaneously for multiple cultures.

Tests of orthogonal cultural identification theory have indicated that, while not strongly related to substance use, cultural identification does differentially affect drug use patterns among Hispanic youth. Analyses of variance conducted on a sample of 7-12th grade Mexican American youth indicated that identification with Hispanic culture was not associated with level of substance use ($F = .46$, $df = 2$, $p = .631$). Those Mexican American youth who showed high Anglo identification, however, were more likely to use drugs ($F = 4.91$, $df = 2$, $p = .008$).

The effects of acculturation also interact with other variables. Amaro et al. (1990) found differences in the effect of acculturation by type of drug, Hispanic subgroup, gender, and education, based on data from HHANES. The results described below are for subjects age 20 and older. For marijuana use, Mexican Americans whose language preference was English were eight times more likely to have used marijuana in the last year, compared to those whose language preference was Spanish. The effect was not as strong among Puerto Ricans. Those who preferred English were five times more likely to have used marijuana in the last year. There were interaction effects for both Hispanic subgroups. Among Mexican Americans, the language preference effect was stronger for females, for those subjects with less education, and for those who were married. Among Puerto Ricans, this effect was stronger among those less educated.

For cocaine use in the last year, the effects of language preference among Mexican Americans were substantial. Those preferring to use English were 25 times more likely to have used cocaine. Again, this effect was not as strong among Puerto Ricans. Last year cocaine use was twice as likely among those preferring English. Interactions were again found for the language preference effect which was stronger among Mexican Americans born in the U.S., and among those with less education. For Puerto Ricans it was stronger among males and for those subjects born in Puerto Rico.

Caetano (1987a, 1987b) has found similar relationships for acculturation with alcohol use. Among Hispanic males, higher acculturation is associated with lower alcohol abstention and higher frequency and quantity of drinking. However, he found a U-shaped function for frequent heavy drinking which occurred highest among low and high acculturated males. The relationship of acculturation to drinking may be even stronger among females. Women in the high acculturation group were 16 times more likely to be frequent high maximum drinkers (drinks weekly or more often and has 5 or more drinks at least once a year). These effects interact with age, differentially by gender. Among males, acculturation effects occurred mostly for older men. There appear to be no age by acculturation interaction effects for Hispanic females.

CONCLUSION

The results discussed above emphasize the complexity of licit and illict substance use among Hispanics. Use will vary depending on type of drug, gender, socioeconomic status, Hispanic subgroup, community of residence characteristics, educational attainment, and acculturation. Estimates of Hispanic substance use that do not take these characteristics into account are likely to obscure important differences that occur among disaggregated samples. The ability to consider each of these factors, however, requires large population studies of sufficient N so that individual cells are large enough for analysis. For example, in order to consider each of the factors described above, the design would look like the following: Gender (2) X SES (3) X Hispanic Subgroup (3) X Acculturation (3) X Educational Attainment (2) X Community Characteristics (3). This design assumes three levels of SES (high, medium, low), three Hispanic subgroups (Mexican American, Puerto Rican, Cuban American), three levels of acculturation (high, medium, low), two levels of educational attainment (dropout, non-dropout), and three levels of community characteristics (inner city, urban non-inner city, rural). In order to obtain 30 subjects per cell, a minimum of 9720 subjects would be required. This number assumes, of course, that each cell is filled with an equal number for each factor. The likelihood of this is not high since the characteristics denoted by each cell are probably not equally distributed. For example, there may be only half as many low acculturated females of high SES. Despite the problems of obtaining a complete sample as described above, this design illustrates the type of drug use epidemiology study that is needed to answer the questions posed by the discussion above.

The answer to the question, "How does Hispanic drug use compare to other ethnic groups," is complex, and dependent on multiple factors. Recognition of this complexity will help avoid simple, unsophisticated conclusions about a most important social problem.

REFERENCES

Amaro, H., Whitaker, R., Coleman, G., & Herrin, T. (1990). Acculturation and marijuana and cocaine use: Findings from HHANES 1982-84. *American Journal of Public Health, 80*, Supplement, 1-7. .

Annis, H.M., & Watson, C. (1975). Drug use and school dropouts: A longitudinal study. *Canadian Counsellor, 9*, 155-162.

ASPIRA. (1983). *Racial and ethnic high school dropout rates in New York City.* Bronx, NY: ASPIRA of New York, Inc.

Austin, G., & Gilbert, M.J. (1989). Substance abuse among Latino youth. *Prevention Research Update*, No. 3. Los Alamitos, CA: Southwest Regional Educational Laboratory.

Bachman, J.G., Wallace, J.M., O'Malley, P.M., Johnston, L.D., Kurth, C.L., & Neighbors, H.W. (1991). Racial/ethnic differences in smoking, drinking, and illicit drug use among American high school seniors, 1976-89. *American J. of Public Health, 81*(3), 372-377.

Caetano, R. (1983). Drinking patterns and alcohol problems among Hispanics in the U.S.: A review. *Drug and Alcohol Dependence, 12*, 37-59.

Caetano, R. (1987a). Acculturation and drinking patterns among U.S. Hispanics. *British J. of the Addictions, 82*, 789-799.

Caetano, R. (1987b). Acculturation, drinking, and social settings among U.S. Hispanics. *Drug and Alcohol Dependence, 19*, 215-226.

Chavez, E.L., Beauvais, F., & Oetting, E.R. (1986). Drug use by small town Mexican American youth: A pilot study. *Hispanic J. of Behavioral Sciences, 8*(3), 243-258.

Chavez, E.L., Edwards, R., & Oetting, E.R. (1989). Mexican American and white American dropouts' drug use, health status, and involvement in violence. *Public Health Reports, 104*(6), 594-604.

Chavez, E.L., & Swaim, R.C. (submitted for publication). Epidemiology of Mexican American adolescent substance use: A comparison of Mexican American and white non-Hispanic 8th and 12th grade students.

DeLaRosa, M.R., Khalsa, J.H., & Rouse, B.A. (1990). Hispanics and illicit drug use: A review of recent findings. *International J. of the Addictions, 25*(6), 665-691.

Fredlund, E.V., Spence, R., & Maxwell, J.C. (1989). *Substance use among students in Texas secondary schools, 1988.* Austin, Texas: Texas Commission on Alcohol and Drug Abuse, January.

Gilbert, M. Jean, & Cervantes, R.C. (1986). Patterns and practices of alcohol use among Mexican Americans: A comprehensive review. *Hispanic J. of Behavioral Sciences*, *8*(1), 1-87.

Johnston, F. (1973). *Drugs and American youth*. Ann Arbor, MI: The University of Michigan Institute for Social Research.

Johnston, L.D., O'Malley, P.M., & Bachman, J.G. (1989). *Drug use, drinking, and smoking: National survey results from high school, college, and young adult populations, 1975-1988*. National Institute on Drug Abuse. DHHS Pub. No. (ADM) 89-1638. Washington, D.C.: U.S. Gov't. Printing Office.

Mensch, B.S., & Kandel, D.B. (1988). Dropping out of high school and drug involvement. *Sociology of Education*, *61*, 95-113.

Morales, A. (1984). Substance abuse and Mexican American youth: An overview. *J. of Drug Issues*, *14*(2), 297-311.

National Institute on Drug Abuse. (1982). *National survey on drug abuse: Main findings 1982*. DHHS Pub. No. (ADM) 83-1263. Washington, D.C.: U.S. Gov't. Printing Office.

National Institute on Drug Abuse (1985). *National household survey on drug abuse: Population estimates 1985*. DHHS Pub. No. (ADM) 87-1539. Washington, D.C.: U.S. Gov't. Printing Office.

National Institute on Drug Abuse (1987). *Use of selected drugs among Hispanics: Mexican Americans, Puerto Ricans, and Cuban-Americans: Findings from the Hispanic Health and Nutrition Examination Survey* (HHANES). DHHS Pub. No. (ADM) 87-1527. Washington, D.C.: U.S. Gov't. Printing Office.

National Institute on Drug Abuse (1989). *National household survey on drug abuse: Population estimates 1988*. DHHS Pub. No. (ADM) 89-1636. Washington, D.C.: U.S. Gov't. Printing Office.

Oetting, E.R., & Beauvais, F. (1990). Adolescent drug use: Findings of national and local surveys. *J. of Consulting and Clinical Psychology*, *58*(4), 385-394.

Oetting, E.R., & Beauvais, F. (in press). Orthogonal cultural identification theory: The cultural identification of minority adolescents.

Oetting, E.R., Edwards, R.W., & Beauvais, F. (1988). Drugs and Native-American youth. *Drugs & Society*, *3*(1/2), 5-38.

Padilla, E.R., Padilla, A.M., Morales, A.P., Olmedo, E.L., & Ramirez, R. (1979). Inhalant, marijuana, and alcohol abuse among barrio children and adolescents. *International J. of the Addictions*, *14*(7), 945-964.

Perez, R., Padilla, A.M., Ramirez, A., Ramirez, R., & Rodriguez, M. (1980). Correlates and changes over time in drug and alcohol use within a barrio population. *American J. of Community Psychology*, *8*, 621-636.

Peters, V., Beauvais, F., Edwards, R., & Oetting, E.R. (1989). Rural drug prevention must target local needs. *OSAP High Risk Youth Update*, *2*(3), 2-4.

Richards, L.G. (1980). The epidemiology of youthful drug use. In Scarpitti and Batesman (Eds.), *Drugs and the Youth Culture*. Beverly Hills: Sage Publications.

Rouse, B. (1987). Substance abuse in Mexican Americans. In Rodriguez, R. and Coleman, M.T. (Eds.), *Mental Health Issues of the Mexican Origin Population in Texas*. Austin: Hogg Foundation for Mental Health, Univ. of Texas at Austin.

Rumberger, R. (1983). Dropping out of high school: The influence of race, sex, and family background. *American Educational Research Journal*, 20(2), 199-220.

Santisteban, D., & Szapocznik, J. (1982). Substance abuse disorders among Hispanics: A focus on prevention. In Becerra, R.M. et al. (Eds.). *Mental Health and Hispanic Americans: Clinical Perspectives*. New York: Grune & Stratton. pp. 83-100.

Schinke, S., Moncher, M.S., Palleja, J., Zayas, L.H., & Schilling, R.F. (1988). Hispanic youth, substance abuse, and stress: Implications for prevention research. *International J. of the Addictions*, 23(8), 809-826.

Spence, R., Fredlund, E.V., & Kavinsky, J. (1989). *1988 Texas Survey of Substance Use Among Adults*. Austin, Texas: Texas Commission on Alcohol and Drug Abuse.

Swaim, R.C., Beauvais, F., Edwards, R., & Oetting, E.R. (1986). Adolescent drug use in three small rural communities in the Rocky Mountain region. *J. of Drug Education*, 16(1), 57-74.

Swaim, R.C., Chavez, E.L., Oetting, E.R., Beauvais, F., & Edwards, R.W. (unpublished manuscript). The effects of gender, ethnicity, and grade on Mexican American and white non-Hispanic adolescent substance use.

Trimble, J.E., Padilla, A., & Bell, C. (1987). *Drug Abuse Among Ethnic Minorities*. NIDA Office of Science Monograph. DHHS Pub. No. (ADM) 87-1474. Washington, D.C.: U.S. Gov't. Printing Office.

Tucker, M.B. (1985). U.S. ethnic minorities and drug abuse: An assessment of the science and practice. *International J. of the Addictions*, 20, 1021-1047.

U.S. Bureau of the Census. (1987). *The Hispanic Population in the United States: March 1986 and 1987 (Advance Report)*. Series P-20, No. 416. Washington, D.C.: U.S. Gov't. Printing Office.

U.S. Department of Health and Human Services. (1985). *Report of the Secretary Task Force on Black and Minority Health*. DHHS Pub. No. (ADM) 85-487. Washington, D.C.: U.S. Gov't. Printing Office.

Velez, C.M., & Ungemack, J.A. (1989). Drug use among Puerto Rican youth: An exploration of generational status differences. *Social Science & Medicine*, 29(6), 779-791.

Watts, W.D., & Wright, L.S. (1988). *A comparison of delinquency, drug use, and related factors among Hispanic and white adolescents*. A report to the Office of Juvenile Justice and Delinquency Prevention. San Marcos, Texas: Southwest Texas State University.

Western Interstate Commission for Higher Education (1987). *From Minority to Majority: Education and the Future of the Southwest*. Boulder, CO: WICHE.

Wetzel, S.R. (1987). *American youth: A statistical snapshot*. Washington, D.C.: William T. Grant Foundation on Youth & America's Future.

Winburn, G.M., & Hays, J.R. (1974). Dropouts: A study of drug use. *J. of Drug Education*, 4(2), 249-254.

Behavioral and Psychological Profiles of Cocaine Users upon Treatment Entry: Ethnic Comparisons

Felipe G. Castro
Elizabeth H. Barrington
Erica V. Sharp
Lino S. Dial
Bu Wang
Richard Rawson

SUMMARY. This descriptive study examined the health-related profile of 112 regular users of cocaine who were recently admitted to an inpatient or to an outpatient drug treatment program. Subjects reported on their health status during the days immediately preceding their entry into treatment. The health profile of these addicted cocaine users was examined in terms of behavioral, psychological and psychiatric measures of health. A *lifestyle shift hypothesis* was examined in these addicted cocaine users using norms from non-addicted "episodic" cocaine users for the behavioral and psychological measures, while using psychiatric norms for the psychiatric measures. This lifestyle shift hypothesis postulates illness progres-

Felipe G. Castro is Director of the Hispanic Research Center, and Associate Professor in the Department of Psychology, Arizona State University. Elizabeth H. Barrington, Erica V. Sharp, Lino S. Dial, and Bu Wang are affiliated with the San Diego State University. Richard Rawson is affiliated with the MATRIX Center.

This research is supported by grant No. DA 05661 from the National Institute on Drug Abuse. We wish to thank the Alvarado Parkway Institute and the MATRIX Center for their participation in this study. The assistance of Debra Gaskin and Chere' Smith-Southerland in the preparation of this manuscript is warmly appreciated.

Requests for reprints should be addressed to Felipe G. Castro, Hispanic Research Center, Arizona State University, Tempe, AZ 85287-2702.

231

sion with greater levels of addiction, a progression manifested by greater severity of dysfunction across several areas of life function. In support of this hypothesis, addicted chronic cocaine users, when compared with episodic, nonaddicted users, exhibited a remarkable unhealthy shift in lifestyle on several lifestyle measures, thus illustrating the manner in which addiction to cocaine appears to deteriorate health status in comparison with a pre-addiction stage of cocaine use or abuse.

Analyses of these health profiles when stratified by ethnicity (Black, Hispanic, and non-Hispanic White) revealed similar patterns of deviation from normalcy in all groups, although the Hispanics exhibited the greatest unhealthy deviations. Further analyses of the Hispanic group by acculturation status indicated that lower acculturation was associated with a worse health status. Implications for evaluation and treatment are discussed.

The point in time when a person that abuses illicit drugs realizes that treatment is necessary is often a low point in that person's life (Washton, 1986). When entering treatment most cocaine users experience a variety of ill effects including somatic distress, malaise, feelings of paranoia. Often they have also lost or jeopardized a job, spouse, or other significant social relationship (Washton & Gold, 1987). Moreover, the drug user's progressive life focus on obtaining illicit drugs usually leads to abandoning or ignoring other life obligations and activities (Westermeyer, 1984). Accordingly, a precipitous and unhealthy "shift" in lifestyle is expected among persons who become so addicted to drugs that treatment is necessary (Marlatt & Gordon, 1985). While this unhealthy shift in lifestyle has been postulated, it has not been examined empirically in addicted drug users including users of cocaine.

Prior evidence from community-based studies suggests that health-related behaviors *do* occur in meaningful clusters or syndromes (Donovan & Jessor, 1985; Harris & Guten, 1979; Hayes, Stacy & DiMatteo, 1984; Istvan & Matarazzo, 1984). In a study of "episodic" cocaine users (early stage, unaddicted users) that were compared with their non-user peers, these early stage, episodic cocaine users exhibited higher frequencies in the consumption of cups of coffee per day and alcoholic beverages per week, along with lower frequencies of relaxation, of healthy meals consumed, and lower scores on indices of daily planning and organization (Castro, Newcomb & Cadish, 1987). These results suggested the occurrence of an unhealthy shift in lifestyle, even among these early stage cocaine users, individuals who reported "enjoying" cocaine use and who still felt in control of their use. Such individuals were likely abusing cocaine, although they had not yet progressed to a stage of dependence that includes increased tolerance, withdrawal symptoms and psychological distress. Similarly, in a community-based study of cigarette smokers and nonsmokers, progressively greater levels of cigarette smoking were related to a lower frequency of healthy behaviors, to a higher frequency of unhealthy behaviors, and to lower levels of intentions to take actions that reduce the risk of cardiovascular disease (Castro, Newcomb, McCreary & Baezconde-Garbanati, 1989).

Thus, with a progressively greater consumption of illicit drugs to the point of addiction/dependence, significant and unhealthy shifts in lifestyle would be expected and have been suggested by previous studies. This unhealthy lifestyle shift, if observed among drug addicts would suggest the need to develop a treatment that addresses various life domains during their recovery from drug abuse. In other words, complete recovery from cocaine addiction may require changes in behavior that transcend a mere abstinence from the use of cocaine and other illicit drugs (Marlatt, 1985). In principle, healthy drug rehabilitation involves normalcy, and/or improvement beyond prior addiction levels across several domains such as the behavioral (exercise, diet), the psychological (beliefs and attitudes) and the psychiatric (emotional distress) lifestyle domains.

The present descriptive study explores the occurrence of unhealthy shifts in selected lifestyle domains (behavioral, psychological, psychiatric) among persons addicted to cocaine who have entered into treatment for their addiction. If progressively greater addiction to cocaine produces greater levels of somatic, psychological and psychiatric illness, then addicted users of cocaine (later stage users who have developed a dependence on cocaine) should exhibit remarkable deviations from normalcy when compared with episodic, earlier stage users of cocaine. Thus, in the present study, we propose a *lifestyle shift hypothesis*, where relative to episodic (not yet addicted) cocaine users, chronic daily (or near-daily) addicted users of cocaine should exhibit remarkable deviations from "normalcy" on health-related measures of behavioral, psychological and psychiatric status.

METHOD

Subjects

The subjects in this study were 112 addicted (chronic, daily or near-daily) users of cocaine who entered a formal inpatient or outpatient drug treatment program in Southern California. In this sample, addiction to cocaine was generally indicated by the person's need for inpatient or outpatient treatment. More specifically, addiction was indicated from the presence of at least three symptomatic criteria necessary for the diagnosis of psychoactive substance dependence. These DSM-IIIR criteria are: (a) substance use in larger amounts or over a longer period of time than the person had intended, (b) unsuccessful efforts to cut down, (c) considerable time spent in procuring the substance, (d) substance use on the job or when discharging role obligations, (e) a reduction of social activities because of substance use, (f) continued use despite the occurrence of problems, (g) increased tolerance, (h) characteristic withdrawal symptoms and (i) substance use to relieve withdrawal symptoms (American Psychiatric Association, 1987). Upon entry into treatment, all subjects were diagnosed as having cocaine dependence of moderate to severe levels, and to be in need of treatment.

This subsample is part of a larger sample of cocaine and methamphetamine users interviewed shortly after they entered an inpatient or an outpatient drug treatment center. Table 1 shows the demographic characteristics of this sample. This sample of addicted cocaine users (n = 112) when compared with a sample of episodic users (n = 25) were somewhat older, consisted primarily of males, and had a lower level of education. As expected, the addicted users' mean frequency of cocaine use episodes per month was considerably higher (M = 11.30) than for the episodic user reference group (M = 6.30) (see Table 1). Thus, the observed behavioral profiles

Table 1

Characteristics of Addicted Cocaine Users and of the
Episodic Users Reference Group

Characteristic	Addicted Users (n=121)	Episodic Users (n=25)	Test of Significance
Age			
M	30.70	25.92	t = 3.89***
SD	6.39	4.66	
Range	(19 to 51)	(20 to 36)	
Sex			
Men	71	7	X^2= 9.05**
Women	41	18	
Education			
High School	70	8	X^2= 11.32**
College	40	14	
Graduate School	2	3	
Cocaine Episodes Per Month			
M	11.30	6.30	t = 2.50*
SD	14.18	7.43	
Range	0 to 90	0 to 30	

*p<.05.   **p<.01.   ***p<.001.

contrasting the addicted users with the episodic users might be influenced not only by level of cocaine use/addiction, but also by group nonequivalances in age, gender and educational level. While the groups differed on these demographic variables, the most important source of difference was the level of cocaine use as measured by frequency of use per month, where the addicted group exhibited a usage level (episodes per month) that was nearly twice that of the episodic users. In addition, the episodic users reported that they still ''enjoyed using cocaine,'' and that they had a hard time turning down cocaine, whereas the addicted users no longer enjoyed nor wanted cocaine, yet based on their dependency, they were unable to stop using cocaine.

Procedure

These subjects were entered into the present study on days three to ten after admission into the inpatient or to the outpatient drug treatment centers. Subjects were entered after detoxification and stabilization, since often subjects were too confused or irritable to respond to a structured interview during the day of admission. A structured interview lasting about one hour was conducted on about day five after admission into the program with subjects agreeing to participate in a longitudinal study of drug-related lifestyle and patterns of recovery from stimulant abuse. There were no remarkable differences in the status of subjects interviewed early or later in this period of detoxification.

The current report examines the data obtained from the first interview but only examines subjects who were regular users of cocaine. Regular use was evaluated by self-report on a four-point scale: (a) have not used more than 10 grams of cocaine in your life, (b) have experimented with cocaine (over 10 grams lifetime) but are not a regular user, (c) have used cocaine regularly usually on weekends, and (d) used cocaine regularly at anytime during the week. Subjects in categories (c) and (d) above were included into this sample. Most of the subjects who did not meet this criteria of regular cocaine use had been admitted to treatment as regular and dependent users of methamphetamine (crystal), and/or were not regular users of cocaine. Some portions of this "intake" interview used a brief induction method to focus the subject on his or her life situation one month prior to treatment entry. Then structured interview questions were asked about events and behaviors that occurred during this period of time. Other questions asked about how the client feels "at the present time."

Instruments

The structured interview consisted of three parts. The first part, "the Drug Use History," asked about past and current patterns of drug use. Its focus was on the use of cocaine, methamphetamine, marijuana, nicotine, and alcohol. The second part, the "Personal Interview," asked about several areas including motivation for treatment, stress and coping patterns, personality variables, and background information. The third part, the "Take Home (In Treatment) Questionnaire," contained *The Lifestyle Survey*, a survey of health-related behaviors, health attitudes, and indices of life satisfaction. The Take Home Questionnaire also included selected scales of the Hopkins Symptom Check List (Derogatis, 1977), items on life values, and other psychosocial measures. While the Drug Use History and the Personal Interview were conducted by face-to-face interview, the Take Home Questionnaire was given to the subject at the end of the face-to-face interview and was collected within one week. Subjects were paid for their participation in this interview upon their return of the Take Home Questionnaire.

Table 2 shows the selected scales drawn from The Lifestyle Survey section of this initial interview protocol, that are the focus of the present report. The four Health Behavior scales (Exercise, High Caloric Foods, Low Caloric Foods, and Complete/Balanced Meals) were developed and validated in prior studies (Castro, Newcomb, & Cadish, 1987; Castro, 1988). The specific health behaviors that define each of these four scales are listed in Table 2, along with the standardized Cronbach's coefficient alpha that was computed for each scale using the present sample of regular cocaine users. The coefficient alpha values from the scales of High and Low Caloric Foods are somewhat lower for this sample of regular cocaine users than they have been for other samples. Nonetheless, based upon their conceptual and practical importance, these scales were retained in the current analyses.

The Psychological Status measures consisted of the Health Motivation Scale, and two single items that measured: (a) level of perceived health relative to peers, and (b) level of daily planning and organization. These two items and the items of the Health Motivation Scale are shown in Table 2. The Health Motivation Scale's coefficient alpha value for the current sample fell somewhat below typical alpha ranges for this scale which have ranged from .80 to .60 in the other subject samples. However, based also upon its conceptual and practical importance, this scale was also retained in the present analyses.

The measures of Psychiatric Status were five scales from the Hopkins Symptom Checklist. The standardized alpha coefficients

Table 2   **Psychological and Psychiatric**
Items for Scales of the Health Behavior Domains

Scale	Item Content	Standardized Coefficient Alpha

HEALTH BEHAVIOR SCALES

Exercise   (.80)

Did Aerobic exercixes for 15 minutes or more (jump rope, jogging, etc.).
Did isotonic exercises for 15 minutes or more (push-ups, weight lifting).
Did stretching exercises to increase flexibilty.
Did an aerobic exercise for 15 minutes or more for the purpose of maintaining my ideal weight.

High Caloric Foods   (.58)

Ate a serving of red meat (6 oz. or more) (beef, pork, etc).
Ate food cooked/fried with lard or containing grease (a saturated fat).
Ate a sweet snack (candy bar, chocolate, jelly beans, etc).
Ate a pastry (doughnut, slice of cake, etc.).
Drank a soft drink containing sugar.
Ate a serving of ice cream (a cone, bowl)
Drank a portion (glass or bowl, at least 4 oz.) of whole milk (not low or nonfat).
Put butter on my food at a meal (not maragine).

Low Caloric Foods   (.49)

Ate a salad of raw vegeatable at a meal.
Ate a fruit.
Ate a serving of lean white meat (6 oz. or more) (fish, poultry).
Ate a dark green, leafy vegetable at a meal (broccoli, spinach, etc.).

Complete/Balance Meals   (.79)

Ate a complete meal (not just a snack).
Ate a balanced meal (with an item from each of these 4 food groups:
(1) milk products, (2) fruits and vegetables, (3) meats, (4) grains.

Note: Items elicit frequency per week except the two items on the Complete/Balanced Meals scale which elicit frequencies per day.

Scale	Item Content	Standardized Coefficient Alpha

PSYCHOLOGICAL STATUS

Health Motivation   (.52)

My usual orientation to health is characterized by:
(1) = I didn't pay attention
(5) = I was almost always concerned

Compared with other persons of my age and sex, I felt that I was:
(1) = Considerably less healthy
(5) = Considerably healthier

My motivation to do something to improve my health was:
(1) = Absent (it was too much trouble, not important)
(5) = Extreme (I was greatly determined to improve my health)

At that time, I intended to participate in a health-improving activity:
(1) = Not at all
(5) = Absolutely yes

Preceived Health Relative to Peers   (--)

Compared with other persons of my age and sex, I felt that I was:
(1) = Considerably less healthy
(5) = Considerably healthier

Daily Planning and Organization   (--)

Regarding my daily planning:
(1) = I seldom planned ahead, I did daily activities as they came
(5) = Almost every daily activity was planned well in advance

= =

PSYCHIATRIC STATUS

Anxiety	(.91)
Depression	(.91)
Somatization	(.91)
Paranoia	(.75)
Hostility	(.89)

for these scales that were computed for this sample are shown in Table 2. All scales exhibited strong alpha coefficients ranging from .75 to .91.

Responses for each of the aforementioned measures were elicited in the past tense. Subjects were instructed to respond, "the way you were (actions and feelings) at the time before you came into treatment." For example, the health behavior items were answered in terms of "times per day," or "times per week," (depending upon the behavioral item), for the period of time "before you entered treatment."

Similarly, the Psychological Status items were answered by prompting the subject to make, "the choice which comes closest to describing how you felt just before coming into treatment." And, the Psychiatric Status items prompted responses on how the subject felt, "during the week before you entered treatment." Thus responses to all these items reflected the subject's status shortly before treatment entry.

For the measures of health behavior and psychological status, data from the group of 25 episodic (earlier stage) cocaine users was used as the norm against which the current sample of (later stage) addicted cocaine users was compared. By contrast, the normative group for analyses using the SCL-90 scales consisted of psychiatric patients. Thus, the level of distress reported by these addicted users of cocaine was compared against the distress levels reported by psychiatric patients, as indicated in norms for psychiatric patients published for the SCL-90 scales (Derogatis, 1977).

For each of the 112 cocaine addicted subjects (the target group), raw scores for the scales and items shown in Table 2 were converted to standardized T-scores based upon scores for these scales and items derived from the group of episodic cocaine users (the comparison group). For any given scale or item, the algorithm used to calculate a T-score yields a standardized deviation score relative to the scale or item mean of the reference or comparison group, i.e., for the present study, the group of episodic cocaine users. A T-score of 50 indicates a mean for the target group which is equal to the mean for the reference group. By contrast, a T-score of 60 (a 10 point difference) indicates a difference of one standard deviation above the score of the reference group, while a T-score of 40 indicates a difference of one standard deviation below the score of the reference group. Clinically, scale score deviating from the comparison group mean (T = 50) by one standard deviation or more (10 T-score points) are considered remarkably different.

RESULTS

Figure 1 shows a profile of health-related behavioral and psychological variables for the group of addicted cocaine users, when stratified by ethnic group: Non-Hispanic Whites, Hispanics, and Blacks. These data are plotted on a T-score grid where the mean scores on the variables of interest for the episodic user (reference) group are standardized to a mean score of 50 with a standard deviation of 10. Significant deviations above or below 50 would be indicative of meaningful differences in the scores generated by the addicted (targeted) group, in comparison with the group used to generate the normative values, i.e., the episodic user group. This figure plots T-score values for the four behavior frequency scales from the Lifestyle Survey: High Caloric Foods (HC), Low Caloric Foods (LC), Exercise (EX), and Healthy Meals (ML). Plotted also are T-scores for the three health-related psychological indices: Health Motivation (HM), Perceived Health Relative to Peers (PR), and Daily Planning and Organization (PN). Also plotted on this figure are scores for the five psychological symptomatology scales obtained from the Hopkins Symptom Check List. These scales were: Anxiety, Depression, Somatization, Paranoia, and Hostility.

For this group of addicted cocaine users, Figure 1 illustrates that on all measures except frequency of Healthy Meals (ML), the deviation shifts away from the normative T-score of 50 were in the unhealthy direction when compared against the norms for the episodic cocaine users, and against the norms for psychiatric patients for the SCL-90 scales. This deviation on the SCL-90 scales is even more striking given that the reference group was psychiatric patients.

On the Behavior Frequency scales, the postulated unhealthy shifts were observed among the addicted cocaine users, with only small differences apparent between ethnic groups. This group of addicted

FIGURE 1. Health-Related Profiles of Non-Hispanic White, Hispanic, and Black Cocaine Addicted Clients upon Entering into Drug Treatment.

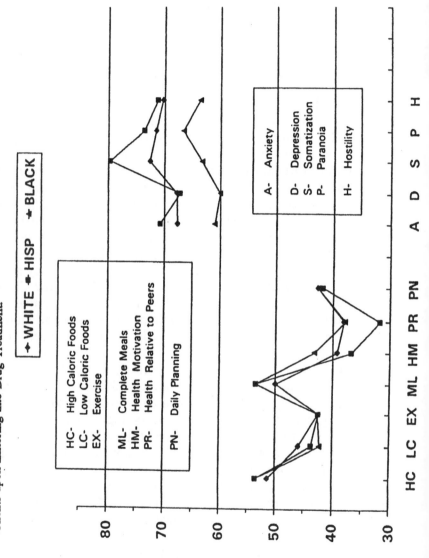

cocaine users showed a slight but insignificant elevation relative to the mean of the episodic user reference group on the High Caloric scale, with these scale scores being (51, 54, and 51) for the White, Hispanic and Black groups respectively. A more remarkable shift was observed for the Low Caloric Foods scale (LC) where the T-scores for the White, Hispanic and Black groups were (46, 44, and 42) respectively. Thus, when compared with episodic cocaine users, these addicted cocaine users consumed healthy low caloric foods at a lower frequency. Similarly, the addicted cocaine users, regardless of ethnicity, did less exercise (42, 42, 43) than did the episodic users. Regarding the frequency of complete/balance meals, the addicted cocaine users reported about equal frequencies (50, 54, 54) as did the episodic users.

Furthermore, for all three of the psychological status variables, the addicted users relative to the episodic users exhibited lower scores, that is scores in the unhealthy direction. On the Health Motivation scale (HM) (see Table 2), the White, Hispanic and Black groups respectively exhibited T-scores of (39, 37, 43). This suggests that these addicted users reported lower levels of motivation to improve their health relative to the episodic users. Similarly, on the index of perceived health relative to peers (PR), the addicted users exhibited considerably lower T-scores of (38, 32, 38) for the White, Hispanic and Black groups respectively. And, for the index of daily planning and organizations (PN), the addicted users also exhibited lower T-scores, these being (43, 42, 43) for these respective groups. Thus, on these psychological indicators of health, the addicted cocaine users exhibited a remarkable and unhealthy shift when compared with the group of episodic cocaine users.

On the five psychiatric symptomatology scales from the Hopkins Symptom Check List (SCL-90), it was noteworthy that despite being compared with psychiatric patients (Derogatis, 1977), the addicted cocaine user group exhibited remarkably elevated scores on all five scales. Here, notable differences were observed across groups, where generally, the Hispanic addicts exhibited the higher scores, with lower scores for Whites and lowest scores for Blacks. Nonetheless, all scale scores for all groups were elevated above 60, thus suggesting a remarkable level of psychiatric distress among these addicted users of cocaine. Scores on the psychiatric distress scales for the White, Hispanic and Black groups respectively were: Anxiety (68, 71, 61), Depression (68, 67, 60), Somatization (73, 80, 63), Paranoia (72, 74, 67), and Hostility (70, 71, 64).

In summary, the profile of scores for each ethnic group, when examined on measures of health behavior, psychological and psychiatric status, provided preliminary support for the lifestyle shift hypothesis. This hypothesis asserts that addiction to illicit drugs (specifically here to cocaine), should produce a remarkable and unhealthy shift in lifestyle, as measured by several indicators of health status.

Within Group Differences for Hispanics and Blacks

In a second set of analyses to examine within-group differences on these lifestyle variables for Hispanic and Black clients of this sample, we conducted one set of correlations for Hispanics (n = 10) and a second set for Blacks (n = 17). For Hispanics, acculturation has been proposed as a major dimension that defines within-group differences in cultural orientation and lifestyle (Cuellar, Harris, and Jasso, 1980). Low acculturated Hispanics are generally Spanish dominant, "traditional" in their orientation to sex roles and life interests, and tend to observe Latin/Hispanic cultural activities more often than do their more acculturated peers. By contrast, acculturated Hispanics tend to be English dominant, may or may not know about their specific Hispanic culture, and may not necessarily participate in cultural activities, perhaps in some cases denying their Hispanic identity, e.g., indicating that they are "not Mexican." A third group, bilingual/bicultural Hispanics are able to participate in both cultures. An acculturation scale developed by Cuellar and his associates (Cuellar, Harris and Jasso, 1980) has been used in several studies as a brief and general measure of acculturation with Mexican Americans. A modified five-item version of this scale developed for use with Hispanics in general has been used previously in a community survey (Castro, 1988) and was used to measure acculturation in this study.

For the Black culture, social class is one major dimension of within-group differences in sociocultural orientation and lifestyle. In the present analysis, the Hollingshead and Redlich index of social position was used as an index socioeconomic status. Table 3 shows the results of correlations between acculturation level in Hispanics and health related variables, and it shows a similar analysis using social class for Blacks.

For Hispanics, lower level of acculturation (being more Hispanic culture oriented) was associated with a lower frequency of exercise and with a higher frequency of consumption of high caloric (less healthy) foods. This behavioral pattern involving low exercise and high consumption of fatty foods connotes an energy imbalance and is consistent with a greater risk of obesity among the less acculturated Hispanics, a pattern corroborated by dietary index data for Mexican Americans in the Hispanic HANES (Health and Nutrition Examination Study) (Marks, Garcia & Solis, 1990). Furthermore,

Table 3

Correlations of Health-Related Variables with Level of Acculturation for Hispanics, and with Socioeconomic Status for Blacks

Variable	Hispanics: Acculturation (n=10)	Blacks: Social Class (n=17)
Exercise	.60*	-.30
Low Caloric	-.07	-.39
High Caloric	-.64*	-.17
Meals-Complete, Balanced	.14	-.46
Health Motivation	.22	-.20
Anxiety	-.64*	.63*
Depression	-.74*	.59*
Somatization	-.41	.01
Paranoia	-.16	.63*
Hostility	-.29	.23

Note: For the acculturation Index, higher scale scores indicate a higher level of acculturation. For the Hollingshead and Redlich Index of Social Position, lower scale scores indicate a higher level of socioeconomic status.

*p<.05.

from the measures of psychiatric distress, lower level of acculturation (greater Hispanic orientation) was associated with greater levels of anxiety and depression. Thus, as indicated on these health-related measures, the more acculturated cocaine addicted Hispanics of this sample exhibited a relatively healthier behavioral lifestyle pattern, along with lower levels of psychiatric distress. For Blacks, there were no significant relationships between social class and the health behavior and psychological measures. By contrast, among the Black subjects, on the measures of psychiatric distress, lower social class was associated with greater levels of anxiety, depression and of paranoia. These results are consistent with prior studies that indicate that social status is generally associated with greater levels of psychiatric distress.

DISCUSSION

The present study examined a lifestyle shift hypothesis which asserts that addicted cocaine users relative to earlier stage episodic cocaine users should exhibit unhealthy shifts on various measures of health status. Such patterns of lifestyle shift were examined in White, Hispanic and Black cocaine addicted subjects. In addition, this study explored within-group differences on these health status measures when evaluated along a dimension of acculturation for Hispanics, and along a dimension of social class for Blacks.

In the present study, data from various measures of health behavior, psychological status, and psychiatric status offered preliminary support for the lifestyle shift hypothesis, that greater addiction to cocaine should be associated with a less healthy behavioral and psychological profile. Moreover, among Hispanics, high acculturation status was associated with a relatively better health status on some of these health-related measures. Data from the HHANES indicates that English speaking (higher acculturated) Mexican Americans and Puerto Ricans are more likely to have used cocaine during the past year than are their Spanish speaking (lower acculturated) peers (Amaro, Whitaker, Coffman, and Heeren, 1990). However, once using cocaine regularly to levels leading to addiction, results from the present study suggest that the less acculturated Hispanics would exhibit less healthy behaviors and greater levels of distress. If this relationship between low acculturation and worse health status is a stable one, then future studies might examine reasons for apparent compromises in health and less adaptive coping that might occur among the lower acculturated Hispanic cocaine addicts. In parallel the present study found among Blacks that lower socioeconomic status was associated with a worse health status on some of these health-related measures.

Overall, the observed similarity in patterns of unhealthy lifestyle shifts for all ethnic groups suggests that cocaine addiction may produce similar health deteriorating effects regardless of ethnic status. Here, cocaine addiction may produce a decline in healthy (low caloric) eating, and in exercise. It may also produce a more extreme decline in perceptions of own health, in the energy and motivation to improve one's health, and in the capabilities for daily planning and organization needed to enact healthy behavior change and/or recovery. Apparently, such addicted cocaine users can no longer recover alone, needing help from others to stabilize and reestablish healthy patterns of diet and exercise in order to recover psychological health, while reducing psychiatric distress and symptomatology. The observed lifestyle shifts of the addicted cocaine users relative the episodic users are only suggestive, since these cross-sectional data cannot confirm the putative temporal ordering of events whereby addiction might precede, may covary with, or may follow unhealthy shifts in lifestyle.

The reason for the apparent and remarkable patterns on psychiatric distress variables when examined by ethnic group are unclear. The most remarkable group differences were observed for the Somatization scale, where Hispanics expressed a greater level of distress over bodily symptoms, and the Blacks expressed the least. Similar differences were observed for the Anxiety and Depression scales. From Table 3, the highest Anxiety and Depression scale scores were apparent among the lower acculturated Hispanics, and also among the lower social class Blacks. Generally, lower acculturation in Hispanics is co-related with lower socioeconomic status (Cuellar & Roberts, 1984). For the present study it might be expected that the discomforts of poverty may be a common source of distress among lower acculturated Hispanics and lower socioeconomic status Blacks.

Complementing the differences between the Hispanic and Black subjects in this sample, the Hispanics exhibited greater deviations from normalcy on two of the three measures of psychological status: Health Motivation, and Perceived Health Relative to Peers. In total, the scores on measures of psychological and psychiatric status suggest that the Hispanics of this sample were somewhat more adversely affected by their addiction to cocaine than were the Black subjects, although in general, all subjects were adversely affected by this addiction.

Treatment Implications

Initial clinical guidelines for deciding between inpatient and outpatient treatment for cocaine abuse have suggested that inpatient treatment is needed in cases involving a greater severity of drug addiction and its sequelae. General clinical indicators of this severity have included the presence of: (1) serious medical or psychiatric problems, (2) severe impairment in psychosocial functioning, and (3) intermittent but destructive health-threatening cocaine use (Washton, 1986). While suggestive, these guidelines still remain broad and require further clarification for truly effective decision making regarding the optimal match between type of treatment and client needs.

The health-related profile described in the present study provides a more detailed view of type and level of dysfunction in three areas of life function: behavioral, psychological, psychiatric. As an indicator of need for life structure and nurturance, an individual client's profile on the health-related measures examined in this study might provide an indicator of that client's relative need for inpatient versus outpatient treatment. Subjects with more extreme deviations from normalcy may be exhibiting a greater deterioration in health and a lower capacity for self care that would contraindicate outpatient treatment and mandate need for admission to a more structured inpatient treatment setting (Washton & Gold, 1987). By contrast, outpatient treatment is less costly and may offer effective treatment in recovery from cocaine addiction in clients with less disrupted lifestyles. Further work is needed to clarify this issue.

Along different lines, a holistic treatment goal may involve re-establishing normalcy across several areas of life function, i.e., change in several health-related behaviors away from the addicted lifestyle. This broader emphasis in planning recovery from addiction would seek to achieve progressive shifts towards normalcy across several behaviors when observed across various phrases of treatment, both in individual clients as well as in groups of clients. Moreover client successes in establishing healthy shifts in their lifestyle might also help safeguard against relapse to the use of cocaine and other illicit drugs (Marlatt & Gordon, 1985).

Study Limitations

The results of the present study are limited by its comparatively small sample of Hispanic and Black subjects. Such small samples may yield results which are not necessarily stable nor representative of results for members of these groups in the larger community. Thus, the observed differences by ethnic group should be considered with caution, perhaps as preliminary indications of the effects of addiction, patterns that should be examined further with larger samples.

As another limitation, the health profiles presented in Figure 1 present values for the group of addicted cocaine users as contrasted with norms for episodic (earlier stage) cocaine users. These observed patterns may reflect differences attributable to cocaine addiction. However, the addicted and episodic groups were also nonequivalent on age, sex and education. Thus, in the present analyses these variables cannot be ruled out as additional sources of variance or confound that could also influence the observed shifts in health profile.

Furthermore, the self-reported responses to the measures included in the present study were obtained by asking subjects to report on how they felt in the recent past, during a specific period of time before they entered treatment. Since persons who enter into treatment may regard themselves as "sick," this self perception would serve as a source of distortion or bias about how sick they may have actually been before entering treatment. While we cannot rule out this source of measurement error, nor ascertain the degree of distortion that it may have introduced, it is certainly true that most cocaine users enter treatment because they are indeed too ill to continue their life as before (Washton & Gold, 1984; Washton, 1986). Thus, we believe that the health-related difficulties reported by these subjects are mostly or entirely reflective of their true health status before entry into treatment.

CONCLUDING NOTE

Greater accuracy in evaluating the health status and treatment needs of cocaine addicted clients at the point of treatment entry may serve to improve client-treatment matching and ultimately improve success in treatment (Finney & Moos, 1986). Here it must be noted that we are still at the initial stages of understanding cocaine abuse and addiction as it may have a unique impact upon certain subgroups of Hispanics and Blacks. While the data from this study suggest that addiction to cocaine has definite ill effects regardless of ethnicity, small but noteworthy effects were indicated in the profiles of the Hispanic and Black subjects observed in this study. If Hispanics, particularly those of lower acculturation are more adversely affected by addiction to cocaine, then future research should further examine any psychosocial factors that may be contributing to such differential effects.

REFERENCES

American Psychiatric Association. (1987). *Diagnostic and statistical manual of mental disorders*–(DSMIII-R). Washington, D.C.: Author.

Castro, F.G., Newcomb, M.D., & Cadish, K. (1987). Lifestyle differences between young adult cocaine users and their nonuser peers. *Journal of Drug Education*, *17*, 89-111.

Castro, F.G. (1988). *The Southern California Social Survey-1988*. Unpublished manuscript.

Castro, F.G., Newcomb, M.D., McCreary, D., & Baezconde-Garbanati, L. (1989). Cigarette smokers do more than smoke cigarettes. *Health Psychology*, *8*, 107-129.

Cuellar, I., Harris, L.C., & Jasso, R. (1980). An acculturation scale for Mexican American normal and clinical populations. *Hispanic Journal of Behavioral Sciences*, *2*(3), 199-217.

Cuellar, I. & Roberts, R. (1984). Psychological disorders among Chicanos, in J.L. Martinez & R.H. Mendoza (Eds.), *Chicano psychology*, (2nd ed.) 133-161. New York: Academic Press.

Derogatis, L.R. (1977). *SCL-90 R, Manual I.* (2nd ed.). Johns Hopkins University.

Donovan, J.W., & Jessor, R., (1985). Structure of problem behavior in adolescence and young adulthood. *Journal of Consulting and Clinical Psychology, 53,* 890-904.

Finney, J.W., & Moos, R.M. (1986). Matching patients with treatments: Conceptual and methodological issues. *Journal of Studies on Alcohol, 47,* 122-134.

Harris, D.M., & Guten, S. (1979). Health-protective behavior: An exploratory study. *Journal of Health and Social Behavior, 20,* 17-29.

Hays, R., Stacey, A.W., & DiMatteo, M.R. (1984). Covariation among health-related behaviors. *Addictive Behaviors, 9,* 315-318.

Istvan, J., & Matarazzo, J.D. (1984). Tobacco, alcohol and caffeine use: A review of their interrelationships. *Psychological Bulletin, 95,* 301-326.

Marks, G., Garcia, M., & Solis, J.M. (1990). Health risk behaviors of Hispanics in the United States: Findings from HHANES, 1982-84. *American Journal of Public Health, 80* (Suppl.) 20-26.

Marlatt, G.A. (1985). Lifestyle modification, in G.A. Marlatt & J.R. Gordon (Eds.), *Relapse prevention: Maintenance strategies in the treatment of addictive behaviors.* New York: Guilford Press.

Marlatt, G.A., & Gordon, J.R. (1985). *Relapse prevention: Maintenance strategies in the treatment of addictive behaviors.* New York: Guilford Press.

Washton, A.M., & Gold, M.S. (1984). Chronic cocaine abuse: Evidence for adverse effects on health and functioning. *Psychiatric Annals, 14,* 733-743.

Washton, A.M. (1986). Nonpharmacologic treatment of cocaine abuse. *Psychiatric Clinics of North America, 9,* 563-571.

Washton, A.M., & Gold, M.S. (1987). *Cocaine: A clinician's handbook.* New York: Guilford Press.

Westermeyer, J. (1984). The role of ethnicity in substance abuse. *Advances in Alcohol and Substance Abuse, 4,* 9-18.

A Structural Equation Model of Factors Related to Substance Use Among American Indian Adolescents

Jeff King
Janette Beals
Spero M. Manson
Joseph E.Trimble

SUMMARY. The present study examined adolescent substance use in an American Indian boarding school population from a multi-causal perspective, with special emphasis on the role of life stress, social support, and depression. Structural equation modeling (Jöreskog & Sörbom, 1989) was employed to test alternative models of the relative influence of such life experiences on the nature and extent of alcohol and drug use. As hypothesized, life stress was positively related to rates of substance use, levels of family support, and depression. However, social support had minimal influence as a mediating factor for substance use.

Alcohol and drug use and abuse are serious social and clinical concerns in many American Indian communities (Beauvais, Oetting, Wolf, & Edwards, 1989; Beauvais, Oetting, & Edwards, 1985; Oetting, Edwards, Goldstein, & Garcia-Mason, 1980; Segal, 1989; Young, 1988). Indeed, their destructive effects are considered to be

Jeff King, Janette Beals, and Spero M. Manson are affiliated with the University of Colorado Health Sciences Center, Denver, CO.
Joseph E. Trimble is affiliated with Western Washington University, Bellingham, WA.
The preparation of this manuscript was partially supported by NIMH Grant No. MH42473-05, NIMH Grant No. MH00833-01, NIAAA Grant No. AA07180-05, and NIDA Grant No. DA06076-01.

the gravest mental health problem facing American Indians today (Abbas, 1982; U.S. Indian Health Service, 1977; National Institute of Mental Health, 1973; Young, 1988). Recent research indicates that among ethnic groups in the U.S., American Indians have the highest, or are among those having the highest, rates of use for alcohol, marijuana, inhalants, stimulants, hallucinogens, sedatives, and heroin (Beauvais et al., 1989; Beauvais et al., 1985; Segal, 1989).

Even more alarming is the observation that 75% of all American Indian deaths are related to alcohol (Young, 1988). Five of ten major causes of death among American Indians are directly attributable to alcohol: accidents, cirrhosis of the liver, alcohol dependency, suicide, and homicide (Andre, 1979; Jones-Saumty & Zeiner, 1985).

Indians begin using drugs and alcohol at an earlier age than their white counterparts (Young, 1988). Okwumabua and Duryea (1987) reported that American Indian youth begin using an array of substances as early as 10 years of age. In a national sample, Oetting et al. (1980) found that 78% of American Indian youth in grades 7-12 have tried alcohol, with 61% reporting use in the last 2 months. Lifetime prevalence rates for alcohol use among American Indian adolescents have been shown to average 80% across the last decade (Beauvais et al., 1989). It is no surprise then, that American Indian adolescents are considered at greater risk for deviant drinking behaviors than many other ethnic populations (May, 1982).

American Indian youth are more likely than White youth to try marijuana and to begin this experimentation at an earlier age (Cockerham, Forslund, & Raboin, 1976; Young, 1988). Inhalant use is twice as high for young Indians than the national average (Beauvais et al., 1985). Toluene-based solvents are among the first drugs used by Indian youth, and often precede the first time drunk (Beauvais et al., 1985).

Much less research has focused on rates of drug use other than alcohol with American Indian youth (Young, 1988). Beauvais et al. (1985) reported that the lifetime prevalence for most drugs is higher than that of non-Indian youth. They also reported that 53% of Indian youth would be considered at risk for drug use, compared with 35% of non-Indian youth.

Attempts to identify and understand the factors contributing to these high rates of alcohol and drug abuse have considered various causes.

Stressful life events have been related to drug and alcohol use among adolescents (Bruns & Geist, 1984; Carman, 1979; Labouvie, 1986; Chassin, Mann, & Sher, 1988). During adolescent development, many new stressors emerge. New academic situations, physical/emotional changes, changing roles in the family, and the need to make life decisions (e.g., career, family, education), are but a few. Several studies have found strong correlations between drug use and number of stressful life events (Bruns et al., 1984; Headlam, Goldsmith, Hanenson, & Raugh, 1979; Newcomb & Harlow, 1986). LaBouvie (1986) suggested that life stress contributes to poor social relations, which in turn leads to substance use as a means to manage these difficulties. Despite the widely recognized stress of life in Indian communities (Bechtold, Manson, & Shore, in press), this aspect has yet to be examined among native youth.

Social support has also been studied in relation to substance use. Viewed as a significant mediating variable, it reduces the impact of stressors which may contribute to substance use (Aneshensel & Huba, 1984; Myers, Lindenthal, & Pepper, 1975; Neff & Husaini, 1982; Segal, Huba, & Singer, 1980). Most efforts have examined both family and friend support (Wills & Vaughan, 1986; Zucker & Gomberg, 1986). During adolescence, friend support becomes increasingly more important than parental support (Zucker & Noll, 1982), and consistently has been linked to substance use (Swaim, Oetting, Edwards, & Beauvais, 1989). Jessor (1987) found that greater orientation to friends than family predicted increased problem behavior, including substance abuse. Wills and colleagues (Wills, 1986; Wills & Vaughan, 1988) found peer support to be positively related to substance use. Smith, Canter, and Robin (1989) also observed that peer influence is the most powerful predictor for level of substance use among adolescents. However, they also noted that family interaction problems may set the stage for the prominence of peer-acceptance issues. Typically, degree of family support appears to be inversely related to rates of substance use (Chassin, Mann, & Sher, 1988; Mann, Chassin, & Sher, 1987; Wills, 1986; Wills et al., 1988). Unfortunately, little of this work has been conducted with American Indians.

Emotional distress has also been linked to adolescent substance use (King & Thayer, in preparation; Russell & Mehrabian, 1977; Watson & Clark, 1984). However, the findings are mixed. Some studies have found negative affect to be minimally related to substance use (Johnson & Matre, 1978; LaBouvie, 1986; Oetting, Beauvais, & Edwards, 1988; Swaim et al., 1989). Others have reported that substance use serves as a buffer to or an escape from negative affect (Aneshensel & Huba, 1983; Blane, Hill, & Brown, 1968; Lex, 1987; Watson & Clark, 1984). Again, questions of this nature are only now being asked about Indian youth.

Most researchers agree that substance use is multifaceted and that causal factors must be studied from a multidimensional perspective (Aneshensel & Huba, 1984; Stein, Newcomb, & Bentler, 1987; Swaim, Oetting, Edwards, & Beauvais, 1989). No one predictor, in isolation, can account for the variability in the nature and pattern of substance use. The most promising models consist of multiple factors that may contribute to substance use (Aneshensel & Huba, 1984; King & Thayer, in preparation; Newcomb & Harlow, 1986; Smith, Canter, & Robin, 1987).

Aneshensel et al. (1984) developed a multi-factor model in which they examined the effects of life stress, social support, illness, alcohol use, and depression. In particular, they argued that life stress would impact on degree of social support, depression, alcohol use, and illness. They also hypothesized that social support mediated the impact of life stress on these factors. Their model for the most part confirmed these hypotheses.

Substance use reaches near epidemic proportions in Indian boarding schools (Dinges & Duong-Tran, 1989). These schools have been the focus of criticism over the years because of their apparent negative influence on the well-being of American Indian students (Kleinfeld & Bloom, 1977; Goldstein, 1974; Krush, Bjork, Sindell, & Nelle, 1966; Manson, Beals, Dick, & Duclos, 1989). May (1982) noted that boarding schools are characterized by a high concentration of high-risk or problem youth. Indeed, in a recent study by Dinges and Duong-Tran (1989), lifetime prevalence rates for alcohol use in a boarding school population reached 93% and 53% were considered to be at an "at risk" level for serious alcohol abuse. Given that approximately 20% of the Indian and Alaska Native student population attends boarding schools, the topic invites close scrutiny (U.S. Department of the Interior, 1988).

The present study builds upon these previous lines of inquiry. Utilizing a model similar to Aneshensel et al. (1984), it examines adolescent substance use in an American Indian boarding school population from a multi-causal perspective, with special emphasis on the role of life stress, social support, and depression. Structural equation modeling (Jöreskog & Sörbom, 1989) is employed to test alternative models of the relative influence of such life experiences on the nature and extent of alcohol and drug use. However, because this paper focuses only on cross-sectional data drawn from a larger study, the "predictive" quality of the findings is theoretical, based on specific hypotheses in regard to presumed relationships among factors.

METHOD

National Center American Indian Adolescent Survey. This report presents data collected as part of a longitudinal biannual survey of American Indian high school students. The data utilized in this paper were gathered in the third wave (November, 1988) of data collection. Wave three contains the measures which were pretested for appropriateness and comprehension during the two previous waves (January, 1988; April, 1988) and subsequently modified based on those results. Subsequent surveys, now totaling four, will allow for longitudinal analyses of the data.

The high school is a tribally-administered boarding school with approximately 200 students in attendance. Seventy-five percent of the students reside in the campus dormitories throughout the school year. The majority of the students belong to five local tribes and come from homes within the state.

Subjects. The sample size of 177 comprises those students who were present for the administration of the survey and who provided complete data on all of the measures of interest. There were 84 male and 93 female participants. Their age ranged from 12 to 19 years, with an average age of 16 years old.

Procedures. A self-report questionnaire was administered to the students twice during the academic year at the same time of day (2nd period, 9:15-10:15 a.m.). Classroom teachers explained the purpose and nature of both the questionnaire and the informed consent to the students. National Center for American Indian and Alaska Native Mental Health Research (NCAIANMHR) faculty and staff were on site to assist with its administration. The students were told that their identities would remain confidential and were encouraged to answer the questions honestly. Most students completed the questionnaire within one hour, during the second and third class periods. Compensation was provided through schoolwide raffle prizes.

Measures. The student questionnaire comprises 11 areas of measurement: (1) sociodemographic data; (2) educational attitudes; (3) cultural affiliation; (4) health characteristics; (5) stressful life events specific to students of this age, educational setting, and cultural background; (6) coping strategies; (7) social support; (8) kind, frequency, attributions, and consequences of substance use; (9) depression; (10) suicidal behavior; and (11) anxiety.

For the purposes of this study, the analyses were restricted to the measures assessing alcohol/drug use, depression, social support, and stressful life events. The Major Life Events scale, recently developed by Lewinsohn and colleagues in the Oregon Adolescent Depression Project (Andrews, Lewinsohn, Hops, & Roberts, in preparation) assesses the occurrence of 14 major life events within the past six months among the adolescent, his/her family, and friends. The Hassles scale is a 20-item measure of recent events also developed by Lewinsohn and colleagues. It was modified to include 10 additional items specific to the Indian boarding school population and setting. Additions to the scale included items concerning religious activities and beliefs (e.g., having to stay at school when ceremonial activities are happening at home), specific issues found in boarding schools (e.g., kitchen duty, distance from family), and cultural issues (e.g., loneliness for others who speak the same tribal language). Students were asked to report those events occurring within the past four weeks and to rate each event (range: 0 = not happen at all and 5 = happen almost every day). Perceived Friend Support and Perceived Family Support are 20-item subscales of the Perceived Social Support Inventory (Procidano & Heller, 1983). These assess perceived level of support from family and/or friends (e.g., "I rely on my friends for emotional support," range: 0 = always false to 5 = always true). Depression was assessed by the

Inventory to Diagnose Depression (IDD: Zimmerman & Coryell, 1988). It is a 22-item scale which refers to depressive symptoms occurring within the past two weeks (e.g., 0 = "I do not feel sad or depressed," to 4 = "I am so sad or unhappy that I can't stand it"). An alcohol and drug questionnaire assessed frequency, quantity, first use, self identification as a user, and other items for both alcohol and drugs. Drug items included those for marijuana, inhalants, and other drugs (i.e., hallucinogens, barbiturates, and amphetamines). Specific items used in these analyses include: Alcohol Use: 3 measures which ask how often the student is currently drinking, (range: 0 = never; 5 = every day), in what amounts (range: 0 = none; 4 = until 'high' or drunk), and self-identification as a drinker (range: 0 = a non-drinker; 5 = a very heavy drinker). Use of marijuana, inhalants, and other drugs were assessed with 2 items each: Frequency of Marijuana Use, Other Drug Use, and Inhalant Use: an item which asks how often student has ever tried a particular drug (range: 0 = never to 4 = every day); and Self Identification as a user item (range: 0 = a non-user; 5 = a very heavy user).

Analytic Strategy. First, measurement models were developed for each construct. The construct of "Life Stress" was comprised of three subscales involving both Hassles and Major Life Events items. Constructs of "Family Support" and "Friend Support" each consisted of 3 subscales. (The "Substance Use" constructs were comprised of the items mentioned earlier and will be discussed in greater detail later.) The "Depression" construct was derived from a single indicator: the sum score of the Inventory to Diagnose Depression (IDD) items.

Structural equation modeling (Jöreskog & Sörbom, 1989) was employed for analyses of the full model containing these constructs and is depicted in Figure 1.

Based on the literature previously reviewed, several hypotheses were developed as guides for the subsequent analyses. Age and gender were considered to be independent or exogenous predictors of each construct. Life stress was postulated to predict perceived family and/or friend support and depression as well as levels of substance use. Both friend support and family support were hypothesized to predict levels of depression and substance use and to mediate the effects of stress on these outcomes. Because the study

Figure 1

American Indian Boarding School Students: Life Stress, Social Support, and Substance Abuse
Trimmed Path Model

$\chi^2 = (176) = 280.38$
Goodness of Fit Index = .875
Adjusted Goodness of Fit Index = .836

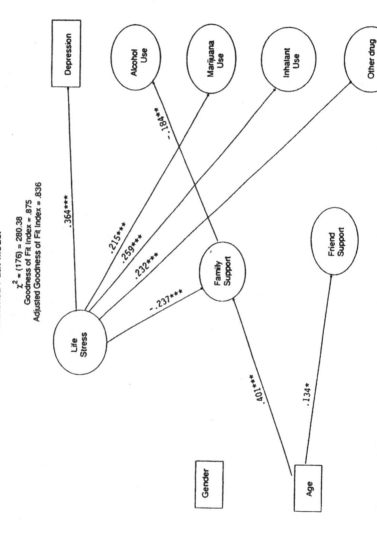

Note: Correlated Equation Error (PSI's) was allowed between Depression and Substance Use Contructs.
LISREL path coefficients are presented in completely standardized foramt.
* p < .10 ** p < .05 *** p < .01

is cross-sectional, prediction is statistically derived based on a theoretical model, rather than derived from repeated measures over time. Thus, the term "predict" will be italicized when discussed in the results section.

RESULTS

Eighty-seven percent of the students indicated they had tried alcohol, with 75% reporting they had used alcohol at least once or twice in the last year. Twenty-five percent reported using alcohol every weekend. Fifty-four percent indicated they have 6 or more drinks when they drink, and of these, 73% answered that they drank until 'high' or drunk. Thirty-seven percent of the students described themselves as moderate drinkers and 14% as heavy or very heavy drinkers.

Seventy-four percent of the students indicated they had tried marijuana. Forty-seven percent stated they used marijuana at least once or twice a month: 42% of these used once or twice a month, 30% used 3-9 times in the last month, and 28% used 10 or more times in the last month. Fifty-six percent of the students identified themselves as current users, and 44% of these classified themselves as at least a moderate user.

Twenty-five percent of the students reported they had tried inhalants, and 31% indicated they had used inhalants at least once in the last year. Of the latter, 33% reported they used inhalants once or twice a month or more. Seventeen percent of the students classified themselves as at least very light users.

Sixteen percent of the students reported using other drugs (e.g., at least once during the last month). Forty-five percent of these users indicated they used other drugs 3 or more times in the last month. Twenty-seven percent of the students classified themselves as very light users or more, and 10% identified themselves as at least a moderate user. Descriptive data for alcohol and drug use are provided in Table 1.

Among the student respondents, 23.2% had experienced 4 or more major life events within the last six months. Thirteen percent of the students met the DSM-III-R criteria for major depression as

Table 1. Frequency of Substance Use for American Indian youth

	alcohol use	marijuana use	inhalant use	other drug use
never	18.1%	48.6%	73.4%	77.4%
1-2 times a year	16.4%		11.9%	
1-2 times a month	37.3%	19.8%	5.1%	9.0%
every weekend	20.3%			
3-9 times a month		14.1%	3.4%	3.4%
several times a week	2.3%			
10+ times a month		13.0%	1.7%	4.0%
every day	1.1%			

Note: Percentages do not sum to 100% because of unanswered items by some subjects.

operationalized by the IDD. Moderate levels of family and friend support were reported (family support: $\overline{X} = 3.21$, SD = .65; friend support: $\overline{X} = 3.43$, SD = .61), with friend support perceived as occurring slightly more often.

While the constructs of life stress, social support, and depression are fairly straightforward, the construct of substance use posed some interesting theoretical questions. Several alternative models present themselves: should these 9 indicators (3 alcohol items, and 2 items each for marijuana, inhalants, and other drugs) be considered as a single construct of substance use or should they be considered separately? Three factor structure models were tested for the alcohol and drug constructs: (a) a single-factor structure of "substance use" which combined all alcohol and drug subscales; (b) a two-factor structure which contained an "alcohol use" factor and a "drug use" factor; and (c) a four-factor structure which contained factors of "alcohol use," "marijuana use," "inhalant use," and "other drug use." Confirmatory factor analyses for these models found the four-factor model to be the best fit for the data (single-factor model $X^2 = 37.05$, df = 27, Adjusted Goodness of Fit Index (AGFI) = .49; Two-factor model $X^2 = 230.68$, df = 26, AGFI = .65; four-factor model $X^2 = 47.91$, df = 14, AGFI = .88). Hence, the four-factor structure for substance use was used in the full model equation.

A full structural equation model was then tested. Initially, a full model was derived such that age and gender were allowed to "predict" all endogenous constructs, life stress "predicted" social support, depression, and substance use, while social support "predicted" depression and substance use. Subsequently, the model was trimmed by fixing to zero those paths which were not significantly different from zero. The final model is presented in Figure 1. The structural analyses revealed that among the exogenous factors, age was positively related to both friend and family support. That is, older students tended to perceive receiving support more than younger students. Gender was not significantly related to any of the constructs.

As hypothesized, life stress was positively related to depression and to all four substance use factors. Specifically, the greater the life stress, the more likely one is to feel depressed and/or to use drugs. Life stress was also negatively related to family support. Students experiencing greater life stress perceived less support from their family. For the most part, social support did not "predict" levels of depression or substance use. However, perceiving greater levels of support from family did "predict" lower levels of alcohol use. It is important to note that although the relationships between these variables are statistically significant, they do not account for much of the variance. However, the low number of subjects may contribute to the greater degree of variation between variables.

DISCUSSION

Previous research has found significant relationships among life stress, social support, emotional distress and substance use. This paper provides additional insight into this phenomena among a

sample of American Indian adolescents. Structural equation modeling was utilized to test the relative and simultaneous influence of
these factors. The results indicate that degree of life stress is significantly related to depression and substance use. Students with high
life stress feel more depressed and use drugs and alcohol more
often than those with low life stress levels. This use may serve as
a means for escape from the effects of these stressors and from the
resultant depressive feelings.

Students with low life stress perceive greater support from their
families, and also are less likely to use alcohol. In the context of a
boarding school, family support perhaps assumes more importance
since the adolescent is away from home. Family support helps
mediate rates of alcohol use for these students. This may be linked
to parents modeling appropriate drinking behaviors. Interestingly,
social support does not appear to be influential in feelings of depression, nor drug use. This finding runs contrary to other research
studies. Indian use of social support may be different than other
ethnic groups, or perhaps the boarding school setting changes the
amount one can rely upon these networks.

The finding that age is positively related to both friend and family support is interesting. That peer support increases with age in
adolescence is a common finding (Zucker & Noll, 1982). However,
one would expect that perceived family support diminishes, rather
than increases, as the student gets older.

Finally, lack of differences in perceived social support across
gender is fairly unique and runs contrary to findings from studies
across diverse ethnic groups (Vaux, 1985). These studies have consistently found that females utilize support networks more than
males.

Because of the cross-sectional nature of the data represented here,
conclusions about the ability of these factors to predict substance
use over time remain theoretical. The longitudinal study from which
the present data were drawn will be used in later analyses to further
explore the causal nature of these relationships. Structural equation
modeling provides many advantages for data analysis: most importantly it offers the ability to test multiple predictors of substance use
simultaneously. In order to fully understand the multifaceted nature
of substance use, future research must encompass multiple factors

in the design and analyses. Further, with structural equation modeling, longitudinal paths can be derived to chart the stability of the dynamics among related factors over time.

The present findings shed light on the role of life stress and support systems in levels of depression and substance use. Life stress has a major influence in rates of substance use, levels of family support, and depression. Social support for Indian adolescents is not as strong a mediating factor as it is for non-Indian adolescents. Future lines of inquiry may extend our knowledge of contributing factors to substance use by addressing students' attribution for their drinking and substance use. Similar questions may address gender and/or age differences in these reasons for using alcohol and drugs. Future studies should also consider the meanings of substance use (and non-use). Finally, careful attention should be given to the nature and importance of family and friend support to Indian adolescents.

REFERENCES

Abbas, L. (1982). Alcoholism among Native Americans. In W. Mitchell & M. Galletti (Eds.), *Native American substance abuse*, 44-54. Tempe, AZ: Arizona State University.

Andre, J.M. (1979). *The epidemiology of alcoholism among American Indians and Alaska Natives.* Albuquerque, NM: Indian Health Services.

Andrews, J.A., Lewinsohn, P.M., Hops, H., & Roberts, R.E. (in preparation). Development and psychometric properties of abbreviated scales for the measurement of psychosocial variables related to depression in adolescents.

Aneshensel, C.S. & Huba, G.J. (1984). An integrative causal model of the antecedents and consequences of depression over one year. *Research in Community and Mental Health, 4,* 35-72.

Aneshensel, C.S. & Huba, G.J. (1983). Depression, alcohol use, and smoking over one year: A four-wave longitudinal causal model. *Journal of Abnormal Psychology, 92*(3), 134-150.

Beauvais, F., Oetting, E.R., Wolf, W., & Edwards, R. (1989). American Indian youth and drugs, 1976-1987: A Continuing Program. *American Journal of Public Health, 79*(5), 634-636.

Beauvais, F., Oetting, E.R., & Edwards, R.W. (1985). Trends in the use of inhalants among American Indian adolescents. *White Cloud Journal, 3,* 3-11.

Beauvais, F., Oetting, E.R., & Edwards, R.W. (1985). Trends in drug use of Indian adolescents living on reservations: 1975-1983. *American Journal of Drug and Alcohol Abuse, 11*(4), 209-229.

Blane, H.T., Hill, M.J., & Brown, E. (1968). Alienation, self-esteem and attitudes toward drinking in high-school students. *Quarterly Journal of Studies on Alcohol, 29*, 350-354.

Bruns, C. & Geist, C.S. (1984). Stressful life events and drug use among adolescents. *Journal of Human Stress, 10*, 135-139.

Carman, R.S. (1979). Motivations for drug use and problematic outcomes among rural junior high school students. *Addictive Behaviors, 4*, 91-93.

Chassin, L., Mann, L.M., & Sher, K.J. (1988). Self-awareness theory, family history of alcoholism, and adolescent alcohol involvement. *Journal of Abnormal Psychology, 97*(2), 206-217.

Cockerham, W.C. (1977). Patterns of alcohol land multiple drug use among rural white and American Indian adolescents. *The International Journal of the Addictions, 12*, 271-285.

Cockerham, W.C., Forslund, M.A., & Raboin, R.M. (1976). Drug use among white and American Indian high school youth. *The International Journal of the Addictions, 11*, 209-220.

Dinges, N.G. & Duong-Tran, Q. (1989). Indian Adolescent Mental Health Screening Project: Replication and cross-cultural validation. Final report to the Mental Health Program, Portland Area Mental Health Service.

Headlam, H.K., Goldsmith, J., Hanenson, I.B., & Raugh, J.L. (1979). Demographic characteristics of adolescents with self-poisoning: A survey of 235 instances in Cincinnati, Ohio. *Clinical Pediatrics, 18*, 147, 151, 154.

Jessor, R. (1987). Problem-behavior theory, psychosocial development, and adolescent problem drinking. *British Journal of Addiction, 82*, 331-342.

Johnson, L.V. & Matre, M. (1978). Anomie and alcohol use: Drinking problems in Mexican American and Anglo neighborhoods. *Journal of Studies on Alcohol, 39*(5), 894-902.

Jones-Saumty, D.J. & Zeiner, A.R. (1985). Sociocultural and psychological factors related to alcoholism among American Indians and Caucasians. *Japanese Journal of Alcohol and Drug Dependence, 20*(4), 367-374.

Jöreskog, K.G. & Sörbom, D. (1989). *LISREL7: LISREL7 user's reference guide.* Mooresville, IN: Scientific Software Inc.

King, J.J. & Thayer, J.T. (in preparation). Psychological distress factors and alcohol and drug use.

Kleinfeld, J. & Bloom, J. (1977). Boarding schools: Effects on the mental health of Eskimo adolescents. *American Journal of Psychiatry, 134*(4), 411-417.

Krush, T.P., Bjork, J.W., Sindell, P.S., & Nelle, J. (1966). Some thoughts on the formation of personality disorder: Study of an Indian boarding school population. *American Journal of Psychiatry, 122*, 868-876.

Labouvie, E.W. (1986). Alcohol and marijuana use in relation to adolescent stress. *The International Journal of the Addictions, 21*(3), 333-345.

Lex, B.W. (1987). Review of alcohol problems in ethnic minority groups. *Journal of Consulting and Clinical Psychology, 55*(3), 293-300.

Mann, L.M., Chassin, L., & Sher, K. (1987). Alcohol expectancies and the risk for alcoholism. *Journal of Consulting and Clinical Psychology, 55*(3), 411-417.

Manson, S.M., Beals, J., Dick, R.W., & Duclos, C.W. (1989). Risk factors for suicide among Indian adolescents at a boarding school. *Public Health Reports*, *104*(6), 609-614.

May, P.A. (1982). Substance abuse and American Indians: Prevalence and susceptibility. *International Journal of the Addictions*, *17*, 1185-1209.

Myers, J.K., Lindenthal, J.J., & Pepper, M.P. (1975). Life events, social integration, and psychiatric symptomatology. *Journal of Health and Social Behavior*, *16*, 421-427.

Neff, J.A. & Husaini, B.A. (1982). Life events, drinking patterns, and depressive symptomatology: The stress-buffering role of alcohol consumption. *Journal of Studies in Alcohol*, *43*, 301-318.

Newcomb, M.D. & Harlow, L.L. (1986). Life events and substance use among adolescents: Mediating effects of perceived loss of control and meaninglessness in life. *Journal of Personality and Social Psychology*, *51*(3), 564-577.

Oetting, E. & Beauvais, F. (1985). *Epidemiology and correlates of alcohol use among adolescents living on reservations*. Paper presented at NIAAA conference, Epidemiology of Alcohol Use and Abuse among U.S. Ethnic Minority groups, Bethesda, MD.

Oetting, E.R. & Beauvais, F. (1986). Peer cluster theory: Drugs, and the adolescent. *Journal of Counseling and Development*, *65*(1), 17-30.

Oetting, E., Beauvais, F., & Edwards, R.W. (1988). Alcohol and Indian youth: Social and psychological correlates and prevention. *Journal of Drug Issues*, *18*, 87-101.

Oetting, E.R., Edwards, R., Goldstein, G.S., & Garcia-Mason, V. (1980). Drug use among adolescents of five southwestern Native American tribes. *The International Journal of the Addictions*, *15*, 435-439.

Oetting, E.R. & Goldstein, G.S. (1979). Drug use among native American adolescents. In G. Beschner & A. Friedman (Eds.), *Youth Drug Abuse*. Lexington, MA: Lexington Books.

Okwumabua, J.O. & Duryea, E.J. (1987). Age of onset, periods of risk, and patterns of progression in drug use among American Indian high school students. *The International Journal of the Addictions*, *22*(12), 1269-1276.

Procidano, M.E. & Heller, K. (1983). Measures of perceived social support from friends and from family: Three validation studies. *American Journal of Community Psychology*, *11*, 1-24.

Russell, J.A. & Mehrabian, A. (1977). Environmental effects on drug use. *Environmental Psychology and Nonverbal Behavior*, *2*, 109-123.

Segal, B. (1989). Drug taking behavior among school aged youth: The Alaska experience and comparisons with lower-48 States. *Drugs & Society*, *4*(1-2).

Segal, B., Huba, G.J., & Singer, J.L. (1980). *Drugs, daydreaming, and personality: A study of college youth*. Hillsdale, NJ: Erlbaum.

Smith, M.B., Canter, W.A., & Robin, A.L. (1989). A path model of an Adolescent Drinking Model derived from Problem Behavior Theory. *Journal of Studies on Alcohol*, *50*(2), 128-142.

Swaim, R.C., Oetting, E.R., Edwards, R.W. & Beauvais, F. (1989). Links from emotional distress to adolescent drug use: A path model. *Journal of Consulting and Clinical Psychology, 57*(2), 227-231.

U.S. Indian Health Service (1977). *Alcoholism: A high priority health problem* (DHEW Publication No. HSA 77-1001). Washington, DC: U.S. Government Printing Office.

U.S. Department of the Interior (1988). Report on BIA education: Excellence in Indian education through effective schools process. Washington, DC: U.S. Government Printing Office.

Vaux, A. (1985). Variations in social support associated with gender, ethnicity, and age. *Journal of Social Issues, 41*(1), 89-110.

Watson, D. & Clark, L.A. (1984). Negative affectivity: The disposition to experience aversive emotional states. *Psychological Bulletin, 96*, 465-490.

Wills, T.A. (1986). Stress and coping in adolescents: Relationship to substance use in urban school samples. *Health Psychology, 5*, 503-530.

Wills, T.A. & Vaughan, R. (1989). Social support and substance use in early adolescence. *Journal of Behavioral Medicine, 12*(4), 321-339.

Weibel-Orlando, J.C. (1985). Indians, ethnicity, and alcohol: Contrasting perceptions of the ethnic self and alcohol use. In L.A. Bennett & G.M. Ames (Eds.), *The American experience with alcohol: Contrasting cultural perspectives* (pp. 201-226). New York: Plenum Press.

Young, T.J. (1988). Substance use and abuse among Native Americans. *Clinical Psychology Review, 8*, 125-138.

Zucker, R.A. & Gomberg, E.S.L. (1986). Etiology of alcoholism reconsidered: The case for a biopsychosocial process. *American Psychologist, 41*, 783-793.

Zucker, R.A. & Noll, R.B. (1982). Precursors and developmental influences on drinking and alcoholism: Etiology from a longitudinal perspective. In *Alcohol consumption and related problems* (Alcohol and Health Monograph No. 1, pp. 289-327). Rockville, MD: National Institute on Alcohol Abuse and Alcoholism.

Zimmerman, M. & Coryell, W. (1986). The Inventory to Diagnose Major Depression (IDD): A self-report scale to diagnose major depressive disorder. *Journal of Consulting and Clinical Psychology, 35*(1), 55-59.

Ethnicity and Drug-Taking Behavior

Bernard Segal

SUMMARY. Alaska, with its predominately youthful population and its "last frontier" ethic, provides an ideal setting to explore what role drugs may play in people's lifestyles, and to learn how such behavior is related to a society that is still attempting to define itself. The present research was undertaken to identify the prevalence of drug use among Alaskan youth, specifically focusing on gaining an understanding of prevalence levels among members of different ethnic groups.

The findings from a study of students in grades 7 to 12 revealed that lifetime prevalence for experience with any chemical substances is extraordinarily high among all youth in these grades. The levels are much higher than that found in comparable aged youth in the lower-48 states. High prevalence levels are also noted for 4th and 6th graders.

A study of the proportion of youth *within* each of the different ethnic groups revealed that drug involvement was very high for Alaskan Natives, American Indians, Hispanics, and students of mixed backgrounds, a phenomenon that is consistent with findings from other research. Blacks and Asian-Pacific Islanders report least use, a finding consistent with other research. Prevalence levels for Whites were less than those for Alaskan Natives, American Indians, Hispanics, but higher than level for Blacks and students of Asian-Pacific Islander backgrounds.

The implications for further research and prevention are discussed. Special emphasis is focused on understanding drug-taking behavior in terms of the meaning it may have within a subculture or ethnic group, rather than approaching the problem of drug use from a unitary perspective.

Bernard Segal is affiliated with the Center for Alcohol and Addiction Studies at the University of Alaska, Anchorage.

INTRODUCTION

Working and living in Alaska, where social, cultural and economic upheavals are part of the Alaskan lifestyle, provides an unusual opportunity to examine drug-taking behavior in a multicultural and transitional society. The economic, social, cultural and climatic forces at work in Alaska all contribute to an extraordinary high level of alcohol consumption and drug-taking behavior across all levels of society (Division, 1990; Lonner, 1983; Segal, 1988). That the adverse health and social impacts of excessive alcohol and other drug use and abuse present a special problem to its people, particularly to its indigenous Natives, is in large part related to the particular nature of Alaska and its people. Any attempt to achieve an understanding of drug-taking behavior in this vast land called the "Last Frontier," needs to start by gaining a perspective on the land and its people.

Alaska's Environment: Geographic and Climatic Features

The geographical and climatic features of Alaska have a significant bearing on the life style of all its people. The state encompasses 586,400 square miles, containing four major mountain chains and 12 major river systems. About one-quarter of the land mass is above the Arctic Circle. The rugged terrain of Alaska is buffeted by extreme variations in climate, ranging during the winter from −60° in the north, west and northeast, to 32° in the southeast. Daylight hours also vary, from total sunlight in the summer and complete darkness in the winter in northern and western areas, to several variations of seasonal daylight and darkness in the interior, Southcentral and Southeastern regions. Transportation in Alaska, due to limited road systems, is largely restricted to airplanes, which makes traveling extremely expensive and any flying highly unpredictable because of weather fluctuations.

Alaska is still very much of an immense wilderness, with many of its Native people living in isolated villages or communities, resulting in unique, adaptive life styles. Their culture and communities, however isolated, have been dramatically impacted by the influx of members of other ethnic groups such as Mexicans, Filipinos and Koreans, and by western technology. While the construction of the trans-Alaska oil pipeline has had a particularly strong social and economic impact on indigenous people, it has also affected all the people of Alaska-Native and nonNative[1] alike (Lonner, 1983). Nevertheless, as Alaska developed Alaskan Natives were suddenly exposed to an intense state of cultural transition, and this transition was in itself a source of much difficulty which contributed to a high level of alcohol consumption (Lonner, 1983; Segal, 1983a, 1988; State, 1975, 1976, 1979).

Alaska's People

Of the currently estimated population of around 537,800 people (as of July, 1987), approximately 52 percent are men and 48 percent women. Alaska's youthful population is represented by a median age of 28.3 years, which reflects the continuing influx of mostly younger people seeking their fortune in the "Last Frontier." Within this estimated population, about 78 percent are nonNative, about 14 percent are Alaskan Natives, about 3 percent are Black, with the remaining 5 percent consisting of Filipinos, Chinese, Japanese, Koreans, Hispanics, and other ethnic groups.

These data compare with a median U.S. population age of 32.3 years, and a gender distribution of 48.8 percent male and 51.2 percent female in 1988 (Hollmann, 1990). The U.S. population[2] by ethnic distribution, reported for 1988, is: White 84.2 percent, Black, 12.3 percent, Asian or Pacific Islander, 2.7 percent, and American Indian or Alaskan Native, 0.7 percent (Hollmann, 1990). The Alaska population appears to contain different proportions of ethnic groups than that reflected in U.S. population data.

Alaska, with its predominantly youthful population and its "last frontier" environment, is a place where drinking and drug use has been found to be prevalent at considerably higher levels than in the "lower-48" states (Division, 1990: Lonner, 1983; Segal, 1983a, 1983b, 1988). Contributing to this high level of drug use is a "macho" ethic that prevails in the state, particularly among many young newcomers. Also linked to Alaska's high prevalence of drinking and drug use is the fact that Alaska remains a developing entity, a place in transition, still struggling to develop its own sense of social and cultural identity. Within this context is an Alaskan Native population whose culture has been significantly impacted by western standards and industrial development. This situation is compounded by a migration pattern in the state tied to a boom-bust economy that involves new arrivals, including members of different ethnic groups, having to adjust to living apart from established family roots while also having to adapt to living in arctic and subarctic environments, characterized by climatic extremes and extended periods of daylight and darkness. These are but a few of the many factors that contribute to place people in Alaska at high risk for both alcohol and drug abuse.

Ethnicity and Drug-Taking Behavior

As noted in publications by the National Institute of Drug Abuse (NIDA) (NIDA, 1987; Trimble, Padilla, & Bell, 1987), there has been an increasing concern about drug-taking behavior among members of diverse ethnic groups. This concern has been intensified because drug use has resulted in specific substance-abuse-related problem behaviors that appear to have become inherent in these different subcultures (Spiegler et al., 1989). Although there are cultural and regional variations among different ethnic groups (cf. Gilbert, 1988), the problem of drug use is nevertheless sufficiently prevalent that it seems to have been integrated into the value systems and life styles of different cultural groups. There is thus a need to generate information on the integration of drug-taking behavior in the construction of role identity over life cycle transitions, as well as a need for information on drug-related socialization practices in a bicultural context (Gilbert, 1988). Furthermore, research is also needed which focuses on the issue of acculturation stress and the relationship between such stress and drinking and drug-taking among different age cohorts within different ethnic groups. In the interest of attempting to begin to address some of these issues, culturally relevant data from Alaska may help to form an information base from which intervention and prevention strategies can be derived that are appropriate for ethnic minorities, particularly Alaskan Natives.

It needs to be noted that in Alaska, the Alaskan Native is a minority population with respect to the larger population. This status, however, varies geographically. Alaskan Natives live in urban centers, relatively large but isolated cities, and in smaller isolated towns and villages. In many of these rural locations the Alaskan Native represents the majority population by number, but they may not control the local government. Many are caught up in the transition from their traditional subsistence way of life to a cash economy. There are no reservations in Alaska akin to those found in the lower-48 states, but there is a similar struggle to maintain tribal government in the face of increasing state and federal regulations. The Alaskan Native students who participated in this study represent those living in large urban centers, smaller rural cities or regional hubs, and small, isolated communities.

Research has shown high prevalence levels of drinking and drug use in Alaska (Segal, 1983a, 1983b, 1988). Although such behavior tends to prevail primarily among young adults (18-25 years) and, to a lesser extent, among older adults (25+ years), youth and adolescents are not immune to involvement in drug-taking behavior. High prevalence levels for drinking and drug use has also been found among this population, and these levels exceeded those found among comparably-aged youth in the lower-48 states (Segal, 1983b, 1988).

The present research examined the pattern and extent of drug-taking behavior among a cross-section of Alaskan youth. The information obtained from the research provides a contemporary and comprehensive review of drug-taking behavior among Alaskan youth. The data takes on particular relevance when it is examined with respect to ethnicity. Specific knowledge of patterns of drug-taking behavior within different ethnic or cultural groups should help foster a better understanding of the phenomena underlying such behavior, as well as contribute to the development of culturally relevant prevention programs.

PATTERNS AND EXTENT OF DRUG-TAKING BEHAVIOR AMONG ALASKAN YOUTH

The current research evolved from a more comprehensive study designed to monitor drug-taking behavior among Alaskan youth

(Segal, 1990). That study focused on obtaining information on the use or nonuse of drugs ranging from legal, socially sanctioned drugs for those of legal age (i.e., alcohol and tobacco products), to illegal and unsanctioned drugs (marijuana, cocaine, stimulants, hallucinogens, depressants, inhalants, heroin, and tranquilizers) taken for social/recreational purposes. A complete description of the study and its findings have been reported elsewhere (Segal, 1990). A brief review of the method follows.

Sampling

The research was conducted during 1987-88, and consisted of an evaluation of 4,129 completed questionnaires obtained from students (51% male; 49% female) in grades 7-12 in ten widely separated school districts. (This research is referred to as the *1988 study.)* One component of the study, in the Anchorage School District (ASD), involved surveying 4th and 6th graders (n = 943, 48% males, 52% female), using a specifically designed questionnaire to correspond to their reading level.

The sampling procedure involved obtaining either a random stratified sample in the larger urban school districts (Anchorage, including 4th and 6th graders, Fairbanks and Juneau) or, in the case of smaller school districts, surveying the entire student body in grades 7-12 present on a given day (Barrow, Bethel, Cordova, Kotzebue, Nome, Seward and Sitka). No sampling was conducted on a reservation site. All participants were part of the general school population considered to be representative of the communities in which they resided.

The study also involved a comparison of findings from an earlier study, undertaken during 1981-82, (Segal, 1983b), which was similarly designed to obtain information about the prevalence of drug-taking behavior among youth in eight of the same communities participating in the current study. (Cordova and Seward were not part of the previous study.) A comprehensive description of this sample and of the procedure for the 1981-82 study is provided elsewhere (Segal, 1983b). Briefly, a total of 3,609 completed questionnaires were analyzed, having been obtained from a sample of students (49% male; 51% female) in grades 7-12. (This research is referred to as the *1983 study.)*

Procedure

For grades 7-12, a self-administered questionnaire was used to obtain information about use or nonuse of drugs. The instrument was pilot tested to assess its reliability and to confirm that its wording was consistent with a seventh grade reading level. The measure demonstrated sufficient content validity to ensure that it adequately assessed use or nonuse of drugs, and the nature and extent of drug use by those students who reported having tried a drug. The 1981-82 questionnaire was similar in content to the one used in the 1987-88 study, but formatted differently. Its reliability and content validity were established (cf. Segal, 1983b). Content validity was achieved by a panel of experts who agreed that the items in the measure were assessing different aspects of drug-taking behavior. Additionally, many of the items used were identical to those asked in the National High School Senior Survey (Johnston, 1988).

The measure for the 4th and 6th grade Anchorage students was pilot tested to ascertain that its word level corresponded to the reading level of the target sample. This measure likewise demonstrated sufficient content validity to ensure its accuracy of measurement.

In an effort to obtain reliable answers from the students, special precautions were taken to protect their confidentiality and anonymity. The students' names were not asked for in any phase of the research. The only identifying information requested on the questionnaire was age, ethnicity, gender and grade; no birth date was asked. Additionally, a series of similar questions were asked within the questionnaire to attempt to check on the consistency of responses. For example, the sequence within question pertaining to use of a particular substance, such as marijuana, started with a question about ever using or not, with the following questions all containing nonuse categories. If a student answered "never tried" and then responded to having tried in the remaining questions, the inconsistency was flagged. Conversely, if a student indicated "having tried" a substance, and the questions following were responded to as not having used, this inconsistency was also noted. Those questionnaires that were found to have inconsistent response pattern were discarded.

Some districts required parental consent in the form of negative response. In these communities post cards were sent to parents informing them that they needed to respond if they objected to their child's participation in the study. An overall negative response rate of less than 1 percent was obtained.

All students who were eligible were asked to volunteer. Few refused, and a return rate of 94.2% was obtained after inaccurate or incomplete questionnaires were discarded. In some locations students actively supported the study by endorsing its administration at School Board meeting, viewing it as a means of helping their school combat the use of drugs.

RESULTS AND DISCUSSION

The data are presented in both tabular and graphic form. In some figures the names of each substance have been abbreviated. The following is a legend to help interpret the abbreviations when the findings are presented graphically.

MJ = Marijuana	DP = Depressants
CK = Cocaine	HR = Heroin
IH = Inhalants	TQ = Tranquilizers
AL = Alcohol	TB = Cigarettes
ST = Stimulants	CW = Chewing/Smokeless Tobacco
HL = Hallucinogens	

PART I. LIFETIME PREVALENCE BY TYPE OF DRUG: TOTAL SAMPLE

The first part of this section presents a brief description of the major findings from the 1988 study and compares these findings with the 1983 results. Its purpose is to convey an overview of the pattern of drug-taking behavior generally found across the state, providing a frame of reference for the specific ethnic studies. The following section conveys an in-depth review of the results pertaining to ethnicity and drug-taking behavior. The 1983 study did not ask for ethnicity,[3] which precluded any comparisons with prior findings on this dimension.

A. Grades 7-12

1. Lifetime Prevalence with a Chemical Substance: 1988 Sample

Table 1 shows the findings related to the percent of students who reported ever having tried a chemical substance; except for alcohol or tobacco half of the students (53.2%) reported having tried marijuana at least once during their lifetime. Over half the students (53.2%) reported having tried marijuana at least once. Conversely, heroin was the least tried (2%). Of the remaining substances, inhalants were the second most experienced (25.7%), followed by stimulants (24.0%). Experience with cocaine (14.4%) and hallucinogens (13.1%) were relatively comparable, but lower than marijuana, stimulants and inhalants. The prevalence of tranquilizers (9.6%) and depressants (9.4%) were also relatively comparable, but lower than cocaine and hallucinogens.

2. Lifetime Prevalence with a Drug by Type of Drug: 1983 and 1988

Figure 1 provides a comparison of the 1983 and 1988 findings (excluding alcohol and tobacco) for the eight comparable school districts. Increases are noted for marijuana (3.6%) and hallucinogens (4.5%), and a larger increase in inhalant use (9.4%) is observable.

Table 1
Lifetime Prevalence by Type of Drug: Total Sample
Grades 7-12
(N=4129)

Substance	Lower[1] Limit	Percent	Upper Limit
Marijuana	51.7	53.2	54.7
Cocaine	13.3	14.4	15.5
Stimulants	22.7	24.0	25.3
Hallucinogens	12.1	13.1	14.1
Depressants	8.5	9.4	10.3
Heroin	1.6	2.0	2.4
Inhalants	24.4	25.7	27.0
Tranquilizers	8.8	9.6	10.5

[1]Upper and lower confidence levels calculated with a .95 confidence interval.

FIGURE 1. Comparison of Lifetime Prevalence by Type of Drug Tried: 1983 and 1988.

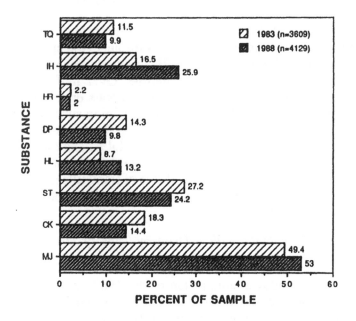

Generally, the pattern of increases and decreases shown in Figure 1 indicate that marijuana retained the highest prevalence level. The increase in inhalants and hallucinogens suggests a possible trend away from more expensive and potentially dangerous drugs (e.g., cocaine) to less expensive, more available, and strongly euphoric-producing substances (e.g., inhalants and hallucinogens). Other substances, it should be noted, are prevalent, and their high prevalence levels should not be overlooked. The overall changes in prevalence levels between 1983 and 1988, however, may be interpreted as reflecting changes in patterns of use.

3. Comparison of the 1983 and 1988 Alaska Samples with the National Household Surveys for 12-17 Year-Olds by Type of Drug Tried: Lifetime Prevalence

Figure 2 compares the 1983 and 1988 Alaska Eight-Community findings for 12-17 year-olds with the 1982 (Miller & Cisin, 1983) and 1988 (NIDA, 1989) National Household Survey's findings for the same age group. The findings show clearly that Alaskan youth, as first observed in 1983, continued to exceed their lower-48 counterparts in every category, and by considerable margins in many instances. Although there are variations in patterns of use in both the Alaska and National Samples, the direction of change for some substances are in the opposite direction. For example, the National Sample showed a decline in prevalence levels for marijuana, hallucinogens, alcohol and tobacco, but the Alaska data showed increases in prevalence for these substances. Declines were noted in the 1988 sample, when compared to the 1983 findings, for cocaine, stimulants, depressants, and tranquilizers. Hallucinogens, however, showed an increase.

Comparisons of the Alaska data (cf., Segal, 1989) with those

FIGURE 2. Comparison of Alaska School and National Household Surveys for 12-17 Year-Olds: Lifetime Prevalence by Drugs Tried.

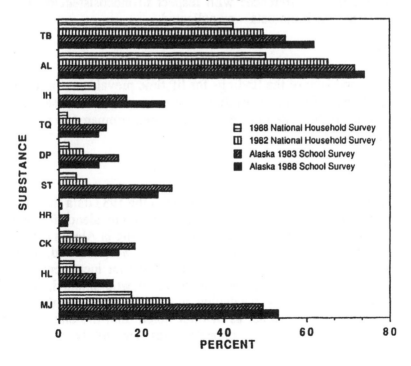

from California, Oregon, and Texas, and with the National High School Senior Survey (Johnston, 1988), revealed that the prevalence levels in Alaska were generally higher than those in the lower-48 states.

The above comparisons suggest that period effects may account for some of the differences that occurred regarding adolescent patterns of drug-taking behavior, but it is also important to note that regional or geographical differences may also contribute to the pattern of drug-taking behavior exhibited by youth. The differences, however, as noted in Figure 2, may be related more to the fact some drugs are used more extensively in Alaska, such as marijuana, than others. In Figure 2, for example, a larger proportion of Alaskan youth have tried different substances, but the pattern of use is nevertheless fairly consistent for the different substances. Segal (1989), in a more detailed comparison of Alaska data with those from the National Household Study, has discussed how the higher prevalence levels found in Alaska may be partially accounted for by methodological differences with respect to inconsistencies in the manner in which the data was collected.

4. Alcohol

A comparison of the findings for lifetime prevalence for alcohol for 1983 and 1988 indicates that there was a slight increase (2.8%) observed for the 1988 (74.5%) sample when compared to the 1983 sample (71.7%).

5. Smoking

A comparison of the 1988 findings with the 1983 data shows that there has been a 7 percent increase in lifetime prevalence for smoking cigarettes. The prevalence level for smoking in Alaska is higher than reported among students in Texas (39.3%) (Fredlund, Spence & Maxwell, 1989). This increase represents an increment in the number of youth having tried cigarettes or who smoked, a trend which is inconsistent with a decline in smoking among adults (Warner, 1989). It is possible, as Warner noted, that the emphasis on low-yield tar and nicotine cigarettes has particularly encouraged smoking among the young, along with an added inducement by advertising directed at youth, particularly young women (Tuckson, 1990).

6. Smokeless/Chewing Tobacco

Data is unavailable for a comparison with the 1983 sample. For the 1988 sample, however, over a third of the sample (38.4%) tried either smokeless or chewing tobacco at least once. This figure is exceptionally high, and is of special concern because of the emerging recognition of the consequences of using smokeless tobacco (WHO, 1988).

B. Grades 4 and 6

Part of the research included a survey of students in grades 4 and 6 in the Anchorage School District (ASD). These findings are included to supplement the above findings by describing the nature of drug-taking behavior that has occurred among younger children. These data will be analyzed by ethnicity in Section II of this report.

Lifetime Prevalence by Type of Drug Tried: 4th and 6th Grades

Inspection of Table 2 shows that drug-taking behavior is present among 4th and 6th graders in varying amounts. Overall, the 4th graders show lower prevalence levels when compared to 6th graders, except for inhalants, which is similar for both grade levels. This finding tends to support the contention that inhalants are used by younger children, and serve as a reminder that such use presents especially dangerous health and social problems (Crider & Rouse, 1988).

Prominent among the findings for the other substances are relatively high prevalence levels for having tried alcohol, followed by experiences with cigarettes, chewing/smokeless tobacco, and marijuana, particularly among the 6th graders.

In summary of Part I, the nature and pattern of drug-taking be-

Table 2
Lifetime Prevalence by Type of Drug: 4th and 6th Grades

	Forth Grade (n=420)		
Substance	Lower[1] Limit	Percent	Upper Limit
Alcohol	44.6	49.4	54.2
Marijuana	1.7	3.4	5.1
Cocaine	0.2	1.2	2.9
Stimulants	0.2	1.2	2.9
Hallucinogens	0.0	0.2	0.6
Depressants	0.0	0.7	0.2
Heroin	0.0	0.2	0.6
Inhalants	10.1	13.4	16.7
Tranquilizers	0.2	1.0	2.0
Smoking	11.2	14.6	18.0
Chewing Tobacco	6.0	8.6	11.2

	Sixth Grade (n=533)		
Substance	Lower[1] Limit	Percent	Upper Limit
Alcohol	51.9	56.1	60.3
Marijuana	7.9	10.5	13.1
Cocaine	0.6	1.7	2.8
Stimulants	2.7	4.4	6.1
Hallucinogens	0.5	1.5	2.5
Depressants	2.1	3.7	5.3
Heroin	0.2	1.1	2.0
Inhalants	10.2	13.1	14.0
Tranquilizers	0.5	1.5	2.5
Smoking	26.6	30.6	34.6
Chewing Tobacco	10.7	13.7	16.7

[1]Upper and lower confidence levels calculated with a .95 confidence interval.

havior found in the sample tends to reflect high prevalence rates for experiences with chemical substances. More than half of the students in grades 7-12 have reported having tried marijuana, nearly one in every three reported having tried stimulants or inhalants, and nearly one out of every five have tried cocaine. Experiences with other drugs are also high, including alcohol and tobacco products. These same trends appear to be evident among 4th and 6th graders. The next section describes detailed findings with respect to prevalence and patterns of drug-taking behavior among students from different ethnic groups.

PART II. ETHNICITY AND DRUG-TAKING BEHAVIOR

Table 3 presents a description of the Alaska sample characterized by ethnic representation. The largest ethnic group, Whites, which is proportionally highest, was included in the series of reports in order to provide a comparison with the other ethnic groups.

It should be noted that for the series of reports that follow the size of the sample is reduced to 3,563 students. This decrease occurred because one of the communities (Sitka) did not include ethnicity on its questionnaire, and because all cases which did not list ethnicity were not included in any of the analyses that follow. (A total of 564 cases were deleted.)

A. Grades 7-12

1. Lifetime Prevalence with a Drug Within Ethnic Groups

Table 4 shows the proportion of students *within* each ethnic group who reported ever having tried a chemical substance (excluding alcohol and tobacco products).

The overall pattern of lifetime prevalence with a drug shows Native American youth with proportionally higher prevalence levels than other ethnic groups. Among those who identified themselves as either an Alaskan Native or American Indian, close to three-quarters of the students within each group (73.9% and 72.6%, respectively), indicated that they tried one or more substances. Over two-thirds of the Hispanic (63.6%) and "Other" students (62.3%) tried a drug. In contrast, less than half the Black students (41.1%) and slightly over half of the Asian-Pacific students (51.3%) tried a drug. More than half (57.2%) of the White students indicated that they tried a drug.

Table 3
Sample Characteristics by Ethnicity
1987-1988
(N=3563)

Ethnicity	n	Percent	Male	Percent	Female	Percent
Alaskan Native	721	20.2	377	10.6	342	9.6
American Indian	73	2.0	46	1.3	27	0.8
Asian-Pacific	113	3.2	61	1.7	52	1.5
Black	129	3.6	71	2.0	57	1.6
Hispanic	77	2.2	41	1.2	36	1.0
White	2275	63.9	1157	32.5	1116	31.4
Other	175	4.9	79	2.2	96	2.7

Grade and Gender

						(Percent)					
	7		8		9		10		11		12
Ethnicity	M	F	M	F	M	F	M	F	M	F	M	F
Alaskan Native	19.9	12.8	7.2	7.2	13.8	14.1	10.9	8.1	12.8	12.4	6.2	7.7
American Indian	2.8	.4	1.8	1.0	1.0	1.5	1.0	.7	.2	.2	.7	.6
Asian-Pacific	.6	1.1	2.1	1.7	1.5	1.2	1.7	1.0	1.7	1.9	2.2	1.8
Black	1.3	.6	3.3	1.7	1.7	1.5	2.1	1.5	.5	1.2	1.8	2.5
Hispanic	1.3	.4	1.2	1.4	.2	1.0	.8	.7	1.2	1.2	1.9	1.2
White	26.6	26.4	34.4	30.6	30.4	26.7	33.9	33.5	33.2	29.0	32.4	37.9
Other	4.5	3.4	2.2	4.0	2.0	3.5	2.1	2.1	.7	1.9	1.9	1.2

Age and Ethnicity

			(Percent)					
	11	12	13	14	15	16	17	18
Alaskan Native	.4	2.4	3.5	3.4	3.4	3.0	3.0	1.0
American Indian	0.0	.2	.3	.5	.4	.3	.1	.1
Asian-Pacific	0.0	.1	.4	.8	.4	.5	.6	.3
Black	.1	.3	.5	.7	.5	.5	.7	.3
Hispanic	.1	.1	.2	.5	.3	.3	.4	.3
White	.1	3.4	10.5	11.0	9.1	11.6	10.5	7.6
Other	.1	.6	1.2	.9	.7	.5	.5	.3

4th and 6th Graders						
(n = 943)						
Ethnicity	n	Percent	Male	Percent	Female	Percent
Alaskan Native	86	9.1	44	4.7	42	4.5
American Indian	30	3.2	10	1.1	20	2.1
Asian-Pacific	40	4.2	20	2.1	20	2.1
Black	65	6.9	28	3.0	37	3.9
Hispanic	30	3.2	15	1.6	15	1.6
White	639	67.8	305	32.4	333	35.3
Other	53	5.6	24	2.5	29	3.1

Table 4
Lifetime Prevalence Within Ethnic Groups: Total Sample
Grades 7-12
(N=3563)

Ethnic Group	Lower[1] Limit	Percent	Upper Limit
Other	60.7	62.3	63.9
White	56.6	57.2	58.8
Hispanic	62.0	63.6	65.2
Black	39.5	41.1	42.7
Asian/Pacific	49.7	51.3	52.9
American Indian	71.1	72.6	74.1
Alaskan Native	72.5	73.9	75.3

[1] Upper and lower confidence levels calculated with a .95 confidence interval.

2. Ethnicity and Lifetime Experiences by Chemical Substances Within Ethnic Groups

Tables 5 through 15 show lifetime prevalence *within* each of the different ethnic groups for each of the different chemical substances, including alcohol and tobacco products.

(a) Marijuana

Table 5 shows a pattern of high prevalence levels for marijuana use within Native American groups. Alaska Natives, for example, showed the highest prevalence (71.3%), followed by American Indians (65.8%), "Other" (55.4%), and Hispanics (53.2%). Black students (35.7%) showed the lowest level, followed by Asian-Pacific Islanders (43.4%). The White students showed a mid-range level of 49.3 percent.

(b) Cocaine

As is observable in Table 6, the highest prevalence for cocaine (including crack) occurs among two ethnic groups, American Indian (20.5%) and Hispanics (18.2%). Prevalence levels for the other

Table 5
Lifetime Prevalence for Marijuana Within Ethnic Groups
Grades 7-12
(N=3563)

Ethnic Group	Lower[1] Limit	Percent	Upper Limit
Other	53.8	55.4	57.0
White	47.7	49.3	50.9
Hispanic	51.6	53.2	54.8
Black	34.7	35.7	37.3
Asian/Pacific	41.8	35.7	45.0
American Indian	64.2	65.8	67.4
Alaskan Native	69.8	71.3	72.8

[1]Upper and lower confidence levels calculated with a .95 confidence interval.

Table 6
Lifetime Prevalence for Cocaine Within Ethnic Groups
Grades 7-12
(N=3563)

Ethnic Group	Lower[1] Limit	Percent	Upper Limit
Other	11.0	12.0	13.0
White	14.5	15.7	16.9
Hispanic	16.9	18.2	19.5
Black	4.7	5.4	6.1
Asian/Pacific	11.3	12.4	13.5
American Indian	19.2	20.5	21.8
Alaskan Native	11.0	12.1	13.2

[1]Upper and lower confidence levels calculated with a .95 confidence interval.

groups are generally comparable except for Blacks (5.4%), who showed the lowest rate and Whites (15.7%), who showed a moderately high level.

(c) Stimulants

Among those ethnic groups trying stimulants (Table 7), American Indian (39.7%) and Hispanic (37.7%) students showed the highest

Table 7
Lifetime Prevalence for Stimulants Within Ethnic Groups
Grades 7-12
(N=3563)

Ethnic Group	Lower[1] Limit	Percent	Upper Limit
Other	15.9	17.1	18.3
White	25.2	26.7	28.2
Hispanic	36.1	37.7	39.3
Black	9.9	10.9	11.9
Asian/Pacific	13.8	15.0	16.2
American Indian	38.1	39.7	41.3
Alaskan Native	13.5	14.7	15.9

[1]Upper and lower confidence levels calculated with a .95 confidence interval.

prevalence levels, followed by White students (26.7%). Black students showed the lowest prevalence (10.9%), followed by Asian-Pacific Islanders. The Alaskan Native (14.7%) and the "Other" group (17.1%) showed mid-range prevalence levels.

(d) Hallucinogens

The highest level of experience with hallucinogens (Table 8), is among Hispanic (24.7%) and American Indian (20.5%) students, followed by Whites (15.5%). Blacks showed the lowest level (6.2%), followed by Alaska Natives (8.7%).

(e) Depressants

Table 9 shows that among students within the different ethnic groups reporting having tried depressants, Hispanics (14.3%) and American Indians (15.1%) showed the highest prevalence levels. The general pattern of use is similar to that found for hallucinogens.

(f) Inhalants

Lifetime prevalence with inhalants, in comparison to the findings thus far, is proportionately higher across all ethnic groups, as shown

Table 8
Lifetime Prevalence for Hallucinogens Within Ethnic Groups
Grades 7-12
(N=3563)

Ethnic Group	Lower[1] Limit	Percent	Upper Limit
Other	12.6	13.7	14.8
White	14.3	15.5	16.7
Hispanic	23.3	24.7	26.1
Black	5.4	6.2	7.0
Asian/Pacific	9.6	10.6	11.6
American Indian	19.2	20.5	21.8
Alaskan Native	7.6	8.7	9.6

[1]Upper and lower confidence levels calculated with a .95 confidence interval.

Table 9
Lifetime Prevalence for Depressants Within Ethnic Groups
Grades 7-12
(N=3563)

Ethnic Group	Lower[1] Limit	Percent	Upper Limit
Other	9.3	10.3	11.3
White	8.4	9.4	10.4
Hispanic	13.2	14.3	15.4
Black	3.3	3.9	4.5
Asian/Pacific	7.0	8.0	9.0
American Indian	14.9	15.1	16.3
Alaskan Native	5.9	6.7	7.5

[1]Upper and lower confidence levels calculated with a .95 confidence interval.

in Table 10. Inhalant use is most prevalent within the Hispanic (35.1%), American Indian (32.9%), White (27.3), Alaska Natives (26.5%) and the "Other" (24.6%) group. Use among Blacks (13.2%) and Asian-Pacific (16.8%) students is also high when compared to their experiences with other substances, but proportionately lower when compared to the other groups.

Table 10
Lifetime Prevalence for Inhalants Within Ethnic Groups
Grades 7-12
(N=3563)

Ethnic Group	Lower[1] Limit	Percent	Upper Limit
Other	23.2	24.6	26.0
White	26.8	27.3	28.8
Hispanic	33.6	35.1	36.6
Black	12.1	13.2	14.3
Asian/Pacific	15.6	16.8	18.0
American Indian	31.4	32.9	34.4
Alaskan Native	25.1	26.5	27.9

[1] Upper and lower confidence levels calculated with a .95 confidence interval.

(g) Heroin

Although the overall prevalence level for experience with heroin is low (Table 11), its use was highest among Hispanic (6.5%) and American Indian (4.1%) students.

(h) Tranquilizers

Among those students having tried tranquilizers within the different ethnic groups (Table 12), Hispanics showed the highest level (16.9%), followed by Whites (11.3%). Alaska Natives showed the lowest use (5.1%), with Blacks (7.0%) having the next highest level.

(i) Alcohol

Table 13 describes lifetime prevalence with alcohol by ethnicity. The prevalence levels are high in relation to other drug use, with American Indian's (87.7%) having shown the highest level, followed by Hispanics (76.6%), Whites (75.1%) and Alaskan Natives (74.5%). Blacks showed the lowest level (58.1%), followed by Asian-Pacific Islanders (72.6%).

Table 11
Lifetime Prevalence for Heroin Within Ethnic Groups
Grades 7-12
(N=3563)

Ethnic Group	Lower[1] Limit	Percent	Upper Limit
Other	1.3	1.7	2.1
White	1.6	2.0	2.4
Hispanic	5.7	6.5	7.3
Black	1.2	1.6	2.0
Asian/Pacific	1.4	1.8	2.2
American Indian	3.4	4.1	4.8
Alaskan Native	1.0	1.4	1.8

[1]Upper and lower confidence levels calculated with a .95 confidence interval.

Table 12
Lifetime Prevalence for Tranquilizers Within Ethnic Groups
Grades 7-12
(N=3563)

Ethnic Group	Lower[1] Limit	Percent	Upper Limit
Other	8.5	7.4	8.3
White	10.3	11.3	12.3
Hispanic	15.7	16.9	18.1
Black	6.2	7.0	7.8
Asian/Pacific	7.9	8.8	9.7
American Indian	7.3	8.2	9.1
Alaskan Native	4.4	5.1	5.8

[1]Upper and lower confidence levels calculated with a .95 confidence interval.

(j) Smoking

Table 14 shows the findings regarding ethnicity and lifetime prevalence with cigarettes. The highest prevalence for having smoked is found among three ethnic groups, American Indians

Table 13
Lifetime Prevalence for Alcohol Within Ethnic Groups
Grades 7-12
(N=3563)

Ethnic Group	Lower[1] Limit	Percent	Upper Limit
Other	72.3	73.7	74.1
White	74.7	75.12	76.5
Hispanic	75.2	76.6	78.0
Black	57.5	58.1	59.7
Asian/Pacific	71.1	72.6	74.1
American Indian	86.6	87.7	88.8
Alaskan Native	73.1	74.5	75.9

[1]Upper and lower confidence levels calculated with a .95 confidence interval.

Table 14
Lifetime Prevalence for Smoking Within Ethnic Groups
Grades 7-12
(N=3563)

Ethnic Group	Lower[1] Limit	Percent	Upper Limit
Other	78.1	79.4	80.7
White	67.3	68.8	69.3
Hispanic	68.6	70.1	71.6
Black	48.0	49.6	51.2
Asian/Pacific	57.7	59.3	60.9
American Indian	80.9	82.2	84.5
Alaskan Native	80.1	81.4	82.7

[1]Upper and lower confidence levels calculated with a .95 confidence interval.

(82.2%), Alaska Natives (81.4%), and "Other" students (79.4%). A large proportion of Hispanic students (70.1%) have also smoked. The lowest prevalence is among Black students (49.6%), followed by Asian-Pacific Islanders (59.3%). The prevalence levels for White students fell in between these groups (68.8%).

(k) Chewing/Smokeless Tobacco

Chewing or smokeless tobacco has been used by many students within each of the ethnic groups (Table 15). This finding is consistent with reports of an increase in smokeless tobacco among adolescents during the past five years (Jones & Moberg, 1988; McCarthy et al., 1986). A particularly high prevalence level has been noted among Alaskan Native youth (Tanner, 1987), a finding which is supported by this study. Alaskan Native youth showed the highest prevalence level (69.6%) for having tried either chewing or smokeless tobacco. Students in the "Other" ethnic category (53.7%) and American Indian youth (53.4%) tied for the second highest level for having tried/used smokeless or chewing tobacco. White youth followed, with 32.5 percent having indicated they tried chewing or smokeless tobacco, Hispanic youth were next (32.5%), followed by Asian-Pacific (23.9%) youth. Black students showed the lowest prevalence level (20.2%) for having tried smokeless or chewing tobacco.

In summary of the findings about drug-taking behavior within ethnic groups, (Tables 5 to 15), Hispanic and American Indian youth, who constituted 2.2% and 2.0% of the sample, respectively, showed a disproportionately high level of prevalence for lifetime prevalence with different chemical substances. This finding is consistent with reports of high levels of drinking and drug use among Hispanic Americans (NIDA, 1987; Spiegler et al., 1989) and American Indians (Oetting & Beauvais, 1981, 1989; Trimble et al., 1987).

The prevalence among Alaskan Natives was also generally high but, except for marijuana, not as high as the Hispanic and American Indian students. Other ethnic groups show variations in their prevalence of drug-taking behavior, but their pattern of use tended to remain fairly consistent across the different substances. Some of these variations may be accounted for by cultural differences within each of the ethnic groups, and by peer influence or encouragement from a group of close friends who mutually support drug use and who use drugs together (Oetting, Edwards, & Beauvais, 1988). Nevertheless, it appears that students in two groups which are eth-

Table 15
Lifetime Prevalence for Smoking Tobacco Within Ethnic Groups
Grades 7-12
(N=3563)

Ethnic Group	Lower[1] Limit	Percent	Upper Limit
Other	52.1	53.7	55.3
White	36.2	37.8	39.4
Hispanic	31.0	32.5	34.0
Black	18.9	20.2	21.5
Asian/Pacific	22.5	23.9	25.3
American Indian	51.8	53.4	55.0
Alaskan Native	68.1	69.6	71.1

[1]Upper and lower confidence levels calculated with a .95 confidence interval.

nic minorities in Alaska–American Indian and Hispanic–are at greatest risk for involvement in drug-taking behavior.

A question which arises after reviewing the above is whether there is a predilection for different ethnic groups to use specific substances. In order to attempt to answer this question a canonical analysis was conducted between the domains of ethnicity and drug use. Canonical analysis, which is an extension of multiple regression and correlation analysis, seeks to derive a linear combination from each of two sets of variables in such a way that the correlation between the two linear combinations is maximized. The canonical variates that are produced are essentially equivalent to the principle components produced by the principal components analysis (PCA), and are interpreted accordingly (Segal, Huba, & Singer, 1980). Although PCA and canonical analysis produce linear combinations of the original variables, canonical correlation analysis does so not with the object of accounting for as much variance as possible within one set of variables, but with aim of accounting for a maximum amount of the relationship between two sets of variables. The results of the analysis are found in Table 16.

Three statistically significant canonical dimensions were extracted. Examination of the first canonical dimension indicates that the

Table 16

Canonical Loadings Between Ethnicity and Drug Use

	Canonical Loadings		
Ethnicity	I	II	III
Alaska Native	-.444	-.850	.049
American Indian	-.062	.050	.633
Asian-Pacific Islander	.956	-.278	.067
Black	.030	.048	-.678
Hispanic	-.015	.207	.377
White	-.233	.819	-.096
Other	-.162	-.083	-.109

Canonical Correlations	.597	.334	.107

Substance	I	II	III
Marijuana	-.046	-.428	.545
Cocaine[a]	-.084	.231	.010
Stimulants	.160	.351	.738
Hallucinogens	-.033	.326	.446
Depressants	.126	.092	.424
Heroin	.027	.085	.297
Inhalants	-.042	.132	.451
Tranquilizers	.054	.281	.090
Alcohol	.203	.169	.505
Cigarettes	-.878	.268	.139
Chewing Tobacco	-.631	-.421	.383

[a]Includes Crack.

highest loading from the ethnicity domain represents Alaskan Natives (−.444) and Asian-Pacific Islanders (.956). The canonical correlation with the corresponding set of drug use variables is .597. Interpretation of this dimension indicates that Asian-Pacific-Islanders showed little use of the different substances while Alaskan Natives tended to try cigarettes and chewing tobacco.

The second pair of canonical dimensions shows high loading on the ethnic domain for Alaskan Natives and Whites. The canonical correlation with the drug use dimension is .334. The loadings in this second dimension indicate that Whites primarily tried stimulants and hallucinogens, while Alaskan Native youth primarily tried marijuana and chewing tobacco.

The third set of canonical dimensions does not yield a very high canonical correlation (.107), but its loading nevertheless reflects the pattern of drug-taking behavior reported above. Within this dimension American Indian and Hispanic students load positively (.633 and .377, respectively) on the ethnic domain, while Blacks load inversely (−.678). Interpretation of the loading on the corresponding drug use domain suggests that American Indian and Hispanic youth tended to have tried most all of the substances, but experienced cocaine and tranquilizers to a lesser extent in comparison to the others, while Black youth tended not to experience these substances.

In all, the pattern of loading found in the canonical analysis, which is consistent with the pattern of drug-taking behavior reported in Figures 5 to 15, suggests that some drugs may be more likely to be used within different ethnic groups than others. Based on this finding, an important research problem that arises is that of determining how different values regarding chemical substances are formed among youth in different ethnic groups.

3. Past Year and Past Month Experience

Figure 3 provides a comparison of past month and past year experience with a drug (excluding alcohol and tobacco). The data represents the proportion of students within each ethnic group from among those who ever tried a drug.

Inspection of the findings indicate that the highest prevalence of use occurred among Whites and Alaskan Native groups, with much lower occurrences having taken place among the other groups.

FIGURE 3. Past Year and Past Month Use by Ethnicity.

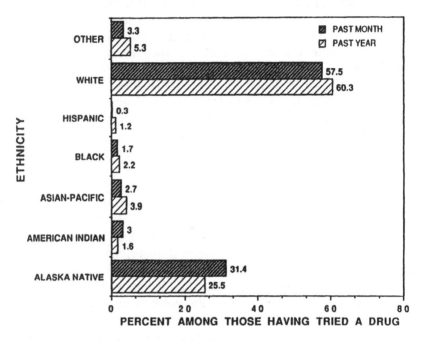

4. *Initiation into Drug-Taking Behavior*

An important element in understanding drug-taking behavior is determining at which ages young people are at greatest risk for initiation into different substances. This question takes on more significance when the focus is on attempting to determine if there are differences in the patterns and prevalence of drug-taking behavior among different ethnic groups.

Innovative research by Oetting and Beauvais (1983) introduced a method for specifically analyzing the acquisition of drug use. According to these researchers, "The method derives from an observation–when a cumulative record of the age of first use for a particular drug is charted (the graph shows what percent of the group have tried the drug at every age), the resulting curve is regular, smooth, and shows certain potentially informative characteristics" (p. 1116). Oetting and Beauvais have called the resulting curve the drug acquisition curve, because it shows how a group acquires exposure to a particular drug. An important aspect of the acquisition curve is that it could be used to show changing trends and to predict future drug epidemiology.

Based on Oetting and Beauvais' (1983) belief that acquisition curves have important implications for drug epidemiology, comparisons were made by ethnic group of the acquisition rates for five of the most prevalent substances (marijuana, inhalants, alcohol, cigarettes and chewing tobacco). The present data, however, are presented is tabular form.

The acquisition data were derived from responses to the following question: "How old were you when you first tried . . . . (name of drug)?" The upper age interval used for this study was 18 years. The results of the analyses are presented in Tables 17 to 21.

(a) Marijuana

The acquisition data for marijuana (Table 17) showed similar trends among the different ethnic groups, but Hispanic, "Other," and Alaskan Native students tended to show higher initiation levels between 12 and 15 years in relation to the other groups.

Table 17
Age of Initiation Into Marijuana by Ethnicity
(Cumulative Acquisition by Age)
Grades 7-12

Age First Tried	Alaska Native	American Indian	Asian-Pacific	Black	Hispanic	White	Other
			Ethnic Group (Percent)				
<10	14.4	13.1	10.5	8.8	12.5	7.1	6.4
11	20.2	17.4	10.5	17.5	22.5	11.8	14.8
12	32.0	30.4	20.7	21.8	25.0	18.0	30.0
13	49.5	60.8	32.9	37.0	35.0	35.5	54.8
14	71.4	80.4	47.2	60.9	52.5	56.8	76.9
15	87.1	91.3	67.6	81.6	72.5	76.4	85.3
16	94.7	93.5	90.0	90.3	92.5	89.8	94.8
17	98.9	95.7	96.1	96.8	97.5	97.4	98.0
18	100.0	97.9	100.0	99.0	100.0	99.4	100.0

(b) Inhalants

The acquisition data for inhalants (Table 18) showed greater variation than observed for marijuana. Blacks, for example, showed the highest level of early use of inhalants, with little increase thereafter until 12, after which there is a more rapid rate of initiation, which peaks at age 16. Hispanics, in contrast, showed a lower initiation rate until age 12, after which there is a dramatic and steady increase until age 17, but the overall prevalence level is lower in relation to the other ethnic groups. Alaskan Native students show a sharp increase in initiation between 11 and 14 years when compared to the other groups.

(c) Alcohol

The acquisition data for alcohol (Table 19) indicate trends similar to age of initiation for inhalants. There was a sharp upturn in initiation after age 11, and a steady acquisition level thereafter, peaking at age 16. Black and Asian-Pacific-Islander students, however, showed less sharp increases in initiation levels in comparison to the other groups.

Table 18
Age of Initiation Into Inhalants by Ethnicity
(Cumulative Acquisition by Age)
Grades 7-12

Age First Tried	Ethnic Group (Percent)						
	Alaska Native	American Indian	Asian-Pacific	Black	Hispanic	White	Other
<10	14.5	20.9	12.6	35.4	22.9	14.2	31.5
11	29.0	29.2	18.9	41.3	22.9	23.2	42.0
12	44.6	45.9	25.2	41.3	22.9	31.8	55.2
13	65.4	54.2	56.5	70.7	42.1	48.9	63.1
14	82.2	70.9	69.0	76.6	57.5	64.4	76.3
15	91.4	87.6	75.3	94.2	72.9	77.6	89.5
16	97.8	91.8	87.8	100.0	92.1	88.1	94.8
17	99.0	96.0	94.1	100.0	99.8	96.4	100.0
18	100.0	100.0	100.0	100.0	100.0	100.0	100.0

Table 19
Age of Initiation Into Alcohol by Ethnicity
(Cumulative Acquisition by Age)
Grades 7-12

Age First Tried	Alaska Native	American Indian	Asian-Pacific	Black	Hispanic	White	Other
			Ethnic Group (Percent)				
<10	18.3	23.8	11.4	21.1	17.9	13.2	16.8
11	27.9	35.7	19.0	26.7	21.5	22.4	26.4
12	43.2	59.4	29.1	30.9	41.1	41.3	47.2
13	64.5	76.3	43.0	49.2	67.9	63.1	72.0
14	81.1	93.2	67.1	70.3	82.2	81.4	85.6
15	93.2	98.3	86.1	87.2	94.7	93.2	93.6
16	97.9	100.0	91.2	95.7	100.0	98.1	97.6
17	99.7	100.0	98.8	99.9	100.0	99.4	100.0
18	100.0	100.0	100.0	100.0	100.0	100.0	100.0

(d) Smoking

Variations are observed among the different ethnic groups with respect to beginning smoking cigarettes (Table 20). Initiation during early exposure contrasts at ten years or earlier among the different groups. American Indian and youth in the ''Other'' group showed the highest levels. Blacks and Asian-Pacific Islanders exhibited the lowest levels. Thereafter all groups showed an increase, but varied with respect to patterns of initiation into smoking. Students in the ''Other'' group, for example, showed a continued increase in initiation after 11 years, peaking at age 14 and remaining constant thereafter. Blacks, in contrast, showed a lower overall involvement with smoking, but vary with respect to initiation until a peak is achieved at age 17. The other groups tended to range in between these two extremes, showing increases after age 11, and peaks at age 16.

(e) Chewing Tobacco

The initiation data for chewing tobacco (Table 21) showed high initiation levels for Alaska Natives and American Indians at early

Table 20
Age of Initiation Into Cigarettes by Ethnicity
(Cumulative Acquisition by Age)
Grades 7-12

| | | | Ethnic Group (Percent) | | | | |
Age First Tried	Alaska Native	American Indian	Asian-Pacific	Black	Hispanic	White	Other
<10	36.3	51.5	33.9	31.6	44.2	40.7	51.7
11	50.9	63.6	38.5	42.6	54.0	52.9	64.2
12	67.5	72.2	55.4	64.9	69.7	69.0	82.2
13	82.2	82.5	72.3	75.4	79.5	80.0	91.6
14	92.2	89.4	76.9	87.7	93.2	88.9	95.5
15	96.1	99.7	80.0	93.0	93.2	94.4	97.1
16	98.9	100.0	90.8	100.0	95.2	98.6	98.7
17	99.6	100.0	95.4	100.0	99.6	99.6	99.5
18	100.0	100.0	98.5	100.0	100.0	100.0	100.0

Table 21
Age of Initiation Into Chewing Tobacco by Ethnicity
(Cumulative Acquisition by Age)
Grades 7-12

| | | | Ethnic Group (Percent) | | | | |
Age First Tried	Alaska Native	American Indian	Asian-Pacific	Black	Hispanic	White	Other
<10	51.1	37.8	25.9	36.3	30.7	34.6	53.4
11	62.3	62.1	33.3	54.2	34.5	45.6	66.4
12	74.9	72.9	40.7	64.9	61.4	57.8	76.2
13	86.1	91.8	62.9	86.3	69.6	70.4	82.7
14	93.6	91.8	81.4	97.0	84.5	82.3	94.7
15	98.2	99.9	92.5	97.0	96.0	92.0	96.9
16	99.6	100.0	99.9	97.0	96.0	97.8	98.0
17	100.0	100.0	100.0	100.0	99.8	99.5	99.0
18	100.0	100.0	100.0	100.0	100.0	100.0	100.0

ages and which continued to rise steadily and peak at age 15. Hispanic students showed a dramatic increase after age 11, which continued to increase steadily until age 15. Overall, the ages between 11 and 14 tended to be the years between which exposure to chewing tobacco was highest.

In summarizing the findings from the acquisition data, it appears that a relationship between chronological age and age of initiation of different drugs can be inferred, and this relationship may also vary with ethnicity. This relationship however, appears to be a complex nonlinear one, that is, age and first experience and ethnicity do not appear to be a direct function of one another. Although different substances were tried at different ages by members of different ethnic groups, there was both overlap and separation for age of exposure to the different substances till age 18. In general, there tended to be a range of years for first experience that extended from 13 to 16 years. After age 16, initiation rates tended to plateau for some drugs and then decline, while other drugs showed a sharp drop in initiation rates after age 16. Initiation ages, however, tended to vary for different ethnic groups. The general pattern, nevertheless, conformed to the findings reported by Segal (1986), who described rates of exposure to different drugs for a large sample of adolescents.

B. Lifetime Prevalence by Ethnicity–Grades 4 and 6: Anchorage School District

As noted previously, a sample of 4th and 6th graders was obtained from the Anchorage School District (ASD). Findings from this sample are included in this report to provide a comparison with the results from the larger sample of students in grades 7-12, and to identify patterns of use among younger children that can be used to identify possible future trends. The results of the findings from students in the 4th and 6th grades in the ASD are found in Tables 22-26. Only those substances (alcohol, marijuana, inhalants, cigarettes and chewing tobacco) which were found to have high prevalence levels are reported. Although there were self-reports of use of hallucinogens (LSD), cocaine and crack, heroin, stimulants, depressants, and tranquilizers, the very limited experience with these substances did not warrant their being described in this report. The data in these figures represents the percent of students *within* each ethnic group who reported ever having tried each of the substances one or more times.

1. Alcohol Use Within Ethnic Groups: Grades 4 and 6

Table 22 shows that over half the students in grades 4 and 6, among all the different ethnic groups, reported having consumed alcohol at least once in their lifetime outside of their home. The general pattern tends to follow that shown in Table 13 for alcohol among the larger sample. Among these primary grade students American Indian youth showed the highest prevalence level (66.7%), followed by Hispanic youth (60%) and by students in the "Other" group (58.5%). Alaskan Native and White students showed comparable levels (52.3%). Asian-Pacific Islander and Black youth showed the lowest levels in comparison to the other groups (50% and 53% respectively). It appears that while alcohol use tends to begin early for all students, American Indian and Hispanic youth may show a higher risk to try alcohol when an opportunity arises.

2. Marijuana Use Within Ethnic Groups: Grades 4 and 6

The pattern of experience with marijuana (Table 23) among the primary graders mirrors that found among the secondary students, in that Alaskan Natives (13.1%), American Indians (13.8%), and the

Table 22
Lifetime Prevalence for Alcohol Use Within Ethnic Groups:
Grades 4 & 6
(N=943)

Ethnic Group	Lower[1] Limit	Percent	Upper Limit
Other	55.4	58.5	61.5
White	49.1	52.3	55.5
Hispanic	56.9	60.0	63.1
Black	49.8	53.0	56.2
Asian/Pacific	46.8	50.0	43.2
American Indian	63.7	66.7	69.7
Alaskan Native	49.1	52.3	55.5

[1]Upper and lower confidence levels calculated with a .95 confidence interval.

Table 23
Lifetime Prevalence for Marijuana Within Ethnic Groups:
Grades 4 & 6
(N=943)

Ethnic Group	Lower[1] Limit	Percent	Upper Limit
Other	9.5	11.5	13.5
White	4.9	6.5	8.1
Hispanic	5.1	6.7	8.3
Black	7.3	9.1	10.9
Asian/Pacific	0.0	0.0	0.0
American Indian	11.6	13.8	16.2
Alaskan Native	11.9	13.1	15.3

[1]Upper and lower confidence levels calculated with a .95 confidence interval.

"Other" (11.5%) groups showed the highest levels of having tried marijuana, followed by Black youth (9.1%). White (6.5%) and Hispanic (6.7%) students showed lower prevalence levels. No use was reported among youth from an Asian/Pacific Island background.

3. Inhalant Use Within Ethnic Groups: Grades 4 and 6

Prevalence levels for inhalants (Table 24) showed variation with respect to use by ethnicity, but Alaska Natives (22.6%) and "Other" (18.9%) groups showed the highest levels. Except for American Indians, who exhibited the lowest prevalence level (6.7%), inhalant use among primary graders in the remaining ethnic groups was generally comparable.

4. Smoking Within Ethnic Groups: Grades 4 and 6

Table 25 shows a prominence of having smoked among all ethnic groups, but Alaskan Natives, American Indian, Hispanic, and "Other" students tended to reveal the highest levels: Alaskan Native students (36%) showed the highest rate, followed by American

Table 24
Lifetime Prevalence for Inhalants Within Ethnic Groups:
Grades 4 & 6
(N=943)

Ethnic Group	Lower[1] Limit	Percent	Upper Limit
Other	17.6	18.9	20.2
White	10.3	12.4	14.5
Hispanic	8.1	10.0	11.9
Black	10.1	12.1	14.1
Asian/Pacific	8.4	10.3	12.2
American Indian	5.1	6.7	8.3
Alaskan Native	19.9	22.6	25.3

[1]Upper and lower confidence levels calculated with a .95 confidence interval.

Table 25
Lifetime Prevalence for Smoking Within Ethnic Groups:
Grades 4 & 6
(N=943)

Ethnic Group	Lower[1] Limit	Percent	Upper Limit
Other	23.6	26.4	29.2
White	19.9	21.5	24.1
Hispanic	27.1	30.0	32.9
Black	23.0	25.8	28.6
Asian/Pacific	15.1	17.5	19.9
American Indian	28.0	31.0	34.0
Alaskan Native	32.9	36.0	39.1

[1]Upper and lower confidence levels calculated with a .95 confidence interval.

Indian youth (31%), Hispanic youth (30%), "Other" youth (26.4%), and Black students (25.8%). Asian-Pacific Islanders showed the lowest level (17.5%) followed by Whites (21.5%) Overall, the pattern shown in Figure 30 approximates that found among the older students.

5. Chewing Tobacco Within Ethnic Groups: Grades 4 and 6

The high level of having tried chewing tobacco found among Alaskan Native youth in grades 7-12 is also uncovered among primary grade students (Table 26). Over a quarter of the Alaskan Native youth (26.7%) have tried chewing tobacco, which is the highest prevalence level among primary graders. Hispanic (16.7%), Black (15.2%) and American Indian (13.3%) students showed high levels of use in relation to the remaining groups.

In summary of the findings from the primary grades, the most striking feature is that the pattern of drug-taking behavior shown among these younger students, when examined with respect to use within ethnic groups among students in grades 7-12, tends to mirror that found among the larger sample. This finding has two clear implications. The first is that it is apparent that there is a trend for ethnic minority youth to be at early risk for involvement in drug-taking behavior. The second is that there may be a proclivity for trying specific substances before others such as cigarettes and smoking tobacco, as well as alcohol and marijuana. Whether or how this pattern may serve as a gateway to other drug use is in need of further research, but Fleming et al. (1989) suggest that cigarette smoking might be the specific precursor leading to multiple drug use.

Table 26
Lifetime Prevalence for Chewing Tobacco Within Ethnic Groups:
Grades 4 & 6
(N=943)

Ethnic Group	Lower[1] Limit	Percent	Upper Limit
Other	2.6	3.8	5.0
White	7.9	9.8	11.7
Hispanic	14.3	16.7	19.1
Black	13.0	15.2	17.4
Asian/Pacific	1.6	2.6	3.6
American Indian	11.1	13.3	15.5
Alaskan Native	23.9	26.7	29.5

[1] Upper and lower confidence levels calculated with a .95 confidence interval.

CONCLUSIONS, IMPLICATIONS, AND RECOMMENDATIONS

Communities throughout the United States have been particularly concerned with the problem of drug and alcohol use among youth for the past 25 years. This interest has been based on the belief that drug use can have catastrophic consequences for youngsters, who are both physically and emotionally immature, for their families, and for their communities. Based on this belief there has been a persistent struggle to understand the values and attitudes expressed by youth toward drugs, and to achieve perspectives on adolescent drug use patterns and trends. Most of this interest, however, has focused largely on white, mostly middle-class, youth (Trimble et al., 1987).

More recently, the very high prevalence of drug and alcohol use among ethnic minorities has stimulated interest in understanding the role and function of drinking and drug use within different ethnic groups in order to counter the problem (Binion et al., 1988; Gilbert, 1988; Newcomb & Bentler, 1986; Oetting, Beauvais, & Edwards, 1988). Westermeyer (1987), however, cautions that whenever a problem arising from drug or alcohol use reaches a critical level in society, particularly among ethnic minorities, there is a tendency to view it as an entirely new and unique phenomenon, when in actuality the behavior may have been in existence for a prolonged period of time. Therefore, before any research is undertaken to ascertain the nature of the psychological, social and cultural interactions that occur within cultural groups with regard to drug use, it is first necessary to understand the ideal and behavioral norms which are associated with drinking and drug use in a given culture. "While certain interactions apply more or less clearly to some drug use, no one model can explain all human behavior with regard to a specific drug, or even one society's behavior *vis-à-vis* its drug of choice" (Westermeyer, 1987, p. 21). Any model, therefore, that attempts to explain drug-taking behavior in a cultural group, first has to gain a perspective on the problem and examine it in terms of the values ascribed to drinking and drug use within a particular cultural group.

The research findings reported in this study represented a first step in the process of understanding drug-taking behavior among different ethnic groups in Alaska. The focus has been on gaining an understanding of prevalence levels and contrasting findings among different ethnic groups.

Overall, the lifetime prevalence for experience with chemical substances in Alaska was found to be high among all youth in grades 7-12. High prevalence levels were also noted for 4th and 6th graders within the Anchorage School District.

Even though the prevalence levels were high, drug-taking behavior is related to availability of drugs. Because of urban-rural differences among the sample the extent to which students obtain and try different substances may have influenced the patterns and extent of the prevalence levels reported herein. The general consistency of the findings across two waves of data collection (1983 and 1988), however, suggest that the availability factor may have had a minimal effect on the findings.

An examination of the proportion of youth *within* each of the different ethnic groups revealed that a great many non-White students tried/used drugs to achieve an altered state of consciousness. Drug involvement within the Alaskan student group was especially high for Alaskan Natives, American Indians, Hispanics, and students of mixed backgrounds (who are represented in the "Other" category), a phenomenon that is consistent with findings from other researchers (Gilbert, 1988; Oetting & Beauvais, 1981, 1987; Skager, Fisher, & Maddahian, 1986). Blacks and Asian-Pacific Islanders reported proportionally less use, a finding consistent with the research of Newcomb and Bentler (1986).

When reviewing the relationship between ethnicity and ever trying chemical substances, including alcohol and tobacco products, *within ethnic groups,* the pattern which emerged indicated that Hispanic and American Indian youth achieved prevalence levels which were disproportionately high with respect to their representation in the sample. Alaskan Natives also showed particularly high prevalence rates for trying marijuana.

The prevalence of smokeless tobacco use, notably chewing tobacco, was also exceptionally high among Alaskan Native youth. Although there may be many reasons for this finding, one contributing factor may be cultural influence. For example, the Alaskan Native culture, especially the Alaskan Eskimo, has been a "chewing culture.'' There is a long history of gnawing on long bones and hides in their culture which was related to survival by obtaining nutrients and making materials from hides (Hild, 1989). It is possible to speculate that as the transition from a subsistence culture to a cash economy society evolved, emphasis on "chewing" decreased accordingly. Within this context it is conceivable that there is a cultural legacy involving chewing, manifested through the use of chewing tobacco. Thus, the introduction of smokeless tobacco to the Native culture may have provided a means of modeling the western culture as well as preserving a cultural tradition of their own.

This conjecture, however, needs to be substantiated by further research which seeks to find answers to such questions as: (a) what is the prevalence of chewing gum among this group? Is it higher than that found among nonNative youth of comparable ages? and (b) What is the prevalence of use chewing tobacco among Alaskan Men and Women?

While the hypothesis stated above is tentative, at best, it was provided to attempt to demonstrate how Westermeyer's (1987) thinking, cited above, may be applied to understand one aspect of drug-taking behavior among Alaskan Native youth. The implication of this preliminary hypothesis is that any attempt to alter the use of smokeless tobacco within the Alaskan Native community may be very difficult because it has to counteract entrenched attitudes and behaviors.

The important question that arises is to what extent are cultural factors involved in drinking and other forms of drug-taking behavior among different cultural groups, especially among Alaska Natives and other nonWhite ethnic groups. Stated differently, the task becomes one of determining to what extent drinking and drug-taking behavior among youth is a symbolic representation of cultural values or traditions within a given subculture. With respect to American Indians, for example, May (1982) stated that ''Particular Indian tribes and cultural groups have been found to be high or low risks for many types of deviance because their traditional tribal customs encourage or do not discourage individualistic, flamboyant behaviors'' (p. 1199). The same phenomena inherent in American Indian and Alaskan Native groups may also be found within cultural subgroups, e.g., Hispanics, who have to adapt to the values and practices of the dominant culture.

The adverse impacts of acculturation stress on youth in different ethnic group or subcultural groups also has to be considered as a factor in drug-taking behavior. Social disorganization, cultural and social change, cultural conflict, and the resulting stress are all involved in the initiation of drug-taking behavior among such youth.

The above findings have important implications. One is that there is a clear need to begin to understand the broad array of social and cultural interactions regarding drug-taking behavior within different cultural groups. While the behavioral and social norms regarding the use of a given drug may closely resemble each other in different ethnic groups, each cultural group may nevertheless ascribe different meanings, values and attitudes to drug use (Westermeyer, 1987). "In societies [such as Alaska, with its ethnic diversity], where ideal and behavioral norms differ with regard to the use of a particular drug, there is likely to be a widespread use of that drug, with all its associated problems" (Westermeyer, 1987, p. 21). Ethnographic studies can help to begin to provide critical information about how cultural attitudes, values, and behaviors interact concerning drug-taking behavior within different ethnic groups.

Another important implication concerns prevention. There is little doubt that there is a need for a concentrated effort to develop education and prevention programs that account for ethnic diversity and which are responsive to the needs of a multicultural society. Prevention programs are usually concerned with changing attitudes about substance use (Simons, Conger, & Whitbeck, 1988). Such change, however, is largely successful among those youngsters who are most susceptible to such influences but do not impact youth who are most at risk for drug involvement (Oetting, Edwards, & Beauvais, 1988). If prevention efforts can be formulated to address the cultural factors within an ethnic group that place youngsters at high risk for drug involvement, then these efforts may be influential. For example, Oetting et al. (1988), state that

Drug involvement [among American Indian youth) is . . . primarily a function of peer clusters; dyads and small groups of close friends who mutually encourage drug use and who use drugs together. Underlying problems, such as poor family conditions and school adjustment difficulties, tend to increase the chances that an Indian child will make friends with other youth who also have problems, and the resulting peer clusters have a higher chance of getting involved with drugs. (p. 29)

Prevention efforts have to focus on changing those factors in the environment that contribute to and reinforce drug-taking behavior, instead of concentrating only on trying to change attitudes about using drugs.

The problem that Oetting et al. (1988) describe applies to all ethnic or cultural groups. The task is to identify and counteract the specific forces or influences within each ethnic group that are related to or influence drug-taking behavior. Such programs may need to start early in a child's development to be effective. The present research findings have provided some preliminary avenues of exploration involving the relationship between ethnicity and drug-taking behavior.

NOTES

1. The term: "Native" is used to refer to Alaska's indigenous people, who may be Yuipic or Inupiat Eskimo, Athabaskan Indians, Tligit or Haida Indians, or Aleuts. "NonNative" refers to all other ethnic groups (e.g., Whites, Blacks, Hispanic, Asian, etc.), who are not indigenous people.

2. Persons of Hispanic origin may be of any race (Hollmann, 1990).

3. Ethnicity was not asked for in accordance with the wishes of several Alaska communities who, because of recent adverse publicity concerning research findings, feared exploitation of the results if ethnicity were used. See the recent issue of *The Journal of the National Center*, Vol. 2, No. 3, Spring, 1989, for a complete discussion of this problem and its impact on conducting research in Alaska. The reverberations have not dissipated, even after nearly ten years.

REFERENCES

Binion, A. Jr., Miller, C. D., Beauvais, F., & Oetting, E. R. (1988). Rationales for the use of alcohol, marijuana, and other drugs by eighth-grade Native American and Anglo youth. *The International Journal of the Addictions, 23*(1), 47-64.

Crider, R. A., & Rouse, B. A. (Eds.) (1988). *Epidemiology on inhalant abuse: An Update.* (Research Monograph Series 85). Rockville, MD: National Institute on Drug Abuse.

Fleming, R., Leventhal, H., Glynn, K., & Ershler, J. (1989). The role of cigarettes in the initiation and progression of early substance use. *Addictive Behaviors, 14, 261-272.*

Fredlund, D. G., MacKinnon, D. O., Anglin, M. D., & Thompson, J. P. (1987). *Substance use among students in Texas secondary school–1988.* Austin, TX: Texas Commission on Alcohol and Drug Use.

Gilbert, M. J. (1988). Alcohol use among Latino Adolescents: What we know and what we need to know. *Drugs & Society, 3*(1/2), 35-54.

Hild, C. (1989, July, 17). Personal communication.

Hollman, J. (1990). *United States population estimates by age, sex, race and Hispanic origin 1980-1988.* Washington, D.C.: U.S. Department of Commerce.

Johnston, L. (1988). *Selected tables from the 1987 National High School Senior Survey.* Ann Arbor, MI: The University of Michigan.

Jones, R. B., & Moberg, D. P. (1988). Correlates of smokeless tobacco use in a male adolescent population. *The American Journal of Public Health, 78*(1), 61-63.

Lonner, T. D. (1983). Major construction projects and changing substance use patterns in Alaska. Anchorage, AK: The Center for Alcohol and Addiction Studies, University of Alaska, Anchorage.

McCarthy, W. J., Newcomb, M. D., Maddahian, E. & Skager, R. (1986). Smokeless tobacco use among adolescents: Demographic differences, other substance use, and psychological correlates. *Journal of Drug Education, 16*(4), 383-402.

May, P. A. (1982). Substance abuse and American Indians: Prevalence and Susceptibility. *The International Journal of the Addictions, 17*(7), 1185-1209.

Miller, J. D., & Cisisn, I. H. (1983). *National survey on drug abuse: main findings.* Rockville, MD: National Institute on Drug Abuse.

National Institute on Drug Abuse. (1989). *National Household Survey on Drug Abuse. 1988.* NIDA Capsules.

National Institute on Drug Abuse (1987). *Use of Selected Drugs Among Hispanics: Mexican Americans Puerto Ricans Cuban Americans.* Rockville, MD: National Institute on Drug Abuse.

Newcomb, M. D., & Bentler, P. M. (1986). Substance use and ethnicity: Differential impact of peer and adult models. *The Journal of Psychology, 120*(1), 83-85.

Oetting, E. R., & Beauvais, F. (1981). *Drug use among Native American Youth: Summary of findings* (1975-1981). Fort Collins, CO: Colorado State University.

Oetting, E. R., & Beauvais, F. (1983). The drug acquisition curve: A method for the analysis and prediction of drug epidemiology. *The International Journal of the Addictions, 18*(8), 1115-1129.

Oetting, E. R., & Beauvais, F. (1989). Epidemiology and correlates of alcohol use among American Indian adolescents living on Reservations. In D. Spiegler, S. Aitken, & C. Christian (Eds.), *Alcohol use among U.S. Ethnic Minorities* (pp. 239-268) (Research Monograph-18). Rockville, MD: National Institute on Alcohol Abuse and Alcoholism.

Oetting, E. R., Edwards, R. W., & Beauvais, F. (1988). Drugs and Native-American Youth. In B. Segal (Ed.). *Drugs & Society, 3*(1/2) 1-34.

Segal, B. (1983a). Alcohol and alcoholism in Alaska: Research in a multicultural and transitional society. *The International Journal of the Addictions*, *18*(3), 379-392.

Segal, B. (1983b). *Patterns of drug use: Report of a state wide school survey*. Juneau, AK: Department of Health and Social Services.

Segal, B. (1986). Age and first experience with psychoactive drugs. The *International Journal of the Addictions*, *21*(12), 1285-1306.

Segal, B. (1988). *Drugs and society: Cause, effects, and prevention*. New York: Gardner press.

Segal, B. (1990). Drug-Taking behavior among school-aged youth: The Alaska experience and comparisons with lower-48 states. *Drugs & Society*.

Segal, B., Huba, G. J., & Singer, J. L. (1980). *Drugs, daydreaming and personality: A study of college youth*. Hillsdale, NJ: Erlbaum.

Simons, R. L., Conger, R. D., & Whitbeck, L. B. (1988). A multistage social learning model of the influences of family and peers upon adolescent substance abuse. *Journal of Drug Issues*, *18*(3), 296-316.

Skager, R., Fisher, D., & Maddahian, E. (1986). *A statewide survey of drug and alcohol use among California students in grades 7, 9, and 11*. Sacramento, CA: Office of the Attorney General.

Spiegler, D., Tate, D., Aitken, S., Christian, C. (Eds.) (1989). *Alcohol use among U.S. Ethnic Minorities* (Research Monograph-18). Rockville, MD: National Institute on Alcohol Abuse and Alcoholism.

State Office of Drug Abuse. (1975). *Alaska state plan for drug abuse prevention*. Juneau, AK. Department of Health and Social Services.

State Office of Drug Abuse. (1976). *Alaska state plan for drug abuse prevention*. Juneau, AK. Department of Health and Social Services.

State Office of Alcoholism and Drug Abuse. (1979). *Alaska state plan for drug abuse prevention*. State Office of Alcoholism and Drug Abuse.

Division of Alcoholism and Drug Abuse. (1990). *State of Alaska alcoholism and drug abuse plan*. Juneau, AK: Division of Alcoholism and Drug Abuse.

Tanner, L. (1987, Feb. 13). *Smokeless tobacco use high among Native teenagers*. Anchorage Daily News, p. B-1.

Tuckson, R. V. (1990). Race, sex, economics, and tobacco advertising. *World Smoking & Health*, *15*(1), 5-6, 8.

Trimble, J. E., Padila, A. M., & Bell, C. S. (Eds.) (1987). *Drug abuse among ethnic minorities*. Rockville, MD: National Institute on Drug Abuse.

Warner, K. E. (1989). Effects of the antismoking campaign: An update. *American Journal of Public Health*, *79*(2), 144-151.

Westermeyer, J. (1987). Cultural patterns of drug and alcohol use: An analysis of host and agent in the cultural environment. *Bulletin on Narcotics*, XXXIX(2), 11-27.

World Health Organization. (1981). *Report of an ARF? WHO scientific meeting on adverse consequences of cannabis use*. Toronto: Addiction Research Foundation.

Planning Programs
for Prevention
of Deviant Behavior:
A Psychosocial Model

E. R. Oetting

SUMMARY. A psychosocial model based on peer cluster theory and aimed at the prevention of deviant behaviors is presented. The fundamental theorem that underlies the model is that deviant attitudes and behaviors are psychosocial in origin, a product of the interaction of psychological, social and cultural characteristics. The model further postulates the following: (1) Adolescence is a critical time in the evolution of deviant behaviors. Prevention programs, therefore, should include a major focus on youth. (2) Deviant attitudes and behaviors are a product of socialization, of learning norms through social interactions. (3) The primary socialization forces in a youth's life consist of the family, the school, and peer clusters. (4) The influence of secondary socialization forces, including the community, religion, the extended family, media, and peers in general, is less than and is usually mediated through the primary socialization links. (5) Any socialization link can transmit deviant norms, but healthy family and school systems are more likely to transmit non deviant norms. (6) Peer clusters can transmit either deviant or non deviant norms, but the major source for deviant norms is likely to be peer clusters. (7) Weak bonds between the child, the family, and/or the school increase the chances that the child will become a member of a deviant peer cluster. (8) Prevention programs to reduce deviant behaviors should reduce risk factors and increase resilience

E. R. Oetting is affiliated with the Tri-Ethnic Center for Prevention Research at Colorado State University.

The concepts presented in this paper have been derived from research supported by grants from the National Institute on Drug Abuse, P50 DA07074, R01 DA06293, R01 DA03371.

313

in order to promote strong bonds between the child, the family, the school, and peer clusters and should ensure that these bonds are utilized to communicate non deviant norms.

Young people can suffer from a variety of problems including physical and emotional illness, accidents, disabilities, and developmental difficulties. The type of intervention program that is needed is usually reasonably clear. Disease can be prevented through vaccination or environmental changes to alter disease vectors. Emotional problems can be treated with psychotherapy and sometimes prevented with psychoeducational programs. Accidents can be reduced by environmental design and training. Access can be increased for the disabled, and youth with developmental difficulties can be educated and trained to optimize their potential. Certainly not all of the answers are known, but there is at least a sense that the forms that prevention should take are known and that progress is being made.

There is a type of problem, however, where there are few clear directions and where progress has been limited: the prevention of deviance. School drop out rates are high. Crime, delinquency, and violence are about as prevalent as they have ever been. Precocious sex is occuring at high levels and, with the advent of the HIV retrovirus, is more dangerous than ever. Finally, although there have been some recent reductions in drug use, it is still endemic among American youth. There have been many attempts to deal with these problems, and some of them have been reasonably successful, but there is no clear, underlying model that encompasses all of these problems and that suggests a direction for future efforts. This paper presents a theory and a model designed to guide the planning aimed at the prevention of deviance.

First, it is essential to define what is meant by deviance and by deviant behaviors, particularly when programs are being planned for minority populations. The term *deviance* has lost much of its respectability among minority groups because it has been used as a weapon of prejudice; some behaviors that are acceptable or typical in minority cultures have been called deviant simply because they are not normative in a majority culture. *Deviance* has also lost some of its precision because it has been applied to minor variations in cultural norms, for example, differences in willingness to "speak up" in a discussion. Despite these misuses, deviance can still be a valuable construct if it is used appropriately. In this discussion deviant behaviors are considered to be those that are usually viewed as culturally inappropriate by the adults in the specific culture in which the child lives *and* that endanger youth; that either produce damage in youth or that adumbrate adult problems. Examples are illicit drug use and criminal acts. These deviant behaviors are legitimate goals for prevention. There are behaviors that endanger people but that are not viewed as deviant in some cultures, and the model only indirectly applies to prevention of these acts. Smoking is a good example. Although smoking creates serious health problems, it is not only accepted but is expected in some cultures. The first task for prevention in such cases is to change cultural norms so that smoking tobacco becomes culturally deviant; then this prevention model would apply. The model would also technically be applicable to culturally disapproved behaviors that do not endanger people, for example, talking back to teachers or parents. Prevention programs that are aimed at behaviors that do not endanger people, however, may merely be attempts to impose cultural conformity, and their value and appropriateness should be carefully assessed before such programs are implemented.

DEVIANCE AND PEERS

A successful prevention effort needs to begin with the recognition that peers play a critical role in developing and maintaining deviance. There are a few severely disturbed adolescents who engage in deviant behaviors because of their psychopathology; most deviant adolescents, however, are linked closely to other youth who share either actively or vicariously in their deviant acts. Peer cluster theory (Oetting & Beauvais, 1986a, 1986b) indicates that deviant behaviors among adolescents are nearly always a function of the interactions of youth in peer clusters. This pattern is consistent in both majority and minority populations (Beauvais, in press; Edwards, 1990; Oetting, Beauvais, & Edwards, 1988; Oetting, Swaim, Edwards, & Beauvais, 1989; Swaim, Oetting, Thurman, Beauvais, &

Edwards, in press). Peer clusters are best friends, couples, or groups of close friends. The youth in these peer clusters spend time together, share ideas, and form their own behavioral norms that can encourage or support deviant behaviors, and they often engage in the deviant behaviors together.

Peer clusters can also be a positive force in the lives of young people. Close friends can mutually reinforce ideas and values that oppose deviance. They can decide that drug use is bad and that drunk driving is wrong. They can mutually support feelings that precocious and/or unsafe sex should be avoided. They can reject criminality and engage in activities that do not provide opportunities for deviance.

Preventing deviance and encouraging non deviant behaviors must therefore alter the formation of peer clusters and change their influence on youth. Two general approaches are possible. One is to directly influence existing peer clusters. The major effects of peer clusters are concurrent; the peer clusters are linked directly to the deviant behavior at the time it occurs. Concurrent prevention programs, therefore, have to change peer clusters by discouraging deviant behavior and attitudes within the peer cluster or by reducing the opportunities for deviant behaviors. The second approach involves early prevention by modifying the precursors that lead to formation of deviant peer clusters. Peer clusters with a high potential for deviance do not form entirely at random. Many youth are attracted to deviant peers because of negative personal, social, and cultural characteristics in their background. Others are innoculated against deviance by strong positive influences in their lives. The most important forces that influence the potential for involvement in deviant peer clusters are the family and the school. There are other factors that affect a child, but they do not have the impact of these primary socialization links.

THE MODEL

Figure 1 presents a general model for prevention. It shows that the major influences on a youth that can encourage or prevent deviance are the family, the school, and peer clusters. The model is

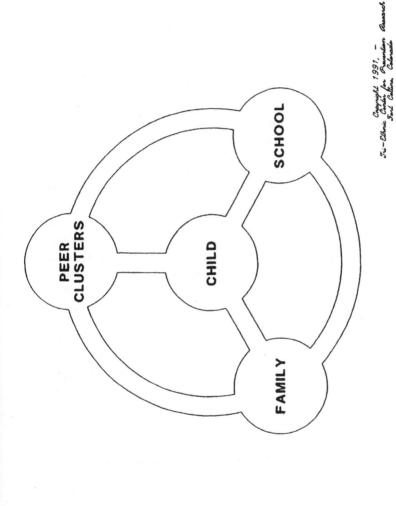

Copyright 1991, –
Tri-Ethnic Center for Prevention Research
Fort Collins, Colorado

Figure 1
A Model for Prevention of Deviant Behavior

317

purposely constructed as a wheel even though topologically the figure would be the same if it were drawn as a surrounding triangle or as a pyramid. The wheel was selected because the visual analogy is direct and graphic and has significant meaning; a wheel is a strong visual and tactile image in the U.S. majority culture, in most U.S. minority culturesm and in fact, in cultures of much of the world. The child is at the center or the hub, surrounded, protected, influenced, and moved by family, school, and peers. There are strong spokes that connect the hub to the rim, that link the child directly to the family, to the school, and to peer clusters. The rim of the wheel is then formed by the bonds between these groups. If all of these bonds are intact–the spokes and the rim–the wheel is a firm structure, and the child is likely to be strong and successful. If any bond is weak or broken, the entire wheel is endangered; other bonds are placed under additional stress and further breakdown is likely. The wheel no longer supports the child.

Primary socialization links. The three elements that make up the rim of the wheel were selected because they are the primary socialization forces for a youth. Nearly all of a child's social learning takes place in these contexts, in activities that are closely associated with either the family, the school, or peer clusters. It is in these primary relationships that the child learns language, attitudes, and beliefs and establishes normative behaviors.

There is a considerable body of literature that links problems with these primary socialization forces to deviance. The family has long been known to be an important factor in the development of the child. The dysfunctional family creates a strong potential for deviance. The drug use literature provides many examples (Adler & Lotecka, 1973; Blumenfield, Riester, Serrano & Adams, 1972; Brook, Lukoff, & Whiteman, 1977; Frumkin, Cowan, & Davis, 1969; Galli & Stone, 1975; Green, Blake & Zenhausern, 1973; Jessor & Jessor, 1977; Oetting & Goldstein, 1979; Pandina & Schuele, 1983; Streit, Halsted, & Pascale, 1974; Tec, 1974). Poor school adjustment is the proximal cause of dropout or expulsion. It is also related to drug use and other forms of deviance (Annis & Watson, 1975; Bakal, Milstein & Rootman, 1975; Brook et al., 1977; Clayton & Voss, 1982; Frumkin et al., 1969; Galli, 1974; Jessor, 1976; Kandel, 1975; Svobodny, 1982). As an example of the importance of peers in encouraging deviance, the single most frequent finding in studies of the correlates of drug use is the link between drug use and the use of drugs by peers, a link that is found in both majority and minority cultures (Adler & Lotecka, 1973; Beauvais, in press; Burkett & Jensen, 1975; Edwards, 1990; Huba & Bentler, 1980; Jessor & Jessor, 1977; Kandel, 1974; Lawrence & Velleman, 1974; McKillip, Johnson & Petzel, 1973; Oetting & Beauvais, 1987; Oetting et al., 1989; Swaim, Oetting, Edwards, & Beauvais, 1989; Tolone & Dermott, 1975; Wechsler & Thum, 1973; Windsor, 1973).

Values, beliefs, attitudes, and behaviors are learned through interactions with people and with other social aspects of the environment, and the model points out that the largest part of that socialization takes place within three contexts: the family, the school, and peer clusters. If these links are to be used to prevent deviance, two factors are important: first, the bonds between these elements of the model must be strong; second, appropriate normative cognitions and behaviors must be communicated through these links. We must begin with the specific elements of the wheel because, if the bonds between the elements are to be strong, each element must be essentially healthy.

There are many characteristics of children that can limit bonding. The most serious problems leading to deviance may be characteristics that make it difficult for children to establish bonds with the primary socialization links. An example would be the "difficult child" syndrome, whose characteristics may be related to genetic factors or very early developmental experiences (see Swaim et al., in press; and Tartar, 1988, for recent reviews). For these children prevention must focus on treatment of the condition or on building substitute socialization mechanisms that discourage deviance. There are other children who develop attitudes or beliefs that prevent them from forming good bonds, and prevention may have to change those characteristics so better bonds can be formed. In a prejudiced environment, being a minority, being disabled, being scarred, having a birthmark, being overweight, or any of hundreds of factors can limit bonding. Primary prevention must be aimed at eliminating prejudice, but the child may also need help in building alternative socialization links while society slowly changes.

There are characteristics of families that prevent adequate bonding. A dysfunctional family cannot form healthy bonds, and family discord, aggression, and hostility have been related to the child's deviant behaviors (Berriel-Gonzalez, Berriel-Gonzalez, Jauregui, & Contreras-Cisneros, 1978; Comstock, 1978; Crites & Schuckit, 1979; DeBarona & Simpson, 1984; Gilbert, 1983; Korman, Trimboli, & Semler, 1980; Matthews & Korman, 1981). Family therapy or psychotherapy for the inadequate parent may be needed, or the child must be provided with an alternative or substitute for this crucial relationship.

A bad school system or even a single truly inadequate teacher can prevent formation of good bonds with the school (Dodson, 1981). Before progress can be made, the school system or its leadership may need to be restructured and destructive teachers need to be either retrained or replaced.

Although there is a higher probability that healthy systems will bond effectively, there is no guarantee. There may be external factors that prevent or limit bonding, for instance, a child might be shuffled between divorced or separated parents or even isolated from parents by illness. Economics can also lead to barriers; reservation-based Native-Americans may have to leave the reservation for long periods to find work and may not be able to take the child along. Although the extended family then frequently becomes the primary family and forms strong bonds, this may not always happen. A child may adjust poorly to grade school simply because the personalities of the child and teacher do not mesh well.

Strong bonds between the child and one or more socialization links do not always assure appropriate bonds with other links. For example, children who are basically healthy and who have strong family bonds are less likely to associate with drug-using peers, but some of them do. There are always children who come from "good" families, who have always had generally good relationships with their families, but who still somehow get involved with drugs during adolescent rebellion. Preadolescence and adolescence are a time of emotional turmoil and of limited cognitive complexity. Even healthy young people can be driven by their immediate needs, can be blind to future disasters, and can make bad choices. When a youth is using drugs within a peer cluster, the peer cluster is transmitting deviant norms. This situation usually places the youth's peers and the family at odds. An analysis of the prevention model would probably show that family-peer cluster bonds are weak–that the family does not know the child's friends and does not like them or approve of them. For example, building bonds between the family and the child's peer cluster may be particularly difficult for a minority family where the child has developed friendships in the majority culture.

Strong bonds with the family may not prevent problems in bonding with the school, particularly for minority youth. The problems of minorities in the school system have been discussed often. Recent papers include Fernandez and Velez (1989); Hare (1988); Robledo (1989); Wehlage, Rutter, Smith, Lesko, and Fernandez (1989). Bonding between minority parents and the school system may be especially difficult. In early human cultures there was no separate school system. Teaching of cultural skills, including the most important skill, language, was the responsibility of the primary family and, to some extent, the tribe. In today's society, in contrast, much of the responsibility for training the child in the culture has been passed on to the schools. The schools, however, are designed to transmit the cultural skills and attitudes only of the dominant majority culture. When the family is successful in that dominant culture and the school is doing its job appropriately, that family's values and beliefs and what they want to teach the child will generally be congruent with those being taught by the school. For members of the dominant culture, there will therefore be at least an implicit bond, and often an explicit bond, between the family and the school.

But the minority family may not participate in this aspect of the dominant culture. The minority family's cultural knowledge, language, cultural skills, values, and beliefs are not necessarily those that the school system was designed to teach or to respond to. There may be no one in the school who speaks the family's language. When that happens, there can be a breakdown of critical links in the model. For further information, Curiel (1991) discusses the barriers that Hispanic parents face in building relationships with the school system.

Strong bonds are, however, only part of the equation. It is also essential that the socialization links formed by these bonds communicate non deviant attitudes and that they do not reinforce deviant behaviors. These attitudinal and behavioral norms are critical; the youth may, for example, have strong bonds with the family, but if the family uses drugs, then the bonds will actually encourage drug use. There are children who live with parents who abuse alcohol and drugs and who do not discourage the child's use. When that happens, the odds are exceptionally high that the youth will go on to form relationships with other youth who have a high potential for deviance. Usually, however, the family and the school try to provide as positive an influence as they can. The family and school are not likely to encourage and support deviance; that is almost always the role of peers.

Peer clusters: A major source for deviant norms. Peer cluster theory states that deviant norms emerge primarily from the links between the youth and close friends (Oetting & Beauvais, 1986a & 1986b). With some exceptions, strong family and school bonds tend to reduce the chance of deviance. Strong peer bonds, in contrast, may be as likely to encourage as to discourage deviance.

When family, school, and peers are *all* bonded together, the peers involved are likely to be non deviant. If the family has strong associations with the child's close friends, those friends are likely to share in the family's values and beliefs and are not likely to behave in ways that are disapproved of by the family. When a child's close friends are bonded strongly to the school, they are likely to have incorporated the attitudes and values promulgated by the school. The peer clusters, in these cases, are not likely to be a source of deviant norms.

For a child to avoid deviance, the forming of strong bonds with a non deviant peer cluster is the final, crucial stage. A breakdown in the bonds with the family or school greatly increases the chances that the child will bond with peers who have a potential for deviance (Oetting & Beauvais, 1987). With the family and school out of the picture, peer relationships then become the major source for norms; and when that happens, the chances that those peer clusters will be a source of deviant norms and that the child will engage in deviant behaviors are greatly increased.

This increase in the potential influence of peers may or may not be accompanied by strong peer bonds. Youth "street gangs," for instance, usually show almost a total breakdown of the links between the youth, the family, and the school and give an appearance of strong internal bonding to peers. The most extreme examples may be the homeless and destitute "street kids" in Mexico and Brazil who form peer "gangs" that totally substitute for a family (Carlini-Cotrim & Carlini, 1988; Leal et al., 1978). In some cases, however, this close bond with friends may be an illusion. Young people may insist that their close relationships with friends are solid, but a closer look may show that is not the case. The youth who has not been able to build strong bonds with the other primary socialization forces may be equally incapable of building really strong bonds within peer clusters. Among highly deviant youth, for example, relationships with peers may be marked by their transitory quality. Anyone who uses drugs may become an "instant friend." These same young people are also likely to talk about being "ripped off" by their friends, suggesting how poorly bonded these friendships are. Despite weak bonding and their fugacious nature, these "instant friends" play the role of peer clusters. They support and maintain deviant attitudes and behaviors and provide the contexts for those behaviors.

Whether the bonds are strong or transitory, the influence of those peer clusters on deviant behavior, particularly in the absence of strong normative influences from the family and the school, can be immense. Building up the links between family, school, and child can reduce the probability of formation of deviant peer clusters, but the essential step is the final one of linking peer clusters into the system so that they become a force for health, not deviance.

SECONDARY SOCIALIZATION LINKS

There are, of course, other socialization forces in the child's life including the community, religion, the extended family, peers, and media that can and do influence the child. These forces affect the child directly by communicating messages about normative behaviors and indirectly by either supporting or undermining the child's primary socialization links.

Community. The most potent secondary socialization force is probably the community. The community provides the broad social environment, the context in which all socialization interactions take place. As such, it has a pervasive influence on nearly everything that happens. In looking at the effect of any single aspect of this background on the child, a specific community influence is likely to be fairly small and almost entirely mediated by the direct relationships with one or more of the primary socialization links. The community, however, influences so many aspects of adjustment that its total impact can be great.

The effects on the child are generally related to the immediate environment, the neighborhood. These effects include physical, emotional, and social health. Physical health can be influenced by water, sewage and garbage control, availability of health services, and protection from violence. Emotional well-being, particularly feelings of security, can also be strongly influenced by fear of violence and by factors such as a stable set of neighbors and local services and businesses. Negative influences can be created by factors such as police hostility or a general atmosphere of prejudice. These negative community characteristics, unfortunately, are more prevalent in impoverished, disadvantaged, minority neighborhoods. The community also provides opportunities for formal peer associations, including transportation and recreational opportunities for youth. These, too, may be less accessible to poor minority youth.

The community has direct and powerful effects on the family and the school and, through them, ultimately on the child. One of the most important influences is economic opportunity for the family. If the family cannot find work, cannot meet financial needs, it is hard for it to provide a stable, supportive environment for the child. The school system that lacks financial or social support from the community is also unable to meet the child's needs.

The community sends messages about expected normative attitudes and behaviors as well. On the one hand, a clean, orderly community with high levels of family involvement in community affairs and with visible anti drug and anti violence programs produces a general message that discourages deviance. On the other hand, the youth living in an impoverished environment with inadequate community services, surrounded not by stability but by transients and failing businesses, whose visible models for success are street hustlers, is picking up messages about normative behaviors that enhance the potential for deviance. Nurco, Shaffer, and Cisin (1984) provide data showing that negative neighborhood characteristics can be strongly related to the use of drugs.

Religion. Religious institutions teach beliefs that tend to counter deviance and also provide other activities and learning experiences. Religious commitment and activity do not preclude deviant behaviors, but they are associated with reduced deviance (Bogg & Hughes, 1973; Brook et al., 1977; Jessor, 1976; Jessor, Jessor, & Finney, 1973; Rohrbaugh & Jessor, 1975; Turner & Willis, 1984). Typically in children and adolescents religion is mediated by the family. Although religions attempt to teach values and appropriate behaviors, they are unlikely to have much effect unless there is a strong family religious orientation to support that teaching. Religious activities that involve youth also act to counter deviance. They not only involve expression of values counter to deviance but also provide opportunities for formal peer associations, generally supervised by adults. These activities compete with the informal peer associations that may encourage deviance.

Extended family. The extended family interacts with the youth less than the primary family, but it provides role models and a sense of generational continuity and cultural stability. In the prevention model the term *family* is not meant to include only the child's biological parents or legal guardians. The actual family referred to in the diagram consists of those adults who live with the child and who are involved in raising that child during these formative years. The term *family* was chosen as a descriptor in the model only because it communicates clearly and quickly and is reasonably accurate for most children. Grandparents, aunts and uncles, baby-sitters, nurses, day care providers, or others should be considered to be the child's family *if* they maintain a close and continuing relationship and are responsible for the child for significant periods of time.

The extended family, then, is not defined by blood or marriage; it consists of those relatives who visit occasionally, who participate in family traditions, and who are identified to the child as relations and part of the family group. These distal members of the family are secondary socialization forces. They may have an influence on the child, but it is negligible compared to the influence of the primary family. When people say things like "It was my grandmother who had the most influence on my life," that grandmother usually had a major role in raising the child and would in this model be defined as part of the primary family, not as extended family.

Peers in general. Although peer clusters provide the primary socialization link, the youth's peers in general are a secondary source of socialization. If, for example, drug experimentation is tolerated and accepted by a large proportion of the youth in a particular school, that general norm increases the chances that peer clusters will engage in drug use. Building general peer norms that oppose deviance is worthwhile. If most youth in a cohort apply strong sanctions against deviance, children seeking peer relationships will have a higher probability of forming peer clusters that include youth with norms against deviance and their own attitudes and behaviors will be influenced in these peer clusters.

There are often larger networks of like-minded friends who share a particular lifestyle. They wear a particular style of clothing, use makeup and have their hair done in a particular style, listen to the same general type of music, engage in similar recreational or school activities, and so on. Walters (1980) was one of the first to categorize these lifestyles and to show that they differed in drug use, and Sutherland (1947) saw differential association with peers who had particular attitudes and values as a potent force in first forming attitudes and then shaping subsequent behaviors. Peer cluster theory, however, points out that, although these lifestyle groups may set a general tone, the dyads or small groups of close friends that form within these broad groups determine the actual behaviors. The larger peer group has an influence, but the influence of the peer cluster is primary.

The effects of peer clusters, peer lifestyle groups, and peers in general can involve complex interactions. Close friends often form islands with clearly defined boundaries that mark them, at least in their own minds, as different. They may build attitudes and engage in behaviors that differ from those of the rest of the group, including deviant behaviors. When there is a high potential for deviance in the peer cluster, the deviant behaviors may become even more extreme because of general intolerance of those behaviors by the peer group as a whole. Those few youth who are drug involved, for example, may form peer clusters that are isolated and rejected by other youth. Their response may be to take pride in and exaggerate their deviant behaviors. The very forces that are likely to reduce overall drug use can act to increase drug involvement of some peer clusters.

Media. One way of viewing media is to see various forms as a constant presence in the child's life, a general part of the environment that has an effect on socialization. Written material, books, papers, texts, comics, signs, posters, and advertisements surround the child, so reading, art, and music are alternative secondary socialization mechanisms. They present the possibility of putting children in touch with cultural concepts and ideas that are not directly related to their primary social contexts. (Recognition of this possibility may be one reason why some strongly conservative subgroups in our society are so concerned with controlling children's access to reading and music; they fear any influence except their own.)

Reading may be the most potent form of media in terms of communicating attitudes and ideas that can either promote or prevent deviance. As a child grows, intellectually and emotionally, reading can have a greater and greater direct influence on attitudes and behaviors, and reading may even be a primary socialization mechanism for adults. Reading has some influence on nearly all young people, but most youth through the period of adolescence have not yet developed a level of cognitive complexity that allows reading to have a primary influence on their attitudes and beliefs; what effect reading has is likely to be mediated through their links to parents, school, and peers. Children comprehend reading within the context of their own experience, attitudes, and beliefs; they generally do not have the ability to translate meaning very much beyond their existing cognitive frameworks. They are likely to interpret what they read within the context of their existing ideas without changing those ideas much. Further, what they do learn is usually tested in their social interactions and is not likely to be incorporated into beliefs and attitudes unless "confirmed" in these interactions.

Considerable attention has been paid to music as a source of deviant attitudes. Art and music can include messages about deviance, but like reading, the major effects occur when the messages are translated through peer clusters. These media can have an effect, and that effect can be serious. When a peer cluster, for instance, becomes obsessed with an idea such as violence or suicide, members can find music, art, or reading materials that provide support for those ideas and can use those media to support their ideas and beliefs. The process, however, is integrally bound up in the mutual reinforcement occuring within peer clusters.

These peer clusters may be embedded in a peer lifestyle group, particularly where there is a particular form of music involved. The youth who identify with a particular style may mark themselves by dress or demeanor, and from the outside these groups may appear to be homogeneous. The peer clusters that exist within a framework, however, may be quite different from each other, and it is within those peer clusters that primary socialization takes place. The choice by a peer cluster to identify with a particular lifestyle group is more likely to be a symptom of the needs and attitudes of its members than to be a cause of deviant behaviors. There may be a particular problem for peer clusters of minority youth if there are no music or art lifestyle groups that include members of their minority group or if those minority lifestyle groups tend toward communication of deviant attitudes.

Television and movies are also secondary socialization factors. The effect of their messages is likely to be mediated by the primary socialization links. Deviant attitudes included in movies and TV will probably not be incorporated into attitudes and behaviors unless they are supported by interactions with deviant primary socialization links, usually peer clusters. Some children spend an exceptional number of hours watching television suggesting the possibility that TV may be a more direct socialization influence for some children. That possibility should be explored, but the passive quality of the interaction with television suggests that for most youth it will retain its status as a secondary socialization force.

Although media are secondary socialization links, they provide a major avenue for prevention programming. A recent book, *Persuasive Communication and Drug Abuse Prevention* (Donohew, Sypher, and Bukoski, 1991), thoroughly reviews the field. Most media efforts, at least in attacking drug abuse, have focused on communicating norms against deviance. The prevention model suggests that media efforts might be effective if they also included attempts to improve bonding between the primary socialization links.

Inclusion of secondary socialization links in the model. The model could have been expanded into another dimension such as a sphere including, for instance, community and peer associational groups in positions orthogonal to family, school, and peer clusters. Other socialization forces such as media could be included as additional dimensions in an N dimensional space. The exercise is tempting, but it would not present as accurate a picture as the model that is presented here. These other socialization forces are secondary, not primary. They are usually related to and their effects mediated by the primary socialization systems–the family, the school, and peer clusters. Prevention programs can and should involve these secondary sources, but special effort should be made to ensure that they are connected to, supported by, and influence the primary socialization characteristics and the links between them.

STAGES IN DEVELOPMENT
AND THE PREVENTION MODEL

The prevention model applies directly to preadolescents and adolescents, where peer clusters are an integral part of socialization. The stages are orthogenetic, and the exact model that should be used for planning prevention programs prior to adolescence depends on the age of the child. Figure 2 shows the stages in development of the model.

The first diagram in Figure 2 shows the social world of the preschool child. The family is the sole primary socialization system during these years. The second diagram shows that during the first few years of school the only primary socialization forces are the family and the school. During those years a child may have playmates and friends, but their impact on the child is not as strong as it will be later; friends are likely to be a secondary socialization force, not a primary one. This second stage begins when children enter school and ends when they begin to be influenced strongly by

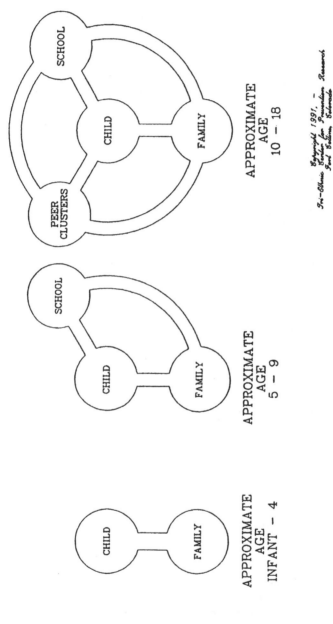

Figure 2
Stages in Evolution of the Psychosocial
Prevention Model in U.S. Culture

330

their peers and when that influence becomes essentially independent of the family and the school. The third model, the general model for prevention that includes peer clusters, becomes applicable at about age 11, when preadolescents begin to form small groups that are cohesive and that survive as groups over extended periods of time from weeks to years. (An interesting hypothesis would be that because of weak family and school bonds, youth who form deviant peer clusters do so earlier than other youth.) The first two stages do not involve peer clusters directly, but these stages are an integral part of peer cluster theory. The earlier interactions between the child, the family, and the school set the stage for formation of peer clusters. Prevention programs for different age groups need to consider these stages of development, focusing efforts on the bonds that are important at each age.

LIMITS OF THE MODEL

Prevention is a term so broad in definition that it can cover almost any program designed to help people, so before utilizing a model it is essential to establish the parameters that limit its applicability. The prevention model is a psychosocial model, concerned with those behaviors that grow out of social behaviors and it would therefore be useful only when a problem involved a vector related to social behavior. Sexually transmitted diseases (STD), for example, involve social behaviors including precocious sex, unprotected sex, promiscuity, and sexual behaviors that lead to torn tissue. As many of these behaviors are deviant within general social norms of both majority and minority populations, the model would be appropriate for prevention of STD.

Because peer cluster theory is concerned with the deviant behaviors of young people, this prevention model is limited to children and adolescents. Despite that limitation, the model is broadly applicable, as many psychosocial prevention programs should target young people. Not only are children at risk for a range of problems, but many adult problems have roots that go back to childhood and adolescence. On the positive side, adult health and competence do not suddenly appear full-blown at maturity; they are outcomes of long growth and development, emerging through a series of stages that are deeply tied to early experience.

There are always individual exceptions that need to be considered. There are situations in our culture where children do not attend school but may, for example, be provided with private tutoring or home schooling. The school system, then, would not enter into the equation; education would be only another function of the family. There are situations where children do not form peer relationships outside the family group. Children of some recent immigrant families attend school but then return to work in a parent's business, with no time for peer group friendships.

There are other children who do not establish peer clusters; they have no best friend nor do they have a group of close friends. It is possible that among these children there are a few who are simply different, who are developing in their own way, self-assured and self-motivated. If so, they are rare. Most children who fail to develop peer clusters in our society are isolated, lonely and shy or are not experiencing developmental tasks that help them develop social skills and independence. They are likely to have problems, both in childhood and later in life. Because their personal and social needs are not being met, they may engage in deviant behaviors in a desperate attempt to meet those needs. If, however, their bonds to parents and to the school are strong and involve communication of non deviant norms, these children without close friends are not likely to develop deviant behaviors; there are no peer clusters to transmit deviant norms.

It is always possible to find specific exceptions to any model, and there are healthy people who passed through systems where one or more of these bonds were weak. The human organism is incredibly resilient, and people must be credited when they have the strength to overcome adversity. Many of those who survived bad situations did so by finding ways to substitute other relationships for the damaged ones, perhaps providing a suggestion for prevention. When primary bonds cannot be formed, substitutes might be found. If a child, for instance, has been unable to establish a positive relationship with a teacher, another adult in the school system may provide an effective substitute, providing a school-child bond. The value of such mentors has been discussed by Guajardo (1990) and Hollifield (1989).

In other situations that seem to be exceptions, the apparent lack of bonding is only on the surface and does not represent what is actually occuring. There are immigrant families where the parents speak little English and appear to have no direct links to the school but whose children are highly successful in school. In this situation, the parent-school bond may be implicit rather than explicit. The parents cannot talk to anyone at the school, but they express a high value for education, insist that their children work hard and do their homework, insist that children learn what the school teaches despite apparent conflicts with the parents' culture, and reward their children for doing well in school. This kind of bond can be effective despite the lack of an actual link between the parents and the school. Caplan, Choy and Whitmore (1992) attribute the academic success of children from Indochinese refugee families to the exceptionally strong family support of education.

One further caveat is that the final model is to a considerable extent culture bound. The model centers on the family, the school, and peers. It applies, therefore, only to those cultures where the child is raised by a primary family, where the school has a strongly established role in socialization, and where the child has interactions with peers that are independent of family and school activities. It would not be an appropriate model where the family and/or tribe were the only means for teaching culturally appropriate skills, attitudes, and behaviors or where there were no peer interactions outside the family until after adolescence.

Although these are limits, they enclose an exceptionally broad domain. The primary family raises the child in most cultures. The school is an important socialization mechanism in most of today's societies, and there are often peer interactions outside the scope of family activities, so the model should apply very generally.

THE PREVENTION MODEL AND CONFORMITY

The basic process of socialization is toward conformity, and this model is a socialization model. Prevention tries to make dysfunctional systems functional and attempts to strengthen weakened bonds. Prevention efforts also dictate to some extent the content of the system, attempting to communicate and firmly establish norms against deviant behaviors that will damage the child. To the extent that the effort succeeds, it does lead to conformity to non deviant norms. Prevention programs, then, might be accused of leading only to social and personal conformity, to building robots with no unique talents and abilities.

The argument is more philosophical than practical. Healthy systems and strong bonds are likely to lead to greater sharing of values, but family values can vary greatly. They can be conservative or radical, respect conformance or demand independence. Adolescence is also a time when youth are likely to experiment with a range of ideas and behaviors, a time of strong needs for both affiliation and independence. Successful prevention programs that build powerful and effective norms against those deviant behaviors that would truly damage the adolescent touch on only one aspect of overall adjustment. They do not necessarily lead to creation of a person who unthinkingly conforms.

In fact, the adolescent with a solid base, with strong emotional links to the family, to school, and to non deviant peer clusters, may be able to use that secure foundation for greater exploration of alternatives. He or she may be more capable of choosing the less traveled and more challenging path.

PLANNING PREVENTION PROGRAMS

The elements of the psychosocial prevention model are substantially the same as those found in other psychosocial approaches to prevention of deviant behaviors, so nearly all prevention programs might be able to fit somewhere within the model. This possibility does not, however, justify any program merely because it happens to deal with one or more of the socialization links discussed here. The model should be used instead to consider the limitations of prevention programs and what might make them more effective.

The prevention model indicates that an effective prevention program must ultimately do one or more of the following: (1) improve the health, competence or strength of the child, the family, the school, or peer clusters; (2) improve the bonds between these elements; or (3) reduce deviant norms or enhance the communication of non deviant norms through these bonds. There are two general types of psychosocial prevention programs: (1) focused programs and (2) broad-based programs.

Focused programs. A focused program is one that is aimed at a limited target, a target defined in terms of specific known risk factors and limited to a relatively narrow subpopulation that is known to be at serious risk for deviance. The aim should be either the reduction of risk factors or the enhancement of characteristics that increase resilience. The targeted subpopulation should be known to be at risk either because its members are deficient or because they are known to be capable of considerable improvement in resiliency.

The first step, therefore, in planning a focused prevention program must be to denote and define the risk factors involved and then to define the subpopulation that is at risk because of these personal or social limitations. The prevention model indicates that, if a focused program is going to lead to an important reduction in deviance, the risk factors should appear somewhere in the prevention model. They can be characteristics of an individual element, weaknesses in the bonds between elements, or inadequate communication of non deviant norms through those bonds.

The elements in the model include the child, the school, the family and peer clusters. As an example of risk factors related to individual elements of the wheel, a group of children may have characteristics that place them at risk. They may have traits that make bonding difficult or that interfere with communication of appropriate norms. These traits can range from relatively rare conditions of serious psychopathology (such as solitary aggressive type of conduct disorder) to traits shared by large numbers of children that merely increase the probability of deviant behaviors (such as sensation seeking or high trait anger). The traits must, however, be true risk factors for deviance. As an example of a prevention program based on a fallacious premise, many prevention programs for drug abuse have been aimed at improving self-esteem, but the research evidence suggests that this is not a particularly strong risk factor for drug involvement.

Focused prevention programs can be aimed at the individual elements of the wheel, but the prevention model suggests that successful reduction of deviance will occur only if the program generalizes so that it influences the strength of the bonds within the wheel and the communication of non deviant norms through those bonds. Two examples may clarify this point further: a prevention program for angry youth and a prevention program for sensation-seeking youth.

High trait anger is a characteristic of the individual. It meets the criterion for a focused program because it has been shown to relate to alcohol involvement of youth and because a specific group of youth can be identified who possess this risk factor. Trait anger can be reduced through anger management training, so a prevention program could be run that attempted to reduce alcohol involvement through anger management training. Such a program might work, and should be tested, but peer cluster theory and the prevention wheel suggest further elaboration.

Peer cluster theory suggests that alcohol use does not occur merely because the youth is angry but that alcohol use and the evolution of the norms that control that behavior derive from the youth's links to primary socialization forces. In this situation these links are most likely to be the family and peer clusters. If the norms for alcohol use are transmitted by the family, then those must be changed. If, however, the family is not encouraging alcohol use, then the source is probably peer clusters. Identification with peer clusters who encourage deviant behavior is, in turn, probably a result of weak bonds with the family and/or the school. It is easy to see how chronic anger could damage those bonds. An early prevention program for angry youth, therefore, not only has to help them deal with their anger but must help them build better relationships with parents and/or deal more effectively with school authorities.

A prevention program dealing with high sensation seekers provides different challenges. High sensation seeking may be less amenable to change than high trait anger, and there may even be some question about the appropriateness of trying to alter it. Whereas high anger is rarely of value to the person, high sensation seeking can, if channeled toward non deviant goals, be a considerable asset. A successful prevention program for sensation seekers, then, must involve an attempt to change the expression of the trait rather than to alter the trait.

Building a successful focused program may also depend on the answers to other questions about sensation seekers. For instance, how does sensation seeking relate to bonding? Whereas high anger is almost invariably a threat to interpersonal bonds with parents and school, sensation seeking may either enhance or detract from bonding, depending on the person and the situation. Before planning a prevention program, we ought to know how sensation seeking influences the bonds with family, school, and peer clusters. Another question is how sensation seeking relates to the transmission of deviant norms. We need to know more about how it influences the communication of deviant and non deviant norms through family, school, and peer clusters.

Although answers are needed to these questions, we are not entirely helpless in the meantime. If peer cluster theory is accurate, a sensation seeker who engages in deviant behaviors will be involved in peer clusters that reinforce deviant norms for that person. A concurrent prevention program, then, would need to involve the peer clusters of sensation seekers, changing them so that they communicate non deviant instead of deviant norms. Donohew and his colleagues, for example, are studying the effect of media on sensation seekers and trying to get the message across to them that it is possible to find excitement in roller coasters rather than drugs (Bardo & Mueller, 1991; Donohew, Lorch, & Palmgreen, 1991). The model indicates, however, that an early prevention program for sensation seekers needs to deal with their links to family and school and suggests studies to find out what factors allow some sensation seekers to build strong bonds with the family and school and keep others from constructing those bonds.

Instead of strengthening bonds, prevention programs may be aimed at decreasing communication of deviant norms. When, for example, a school runs an anti drug program such as "Just Say No," it is trying to use its existing bonds with students in order to transmit anti drug norms. The children with strong school bonds are likely to incorporate these beliefs. The problem is that children with weak bonds to the school are those least likely to be influenced by the program; the children who need it most may be influenced the least. Because of their hostility toward the school, they may in fact reject the norms the school is trying to communicate and actually move toward deviance.

In general, focused prevention programs can be effective when they are attacking key elements of the model. The model suggests, however, that the overall effectiveness of these focused programs will depend on several factors. The most important is probably whether or not the focused prevention program is aimed at a critical problem in the system. Is it altering characteristics that are actually involved in the production of the deviant behavior? Is it reaching the subgroup of the population that is at risk because of those characteristics? Focused prevention programs might become more effective if they followed on through the model, building in follow-up programs that assured transfer of the focused program to strengthening of the other elements of the model and of the bonds between them.

Broad-based programs. Whereas the focused program is aimed at a specific limited set of risk factors, broad-based programs attempt to generally reduce risk factors or to develop greater resilience in an entire population or cohort. Developers of broad-based programs usually provide a wide range of attacks on the problem. Some of these attacks may be focused programs aimed at high-risk youth. Others may be more general programs aimed at increasing resiliency and further reducing risk to low-risk youth. Although the analysis of each individual program is the same for focused and broad-based programs, there may be differences in philosophy and approach. It is possible to have a broad-based program that clearly targets known risk factors and specific subpopulations, a program that is really just a set of focused programs. More often, the individual parts of broad-based programs are aimed at wider segments of the cohort and are not specifically targeted at high-risk subpopulations, meaning that broad-based programs are more likely to be planned to have "something for everyone."

Broad-based programs are also more likely to include individual programs aimed at secondary, rather than primary, socialization links. A focused program needs to have a strong influence on one or more elements of the prevention wheel, as high-risk youth have serious problems with one or more of those elements. A broad-based program can have a more diffuse influence and still be effective for low-risk children. Prevention programs might be aimed, for example, at improving links to the extended family, a secondary socialization force that is a probable source of non deviant norms.

Economic improvement in the community can be an important factor in enhancing the well-being of the family. The community might develop supervised recreational facilities, providing opportunities for formal peer activities that compete with the informal peer activities that tend to be more related to deviant behaviors. The media can clarify community, school, and family norms, making it clear that there is strong opposition to deviance.

The danger lies in the fact that it is typically much easier to reach low-risk youth. Because low-risk youth have good bonds with family and school, they are more available and more susceptible; those parts of the program that are aimed at low-risk youth are easier to present and the children are more likely to respond favorably, without resistance and/or hostility. There are also many more youth at low risk, so a program that has a small effect on a lot of youth may look very good. Over time, it is so much easier to work with these low-risk youth that a program can drift away from its original goals; less attention is paid to the high-risk youth, and their deviant behavior may remain unchanged.

The prevention model also suggests that there may be important aspects of prevention that may have been largely ignored in broad-based programs. It is not only the spokes of the wheel that must be maintained but the rim as well. For example, only a few programs have looked at the bond between families and the school, yet this connection may be critical, particularly for minority families where there are communication problems or in families where the parents themselves failed in school. There are no well-known programs specifically aimed at improving the bonds between parents and peer clusters or peer clusters and the school.

CONCLUSION

The prevention model provides a convenient theoretical framework for analyzing and planning prevention programs. The model focuses on children and adolescents because most deviant behaviors are initiated during these developmental periods and the factors that create risk for later deviance are likely to be present during these years. The model suggests that the child develops deviant or non deviant norms through relationships with primary socialization links: the family, the school and peer clusters. Prevention programs based on this model must either reduce risk factors or increase resiliency. Programs can be aimed at (1) an individual element of the model–the child, the family, the school, or peer clusters; (2) improving the bonds between the elements; and/or, (3) reducing transmission of deviant norms through these primary socialization links. There are two general types of prevention programs, focused programs and broad-based programs. Focused programs for high-risk youth must be aimed at the primary socialization links in the model if they are to be effective. Broad-based programs may consist of a variety of more diffuse programs aimed not just at high-risk youth but at youth with lower potential risk; they are more likely to be effective if they have a strong impact on one or more elements of the prevention model. The prevention model provides a graphic visual image that is easy to remember and that helps organize thinking about prevention of deviance. It is a useful tool that can be used to improve the efficacy of prevention programs and ultimately can help reduce the problems that young people encounter because of drug use, dropout, and delinquency.

REFERENCES

Adler, P. T., & Lotecka, L. (1973). Drug use among high school students: Patterns and correlates. *International Journal of the Addictions, 8,* 537-548.

Annis, H. M., & Watson, C. (1975). Drug use and school dropout: A longitudinal study. *Canadian Counsellor, 9,* 155-162.

Bakal, D., Milstein, S. L., & Rootman, I. (1975). Trends in drug use among rural students in Alberta: 1971-1974. *Canadian Mental Health, 24*(4), 8-9.

Bardo, M. T., & Mueller, C. W. (1991). Sensation seeking and drug abuse prevention from a biological perspective. In L. Donohew, H. E. Sypher, and W. J. Bukoski (Eds.), *Persuasive communication and drug abuse prevention.* Hillsdale, NJ: Lawrence Erlbaum.

Beauvais, F. (in press). Drug use of friends: A comparison of reservation and non-reservation Indian youth. *Journal of the National Center for American Indian and Alaska Native Mental Health Research.*

Berriel-Gonzalez, R. E., Berriel-Gonzalez, M. E., Jauregui, R., & Contreras-Cisneros, G. (1978). General characteristics of patients using volatile substances admitted to the Centro de Integracion Juvenil "Leon." In C. W. Sharp & L.

T. Carroll (Eds.), *Voluntary inhalation of industrial solvents.* Rockville, MD: National Institute on Drug Abuse.

Blumenfield, M., Riester, A. E., Serrano, A. C., & Adams, R. L. (1972). Marijuana use in high school students. *Diseases of the Nervous System, 33*(9), 603-610.

Bogg, R. A., & Hughes, J. (1973). Correlates of marijuana usage at a Canadian technological institute. *International Journal of the Addictions, 8*, 489-504.

Brook, J. S., Lukoff, I. F., & Whiteman, M. (1977). Correlates of marijuana use as related to age, sex and ethnicity. *Yale Journal of Biological Medicine, 50*, 383-390.

Burkett, S. R., & Jensen, E. L. (1975). Conventional ties, peer influence, and the fear of apprehension: A study of adolescent marijuana use. *Sociological Quarterly, 16*, 522-533.

Caplin, N., Choy, M. H., & Whitmore, J. K. (1992). Indochinese refugee families and academic achievement. *Scientific American, 266*(2), 36-42.

Carlini-Cotrim, B., & Carlini, E. A. (1988). The use of solvents and other drugs among homeless and destitute children living in the city streets of Sao Paulo, Brazil. *Social Pharmacology, 2*(1), 51-62.

Comstock, B. (1978). Psychological measurement on long-term chronic inhalant abusers. In C. W. Sharp & L. T. Carroll (Eds.), *Voluntary inhalation of industrial solvents.* Rockville, MD: National Institute on Drug Abuse.

Clayton, R. R., & Voss, H. R. (1982). *Technical review on drug abuse and dropouts.* Rockville, MD: National Institute on Drug Abuse.

Crites, J., & Schuckit, M. A. (1979). Solvent misuse in adolescents at a community alcohol center. *Journal of Clinical Psychiatry, 40*, 39-43.

Curiel, H. (1991). Strengthening family and school bonds in promoting Hispanic children's school performance. In M. Sotomayor (Ed.), *Empowering Hispanic families: A critical issue for the 90's.* Milwaukee, WI: Family Service America.

DeBarona, M. S., & Simpson, D. D. (1984). Inhalant users in drug abuse prevention programs. *American Journal of Drug and Alcohol Abuse, 10*(4), 503-518.

Dodson, J. (1981). Conceptualizations of black families. In H. T. McAdoo (Ed.), *Black families.* Beverly Hills, CA: Sage Publications.

Donohew, L., Lorch, E., & Palmgreen, P. (1991). Sensation seeking and targeting of televised anti-drug PSAs. In L. Donohew, H. E. Sypher, and W. J. Bukoski (Eds.), *Persuasive communication and drug abuse prevention.* Hillsdale, NJ: Lawrence Erlbaum.

Donohew, L., Sypher, H. E., & Bukoski, W. J. (Eds.) (1991). *Persuasive communication and drug abuse prevention.* Hillsdale, NJ: Lawrence Erlbaum.

Edwards, R. W. (1990). Peers of dropouts: Drug use and delinquency. Doctoral dissertation, Department of Psychology, Colorado State University, Ft. Collins.

Fernandez, R., & Velez, W. (1989). *Who stays? Who leaves? Findings from the ASPIRA Five Cities High School Dropout Study.* Washington, DC: ASPIRA Institute for Policy Research.

Frumkin, R. M., Cowan, R. A., & Davis, J. R. (1969). Drug use in a Midwest sample of metropolitan hinterland high school students. *Corrective Psychology*, *15*, 8-13.

Galli, N. (1974). Patterns of student drug use. *Journal of Drug Education*, *4*, 237-248.

Galli, N., & Stone, D. B. (1975). Psychological status of student drug users. *Journal of Drug Education*, *5*, 327-333.

Gilbert, J. (1983). Deliberate metallic paint inhalation and cultural marginality: Paint sniffing among acculturating California youth. *Addictive Behaviors*, *8*, 79-82.

Green, M. G., Blake, B. F., & Zenhausern, R. T. (1973). Some implications of a survey of marijuana usage by middle-class high school drug users. *Proceedings of the 81st Annual Convention of the American Psychological Association*, *8*, 679-680.

Guajardo, M. (1990). *Mentoring minority adolescents: Creating champions*. Paper presented at the National Dropout Prevention Conference, Nashville, TN.

Hare, B. (1988). Black youth at-risk. In *The state of Black America*, pp. 81-92. New York: National Urban League.

Hollifield, J. (1989). Typology sets the stage for dropout prevention action. In *Valued Youth Anthology* (pp. 1-4). San Antonio, TX: Intercultural Development Research Association.

Huba, G., & Bentler, P. M. (1980). The role of peer and adult models for drug taking at different stages in adolescents. *Journal of Youth and Adolescence*, *9*, 449-465.

Jessor, R. (1976). Predicting time of onset of marijuana use: A developmental study of high school youth. *Journal of Consulting and Clinical Psychology*, *44*, 125-134.

Jessor, R., & Jessor, S. L. (1977). *Problem behavior and psychosocial development: A longitudinal study of youth*. New York: Academic Press.

Jessor, R., Jessor, S. L., & Finney, J. (1973). A social psychology of marijuana use: Longitudinal studies of high school and college youth. *Journal of Personality and Social Psychology*, *26*, 1-15.

Kandel, D. (1974). Inter- and intragenerational influences on adolescent marijuana use. *Journal of Social Issues*, *30*, 107-135.

Kandel, D. (1975). Reaching the hard-to-reach: Illicit drug use among high school absentees. *Addictive Diseases: An International Journal*, *1*, 465-480.

Korman, M., Trimboli, F., & Semler, I. (1980). A comparative evaluation of 162 inhalant users. *Addictive Behaviors*, *5*, 143-152.

Lawrence, T. S., & Velleman, J. D. (1974). Correlates of student drug use in a suburban high school. *Psychiatry*, *37*, 129-136.

Leal, H., Mejia, L., Gomez, L., & Salinas de Valle, O. (1978). Naturalistic study on the phenomenon of inhalant use in a group of children in Mexico City. In C. W. Sharp and L. T. Carroll (Eds.), *Voluntary inhalation of industrial solvents*, Rockville, MD: National Institute on Drug Abuse.

Matthews, R. W., & Korman, M. (1981). Abuse of inhalants: Motivation and consequences. *Psychological Reports, 49,* 519-526.

McKillip, J., Johnson, J. E., & Petzel, T. P. (1973). Patterns and correlates of drug use among urban high school students. *Journal of Drug Education, 3,* 1-12.

Nurco, D. N., Shaffer, J. W., & Cisin, I. H. (1984). An ecological analysis of the interrelationships among drug abuse and other indices of social pathology. *International Journal of the Addictions, 19*(4), 441-451.

Oetting, E., & Beauvais, F. (1986a). Peer cluster theory: Drugs and the adolescent. *Journal of Counseling and Development, 65*(1), 17-22.

Oetting, E. R., & Beauvais, F. (1986b). Clarification of peer cluster theory: A response to Peele, Cohen and Shaffer. *Journal of Counseling and Development, 65*(1), 29-30.

Oetting, E. R., & Beauvais, F. (1987). Peer cluster theory, socialization characteristics and adolescent drug use: A path analysis. *Journal of Counseling Psychology, 34*(2), 205-213.

Oetting, E. R., Beauvais, F., & Edwards, R. W. (1988). Alcohol and Indian youth: Social and psychological correlates and prevention. *Journal of Drug Issues, 18*(1), 87-101.

Oetting, E. R., & Goldstein, G. (1979). Drug abuse among Native American adolescents. In G. M. Beschner & A. S. Friedman (Eds.), *Youth drug abuse: Problems, issues and treatment.* Lexington, MA: Lexington Books.

Oetting, E. R., Swaim, R. C., Edwards, R. W., & Beauvais, F. (1989). Indian and Anglo adolescent alcohol use and emotional distress: Path models. *American Journal of Alcohol and Drug Abuse, 15*(2), 153-172.

Pandina, R. T., & Schuele, J. A. (1983). Psychosocial correlates of alcohol and drug use of adolescent students and adolescents in treatment. *Journal of Studies on Alcohol, 44,* 950-973.

Robledo, M. (1989). The prevention and recovery of dropouts: An action agenda. In *Valued Youth Anthology* (pp. 1-4). San Antonio, TX: Intercultural Development Research Association.

Rohrbaugh, J., & Jessor, R. (1975). Religiosity in youth: A personal control against deviant behavior. *Journal of Personality, 43,* 136-155.

Streit, F., Halsted, D. L., & Pascale, P. J. (1974). Differences among youth users and non-users of drugs based on their perceptions of parental behavior. *International Journal of the Addictions, 9,* 749-755.

Sutherland, E. H. (1947). *Principles of criminology* (4th ed.). Philadelphia: Lippincott.

Svobodny, L. A. (1982). Biographical, self-concept and educational factors among chemically dependent adolescents. *Adolescence, 17,* 847-853.

Swaim, R. C. (in press). Childhood risk factors and adolescent drug and alcohol abuse. *Educational Psychology Review.*

Swaim, R. C., Oetting, E. R., Edwards, R. W., & Beauvais, F. (1989). The links from emotional distress to adolescent drug use: A path model. *Journal of Consulting and Clinical Psychology, 57*(2), 227-231.

Swaim, R. C., Oetting, E. R., Thurman, P. J., Beauvais, F., & Edwards, R. (in press). American Indian adolescent drug use and socialization characteristics: A cross-cultural comparison. *Journal of Cross Cultural Psychology.*

Tarter, R. E. (1988). Are there inherited behavioral traits that predispose to substance abuse? *Journal of Consulting and Clinical Psychology, 56*(2), 189-196.

Tec, N. (1974). Parent-child drug abuse: Generational continuity or adolescent deviancy? *Adolescence, 9,* 350-364.

Tolone, W. L., & Dermott, D. (1975). Some correlates of drug use among high school youth in a midwestern rural community. *International Journal of the Addictions, 10,* 761-777.

Turner, C. J., & Willis, R. J. (1984). The relationship between self-reported religiosity and drug use by college students. In S. Eiseman, J. Wingard, and G. Huba (Eds.). *Drug abuse: Foundation for a psychosocial approach.* Farmingdale, NY: Baywood.

Walters, J. M. (1980). Buzzin': PCP use in Philadelphia. In H. W. Feldman, M. H. Agar & G. Breschner (Eds.). *Angel dust.* Lexington, MA: D. C. Heath.

Wechsler, H., & Thum, D. (1973). Drug use among teenagers: Patterns of present and anticipated use. *International Journal of the Addictions, 8,* 909-920.

Wehlage, G., Rutter, R., Smith, G., Lesko, N., & Fernandez, R. (1989). *Reducing the risk.* Philadelphia, PA: Falmer Press.

Windsor, R. A. (1973). Mood modifying substance usage among 4H and non-4H youth in Illinois. *Journal of Drug Education, 3,* 261-273.

Overview of Selected Federal Efforts to Encourage Minority Drug Abuse Research and Researchers

Catherine S. Bolek
Julius Debro
Joseph Trimble

SUMMARY. This article contains three sections. The first part is a brief overview of National Institute on Drug Abuse's (NIDA) ethnic minority research and research training efforts initiated between 1986 to 1991. The second part contains excerpts from a report entitled "Research Monograph: Drug Abuse Research Issues at Historically Black Colleges and Universities" submitted as a final contract deliverable to NIDA. The third part is a summary of the proceedings of a NIDA sponsored conference, entitled "Toward the Development of Ethnic Minority Drug Abuse Research and Researchers."

SECTION I

A Brief Overview of NIDA's Ethnic Minority Research and Research Training Efforts–1986 to 1991

National concern over the issue of drug abuse has stimulated a major effort on the part of the Federal government and its agencies

---

Catherine S. Bolek is affiliated with the University of Maryland Eastern Shore; Julius Debro is affiliated with the University of Washington; and Joseph Trimble is affiliated with Western Washington University.

The authors wish to acknowledge the contributions of all those who assisted in the development of the material contained in this chapter. Special acknowledgement is given to contributions of Janis Brose, Ernie Chavez, Leo Hendricks, and Nolan Zane whose work appears in the two final reports.

to identify effective ways of preventing, deterring, and/or treating this behavior. Federal support for such efforts has been continuous for over three decades with associated costs rising into the tens of billions of dollars. While national survey figures indicate a general downturn in drug use during this period, a critique of the drug abuse research literature (Rebach, Bolek, Russell & Williams, 1992), suggests that minorities, in particular, continue to be at significant risk for a number of life threatening outcomes. These outcomes include an increased risk for mortality from infectious disease such as AIDS ". . . homicide resulting from drug trafficking, suicide or accidents as a consequence of drug or alcohol use, criminal justice actions resulting from drug trafficking or use, and negative effects on school, job, general health, family, and community." The authors report that ". . . although the epidemiological evidence clearly indicates the risks faced by minority group members, the review of this body of literature indicates that robust, effective prevention and treatment models have yet to emerge."

During this same period, Federal agencies, with the prompting of the Congress and White House, attempted to recruit ethnic minority scholars into their research grants and contracts activities. Specific set-asides and minority focused programs were initiated by such Federal organizations as the National Institutes of Health and the Alcohol, Drug Abuse and Mental Health Administration (ADAMHA). The first section of this chapter will provide a brief discussion of the efforts of one of the ADAMHA Institutes, The National Institute on Drug Abuse to, address these issues.

The National Institute on Drug Abuse

The National Institute on Drug Abuse (NIDA) was established by law in 1974 as one of three ADAMHA Institutes, a Public Health Service Agency within the Department of Health and Human Services. According to its mission statement, "NIDA is authorized as a research Institute to study the causes and consequences of drug abuse and ways of improving our ability to treat and prevent drug abuse and to collect information on the incidence and prevalence of drug abuse. Since its inception, NIDA has been the lead federal agency responsible for reducing the demand for illicit drugs.

Through the congressional reauthorization process, NIDA has been directed to carry out its mission using various mechanisms such as research grants and contracts.''

NIDA supports more than 900 grants awarded to many of the Nation's major research and medical facilities. In addition, NIDA operates its own Addiction Research Center located in Baltimore, Maryland. Review and scientific administration of research grants and contracts and related support activities are managed by approximately 300 full-time staff. NIDA's Fiscal Year 1990 budget was approximately $400 million.

NIDA's Special Populations Research Programs

In an attempt to address many of the issues presented earlier, NIDA created and continues to support a number of research and research training programs aimed at ethnic minority populations. Through an annual commitment of resources and staff, NIDA's program goals focus on the following issues: (a) increasing the participation of minority researchers in its grants and contracts programs; (b) support for basic research on important issues that will increase the understanding of drug abuse among populations who have an above-average risk; and, (c) developing improved methods for diagnosis, prevention and treatment of drug abuse among these populations. To meet these goals, NIDA established the Special Populations Research Programs, which in turn, initiated three primary activities: (1) the implementation of a research training program for minority scholars; (2) the creation of minority specific grant mechanisms; and (3) the development of an annual evaluation and reporting activities.

In the mid-1980's, NIDA developed a program of research and research training opportunities for ethnic minority researchers and academics. In cooperation with other ADAMHA Institutes and Offices, NIDA has participated in the Minority Access to Research Careers Program, the Minority Institutional Research Development Program, the Minority Supplemental Awards Program, the Minority High School Apprenticeship Program and other grant and contract programs. Annual awards through these initiatives are made to applicant institutions to support a variety of activities including undergraduate, pre- and post-doctoral training, investigator initiated grants and cooperative agreements.

Many minority institutions and minority investigators have applied for research support through these grant mechanisms. However, the funds made available generally represent a small percentage of the total funds available to all Institutes of Higher Education (IHE). The complex restrictions, narrow focus, and long waiting periods associated with many minority grant programs when coupled with limited dollars may have reduced some enthusiasm for participation in these programs.

In addition to grant programs, NIDA developed the Special Populations Research Development Seminar Series. The purpose of the series was to provide minority scholars with an opportunity to develop a fundamental understanding of the language and process of drug abuse research. Particular emphasis was given to developing an understanding of drug abuse science and associated research methodology. The seminars focused on the development of theory based research proposals that employ quantitative analytic methods. The seminars also presented an overview of NIDA's research grants and contracts process from preproposal through submission and review to award. The objective of the series was to stimulate the development of the minority scholars competitive research skills. NIDA staff worked with the participants in designing an individualized training program and in selected mentors.

Initiated in 1985, the seminar series has remained an integral part of NIDA's minority research training efforts. In the pilot seminar delivered in 1986, minority scholars from universities and colleges across the country were invited to participate in a series of lectures, demonstrations, and discussions, which were accompanied by individual consultation and mentoring. The purpose of these activities was to stimulate the development of highly competitive investigator initiated (R01) research proposals.

Under the guidance and largely voluntary efforts of many of the researchers participating in this volume, proposals were submitted by the participants usually within six months of completing the training. By 1991, dozens of minority scholars had participated in seminars specifically tailored to meet the unique needs of those attending. For example, seminars have been developed for faculty and research associates of Historically Black Universities and Colleges; the faculty of the colleges and universities located in Puerto Rico, and for clinicians, academics and community service providers serving American Indian and Alaska Native populations.

In general, the training consisted of two parts. A series of formal workshops and an individual mentoring program. The training consisted of one or more group meetings for the purpose of identifying NIDA's research interests; assessing the strengths and weaknesses of the seminar participants' research skills and plans; providing an indepth understanding of the grants preparation, submission, review and award process; and, other grant related guidelines. Moreover an effort was made to match the participant with a mentor (generally a senior grantee who had served on a peer review committee) and a Federal Project Officer (generally one with a track record of scholarship in a related field of research). In this collaborative manner, the neophyte grantee would refine and submit these proposals to any one of a wide variety of grant programs. In addition, a computer based grants mentoring program was introduced into the series in 1991.

Each seminar effort was assessed using pre- and post-test evaluations that are administered to all participants. In addition, faculty were asked to provide overall evaluations and recommendations for future seminars. Objective measures such as the number of grant applications submitted by participants and the results of the peer review were used to assess the success of the series.

These efforts have resulted in the increased participation of ethnic minority principal investigators. Secondary benefits include the selection of several seminar graduates to serve on Initial Review Groups (IRGs), to present and publish articles in NIDA sponsored monographs, and to serve as mentors to colleagues and graduate students. Funded projects resulting from these efforts included: (a) studies that examine drug abuse among the homeless; (b) prevention programs aimed at minority youth; (c) epidemiologic studies of the nature and extent of drug use among sub-groups in minority populations; and (d) community demonstration projects aimed at preventing the transmission of AIDS in the Black Community.

Notably, this effort produced an increase in the number of minority grantees however much of the credit goes to the research community who volunteered as unpaid mentors. These mentors frequently provided outside funds to seminar participants for travel and other resources necessary to complete the proposals.

The last component of the Special Populations Research Programs was the responsibility to review current efforts and to identify new directions for future program development. To meet this requirement, NIDA staff developed a number of contract mechanisms the purpose of which was to: (a) examine NIDA's efforts to increase the participation of minorities in its grant and contract programs; (b) focus research on the prevention and treatment of drug abuse among minority groups; and, (c) to develop a set of research recommendations to serve as the basis for future programs. The following sections provide excerpts and summaries of two representative examples of program evaluation.

SECTION II

Summary Report–Drug Abuse Research Issues at Historically Black Colleges and Universities

Historically Black Colleges and Universities (HBCUs) have played a significant role in the education of African Americans; made outstanding intellectual and scientific contributions that are indispensable to the broader society, and served as centers for African American Culture. However, these institutions have had little success in securing a place on the Federal biomedical and behavioral agenda. This section provides a summary of an initial attempt on the part of NIDA to enhance the participation of the faculty and research associates of HBCUs in its research programs in general, and in careers in drug abuse in particular. These efforts are based on the need of the Institute to: (1) identify and remove any barriers to fair and open competition; (2) solicit actively research proposals; (3) provide a research support base for research conducted by HBCU faculty, research associates, and students; and, (4) stimulate private sector involvement.

To meet these goals, NIDA published a Request for Contracts in 1988 and subsequently awarded a competitive contract to Clark-

Atlanta University under the direction of Dr. Julius Debro, Former Chairman of the Department of Criminal Justice, currently Associate Dean, Graduate School, University of Washington. The purpose of the contract was to assemble an advisory panel whose membership was to be made up of HBCU administrators, faculty, research associates, and graduate students. Panel members were assigned the responsibility of examining barriers to research participation and reporting their findings to the group.

A major contract requirement was the development of a report that would provide information on the following topics: (1) identification and summary of drug abuse research conducted by HBCU faculty and research associates; and (2) identification and review of research opportunities and barriers at HBCUs. The following is an excerpt taken from the final report.

RESEARCH MONOGRAPH:
DRUG ABUSE RESEARCH ISSUES AT HISTORICALLY BLACK COLLEGES AND UNIVERSITIES

Excerpts Taken from: *Eliminating Barriers to Research Careers*

–Julius Debro, D. Crim

Barriers to conducting research exist at all colleges and universities, but they are exacerbated at Historically Black Colleges and Universities. The barriers become more pronounced because of the ever present lack of adequate financial resources to properly administer the university. Black colleges were born in poverty and have never been able to break free from that cycle of poverty. For almost a century, they were denied equal funding from state governments and private foundations and frequently funds which were collected from taxes in the Black community were diverted to white schools. The largest endowment among the HBCUs is less than 50 million dollars, the smallest less than 7 million.

This essay will discuss some of the most common barriers which constrain scholarly research and grant procurement and administration at Historically Black Colleges and Universities. The data for this article were collected from social science researchers who participated in a series of National Institute of Drug Abuse (NIDA) conferences. In addition, the author has spent over a decade teaching and administering research grants at two HBCUs, one private and one public institution. Over the years, formal and informal interviews concerning the benefits and pitfalls of conducting research at Black colleges have been conducted with hundreds of HBCU scholars, administrators, staff, and trustees, from over 50 public and private institutions.

In most of the HBCUs, research has never been given top priority. Most of the HBCUs do not have expert researchers who can train or assist young professors on campus. Teaching has always ranked number one in terms of priority. Faculty members are encouraged to spend many hours in consultation with students over and above the number of office hours which are quite often dictated by department chairs and deans. At one graduate school, the dean dictates the amount of hours as well as the number of days one should have office hours.

Those colleges and universities that have been involved in research have made important contributions. Prior to 1960, some of the most important social science research published in this country was produced by Black scholars at HBCUs. Since the 1970s, most of the published research conducted by Black doctorates within the last two decades have been conducted at major white universities. There are several reasons for this shift. One primary reason for the shift of research away from Historical Black Colleges has been the unspoken assumption of grant-makers in both the private and public sector that Black and white scholars at predominantly white universities are more qualified to conduct scholarly research.

The paucity of graduate programs and students at Black colleges presents a major constraint to the research process. Within the HBCU community, there are only seven schools with graduate programs out of a total of 105 Historically Black Colleges. Only the graduate schools have students that can assist with research. However, those few schools which do have Ph.D. programs are unable to compete for the limited pool of Black graduate students because they cannot offer funding opportunities. Furthermore, there is an unofficial policy among the major funding programs to channel the most promising students to predominantly white schools. Even at some of the graduate schools, research assistants may be difficult to obtain because chairs are reluctant to approve expenditures for graduate research assistants, even though the money may be in the grant budget. HBCUs cannot begin to compete with wealthier predominately white institutions in terms of facilities and staff since they often do not have money for secretarial assistance and for library materials and little if any money is available for faculty to travel to conferences, and most have outmoded instrumentation for research.

The libraries of HBCUs are notoriously limited. Current issues of journals are often missing or they have not been ordered by the library. Books are quite old and computerization does not exist. Special collections are not often complete. One respondent indicated that he/she must leave their institution and travel over 50 miles to get to the library of a major white institution to conduct library searches and that the institution does not even have one SPSSx statistical package for conducting social science research.

Ironically, professors are expected to publish to gain tenure, despite the economic, social and psychological barriers erected by their administrations. Monies are not provided for attending professional meetings. Most HBCUs follow the general criteria for promotion, i.e., scholarship, teaching, and public service. Scholarship is defined as publishing and teaching. Teaching is seen as the most important phase of scholarship but trying to identify what constitutes a good teacher is still somewhat illusory. In tenure and promotion hearings, most of the weight for scholarship is given to publications yet very few of the professors find the time or receive the necessary support to spend time writing papers. Most of the publications are in non-refereed journals or in popular publications such as *Ebony*, *Essence*, *Jet*, or in monographs commissioned by government agencies or foundations.

Grants Administration at HBCUs

The barriers to administering a grant are numerous. One such barrier is that of not providing adequate resources for departments to compete for grants. Some departments have no typewriters, computers, nor copying equipment to complete their research proposals. One faculty member at Howard Medical School wondered out loud as to "why hundreds of thousands of dollars generated in indirect cost was insufficient to provide air conditioning and well heated labs or why faculty members had to throw out experimental results because excrement leaked into their laboratories from the animal facilities above, or water had dripped down from the roof."

Excessive teaching loads are a major culprit hindering research at HBCUs. Most professors teach a minimum of four courses per semester. Some colleges require teaching five courses or more, depending on student enrollment. Research is considered an extra task at some HBCUs and one cannot "buy" off one's time by having a research project. Once the grant is received, release time is not given to complete the work of the grant. Professors are expected to complete their normal work load as well as to work on the grant. Research is seen as an additional load rather than as part of the regular college/university expectations.

Day to day resources such as newspapers, journals, *Federal Register*, etc., are not available for professors to scan for grant opportunities. Faculty members with grants complain that it is better to do nothing than try and administer a grant. The grants office or the department chair attempts to control each and every expenditure up to and including the purchase of stamps for correspondence.

Clerical assistance is difficult to obtain when professors are writing grants. Some chairs of departments generally believe that clerical assistance is only for the chair and not for faculty. Other departments have no clerical assistance and must rely on secretarial help from the dean's office or generate secretarial help themselves. Most information concerning grant related activities are received by administrators at college/universities. This information is generally not disseminated to faculty or if disseminated it is not done in a timely manner. Most of the colleges/universities do not have a grants and contracts unit, thus, the information may go to the vice presidents or to the deans who may or may not release the information.

Quite often faculty members receive no rewards for obtaining grants for the college/university. The obtaining of a contract/grant may create hostility which is directed at the recipient because he/she has gained a degree of independence and no longer has to rely on the chair, the dean, the vice president for a computer, supplies, a desk, etc. The professor may be penalized by not receiving a small increase in salary, by receiving a poor evaluation or by having the grant taken away.

It would be unfair to identify the barriers to research at HBCUs without explaining how those barriers emerged and why they persist. For instance, one major reason why Black college administrators do not facilitate their faculty to engage in scholarly research is that the college has very little to gain economically from research. Because HBCUs are constantly functioning on the edge of bankruptcy, they have not been permitted the luxury of long term planning. For instance, the academic status of a university is dependent upon two basic criteria: the quality of entering students (usually measured by standardized test scores) and the quality of the faculty (measured by numbers of publications in referee journals). So although HBCUs would increase their academic standing in the long-run, if they facilitated scholarly research, in the short term, they see this research as only enhancing the career of the individual faculty member. Also, there is the underlying concern that if faculty publish, they will be more marketable and consequently might leave their university for more lucrative salaries. Likewise, a faculty member who acquires more independence, since he/she can purchase supplies and travel to conferences, is less dependent upon the benevolence of the dean. Since integration, HBCU administrators and presidents have been fearful of losing their faculty and attempt to keep them by overloading their teaching and counseling responsibilities.

Teaching, however, results in immediate payback, since student aid represents a large portion of the federal assistance received by HBCUs. Since the 1970s, student aid has accounted for a significant portion of the Federal government's contribution to black colleges. In 1978, student aid accounted for 53 percent of the federal funds allocated to black institutions. By 1985, it had been decreased to 36.8 percent, with another 13.5 percent designated for Program Evaluation, Fellowships, Training and Facilities.

How can barriers be eliminated? One of the major ways of eliminating barriers is providing greater autonomy for faculty. Faculty members at HBCUs are not seen as a valuable asset by administrators. All major decisions are made by the president with the faculty having little, if any, input into those decisions.

Decision making should be de-centralized. Now decision making is highly centralized and nothing can be done if the act requires an administrator's signature until that administrator returns. Administrators are often unavailable to faculty primarily because they are constantly attending meetings with other administrators trying to solve problems which are often unsolvable. They spend their time in meeting after meeting impressing each other with how important they are in the scheme of things at the college or university. Faculty members must be given power to make decisions.

Faculty meetings, while important, serve only a limited purpose on campus. At one school, the president attended all of the faculty meetings and made a mental note of those faculty members who did not attend or who raised serious questions concerning the administration of the institution. Most of the faculty members at HBCUs do not attend faculty meetings because they realize that faculty members have very little power to bring about change on campuses.

Faculty members are generally non-union and act as individuals rather than as a collective body. Those faculty members who become active in campus matters are soon fired, or become so discouraged that they either leave or give up, returning only to campus to teach their course and leaving soon after to become involved in their own outside activities or in consulting. Morale among some faculty members was very low. Not only do faculty members suffer from poor research conditions, but they suffer from a malaise caused by many years of insecurity. This insecurity was caused by a lack of power, by salaries still being among the lowest in the academic community, and by an inability to make changes to improve the campus climate. Some faculty members who have tried to make a difference have been punished by the administration by not getting raises or by being denied promotions.

HBCU faculties like students have changed over time. They have changed primarily because of the Civil Rights Movement. Major white colleges now recruit the best and the brightest whereas before the civil rights movement Black colleges had a monopoly on these resources. Black faculty at all major institutions are in great demand and many of the Black faculty members leave Black colleges and universities and go to major universities. Those faculty members who are left are those who are dedicated to providing quality education to Black students regardless of the barriers that exist. In some sad cases, HBCUs are left with those scholars who are not longer marketable because they have not had the time or resources to publish in their field.

The diversity of faculty members continues to increase. There are now large numbers of foreign faculty members, Indians, Koreans, Chinese, Africans, Vietnamese, as well as whites and Hispanics. In the vast majority of cases, Black colleges provide the foreign scholar with his/her first academic employment opportunity in the United States. Many remain at Black schools, while many later are able to use their experience to obtain employment at Historically White Colleges or Universities.

Foreign faculty members have become increasingly attractive to Black colleges because they are willing to work at lower salaries until they gain experience. They also tend to hold degrees in fields in which there are few Black Ph.D's (e.g., Mathematics, engineering, physics, computer science, etc.). Black colleges have always welcomed the diversity, including the hiring of women to teach on their campuses. However, HBCU administrators should be aware that most foreign faculty members do not integrate into Black communities where Black faculty members have provided leadership for decades. Although many foreign scholars have made important sacrifices to teach at Black schools, their initial motivation for teaching at an HBCU is often entirely different than the motivation of Blacks and some whites who are teaching at those same institutions. For instance, during the Civil Rights Movement, many white scholars left prominent white institutions to teach at HBCUs and in the late 1970s, many Black scholars also opted to leave comfortable positions at elite white universities "to give back something to the Black community."

Barriers for conducting research at HBCUs are many but they are not insurmountable. Some of the most important research has been conducted in inferior laboratories with inferior equipment by professors who were dedicated to making a difference. While there are many barriers to conducting research at HBCUs, there are also many rewards. One conference participant indicated that training for a Ph.D. occurred at a major white university, but there was a desire to teach at an HBCU because of the ability to conduct research on Black people that is valued as "true" research. White universities quite often do not value Black research or publishing in Black journals so it is difficult to obtain tenure.

Another participant indicated that while there are many barriers at HBCUs, those barriers can be overcome by flexibility and versatility. One has to be very flexible at HBCUs because of many of the barriers one must overcome and one must be versatile because of the many duties one must perform . . . "If you are not able to be patient, able to be flexible, able to take what is being offered, i.e., playing the hand that is dealt you, you're not going to be able to be successful in an HBCU." "I do think, despite the constraints, it's worth it to be at an HBCU to make a contribution, even if you don't stay forever."

CONCLUSION

The following suggestions are made for improving research at Historically Black Colleges:

1. Reduce the teaching load from four/six courses to a maximum of three per semester;
2. HBCUs must make the transition from a traditional teaching institution to more of a research institution;
3. Increase the amount of graduate programs;
4. Establish peer-review committees;
5. Increase facilities for research;
6. Must identify the less competitive, easier to get, less expensive grants. These grants should be applied for and young professors should be encouraged to obtain these grants;
7. Faculty must be provided with research conditions comparable to major universities. At one HBCU, the computer was not included in a statistics class until 1984. Data had to be sent to a major white university for processing. The turnaround time for data return was approximately two and one half weeks;

8. Funds to develop a research proposal must be made available as well as providing release time for such endeavors.
9. Salaries must be increased;
10. Major universities must offer summer workshops for the development of black research faculty and;
11. Faculty must be given greater autonomy.

SECTION III

Conference Summary—"Toward the Development of Ethnic Minority Drug Abuse Research and Researchers"[2]

–Joseph Trimble
–Ernie Chavez
–Nolan Zane
–Janis Brose

Under an ADAMHA 1% Evaluation Contract mechanism, NIDA funded a one year project aimed at examining the Institute's efforts to increase the participation of American Indian/Alaska Native, Hispanics, and Asian Pacific Islanders in its grants and contracts programs. The following material is an excerpt from the final report submitted to NIDA December, 1991.

Conference Objectives

The purpose of the conference was to accomplish the following tasks:

1. To develop panel meetings for the purpose of examining, from a rigorous scientific perspective, clinical, behavioral and research training issues related to drug abuse and American Indian/Alaska Natives, Hispanics, and Asian Pacific populations;
2. To identify and select American Indian/Alaska Native, Hispanic and Asian Pacific scholars actively participating in drug abuse research who may serve as chairmen, presenters, discussants and in other related roles;

3. To convene three, two-day conferences (one for each of the following groups):
   • American Indian and Alaska Native scholars;
   • Hispanic scholars; and
   • Asian Pacific scholars.
4. To prepare a publication quality review of drug abuse research and research training related issues including a set of recommendations regarding research and research training needs and opportunities.

Thirty-four participants were invited to attend the two day meeting. Each of the three ethnic groups had reasonable balance of participants representing a number of academic orientations and research interests. In addition, several prominent scholars and policy planners were in attendance some of whom delivered invited addresses.

Summary of Ethnic Specific Issues and Recommendations

This section focuses on training and methodological issues with respect to substance abuse research for each ethnic group, namely, American Indian and Alaska Native, Asian Pacific, and Hispanic populations. Because the discussion process and content varied somewhat across the different ethnic conferences, the issues and recommendations for each ethnic population are presented in a format that best captures the conference proceedings for that particular group.

American Indian and Alaska Natives

The primary discussions focused on training and funding strategies that could generate more research on American Indian and Alaska Native communities.

High school mentorships are needed to interest promising students in ADM (Alcohol, Drug Abuse, and Mental Health) issues. There is a need to redefine ADM research careers for them as positive and important. A significant step in this direction would be to go beyond the current definition of high school pre-college training programs which are now mostly basic science and engineering oriented.

Most Indian pre-doctoral students and post-doctoral trainees have more financial obligations than other students. They must support children and families, therefore the individual award levels might need to be higher. Some awards require a substantial amount of work which detracts from learning/scholarship experience of Indian students. It is important that universities be monitored or kept from requiring work from trainees. There are two other problems associated with institutional awards. First, the Federal government typically pays only 50% of the stipend and the remainder must be covered by the host institution. This arrangement does not provide much incentive for universities and other institutions to initiate training programs. Second, typical awards are only for the trainee stipends and contain only an additional $1500 to support the actual training involved. This is far too little support for departments and universities to host trainees.

Given the greater financial and educational needs of Indian trainees, longer terms of funding are required for training programs if they are to be effective in developing viable social science careers for Indian students. In the past, some training has been defunded after a few years (usually five years or less) even when they have succeeded in recruiting and training Indian students. Institutions with productive training records should be refunded to assure the consistent development of Indian researchers. Also, training programs must be interdisciplinary to adequately address Indian substance abuse and related issues. One of the major goals of pre and post-doctoral training should be directing individuals towards the acquisition of small grants, first awards and other support.

Recommendations

- Establish more individually awarded, long-term training opportunities for Indian students as sponsored by ADAMHA, IHS, etc. Special outreach efforts must be made within these programs to make Indian students aware of these training opportunities.
- Develop more university-based training programs for Ameri-

can Indians that involve intensive mentoring experience with experienced scholars.

- Initiate high school programs that are add-ons to existing R01 grants (focused on Indian substance abuse issues) which are designed to give students exposure and training for the summer.
- Develop programs to train post-bachelors, post-masters Indian practitioners (RN, MSW, MPH, others) in substance abuse research. Such training must be coordinated among a consortium of available scholars and university programs.
- Establish a short term (6 months-1 year) post-doctoral program in conjunction with IHS to enhance research training for IHS employees.
- Expand the utilization of MARC for Indians and obtain greater commitment of training funds from the granting agencies.
- Allocate greater funding support for MIRDP and supplemental awards that are associated with promising research programs from institutions with high Indian populations.
- Develop a self-paced, packaged program in cross-cultural methodology in substance abuse which would be available to college classrooms.

Acquisition of Research Grants

In view of the paucity of research awards for projects that examine American Indian substance abuse issues, there is a great need for NIDA to facilitate more funding opportunities using a variety of mechanisms. First, it is important to intensify the training and mentorship of new investigators to broaden the number of investigator initiated proposals and the pool of principal investigators. Second, it would be helpful to encourage collaboration of Ph.D. and highly qualified Master's level people in proposals. Third, given the progressive reduction in research funding, it is important that joint funding of research projects occur between NIDA, Indian Health Service, and Bureau of Indian Affairs. One way would be to supplement awards across institutes regardless of where the R01 resides, and this would be especially important in examining issues of co-morbidity. Incentive would be given to institutes that cross fund. There may also be a need to redefine the memorandum of agreement that the Indian Health Service has with ADAMHA. The Indian Health Service should redefine its scholarship program in terms of research. Fourth, ADAMHA should recognize the centrality of start-up and termination activities in community relations with research awards to Indians.

Recommendations

- Develop regional centers on ethnic minority substance abuse research whose functions will include:
  a. coordinate and disseminate information in the area of minority substance abuse research (e.g., may utilize Public Health Network as one source for information dissemination);
  b. provide resource information on personnel and colleges/departments/programs in this area who can provide expertise in the area of cross-cultural research methodology in substance abuse (e.g., extensive resume file). (The National Criminal Justice Reference Service may serve as a model for the dissemination component of these centers.); and
  c. provide a listing of training programs available which promote scholars/researchers in this area.
- Establish a consortium of Indian research scholars to support research and proposal efforts.
- Compile a compendium of final reports of all Indian-relevant research funded over the past ten years.

Grant Review and Award Process

There should be an emphasis on the identification and nomination of qualified American Indian scholars to act as reviewers at all levels. The Institute needs to take seriously its commitment to bring in new scholars to orient them to the Internal Review Group process.

- Develop a standing advisory/policy committee on ethnic minority research which performs the following functions:
  a. monitors appointments to review committees;
  b. monitors RFPs & RFAs;
  c. monitors policy decisions; and
  d. is involved in policy making decisions.
- Establish annual reviews for IRG members for the Ethnic Minority and the Women's Mandate criteria.
- Develop an accounting of all research and training proposals submitted to NIDA and other ADM agencies within the past five years and their subsequent disposition. Categories reported on should be: (1) Proposals submitted by Indian and Native scholars; and (2) Proposals submitted with a focus on Indians.
- Conduct a systematic evaluation of the strengths and weaknesses reported by IRGs as characterizing research and training proposals submitted by Indian and Native scholars and/or whose primary focus is Indian and Native populations.
- Issue a special edition of a journal addressing the implications of the recent ADAMHA mandate on the inclusion of ethnic minorities and women in research proposals.
- Issue an RFA for the development of culturally-sensitive instruments. The initial process could take the form of (1) a colloquia series over a period of time, or (2) a series of conferences (e.g., Western Behavioral Sciences in Fort Collins, Colorado, on instrument development).
- Issue an RFA/RFP for innovative cross-cultural explanatory model development and validation.

Hispanic Americans

In addressing the training and research issues of Hispanic populations specific formal recommendations were drafted. These recommendations and their rationales are presented below.

Recommendations

- Increase the numbers of Hispanic researchers on R01 and PO funded grants. Specifically increase the total number of grantees by 50% over a five year period.

This goal is to be accomplished through the following mechanisms: (a) establish training mechanisms to achieve this goal and expand training programs such as those already in place through NIDA's special populations training, (b) establish joint venture training centers, and (c) earmark funds for technical assistance to Minority PI's.

- Increase the Institute's portfolio of culturally relevant and responsive research.

This research should lead to meeting the special needs and assist in our understanding of issues within special populations. Given the mandate by ADAMHA to include women and minority populations within R01 grants, terms such as culturally-sensitive and culturally relevant must be defined. Appropriate methodology must be incorporated into research projects which include special populations.

- Stimulate the development of new explanatory theories, techniques, and instrumentation with special populations.

Special grant initiatives are needed to support research that focuses on theory and instrument development with special populations. This type of research requires consistent funding for multi-year projects.

- Establish mechanisms to communicate relevant research and their application to the community in order to reduce the prevalence of drug and alcohol use within Hispanic populations.

Such projects are needed to increase the technical information available on appropriate methodologies for the study of Hispanic populations. Technical assistance programs also would serve to increase the awareness of the importance of cultural issues in contributing to solutions for reducing drug and alcohol use within Hispanic communities.

- Develop mechanisms to guarantee the institutionalization of the need to conduct culturally relevant research with ethnic and minority populations.

Some possible mechanisms involve the creation of an external scientific advisory board to the Director and establish an office for research with special populations which will coordinate efforts within the agency.

Asian Pacific Americans

With respect to Asian Pacific issues, recommendations are presented to (1) increase the pool of researchers who would study substance abuse and use within Asian Pacific communities in a culturally salient fashion and (2) improve the methodological strategies that are applied to Asian Pacific substance abuse issues. Before recommendations are presented, the major issues and problems to which the recommendations are directed are discussed.

Training Issue: Lack of and Little Educational Support for the Development of Asian Pacific Researchers

Several factors work to severely limit the number of talented, young Asian Pacific individuals who could become effective researchers. First and foremost, social science careers often are not seen as legitimate or economically viable careers by most Asian Pacific families. This socialization effect begins very early so that by high school most Asian Pacific students are disinclined to pursue social science careers. This is in direct contrast to the great interest among Asian Pacific youth in pursuing careers in the natural sciences and in medicine. Second, the image of Asian Pacific Americans as a "model minority" who have avoided substance abuse problems has created the impression that little empirical work is needed in this area which, in turn, contributes to the impression that such careers will have little marketability. Finally, even for those interested in social science careers, there are few mentors who can support students in following through on these aspirations. All these influences operate to exclude social science as an attractive occupational alternative in the Asian Pacific American's "folk theory of success."

At the professional level other problems exist. The diversity of

Asian Pacific groups in language, immigration experiences, etc., as well as the practical problems of obtaining adequate sample sizes widely distributed, relatively small populations makes conducting research on Asian Pacific communities particularly difficult. Thus, even if an Asian Pacific individual actually becomes a social scientist, these difficulties in conducting the required empirical work reduces the perceived viability of making Asian Pacific substance abuse as a major career focus.

Recommendations

• Establish training mechanisms for the development of Asian Pacific researchers at the earlier stages of the educational continuum (e.g., high school and undergraduate programs).
• Co-sponsor with the other Institutes a social science fair for Asian Pacific students. The fair would function to provide national recognition for promising Asian Pacific youth interested in pursuing social science careers and allow them to network with the few Asian Pacific researchers who may serve as their mentors in the future. (Note: Seven medical schools sponsored such a fair in Atlanta that was attended by 18,000 students.)
• Develop postdoctoral training programs to "retool" foreign Asian Pacific researchers (with at least permanent resident status) who demonstrate interest in redirecting careers to study Asian Pacific substance abuse.
• Encourage MARC (Minority Access to Research Careers) and other related programs to place students with research faculty who work in research settings that focus on Asian Pacific issues related to substance abuse (e.g., mental health, health, etc.).
• Develop a Center of Excellence that will serve as the focal training base for undergraduates, graduate students, and postdoctoral scholars. The center would provide an extensive core of training opportunities, and, more importantly, a critical mass of Asian Pacific researchers who would serve as mentors.

Issue: Lack of Funding Opportunities
for Asian Pacific Researchers

The funding of substance abuse research that focuses on Asian Pacific Islanders is quite low, and this trend can be largely attributed to several conditions. First, few Asian Pacific researchers are experienced in the grants procurement process. Second, few Asian Pacific social scientists participate on NIDA's IRGs so that issues that often confront research on Asian Pacific communities may not be fully addressed by these review groups. Those Asian Pacific researchers who do participate often have not been socialized to the role of an IRG member. This inexperience tends to diminish their impact on the review committee. Finally, most grant training programs have been inadequate because they have tended to be one-time workshop training experiences with little follow-up technical assistance. This individually-based, on-going technical support is critical as grant skills depend heavily on "hands-on" experiences.

Recommendations

- Continue and expand the Minority Research Development Seminar Series which has been successful in training and involving more ethnic minorities in substance abuse research.
- Develop an orientation program to socialize more Asian Pacific researchers for participating effectively in NIDA's IRGs. This program would have the following objectives: (a) initially involve Asian Pacifics as ad hoc reviewers on IRGs; (b) as these reviewers develop experience, place them on a NIDA IRG, and network them with senior Asian Pacific scholars who have IRG experience; (c) once these scientists become experienced IRG reviewers, have them mentor other Asian Pacific researchers for IRG participation.
- Charge the Center of Excellence with the responsibility of (a) developing and identifying Asian Pacific researchers who could be effective grant reviewers for NIDA, and (b) maintaining a mentorship/technical assistance program that promotes grant proposal activities among Asian Pacific scientists.

Issue: Need for More Technical Assistance to Increase Research Opportunities for Asian Pacific Scientists

The collection of Asian Pacific researchers whose work focuses on Asian Pacific American substance abuse consists of a relatively small number of scientists that are widely distributed across the mainland United States, the Pacific Islands, and Canada. This wide geographical distribution of a small number of researchers has impeded the development of a cohesive network of researchers who would share resources, data, grant strategies, and research theory and technology. Special technical assistance efforts are required to increase the likelihood that those persons who are committed and interested in Asian Pacific substance abuse research will be aware of and have access to appropriate resources and grant opportunities.

Recommendations

- Award technical assistance contracts to a number of Asian Pacific agencies or individuals for the purpose of their becoming familiar with all NIDA funding programs and research projects. These agencies and individuals who are already embedded in Asian Pacific networks essentially become the information "brokers" for NIDA.
- Establish a staff position as the designated contact for the Asian Pacific researcher community.
- Establish a resource center that would serve as a clearinghouse for Asian Pacific research and funding opportunities. The center would be the central data bank on Asian Pacific substance abuse. It would provide information on research findings concerning Asian Pacific substance abuse issues, culturally appropriate research methodology, research projects completed, current research projects being funded, grant opportunities, and the identification of all individuals involved in Asian Pacific substance abuse research.

Research Issue: Conceptual and Definition Problems

There are numerous conceptual problems that have hindered significant progress in research on Asian Pacific substance abuse.

First and foremost, the survey studies that have examined Asian Pacific populations usually have not differentiated among specific Asian Pacific groups in their samples. This is a serious shortcoming because the Asian Pacific groups which appear at highest risk for developing substance abuse problems have seldom been studied or have not been separately identified in previous research. Any examination of Asian Pacific American substance use and abuse patterns must address the wide range of diversity among different Asian Pacific groups. Concomitant with this inter-group diversity are important within group differences in terms of acculturation, ethnic identity, primary language dialect, country of origin, etc.

Too often substance abuse research on Asian Pacific Americans has been focused at a descriptive level in which ethnic differences are examined. The distinction between ethnic and cultural differences is an important one to make because it appears that the latter constitutes the more proximal determinants of substance use and abuse. Ethnic differences refer to variations on those personal-social characteristics (e.g., social class) which an individual tends to have simply by being a member of a certain ethnic group. Cultural differences, on the other hand, imply certain differences in attitudes, values, and perceptual constructs as a result of different cultural experiences. Whereas the former simply involves group membership, the latter constitutes a host of socio-psychological variables which are linked to different cultural lifestyles and perspectives. Ethnicity implies cultural differences but often these socio-psychological variables have not been directly assessed in Asian Pacific substance abuse research.

Finally, it may be wise to reappraise the way in which acculturation, cultural identity, and cultural conflict are conceptualized and measured. These variables constitute one of the most important domains of individual differences within Asian Pacific groups. For example, previous research has assumed that acculturation and cultural identity development reflect a bipolar model. In other words, to be highly acculturated in Western culture presumes low acculturation in East Asian or Pacific Islander culture. Some researchers have suggested that a person's identification with one culture is independent or orthogonal to his or her identification with another culture. If applicable to Asian Pacific acculturation and cultural identity, this orthogonal model of cultural identity implies a change in how acculturation variables are measured.

Recommendations

- Establish standard identification procedures in which specific Asian Pacific groups are differentiated in study samples.
- Prioritize studies that examine cultural variables that are directly associated with ethnic differences.
- Develop more comprehensive theoretical models of culture conflict, one of the most widely implicated variables related to substance abuse among Asian Pacific youth.
- Sponsor studies that compare different models of acculturation as applied to Asian Pacific adaptation patterns.
- Sponsor studies that examine substance abuse patterns of previously neglected groups, which include: Pacific Islanders, South East Asian refugees, Asian Pacific elderly, and Amerasian children.

Issue: Methodological Problems

Basic epidemiological data on the prevalence of Asian Pacific substance abuse is sorely lacking because standard national sampling strategies cannot be applied to Asian Pacific populations which tend to be relatively small in numbers and widely distributed across the United States. Even if the sampling problems could be circumvented, the following methodological difficulties must also be considered. First, a number of problems can occur when using self-report measures with Asian Pacific populations. Many Asian Pacifics whose primary language is not English may have difficulty in responding to items that have very little context in terms of time, place, and person. Most East Asian languages are very contextualized in that the context often establishes the tense, status of the person, etc. Also, there is often significant stigma and shame associated with having personal problems such as substance abuse that impair a person's ability to fulfill role responsibilities and obligations to the family or community group. Consequently, self-report responses may vary greatly depending on the public or private nature of the measure's administration.

Second, most studies are "ahistorical" in that they are not comparable with studies conducted on Asian Pacific samples from the country of origin. Without this comparability, valuable information on the process of acculturation and its relationship to substance use (e.g., the development or maintenance of protective drinking attitudes in East Asian countries and changes in these attitudes with acculturation). Third, previous studies comparing ethnic groups in alcohol use have confounded physiological differences in alcohol-related sensitivity with differences on socio-cultural factors such as acculturation. Research designs that can assess the interactive effects between physiological and socio-cultural factors are needed to examine the protective influences that have been implicated in explaining low drug use among certain Asian Pacific groups. Finally, as structural variables, it is clear that cultural variables often have interactive effects with other variables such as stressful life experiences. Most studies on Asian Pacific substance abuse have tested for cultural main effects rather than investigating these interactions.

Recommendations

- Develop innovative sampling strategies for rare elements.
- Conduct a series of studies that examine the appropriateness for Asian Pacific populations of the most frequently used measures in substance abuse research.
- Collect data on international samples to clarify the effects of immigration and acculturation on substance use.
- Set as priority the funding of studies that examine how cultural variables interact with other predictors of substance abuse in Asian Pacific populations.
- Develop a monograph on theoretical and methodological issues that confront research focused on Asian Pacific communities. Use monograph as resource in the training of Asian Pacific researchers and in educating IRG members.

SUMMARY RECOMMENDATIONS

Recommendation 1

NIDA and the other Institutes should strive to increase the number of R01 awards to ethnic minority researchers. This would also serve to increase the available pool of ethnic and minority researchers for service on review and advisory committees.

Recommendation 2

Increase the availability of existing research with ethnic minorities, as well as making future research more available to community organizations through better information transfer.

Recommendation 3

NIDA and the other Institutes should attempt to enhance the sophistication and development of new scientific methodologies with special populations.

Recommendation 4

Given the reorganization of NIDA into NIH, the Director of NIH should develop a Scientific Advisory Board on ethnic/minority issues. This board would be responsible for assisting the Director in developing training programs and consult with the Director on methods for enhancing research with special populations.

CONCLUSION

Given the uneven performance of many Federal agencies in terms of "actual" support for minority access to sponsored programs and activities, NIDA appears to have made some progress in addressing this issue. It should be noted that the unique contributions of the authors whose work appears in this volume are directly responsible for the development and implementation of many of NIDA's minority research initiatives during the 1980's. While NIDA's contributions were significant, the contributions of the outside community of concerned researchers were equally significant. Without the voluntary collaboration of these researchers, the program would not have experienced its current high level of success.

This rich collaboration produced many positive results. For example, increases in the number of minority researchers receiving grant support; in the number of minorities and women serving on the peer review committees; and in the number of NIDA staff who are minorities is a noteworthy accomplishment.

To ensure that this trend continues and is enhanced, minority researchers should monitor the activities of this Institute; provide constructive criticism as warranted; and support the efforts of colleagues and graduate students who are seeking research support from this Institute.

NOTES

1. Portions of this section were taken from *Eliminating Barriers to Research Careers* (Debro & Bolek, 1990).
2. See Trimble et al. (1991).

REFERENCES

Debro, J. J. and Bolek, C. (1990). *Drug abuse research issues at historically Black colleges and universities.* Atlanta: Department of Criminal Justice and Administration, Clark Atlanta University.
Executive Order 12320, Federal Register, Vol. 46, Number 180, September 17, 1981.
Garrison, H. H. and Brown, P. W. (1985). *A staff Paper. Minority Access to Research Careers: An Evaluation of the Honors Undergraduate Research Training Program.* Washington, DC: National Academy of Science, National Academy Press.
Rebach, H., Bolek, C. S., Russell, R., and Williams, K. (1992). *Substance Abuse Among Ethnic Minorities in American: A critical annotated bibliography.* New York: Garland Press, 1992.
Report and Recommendations. (1987). Symposium, "Alliances: An Expanded View," National Academy of Sciences, Washington, DC, September 23-25.
Report to DHHS-Impact of Executive Order 12320 as it Relates to Programs

Administered by the Department of Health and Human Services on Private Historically Black Colleges and Universities–Purchase Order SA-87-2559. (Linton, Mields, Resler & Cottone, Ltd, April, 1988.)

Thomas, G. E. (1986). *The Access and Success of Blacks and Hispanics in U.S. Graduate and Professional Education*, a working paper for the Office of Scientific and Engineering Personnel National Research Council, National Academy Press, Washington, DC.

Trimble, J., Zane, N., Chavez, E. and Brose, J. E. (1991). *Towards the Development of Ethnic Minority Drug Abuse Research and Researchers: Conference Proceedings and Recommendations*. Rockville, MD: Office of Special Populations Research, National Institute on Drug Abuse.

Trimble, J. E., Padilla, A. M., Bell (Bolek) C. S. (Eds). (1987). *Drug Abuse Among Ethnic Minorities*. Washington, DC: Office of Science Monograph Series (ADM 87-1474), National Institute on Drug Abuse.

U. S. General Accounting Office. (1988, May). *Minority Representation: Efforts of the Alcohol, Drug Abuse and Mental Health Administration*, GAO/HRD-88-49, Washington, DC.

U. S., DHHS, *Report of the Secretary's Task Force on Black & Minority Health*, Volume I: Executive Summary. Washington, DC, August, 1985.

U. S., DHHS, PHS, HRSA, Bureau of Professions, Office of Data Analysis and Management, *Location Patterns of Minority and Other Health Professionals*, DHHS Publication No. HRS-P-OD 85-2, August, 1985.

Index

from cocaine use, general
population 160
Music influence. *See* Media

National Institute on Drug Abuse
(NIDA), ethnic minority
research and training efforts
of, overview 345-350
toward Historically Black
Colleges and Universities
participation enhancement,
report summary 350-359
recommendations for ethnic
minority research/funding,
summary 373
for Alaskan Natives 360-364
for American Indians 360-364
for Asian Pacific Americans
366-372
for Hispanic Americans
364-366
National Institutes of Health (NIH),
role of in research funding
2-5
Native Americans. *See* American
Indians

PCP use, by homeless Blacks 131,
145
Peer clusters, defined 316,322. *See
also* Peer influence
Peer influence on adolescent/youth
substance use 31,195,255,
263-264,265; *mentioned*
315-340
Personality factors related to
substance use 33,161-162
Physiological reactions to alcohol
use
by American Indians 34
by Asians 34,187,190-192
Predictors of substance use
acculturation 28-29
age 28-29

gender 28-29
of health problems 26
in cross-sectional studies, control
of 40
race 28
relationships among variables 69
social influences 31-32
Prevalence studies on substance use,
research issues regarding
61,67
Prevention programs
cultural sensitivity issues
34,38-39
experimental designs 70-71
Prisoners. *See* Criminal activity
Proposals for research. *See* Grants,
application for
Psychiatric disturbance related to
substance use
by adolescents 255-256,263
by African Americans 32-33
alcohol use related 26
cocaine use related 161-162,232,
illus. 238-239,243-244
study of 237,240, *illus.*
242,243-244
co-morbidity 161-162
depression 32-33
diagnosis of 35
among homeless 125,141,144,
145
Psychological impairments of
cocaine users 232, *illus.*
238-239,243
study of 234-237,240, *illus.* 242,
243
Psychological well being of
adolescents, relation to
substance use 81
Psychometric rigor of data collection
40,66-67
and reliability of data 10,39-40,
66
and validity of data 10,24,39-40,
66,158-159,173-174

*For Product Safety Concerns and Information please contact
our EU representative GPSR@taylorandfrancis.com Taylor & Francis
Verlag GmbH, Kaufingerstraße 24, 80331 München, Germany*

T - #0082 - 270225 - C0 - 212/152/22 - PB - 9781560230236 - Gloss Lamination